Close-up on

SUNSET BOULEVARD

Also by Sam Staggs

*All About "All About Eve": The Complete Behind-the-Scenes
Story of the Bitchiest Film Ever Made*

MMII: The Return of Marilyn Monroe

Sam Staggs

St. Martin's Press 🜨 New York

Close-up on

SUNSET BOULEVARD

Billy Wilder, Norma Desmond,

and the

Dark Hollywood Dream

www.stmartins.com

Design by James Sinclair

Library of Congress Cataloging-in-Publication Data

Staggs, Sam.
    Close-up on Sunset Boulevard : Billy Wilder, Norma Desmond, and the dark Hollywood dream / Sam Staggs.
        p.   cm.
    ISBN 0-312-27453-X
        1. Sunset Boulevard (Motion picture)   2. Wilder, Billy, 1906—Criticism and interpretation.   I. Title.

PN1997.S845 S73 2002
791.43'72—dc21

                                                                        2001048989

First Edition: April 2002

10   9   8   7   6   5   4   3   2   1

In memory of Pauline Kael
(1919–2001)

About *Sunset Boulevard*, she wrote:

The whole enterprise exudes decadence like a stale, exotic perfume. You might not want to smell it every day, but then in 1950 you didn't get the chance: it was certainly a change from oceans of rosewater, lilies of the San Fernando Valley, and the scrubbed, healthy look.

contents

No memory of having starred
Atones for later disregard
Or keeps the end from being hard.
    —Robert Frost, "Provide Provide"

So this is where people come to live; I would have thought it a
city to die in.
    —Rainer Maria Rilke, *The Notebooks of Malte Laurids Brigge*

Voice-Over, 1948

Yes, this is Romanoff's in Beverly Hills, California. The famous restaurant on Rodeo Drive, not far from Sunset Boulevard. Tonight's a busy night, lots of stars at dinner. The prince himself, Michael Romanoff, has just seated Samuel Goldwyn and party. The mogul and the prince are buddies.

By the way, Michael Romanoff is no more a prince than Sam Goldwyn is. Mike is really Hershel Geguzin from Poland, a tailor's son. Or maybe he's from Lithuania. Anyway, the closest he ever came to the Czar was when Russian soldiers rounded up his relatives. But if he wants to bill himself as Prince Michael, part of the dynasty, nobody cares. After all, everybody in the place is royalty if you don't look too close.

Glance around the room. That's Gable at the bar, talking to Jimmy Stewart. Over there at a corner table by the window, with a new man, the blonde is Lana Turner. Now a little to the left of her, keep turning and who do you see? Jane Russell, Robert Mitchum, Cornel Wilde. Lizabeth Scott. John Huston, Bogart and Bacall. Other nights you'll see Richard Widmark, Barbara Stanwyck, Eddie Robinson, Mary Astor.

Now the other way, and take a close look at the booth to the side of the bar. Goldwyn and his wife. They're with a younger couple, Billy Wilder and his fiancée, Audrey Young. Goldwyn has just said something to Billy in Yiddish, Billy answers in German, and Audrey wants to know what it means. All four of them talking at the same time, when out of the corner of his eye Billy Wilder sees an unsteady old man near their table. The man's untidy suit has a couple of spots on it and his cuffs are frayed. The white shirt he's wearing might have been fresh the day before yesterday.

This old man is very tall in spite of his sagging shoulders. He seems stooped forward to eavesdrop. But a glance at the face tells Billy Wilder the man's not interested in anything they say at the table. His grayish face looks like worn asphalt, his hair is even grayer, and his nose could double as an umbrella hook.

Talk and merriment drain from the table. The tall, gray old man sways like a tree in winter, points his long index finger at Goldwyn, and speaks in the courtly tones of the Old South. "Here you are, you son of a bitch."

"Drunk," one of the women mutters.

"Son of a bitch," the man declaims to the stricken producer. "Here *you* are, and I ought to be making pictures, I'm the one—"

Frances Goldwyn, Samuel's wife, will not hear another word from this old fool. "Get away from here," she hisses. "Get away, you silly old man."

Kicked by her words, the man lapses into the noise and gaudy elegance of Romanoff's and is heard from no more. Sam Goldwyn's face looks as if he has felt the shaky earth wince far below.

"Do you know him?" demands his wife. "Who the hell is he?"

"That man," Goldwyn answers after a long moment of recovery, "was D. W. Griffith."

This little scene won't make the columns tomorrow, but a few months from now you'll read about D. W. Griffith. He's an old-time movie director and when he dies on July 24, 1948, the papers will run respectful notices. They'll say he pioneered the art of motion pictures, that he directed hundreds of silents including *The Birth of a Nation* and *Intolerance*, and that he was washed up even before talkies came in. They'll mention that he hasn't directed a picture since 1931, a flop called *The Struggle*.

If you drop in at Griffith's funeral, you'll have no trouble finding a place to sit. In fact, only half the seats at the Hollywood Masonic Temple will be filled, so you and everyone else gathered outside the auditorium to watch has-been celebrities will be invited in to fill the empty seats. You might find yourself near Lionel Barrymore or Mack Sennett. Or behind Blanche Sweet, Richard Barthelmess, Walter Huston, Raoul Walsh, Mae Marsh, Donald Crisp. If you're really lucky, maybe you'll sit next to Mary Pickford or Erich von Stroheim.

On several of these faces you may detect a sneer directed at two of the honorary pallbearers, Louis B. Mayer and Samuel Goldwyn. That's because Griffith's friends think these two could have given the old man something to keep him busy in his final years. But didn't.

There'll be a eulogy by screenwriter and producer Charles Brackett, who's president of the Academy of Motion Picture Arts and Sciences and never met D. W. Griffith. Brackett's latest picture, written as usual with Billy Wilder, is *A Foreign Affair*. Brackett will stand up at the funeral and say, "When you've had what he'd had, what you want is the chance to make more pictures, unlimited budgets to play with, complete confidence behind you. What does a man full of vitality care for the honors of the past? It's the present he wants, and the future. There was no solution for Griffith but a kind of frenzied beating on the barred doors. He lies here, the embittered years forgotten, David Wark Griffith, the Great."

A speech that's rather fine and florid, and that in no way resembles the screenplay Brackett and Wilder will soon write, called *Sunset Boulevard*, about a murder in one of those great big houses, with an old-time movie star involved, one of the biggest. *Sunset Boulevard*, brutal boulevard, will be their mordant elegy to the silent-picture era. And, by a decree of cross-eyed fate, it will also be the picture that ends the collaboration of Billy Wilder and Charles Brackett.

chapter 1

A La Recherche de Norma Desmond

The seed of *Sunset Boulevard* was not necessarily the pathetic story of D. W. Griffith, although that encounter at Romanoff's and the subsequent funeral must have stirred the psychological sediment of Billy Wilder and of Charles Brackett. No doubt the sere and cautionary case of the broken giant also kicked the psyche of Brackettandwilder, their conjunctive moniker during the years when, according to Wilder, they formed "the happiest couple in Hollywood."

In a broader sense, however, *Sunset Boulevard* was all about has-beens. And about *all* has-beens. Then, as now, the formerly famous haunted the purlieus of Los Angeles, the only company town in the world whose by-products gnash their teeth in endless hope of resurrection.

Billy Wilder's mind was a magnet for such irony. And although in 1948 he was nearing the climax of his artistry as a filmmaker, he had the nerves of an ex-German Jew. The terror and desperation Wilder saw in Hollywood must have jarred memories of Weimar and the rising hysteria he left behind him in the thirties.

Born in Poland in 1906 and raised in Vienna, Wilder moved to Berlin in 1926, and worked at various film studios, including UFA. In 1933, when Hitler took over Berlin, Wilder escaped to Paris. There he codirected (with Alexander Esway) his first film, *Mauvaise Graine*, which opened in the summer of 1934. But Billy Wilder didn't stick around for the premiere. Already, on January 22 of that year, he had wisely sailed for the United States on the *Aquitania*. Hoping for picture work in America, he landed with slender prospects. "I came here because I didn't want to be in an oven," Wilder said many years later.

In the words of Ed Sikov, Wilder's most recent biographer, "Billy and [his first wife] Judith eloped to Yuma, Arizona, on December 22, 1936, six months after he married Charles Brackett." Sikov's hard-edged assessment of both matches is beyond dispute: "Wilder's marriage with Judith produced two children and a lot of acrimony. His marriage with Brackett produced a lot of acrimony and eleven of the best, most successful films Paramount ever made."

If anyone ever films the Wilder–Brackett marriage, they might almost think of Groucho Marx and Margaret Dumont while writing the screenplay. Charles Brackett, of course, wasn't daft and he was nobody's gaga sidekick, but he did possess the sort of upper-crust Eastern credentials that, in movies, used to signal "high-class," "old money," and "urbane gentleman." A polished Republican, Brackett seemed, on the surface at least, the antithesis of Wilder, the hyper, street-smart immigrant. Teaming the two writers, as Paramount did, opened up screwball possibilities.

Wilder was a scamp, while Charles Brackett lived so respectably that, by Hollywood standards, he seemed rather square. The son of a banker, Brackett was born in 1892 in Saratoga Springs, New York. He graduated from Williams College and Harvard Law School. While at Harvard he began writing short stories. Later he wrote several novels. One of these, *Weekend*, published in 1925, drew the attention of Harold Ross, founding editor of *The New Yorker*. Ross made Brackett drama critic of the magazine, a post he held from 1926 to 1929.

Hollywood began buying stories from Charles Brackett in the 1920s, and in 1930 RKO enticed him to go west. Like many writers from the East, he disdained the studio assembly line approach to writing. So he went home. Soon, however, Paramount's blandishments lured him to Hollywood again, and in 1932 he signed a contract with that studio as a staff writer. Some half dozen scripts followed, not one of them noteworthy, until someone at Paramount had the crazy-brilliant idea of caging Brackett with Wilder.

The matchmaker in this case was Manny Wolf, story editor and head of the Paramount writers' department. Perhaps Wolf had heard the old chestnut about putting a typewriter into a room full of monkeys and the probability that eventually they would write *Hamlet*. And perhaps this was his experimental version of that theory.

One day, Wolf called Brackett to his office. "Charlie Brackett, meet Billy Wilder," Wolf said. "From now on you're a team." With Billy Wilder and Charles Brackett in the same room there were monkeyshines aplenty, screeching fights and endless chatter, but eventually they did use that typewriter for their own tragical historie, and it became the climax of their career. Only, the prince turned into Norma Desmond, there was something rotten in Hollywood, and a funny thing happened on the way to a comeback.

A lot of funny things, in fact, and some not funny at all, for on the road to *Sunset Boulevard* Brackettandwilder created—with help, in some cases, from other typing monkeys—the following films: *Bluebeard's Eighth Wife* (1938), *Midnight* (1939), *What a Life* (1939), *Ninotchka* (1939), *Arise, My Love* (1940), *Hold Back the Dawn* (1941), *Ball of Fire* (1941), *The Major and the Minor* (1942), *Five Graves to Cairo* (1943), *Double Indemnity* (1944), *The Lost Weekend* (1945), *The Emperor Waltz* (1948), and *A Foreign Affair* (1948).

Who was the world's most famous has-been in 1948? At the time of *Sunset Boulevard* it was surely Greta Garbo, although the term was never applied to her. It didn't fit. After all, Garbo had left pictures in 1941 of her own volition, and from then until her death in 1990 she could have named her price for a triumphant return to movies at any studio in the world. Garbo, whether working or retired, was always big news.

Billy Wilder, however, had his own way of beholding, and to his eye Garbo looked like a magnificent remnant of Hollywood in its great years of muteness. Because he was not only a writer but a connoisseur of painting and sculpture, he saw silent pictures not as lacking words but rather as civilization's newest form of visual art. Garbo's face, to Wilder as to countless millions, amounted to a work of art, whether silent or speaking. Her enormous will—forsaking the stardom that others lusted for—along with the implied sadness in her beauty, augmented the Garbo legend. Perhaps more than anyone, she embodied the essence of movies. (That was in 1948, when Marilyn Monroe was just a twinkle in Hollywood's eye.)

Whether Billy Wilder entertained such elaborate Garbo thoughts or not, we don't know. But soon after he and Brackett began planning "a new film about an old silent screen star who had a few problems," Wilder invited Garbo to his house at 704 North Beverly Drive for a drink. He had known her since *Ninotchka*, the Lubitsch film that he, Brackett, and Walter Reisch wrote at MGM.

Reisch came to Billy's house, too, and they told Garbo some of their latest story ideas. Like so many others, they naively thought they might lure her back into pictures. At one point Wilder told Garbo about the death mask he had seen at the Louvre, titled *L'Inconnue de la Seine*, supposedly the image of an unknown woman drowned in the river. Wilder's embryonic story had the woman narrating her life in flashback as the picture unfolds. Presumably, she was narrating from her watery grave in the Seine, as William Holden came to narrate *Sunset Boulevard* in one long flashback from Norma Desmond's swimming pool. Garbo, of course, was not lured.

Reclusiveness is an essential part of the stereotype of every has-been. Without the disdainful seclusion that has kept her home for twenty years, Norma Desmond would resemble any difficult ex-actress. Her removal from life, however, magnifies the dark allure. A similar removal that occurred in real life impressed Wilder during the writing of *Sunset Boulevard*.

Two of Billy's old friends from Germany, the pioneering director Joe May and his wife, Mia, fled to Hollywood about the same time as Wilder. Unmoored in a strange new land, they spiraled downward into melancholy decline. Joe May was reduced to hack work. Eventually, with financial help from Wilder and others, the Mays opened a restaurant in Los Angeles called the Blue Danube. Mia May, once a star in her husband's films, now cooked goulash. But not for long. The restaurant closed soon after it opened. The Mays, broken by failure and shame, locked themselves away and almost never left home.

Garbo, talking corpses, careers in collapse, and ex-actresses slinging hash—it's impossible to measure their weight on Wilder and Brackett. It's equally difficult to pinpoint the moment when *Sunset Boulevard* emerged in recognizable form, with Gloria Swanson marked forever as the archetype of Has-been, for the picture started out as a comedy with Mae West.

After toying with the idea of a story about a former queen of burlesque, Wilder and Brackett thought of Mae for the lead. But when they propositioned her about starring in this new picture as an old vamp with a dead monkey and a new gigolo, she didn't go for it.

Perhaps she recognized herself in Norma Desmond. Mae, too, kept monkeys as pets. When one of them died she grieved inconsolably, missing the premiere of *I'm No Angel* owing to one such demise. The time she and Garbo spent an evening together, Mae talked nonstop about her favorite subjects, monkeys and musclemen.

Gigolos? Mae considered them "nice boys" (for gals who lacked what Mae had so much of). She couldn't see herself, however, paying a man's upkeep in return for favors, not even in a picture story. Mae, in fact, thought it should be the other way around. Years later Wilder said, "The idea of Mae West was idiotic because we only had to talk to her to find out she thought she was as great, as desirable, as sexy as she had ever been." Approaching sixty, Mae couldn't imagine herself as anything less than torrid—onscreen or off. She hadn't made a picture in years, but Wilder didn't bring that up.

A. C. Lyles, a Paramount producer who had known everyone on the lot since he started as office boy to studio founder Adolph Zukor in 1937, pointed out that since Mae West was accustomed to writing her own material, she might also have balked at a script written by others. "She would certainly have wanted to rewrite it," declared Lyles.

Turned loose on the script, would Mae have kept the famous lines? Imagine the hip wiggling, the eye rolling, and the suggestive slant she'd give to "I *am* big. It's the pictures that got small." From Mae's mouth, "I'm ready for my close-up" wouldn't be addressed to DeMille but to a young stud, and she'd make it clear she didn't mean a camera shot.

Wilder was right; she would have turned *Sunset Boulevard* into "a kind of Laurel and Hardy picture." For starters, she didn't take Hollywood seriously enough to convey Norma Desmond's clawing desperation. Arriving from New York in the early thirties, Mae told reporters: "I'm not a little girl in a big town. I'm a big girl in a little town." Kidding the movies, kidding sex, Mae West refined the shtick she had derived from the rowdy ribaldry of burlesque.

Nor had Mae appeared in silent pictures. Silents—the source of Norma Desmond's melodramatic posturing—were alien to Mae's brand of comedy. Silent film was the wrong medium to express comic horni-ness, and Mae was always comically horny. She was smart to wait for talkies, since they conveyed the adenoidal innuendos and the Brooklyn double entendres of her acting style. The only thing Mae West had in common with Norma Desmond was audacity. Filming *Myra Breckinridge* (1970), her first movie in twenty-seven years, Mae declared: "I'm not making a comeback. I never went away."

"We needed a passé star who has gone down the tubes," Wilder said, recalling the hunt for Norma Desmond. "And the reason we needed a *real* passé star to play her was because it's very difficult to find a woman in her sixties, let us say, who is undiscovered—where was she until sixty? It would be hard to believe she was ever a big star. So we went after one who had been big."

Next stop, Mary Pickford. Wilder sums it up in a sentence: "Mr. Brackett and I went to see her at Pickfair, but she was too drunk—she was not interested." Pickford biographer Scott Eyman gives a different version. According to him, "Pickford said she adored the script . . . but she demanded a major structural alteration: The screenwriter/gigolo must be made completely subordinate to Norma Desmond; there must be no question about who was to be the star of the picture."

The same biographer offers a glimpse of Pickford in retirement that evokes Norma Desmond's Chaplin imitations and the bridge parties for her old friends, the silent movie "Waxworks": "She would throw parties for . . . Constance Collier, D. W. Griffith, Dorothy and Lillian Gish. . . . At these parties, Mary would offer an after-dinner turn, a scene between Elizabeth I and Mary Queen of Scots, with Pickford playing both parts."

chapter 2

When Queens Collide

*N*ext, Pola Negri flitted across the joint mind of Brackettandwilder. The Polish-born Negri possessed a mysterious background befitting Norma Desmond and her ilk, and by the late 1940s she, too, lived in seclusion. Several contradictory versions of this approach have been told, making it unclear whether the team actually offered Negri the role or only talked about it. The upshot, however—assuming that contact actually was made—resulted in the sputtered refusal of the proud, forgotten star to become food for vultures.

Little is known of Pola Negri, or perhaps the problem is that too much is known. At one time, however, people knew a great deal about her, or thought they did. Still, the very first question remains unsettled after a hundred years: was she the daughter of a down-at-heels Polish noblewoman and a Slovak tinsmith, or did a Gypsy violinist beget her on a peasant maiden as his caravan passed through the Polish town of Lipno? And did the conception of Barbara Apolonia Chalupiec (a surname which, when pronounced, sounds like a sneeze) take place in 1894, 1896, 1897, or 1899?

Like her younger neighbors from the country next door—Zsa Zsa, Eva, and Magda Gabor—Pola Negri air-brushed her past and took the first sleeper car out of Warsaw in the direction of stardom. In 1917 she appeared on the Berlin stage in a Max Reinhardt production. This success brought her to the attention of Lubitsch, who starred her in *The Eyes of the Mummy* and *Carmen* in 1918, and in other pictures later on.

Arriving in Hollywood in 1923, Negri found the throne of Paramount occupied by Gloria Swanson, a mere commoner. "That's Countess Pola to you," the foreign woman might have informed Swanson if the two detested one another as much as the studio's publicity mill prodded them to. Pola would have been half-right, for she had shed her husband, Count Eugene Dambski, only recently, a little before her advent in the Kingdom of Make Believe.

The crisis of precedence was solved when Swanson married Henri, Marquis de la Falaise de la Coudraye, in 1925—only to be unsolved two years later when Pola married Prince Serge Mdivani, who claimed royal blood from the ancient lineage of Georgia, Stalin's homeland. Prince Serge was, above all, a royal pain, and so was his brother David, who for a time functioned as the husband of silent star Mae Murray. A biographer once dubbed them "million-dollar studs," referring to the average amount paid by a rich woman to divorce one of them. It was sometimes whispered that the Mdivanis grew up far from any palace, on a sheep farm in the old country.

Between husbands La Negri carried on panting affairs with Chaplin and Valentino. When the great Latin lover died in 1926, she swooned for the cameras in her $3,000 mourning outfit. Despite her passion schedule, she found time to star in *Bella Donna, The Cheat, Lily of the Dust, Flower of Night*, and other films equally florid. Her perfumed acting matched the aroma of the titles, for on screen Negri did everything that Swanson did not do. She overacted, chewed the scenery, lolled on luxurious beds, flung herself about on divans, and flared her nostrils. To rev up her emotional heat, Pola Negri demanded that the floor of her dressing room be strewn with fresh orchid petals.

For recreation, she strolled up and down Sunset Boulevard with her pet leopard on a leash.

Paramount, like London in the sixteenth century, had one queen too many. Which one would reign, and which one lose her head? That question led to the affair of the cats.

While it is an established fact that Pola walked a leopard (or was it a tiger, after all, as a few reports insist?), she reputedly suffered from ail-urophobia. Only a specialist in psychiatry can say whether fear of the house cat excludes or encompasses fear of its fiercer relative. Other versions of the story abound. No, no, they insist, Gloria Swanson and not Pola Negri hated cats and so Pola rounded up a multiplicity of the creatures and unleashed the disgruntled felines in Gloria's dressing room (or possibly the set of her current picture). Swanson, ill and terrified, retreated to her mansion.

In her autobiography, *Memoirs of a Star*, Negri wrote that "every unkind thing that was said about me was attributed to Gloria Swanson, so that the Paramount publicists could keep interest high in our imaginary fight." She admits to being superstitious about cats and adds that Swanson adored them. Someone released "a herd of felines" on the set her first day of work at the studio, and a black cat indeed raced in front of her. "I fled back inside," Pola recalled, and sent word that she could not work because "it would be fatal to start the picture today."

Swanson called the feud rumors "pure nonsense." In an attempt to squelch them, she gave a dinner party to which she invited Pola, Charlie Chaplin, and several others. Since Swanson didn't allow photographers in her house, no one snapped a picture of the two queens together. "So far as the world knew," Swanson mused, "instead of sitting down to a fancy dinner, Pola Negri and I had spent that night dreaming up hateful things to do to each other."

The decline of Pola Negri began not long after the death of Valentino. Perhaps the public found her histrionic keening out of control. Or maybe she simply ran out of flamboyance and had no solid acting talent to fall back on. Sound might have done her in if mawkishness hadn't, for her accent remained as pungent as her emotional displays.

Negri left Hollywood and returned to Europe, where she made films in several countries during the thirties. One of these, *Mazurka*, filmed in Germany in 1935, became Hitler's favorite picture. Rumors of a romance between Pola and the Führer sent her ballistic. She sued the French magazine *Pour Vous* for printing the rumor, and collected a bundle. Her wardrobe mistress discounted the Nazi romance. "Miss Negri is herself a dictator," she said. "She would never take orders from Hitler."

During the war Pola lived in New York. Maggie Lewis, a former actress, recalled meeting her there in the midforties. "She had an Addams Family look," Lewis said. "The hair was dyed black and the skin was dead white. She had that old silent-screen look." One day Lewis asked, "You worked under Lubitsch, didn't you, Miss Negri?" Lewis imitates the accent: "Did I vork under Lubitsch? I vorked under Lubitsch—and Lubitsch vorked under me." (According to Lewis, it may or may not mean what it suggests.)

Pola Negri appeared in no films between 1943 and 1964, when she made a comeback in *The Moon-Spinners* with Hayley Mills. Pola remembered how to be a star, and in the picture she made a star's entrance—"sitting in an ornate chair with its back to the viewer, with only her hand visible. At first glimpse, she is busily cleaning her jewelry, dipping a large diamond necklace into a glass of champagne and then scrubbing it with a little brush. She wears gold brocade and a mink stole. Her thick black hair is arranged in a simple pageboy, with an elaborate braided chignon on top."

That entrance was also her exit. Demand was small for elderly ladies who looked like Vampira crossed with Marilyn Manson. Pola Negri settled in San Antonio, Texas, where she lived in peaceful seclusion until her death in 1987.

Every gossip I know descended on me with the information that in San Antonio, Negri spent the last twenty-five years of her life with a wealthy lesbian lover. True or false? Written confirmation proved elusive. Even the archgossip, Axel Madsen, in his cultish book *The Sewing Circle: Hollywood's Greatest Secret—Female Stars Who Loved Other Women*, holds his tongue. He supplies a mere tidbit from Tallulah Bankhead, who supposedly called Negri "a lying lesbo." The context of Bankhead's remark remains obscure.

David Shipman, however, in *The Great Movie Stars: The Golden Years*, recounted a telltale anecdote. Writing in the seventies, when sexual secrets of the stars were still discussed through gauze, Shipman nevertheless said a mouthful: "Pola Negri later retired to San Antonio with a friend, a Texas heiress . . . and made headlines some years later when the woman married and she threatened to sue—but she didn't; soon after, the heiress divorced and the ladies were reunited."

chapter 3

The Happiest Couple in Hollywood

A s the year 1950 approached, the flamboyant myths of Hollywood ripened, unharvested, in the sun. For more than fifty years a great glamorous divinity—in effect, the New World's technological metamorphosis of Greek and Roman deities—had created and destroyed, battled monsters, reveled and sorrowed, raped, ravaged, wept, and loved. These Californian gods and goddesses, sweeping in from every corner of the globe, brought on their wings more than jolly new entertainments or a revised pagan cult. Already, in just a half century, they had restructured the desires and principles of entire civilizations. In homage to this pantheon, Celebrity was now heralded as the fairest grace.

So far, however, no local Hesiod or Ovid had collected and codified the stunning stories, the fabulous exploits of movieland Olympus. There had been vignettes, meaning sanitized movies about the movies, with stars playing stars, but these pictures amounted to little more than industry PR. They left out the cruelty and the rock-bottom heartbreak.

In their book *Hollywood's Hollywood*, film historians Rudy Behlmer and Tony Thomas trace the fascination of behind-the-scenes stories to 1908, when Vitagraph, a New York production company, filmed *Making Motion Pictures: A Day in the Vitagraph Studio*. In that early film, moviemakers established the formula for portraying themselves. Since then, most movies on the subject have been variations on that first scenario, which Behlmer and Thomas summarize: "In the executive office of Vitagraph a script is being considered. A director and supervisors enter, receive their instructions, and proceed to the studio in the Flatbush section of Brooklyn. Preparations begin, actors and actresses are made up, and performers and crew are shuttled in studio cars to the location.

"After the scene is shot, everyone returns to the studio where, following a quick meal at the Vitagraph lunch counter, the studio scenes are rehearsed and photographed. All the necessary equipment for the different effects are shown. After the picture is finished, it is projected, and the audience sees *Love Is Better Than Riches*, the story within a story, in its entirety."

Dozens of self-referential silent pictures followed, including *Mabel's Dramatic Career* (1913), directed by Mack Sennett and starring Mabel Normand, Chaplin's *His New Job* (1915) and *Behind the Screen* (1916), and Cecil B. DeMille's *We Can't Have Everything* (1918). In the latter, a sequence depicts a director filming a harem scene—DeMille's witty hommage to himself.

One of the most significant of these silents bore the straightforward title *Hollywood*. Released in 1923, this spoof follows an obtuse wannabe actress from the Midwest to Hollywood, where she bumps into all the stars and fails to recognize a single one. It's impossible to say much about the picture, because no negative or prints survive. Yet its influence seems marked. It's likely that Billy Wilder saw the movie as a youngster in Europe, and Charles Brackett as a man about New York.

Produced by Famous Players–Lasky (soon to become Paramount Pictures), *Hollywood* included more than eighty cameo appearances by stars and personalities of the time: Mary Astor, Cecil B. DeMille, Sid Grauman (of the Chinese Theatre), William S. Hart, Pola Negri, Anna Q. Nilsson, Mary Pickford, and Gloria Swanson. A still reproduced in Behlmer and Thomas's book shows silent star Nita Naldi in the backseat of a Norma Desmond–type car, with scowling, uniformed chauffeur in attendance. Is the resemblance purely coincidental, or does it foreshadow *Sunset Boulevard*?

Another scene in *Hollywood* was worthy of Billy Wilder himself. The young actress, seeking work at the "Christie Comedies" studio, stands in the employment line near a corpulent man who moves aside to offer her

his place. When the man eventually steps up to present his own credentials, the window is slammed in his face and the CLOSED sign shoved into
view. The camera moves into close-up . . . and Fatty Arbuckle gazes at the
forlorn, one-word verdict. This was one of Arbuckle's few appearances
onscreen after the 1921 rape scandal that ruined his career. The daring,
poignant inclusion of Arbuckle reeks of the "bad taste" that Wilder has
been accused of throughout his career. Who knows; if Arbuckle had
been alive when *Sunset Boulevard* was made, Wilder might have seated him
at the bridge table with Norma Desmond and the Waxworks.

The studio-and-stars genre continued into the era of talking pictures,
with *What Price Hollywood?* (1932), *The Death Kiss* (1933), *Hollywood Boulevard* (1936), *A Star Is Born* (1937), to name only a few. ("I loved *What Price
Hollywood*," Wilder said, "and I loved the original *A Star Is Born*.")

The genre mutated in the forties to become the all-star musical entertainment awash in patriotism and packed with famous personalities: *Star
Spangled Rhythm* (1942), *Thank Your Lucky Stars* (1943), *Hollywood Canteen*
(1944), and the like.

The influence of these myriad earlier pictures on Wilder seems mini-
mal. Billy Wilder at the movies, watching Hollywood's flattering portray-
als of itself, is like Shakespeare attending the plays of John Lyly, Robert
Greene, Thomas Kyd—his forerunners and contemporaries—and then
going home to write *Othello.*

Sunset Boulevard is an extreme work, full of bile. It's as black as obsid-
ian, and as lustrous. This is, indeed, Billy Wilder's *Othello*, his *Paradise Lost*,
and also his *Day of the Locust*. Watching it is a painful pleasure because our
illusions are mangled along with those of every character. A half century
later it's still ahead of its time, for it's not only everybody's autobiography in Hollywood—one long in-joke—but also an accusing finger
pointed at the film industry's oversupply of dreamers. (Those dreaming
fans "out there in the dark" also stand warned.) A bitter comedy and a
tragedy of absurd ambition, the film is a vivisection of success and
celebrity, of Hollywood, America, and the world. Whatever the measure
of that success—small, medium, large—in *Sunset Boulevard* it's shrouded
in noir.

The emotional color scheme of *Sunset Boulevard* ranges from twilight shadow to haunted midnight, brightening occasionally to ominous afternoon but shading back, always, to darkness visible. Wilder's palette subsumes the conventional tones of film noir and adds a wash of melodrama. If most forties films noirs could be called "men's pictures," *Sunset Boulevard* is the great aberration: it's a "women's picture" where the tears turn to dust. It's *Mildred Pierce* with a swimming pool through the eyes of Euripides.

What's unique about *Sunset Boulevard*, however, is not its noir thesaurus but rather the subject and style of this tableau. That's because no other filmmaker dared paint Hollywood stark naked. Or if they dared, they lacked the Wilder touch, meaning Billy Wilder's technique, his bravado, his genius, and his gift for humanizing even a Godzilla ego like Norma Desmond's. Better than anyone who preceded or followed him, Wilder knew how to mirror the backside of the silver screen as a kind of purgatory.

With silent laugh track.

That mirror was cracked, or at least opaque, on the day in autumn 1948 when cynical, jaded Billy Wilder (those clinging journalistic epithets say so much about him, and so little) and his milder cohort, Charles Brackett, settled down to their next big project. *Sunset Boulevard* would prove unruly. So unmanageable was it, in fact, that shooting would start minus a completed script, proceed without one, and only when the picture was nearly over would anyone know how, or why, William Holden's character ends up dead in Norma Desmond's pool.

Earlier in 1948—on February 12—*A Foreign Affair* had wrapped. It was produced by Brackett, directed by Wilder, and written by them and Richard L. Breen. On May 26, the Brackett–Wilder picture *The Emperor Waltz* was released after a two-year delay. The reason for that delay was obvious to anyone who saw it: the picture was no good. Wilder hated it; Brackett called it a "stinker."

On June 8, Charles Brackett's wife died at their home on Bellagio Road in Bel-Air. They had been married for twenty-nine years. The reclusive Elizabeth Fletcher Brackett spent her later years as an alcoholic.

In better days, however, the Bracketts gave Sunday luncheons that a writer for *Life* magazine once described as "Hollywood's equivalent of Mme. de Staël's salons in eighteenth-century Paris." The writer continued, "To them troop the most entertainingly articulate writers, actors, actresses, and assorted geniuses in the craft. Brackett, who is an appreciative listener as well as an excellent raconteur, presides over them with solicitude and grace. In this function he is ably assisted by his wife, a kindly but witty lady whose occasionally corrosive remarks have from time to time been attributed to Dorothy Parker."

Christopher Isherwood, in his diary, took a different view. "Sunday lunch we went to the Bracketts'—why, God knows," he wrote. Again: "Yesterday a really funereal party at the Bracketts'." Another time he included the Bracketts among "perhaps the most boring people I've ever known."

The Bracketts' modern stone house was incongruously furnished in the outmoded elegance of bygone times: tasseled lamps, Tiffany vases, red plush sofas and chairs bedizened with antimacassars. According to a Wilder biographer, one saw, at those Sunday gatherings, "ladies and gentlemen sitting in Belter chairs around Belter card tables playing cribbage with an antique cribbage board." The Bracketts had, apparently, attempted to re-create the nineteenth century in ultramodern L.A. Their friends no doubt smiled condescendingly at their decor; it would take several decades for nostalgia to reinstate all things Victorian.

It's possible that Brackett and Wilder consciously re-created, or at least alluded to, those Brackett card parties when they gathered Norma Desmond and the Waxworks to play bridge among the fusty elegance of Hollywood's bygone times.

There was more to come for Wilder and Brackett in the eventful year 1948. *A Foreign Affair* opened in New York on July 7 and in Los Angeles July 22. On July 27 Brackett eulogized D. W. Griffith.

When *A Foreign Affair* went into general release in August, Paramount found itself in a tedious predicament. Various government officials protested the film's subject matter, which they felt reflected negatively on American forces in Berlin. And understandably so, for this was long before *M*A*S*H*. World War II movie propaganda had accustomed the 1940s public to rather chaste GIs endowed with boyish bravery who let off steam through horseplay. These boys wrote letters to Mom and their girls back home, and their mild lust came no closer to climax than ogling pinups of Betty Grable.

Suddenly, thanks to this brash new Wilder movie, the American army was shown stripped of apple pie scruples. Randy, raunchy, and amoral, these men were black market entrepreneurs and every bit as cynical as . . . well, Billy Wilder. And the Germans, now America's friends, were barely de-Nazified. Marlene Dietrich, singing "Black Market" in a seedy cabaret, makes every raunchy suggestion in the book.

Paramount, in a position to say "I told you so," probably did. The studio had squirmed over *A Foreign Affair* from the outset. For starters, the title made them nervous; the front office suggested a string of bland substitutes, including *Love in the Air, Operation Candybar,* and *Two Loves Have I.* Studio executives also thought the script went too far. Brackett and Wilder, near the height of their artistic testosterone and still riding the prestige of their 1945 Oscars for *The Lost Weekend,* prevailed with both title and sceenplay.

A Foreign Affair still packs a wallop. No wonder it raised a ruckus then. Following the protests of individual government officials, Billy Wilder was denounced on the floor of the House of Representatives for treating Germans and Americans with equal irreverence. (Translation: His picture savaged a prudish Iowa congresswoman played by Jean Arthur, rather than making her morally superior to Dietrich's magnificent slut.) The Department of Defense, joining the outcry, issued a statement of exquisite hypocrisy, denying any resemblance between the film's GIs and American soldiers.

According to some sources, Paramount pulled the picture from a number of theatres not long after release. It's unclear, however, whether the studio really took such drastic steps in the marketplace, or whether it merely threatened.

It's suprising that Charles Brackett and Billy Wilder ever completed one good script, let alone all those famous ones that established them among Hollywood's greatest writers. For they were a pair of cutups and loafers.

That, at least, would surely have been the impression of a casual visitor to their office in the closing months of 1948, when *A Foreign Affair* was behind them and they couldn't get a grip on their story of a forgotten silent star in a ramshackle palazzo.

Successful collaboration demands two or more strong personalities who recognize their strengths and acknowledge their weaknesses. (Asked once, during negotiations for a Screen Writers' Guild contract, to define a team, Brackett replied, "Whom God hath joined together.") Writers with implacable egos should work alone. Certainly, neither Wilder nor Brackett was deprived of ego. As movie veterans, however, they accepted the total collaboration required in filmmaking at every step. In more personal terms, neither man denied his lack of one key component in screenwriting genius.

Brackett wrote polished modern prose. He had learned to plot novels, and that knack carried over to his scripts. But pizazz? There his writing sagged.

Wilder was all pizazz—in German. His greatest liability, however, was his English. He spoke it fluently, and wrote with equal fluency. He was as witty in his new tongue as in the old. To an artist, however, a foreign language remains elusive in most ways that count. Every language, deep down, is a secret code whose nuances and occult signs vibrate most clearly to a native. Rare is the writer who achieves sublimity in a language not his own. An aphorism of E. M. Cioran specifies the challenge: "To change languages is to write a love letter with a dictionary."

Wilder's other gifts towered: a former journalist and screenwriter in Berlin, he had the German linguistic world in his mouth, from *Hochdeutsch* to Austrian dialect and Yiddish. He also spoke French. Crammed into his head was the irony, the wit, the polyglot culture, high and low, of Western Europe. And all of it spiced with the bitter herbs of a Jew despised by the guardians of his birthright.

Various accounts have been told of the workaday world of Brackett and Wilder. The best way, perhaps, to look in on them so long after the fact is to reconstruct a typical writing day, with its noisy shenanigans, raucous quarrels, and—once they settle down—the miraculous result of their uneasy partnership, those classic pages of film script.

When veteran Paramount producer A.C. Lyles first started work for studio head Adolph Zukor in 1937, he used to drop by their office on his rounds. "I remember Charlie Brackett on the couch," Lyles says, "with his shoes off in stocking feet, and Billy in the chair across the way." That might be called the "snapshot version" of Billy and Charlie. The "live action sequence," according to others who saw them, sets Wilder in agitated motion, pacing, gesticulating, chain-smoking (cigarettes stubbed out in favor of cigars, then back to cigarettes and never a complaint from Charlie about secondhand smoke), flourishing a cane as he uproots Brackett from the couch and sprawls on it himself.

Brackett, less kinetic, walks from couch to chair. "Never stand when you can sit" seems to be his motto. "His only form of exercise is moving the pegs up and down a cribbage board." Static body, vigorous mind: these Brackett qualities balance Wilder's fitful nerves. An observer noted that "Brackett conveys an impression of sound metabolism and repose, which his friends find soothing."

A.C. Lyles, still in his teens in the late thirties when he started at Paramount, was "in everybody's office" on errands for Zukor. "Charlie and Billy would stop me and ask, 'What's going on around here?' It wasn't only gossip they wanted from me. They were interested in the various Paramount productions. You see, I first knew them before Billy started directing pictures. They were considered such big writers. I was in awe of them."

Asked to describe their offices in the Writers' Building, Lyles mentions their suite, which included a secretary's office as a kind of anteroom. He continues, "The office where they worked was about the size of this," indicating his own large, high-ceilinged space in the William S. Hart Building, across from the commissary dining room on the Paramount lot. "The size of this" translates roughly into the square footage of a small one-bedroom apartment; indeed, there was a large "bedroom" in the suite, where both men napped every day after lunch. In the smaller room—dubbed the game room—they played cribbage, entertained sundry visitors, and wrote when they felt like it.

"One of the best things about a collaborator," Wilder said, "is that he stops you from committing suicide. It's fun to arrive in the morning and you have forty-five minutes of bitching about your wife, and how lousy the food was, and you saw a picture and it stank. It establishes a good atmosphere before you get going on your own crap."

Wilder, "a fountain of energy, of ideas and enthusiasm, of sarcastic banter, compliments, and anecdotes," had a short attention span. No doubt the greatest value of his collaborator wasn't "suicide prevention" but simply a shield from ennui. "Writing," Wilder confessed, "is a very, very dull and boring, dreary thing."

Wilder knew what would happen without his partner in the same room: "At the end of the day, he has seven pages and I have nothing, because I read the pornographic novel, or I wrote letters, or I slept."

Another inside look at Brackett and Wilder was published in *Life* magazine in 1944. The piece, by Lincoln Barnett, more closely resembles a *New Yorker* profile than the usual quickie treatment of the Luce magazines. One reason for such journalistic depth, perhaps, was because, as Barnett stated, "they boast a kind of prestige and independence no other writers in any major studio have attained."

Translated into financial terms, their prestige amounted to roughly $2,500 per week, per writer. As "executive writers," they had reached the happy plateau where they had the "freedom to evolve their own ideas and try experiments that run-of-the-mill, thousand-dollar-a-week writers could not attempt."

For writers who require absolute quiet in order to work, the Brackett and Wilder suite sounds maddening. "Their office has a kind of convivial coffeehouse atmosphere," according to the *Life* profile. "Idling actors and writers drop in every few minutes to grouse or gossip."

In his recent biography of Wilder, Ed Sikov telescopes the workplace donnybrook into a quick-cut montage: "Work, talk, cards, gossip, lunch, naps, work, talk, and work." Most of the men's friends agree that Wilder served as catalyst for the carnival atmosphere. The composer Miklós Rózsa, recalling his first meeting with the team, said that "the volatile Wilder was all jokes and wit and couldn't sit still for a moment." Brackett, on the other hand, was "cool, composed, and well behaved."

Brackett, mindful of his upright Yankee background, sneaked in the semblance of a work ethic. In 1955, recalling his years with Wilder, he said that their method began "with talk—seemingly endless talk—but all of it directed towards the project." If Paramount brass had overheard their employees' endless talk, they perhaps would have considered it time wasted. But any writer, any collaborator, knows better. The stream of repartee, gossip, grousing, and small talk loosens up the unconscious. It's a purgative for ideas and plots and dialogue reluctant to come out.

"The only reliable peg I know on which to hang a story is character," said Brackett. And what a character she was—Norma Desmond, who emerged long before Joe Gillis, Max, or any of the others in *Sunset Boulevard*. Before the team had an inkling of the plot or a scrap of dialogue, they had Norma Desmond. Wilder said later that they had glimpsed her "five years before we actually got around to it." Not until 1948, however, did they close the office door and start getting acquainted with their star of stars.

"What sort of story shall we do?" asked Brackett. For once, Wilder had no reply. So they opened the door, the visitors came and went, someone suggested "a relationship between a silent-day queen and a young man."

Yes! They envisioned the movie queen sealed away in an immense run-down mansion on Sunset Boulevard; both men had seen such places. They beheld her dusty mementoes, her clutter of furniture sufficient for a remake of *Intolerance*, and they saw the nice young man, maybe from the Midwest, down on his luck, unable to make it in Hollywood.

And then what happens? The question hung in the air. Brackett and Wilder didn't have writer's block; professional writers seldom use the term, considering it an amateur's indulgence. But they had reached an impasse.

A thousand details came to mind, but details don't make a screenplay. They turned the problem this way and that, they scrutinized it, discussed it, and what they came up with was an ex-movie queen and a young man. And then what happens?

At times the merriment in their suite verged on hysteria. At other times the two men quarreled, yelled, insulted one another with wild recriminations. Someone even hurled a telephone book, or so it was rumored around Paramount. As the summer of 1948 lapsed, blank pages stayed blank.

Stymied by a pivotal turn of plot in *Sunset Boulevard*, Wilder and Brackett took on a third writer, D. M. Marshman Jr., who had written about movies for *Life*. Wilder has said very little about the new partner and his contribution. According to Gloria Swanson, however, Marshman was invited to a screening of *The Emperor Waltz*, the 1948 film that both Brackett and Wilder preferred to forget. Marshman criticized the film in such impressive terms to the cowriters that he was invited to collaborate with them on a future movie. According to a Paramount interoffice memo, Marshman was put on the payroll August 9, 1948. His job description: "To develop the story line."

The Third Man

Let D. M. Marshman Jr. equal X.

Hired by Brackett and Wilder to help them plot *Sunset Boulevard*, he remains the unknown quantity in this screenwriting equation. It's true, as a recent Wilder biographer points out, that Paramount paid Marshman and Wilder more for *writing* than they paid Brackett. Brackett, however, received $130,000 as producer. Wilder got $211,416 for writing on top of his director's fee of some $90,000. Marshman was paid $11,600. But at best these figures are misleading, at worst meaningless.

Paramount, like other studios, used every available technique to burnish its account books. The right hand didn't know what column of figures the left hand was adding or subtracting. Hollywood bookkeeping has always been a crafty blend of voodoo economics and fairy-tale accounting. Trying to prove, or disprove, anything by these long-ago figures is like pegging your life to newspaper horoscopes.

Billy Wilder has more or less confirmed Swanson's account of how Marshman came aboard. "He was bright," Wilder said, "and we thought we might go stale so we brought in somebody to kick ideas around." Asked why Marshman never worked with him again, Wilder replied that "he went to Fox and then he was working for Hublein—you know, cocktails and Hiram Walker. Then I saw him again and he was sort of a girdle merchandiser. I don't know what happened to him."

Marshman appears to have only one other screenwriting credit, a 1953 Fox film called *Taxi*.

Nancy Olson, who plays Betty in *Sunset Boulevard*, has only vague memories of him on the set. When I asked her about Marshman, she said, "What on earth was he doing there?" I inquired whether he spent time on the set during production. She said, "He was always moaxing around." (Later I asked the meaning of the verb "to moax." She said, "That means hanging around when you're not really vital. Nothing derogatory, though; just superfluous." She decided it must be a Wisconsin word, remembered from her Midwestern childhood.)

Marshman's contribution, whatever the extent of it, undoubtedly adds up to a few pages. It's impossible to ferret out clues from internal evidence, and the external evidence—given here in toto—yields a paltry sum.

Sometime between August 9 and December 21, *Sunset Boulevard* was born. More specifically, the first act was born.

Screenwriters have always thought in terms of acts one, two, and three, a reflection of the theatrical origins of the screenplay. Bookstore shelves today display dozens of how-to books on script writing, and they all emphasize the importance of the three-act structure. Billy Wilder, perhaps more than any Hollywood writer, talks in these terms. Through-out his long career he seldom gave an interview without mentioning the absolute necessity of thinking and writing in three acts. In Cameron

Crowe's book *Conversations with Wilder*, published in 1999, there's a section called "Billy Wilder's Tips for Screenwriters." Among them:

—"If you have a problem with the third act, the real problem is in the first act."

—"The event that occurs at the second-act curtain triggers the end of the movie."

—"The third act must build, build, build in tempo and action until the last event, and then that's it. Don't hang around."

Although Wilder and Brackett knew the rules of dramatic construction from Aristotle to tipsheets of the Screen Writers' Guild, real plot development on *Sunset Boulevard* began only after D. M. Marshman Jr. opened Brackettandwilder into a ménage à trois. It's possible the senior partners were inhibited by the hornet's nest stirred up by *A Foreign Affair*. Not the reaction in Washington, but rather the one at Paramount, because another controversial script could mean a studio clampdown (for financial reasons) and moralistic Production Code censorship, as well, first of their script and subsequently of their movie.

Suddenly, Hollywood seemed a dangerous place. With recent controversy in their wake, a red scare that had metastasized, and the film industry's yellow streak widening daily, Wilder and Brackett went further underground than usual at the outset of *Sunset Boulevard*. Remembering the insipid titles offered by the studio in lieu of *A Foreign Affair*, they dumbed it down before anyone else had the chance. Paramount wanted stupid titles? Give 'em *A Can of Beans*, which was, for a time, the unattractive working title of their new script.

During the months from August to December 1948, Brackett, Wilder, and Marshman completed the first thirty pages of dialogue and narrative of *Sunset Boulevard*. Except for the opening sequence in a morgue, which was filmed but cut before general release, the script includes substantially all of the action and dialogue in the opening section of the picture. Even in those early stages, it's a well-crafted piece of writing, obviously the polished work of professionals.

Fortunately, the picture soon got a new and improved title. The thirty-page fragment on yellow paper, dated December 21, 1948, was designated "For Limited Distribution." On the second page is a note from the writers: "This is the first act of *Sunset Boulevard*. Due to the peculiar nature of the project, we ask all our coworkers to regard it as top secret. Brackett & Wilder."

Based on this installment, Paramount gave a vote of confidence to the team by green-lighting the production. From long experience, the studio did not require a finished script from these two. Brackett and Wilder, long before, had formed the habit of going into production with only a partial screenplay, but this time they were stingier than ever. After that initial thirty-page hors d'oeuvre, they doled out pages with ration book paucity, and their obfuscation worked as planned. The picture was budgeted, cast, and in production before anyone at Paramount—or at the Production Code Administration, known variously as the Hays Office and, after 1945, as the Johnston Office—realized exactly what it was about.

At this early stage, Joe Gillis was called "Dan Gillis." The producer was "Kaufman" and not yet Sheldrake. Gillis was to drive a "1941 Buick convertible" rather than the 1946 Plymouth that William Holden drives in the film. Norma Desmond's car was to be "an old Rolls-Royce." (Two months later they changed the Rolls to a Hispano-Suiza. Only later did the writers hit upon an outré Isotta-Fraschini with leopard upholstery to contain Norma and her entourage.)

Driving Miss Desmond

Norma Desmond's Isotta-Fraschini, the ultimate star car, matches Norma herself: it's exotic, expensive, hard to handle, and outdated. And not rare during the silent era: in the 1920s an Isotta dealership was located on Sunset Boulevard.

The car's history begins in Milan in 1898, when Cesare Isotta and the three Fraschini brothers formed a company to import Renaults into Italy. By 1902, they were producing their own automobiles.

At first the Isotta's main market was Europe, though transatlantic sales soon caught up. By the early twenties the Isotta-Fraschini had become one of the world's most prestigious and desirable automobiles. King Victor Emanuel of Italy owned one; so did Queen Marie of Romania, the Empress of Abyssinia, Prince Louis of Monaco, and the Aga Khan. In Hollywood, Isottas transported Clara Bow, Jack Dempsey, and William Randolph Hearst. Rudolph Valentino ordered a two-seater speedster with an all-aluminum body, but the car was not finished before the actor's death.

According to the authors of *The Automobile: The First Century*, the Hispano-Suiza held "the edge in chic over its main rival in the Continental carraige trade, the Isotta-Fraschini. . . . Those who have driven both cars say that the Hispano was without a doubt the better-handling vehicle. 'In comparison,' they said, 'the Isotta drove like a truck.' Perhaps it is because the Hispano was designed for the man who drove himself, while the Isotta was meant to be driven by a chauffeur, who would not complain."

The Depression wiped out the Isotta-Fraschini as thoroughly as talking pictures wiped out Norma Desmond. By 1933, with virtually no sales, the company was sold to an aircraft manufacturer. Isotta attempted a comeback after World War II, but the road such extravagant cars once had traveled no longer existed. Even Paramount couldn't afford one; the Isotta-Fraschini in *Sunset Boulevard* came from a rental firm.

Norma Desmond's automobile eventually returned home, or almost. Today it's on exhibit at the Museo Dell'Automobile, in Turin, one of the world's largest car museums. It arrived there in 1972 with the interior stripped of its leopard skin upholstery and such accoutrements as the gold-plated car phone. On the doors, however, her regal crest proudly announces that this vehicle once belonged to ND.

The main difference between this early version and the subsequent shooting script has to do with Norma's writing project. Here it's her memoirs and not a mad, unfilmable screenplay that she's working on. She tells Gillis: "It's a book about me. I've been writing it for years. It's about the glory that was Hollywood, and the grandeur that was us. Young man, you just don't know!"

On February 14, 1949, Brackett and Wilder turned in another fragment of their script, bringing the total number of pages to fifty-three. In an accompanying memo, they summarized changes made and changes still to come:

(1) Dan Gillis' name is now Dick Gillis. Kaufman's name will be Millman; (2) The Desmond house is not quite as dilapidated as originally indicated. It is enormous, musty, somber—but no tattered old hangings, and no newspapers littering the lawn; (3) Norma Desmond's writing project is not her memoirs, but a script about Salome on which she has been working many years—a vehicle in which she hopes to have a comeback; (4) The room above the garage in which Gillis is quartered is not an enormous storage space, but a chauffeur's room. It has no lock on the door, the lock having been gouged out. As he cannot lock the door at night, Gillis puts a heavy chair in front of it.

It is here, too, that the car is temporarily a Hispano-Suiza, described in voice-over by Gillis: "The whole thing was upholstered in Russian leather, and had one of those car phones, all gold-plated. To me it was like riding in the Black Maria."

These changes, minor but intriguing, suggest that delays on the part of Wilder and Brackett had less to do with the picture's story line than with horse trading. The horses in question—Wilder might well have suffixed the word "asses" to the metaphor—were, of course, those stock villains of the industry, studio bosses and Production Code censors. No doubt Brackett and Wilder could have turned in an almost-final draft if they had wished. After all, despite the carnival atmosphere in their office, these were two of the most disciplined writers in town.

Perhaps one reason they got away with such an unorthodox script timetable was that Paramount had no equivalent of Darryl F. Zanuck. Had Brackett and Wilder worked at 20th Century–Fox, under Zanuck, they would have been required to turn in for his personal approval a completed script before anything took place in front of the camera. Zanuck, with his keen instinct for story and dialogue, would have made his revisions, the majority of which would then have been incorporated in the shooting script.

By 1949, however, Adolph Zukor, the Hungarian émigré who founded Paramount, was seventy-seven years old and functioned merely as a figurehead chairman of the board. Barney Balaban was president, and Y. Frank Freeman vice president in charge of production. If any one of these men had a keen instinct for good writing, it remained a secret. Billy Wilder's pun on vice president Freeman's name indicates his opinion of the studio's upper echelon: "*Why* Frank Freeman? A question nobody can answer." More plainly, Wilder dubbed him an "idiot."

As for casting, Brackett and Wilder knew who they wanted from day one. When they turned in those first thirty pages on December 21, 1948, they had listed the following on page two under the heading, "The Actors We Hope to Get": Montgomery Clift as Gillis, Gloria Swanson as Norma Desmond, Erich von Stroheim as Max von Meyerling, and "a new face" to play ingenue Betty Schaeffer. (Joseph Calleia was their first choice to play Sheldrake, the producer. The part eventually went to Fred Clark.)

A New Face

Nancy Olson, who got the part of Betty Schaeffer, doesn't know how Billy Wilder chose her. "It's possible he watched my screen test from the year before," Olson speculates. "He had seen me around Paramount, where I was under contract. He saw me in the commissary."

A journalist once described Olson as "the original success kid" who "started at the top. Unlike many young players, she served no period of apprenticeship at the studio, no posing for cheesecake, no dating of executives or executives' sons, no playing of starlet bits. Right off she was assigned starring roles."

Milt Lewis, a talent scout from Paramount, attended a production of Molnar's *The Play's the Thing* at UCLA, where Olson was a drama student. Olson's performance as the actress impressed the scout, who came backstage afterward and invited her to the studio for an interview. A screen test followed, Olson signed a contract, and she also stayed in school.

Sometimes, loitering about the studio between appointments, she would haunt the music department. There she got to know Jay Livingston and Ray Evans, the songwriters who composed "Buttons and Bows," the song heard at the New Year's Eve party in *Sunset Boulevard*. Evans and Livingston appear for a few seconds at the piano, performing their own song. Olson became such a regular visitor to their Paramount office that they came to expect her, like the studio letter carrier delivering mail.

No one guessed that twelve years later, when Olson married Alan Livingston in 1962, her pal Jay Livingston would become her brother-in-law.

In spite of D.M. Marshman's help with plot structure, one thorny problem persisted: What to do with the theme of the passé star and the hungry writer who, in Wilder's words, "wanted a pool, got a pool, and ultimately drowned in a pool." Years later Wilder said, "We had not written the third act yet, but we knew they fished him out of a pool."

Despite these starts and stops on the *Sunset Boulevard* script during the close of 1948 and the early months of 1949, Paramount hired stars, built sets, sewed costumes, and footed the bills without undue fuss or worry. One reason for studio insouciance was the known professionalism and the financial track record of Wilder and Brackett. Another reason was the "safe" material, for no one dreamed this picture would be so iconoclastic.

By long tradition and a moguls' agreement, Hollywood pictures about Hollywood emphasized glamorous success and backstage schmaltz. Stars in such movies didn't finance gigolos, and they certainly didn't kill—not even hack writers—though they might sometimes commit suicide, as did Frederic March, playing Norman Maine in *A Star Is Born* (1937). (Norma Desmond's name is perhaps an oblique allusion to that earlier has-been.) And such cruel downers as *The Barefoot Contessa* and *What Ever Happened to Baby Jane?* were not yet conceived.

The lord high executioner of industry censorship, Joseph I. Breen, was not so easily mollified as the Paramount bosses. By April 11, 1949, a week before shooting was to begin, Luigi Luraschi of the studio's censorship department submitted eighty-eight pages of the script. Ten days later Breen replied, "Inasmuch as this material is incomplete, we cannot, of course, render an opinion as to the acceptability of the entire story. However, as far as this material goes, we are happy to report that it seems to meet the provisions of the Production Code."

Breen did, however, point out the following unacceptable details: "Page 12: Please eliminate Gillis' line 'I'm up that creek and I need a job.' Page 27: Please eliminate Gillis' line ' . . . and the wind *goosing* that organ once in a while.' Page 46: Please eliminate the reference to Miss Desmond having been married three times." Breen won two out of three in this round. The first objectionable line became, "I'm over a barrel. I need a job." *Goosing* turned into *wheezing*. But Norma Desmond's marital past was not revised.

New pages dribbled in, and also revised pages, first to Luraschi at Paramount, and from him to Breen, with frequent correspondence between the two men. Most pages were acceptable on this piecemeal basis.

On May 24, 1949, when shooting had been underway for five weeks, Breen wrote worriedly to Luraschi:

> We have read a considerable number of recently dated pages for your proposed production *Sunset Boulevard*. Inasmuch as we have never read the final sequence for this script, we do not know whether the overall story meets the requirements of the Production Code.
>
> The most recent of this material seems to indicate the introduction of a sex affair between Gillis and Norma Desmond which was not present in the earlier material. Whether or not this overall story will carry a sex affair, we cannot say. However, it seems to us at this point that there is no indication of a voice for morality by which the sex affair would be condemned, nor does there appear to be compensating moral values for the sin.

Only on July 20, 1949—more than a month after the picture wrapped—did Breen approve the script. Appended to his letter was the usual caveat: "You understand, of course, that our final judgment will be based on the finished picture."

Many years later, as Wilder neared the end of his directing career, he said: "There are times when I wish we had censorship, because the fun has gone out of it, the game that you played with them."

The Script

If you read any version of the *Sunset Boulevard* script, whether published or unpublished, you may get the eerie feeling that Norma Desmond, Joe Gillis, and the others didn't say certain things quite the way they're printed on the page. You'll be absolutely right.

The terms "script," "screenplay," and "shooting script" mean more or less the same: a blueprint used first by art director, costume designer, and other specialized technicians, then by director and actors. If you read a published "screenplay" or "script," you're reading something different from the actual dialogue you hear from the screen. That's because changes are made every day during filming—by producer, writers, director, or actors. The only way to read the exact words spoken by actors in a film is from the "release dialogue transcript," a stenographic record of every utterance. (The term "cutting continuity" is sometimes also used to mean not only the dialogue as heard on screen but a precise written description of shots, camera angles, and the like.)

Release dialogue transcripts are almost never published, and it's ridiculous that they are not. Why are copyright holders—the studios—so obtuse? The "release dialogue" is usually more polished than the dialogue in the shooting script. And a release dialogue transcript is always made, only to sit in somebody's file cabinet or in an archive collection.

In the case of *Sunset Boulevard*, I used a version published by the University of California Press in 1999. Edited by Jeffrey Meyers, it's the closest thing available to an uncorrupt text. Even so, it's plenty corrupt.

For starters, the sole author credited on jacket and spine is "Billy Wilder." Only the title page carries, in smaller print, "screenplay by Charles Brackett, Billy Wilder, and D. M. Marshman Jr."

In his introduction, Meyers writes that "this edition of *Sunset Boulevard* makes it possible to get as much pleasure from reading the taut, highly intelligent screenplay as from seeing the film. It also enables the reader to savor some of Wilder's greatest lines." He means, of course, some of Brackett and Wilder's greatest lines, and perhaps some good lines by Marshman.

But one doesn't get exactly the same pleasure from reading his edition as from seeing the film. I made my own release dialogue transcript by endlessly starting and stopping the VCR and changing every syllable in the script to conform with the exact lines spoken by the actors. The script that Meyers used runs 117 pages, and on 108 of those pages I corrected discrepancies between the written text and the spoken! These corrections ensure that all *Sunset Boulevard* quotations in this book come verbatim from the film.

This problem is widespread. If you read James Agee's published script of *The African Queen* you encounter a lot of fussy, uninspired dialogue that someone—John Huston? Katharine Hepburn?—had the good sense to make charming. Published versions of Joseph L. Mankiewicz's *All About Eve* screenplay zip along, but the zip differs markedly from the release dialogue.

The Citizen Kane Book, by Pauline Kael, contains both the shooting script and cutting continuity of *Citizen Kane* by Herman J. Mankiewicz and Orson Welles. It's a textbook example of the before and after of screenwriting.

chapter 4

Chaz

To James Larmore Jr., Charles Brackett was his grandfather, Pop-Pop. That nickname changed to Gramps when Larmore reached puberty and during his teen years, wishing to sound more grown up, he started to call his grandfather Chaz.

Larmore's father, James Larmore Sr., married Alexandra Brackett, the daughter of Charles and Elizabeth Brackett, during World War II, when he was a soldier. Before that, he had been a chorus boy. Later he became assistant to his father-in-law, Charles Brackett. He also appeared in a minor role in *A Foreign Affair*.

I tracked down Brackett's grandson because I thought he might tell me something new about the working relationship of Brackett and Wilder. During their heyday it was assumed that Brackett supplied the sophistication, the erudition of a script, and that he also polished Wilder's vulgar edges. The energy and outrageousness in their pictures, said Hollywood conventional wisdom, came from Billy.

The prevailing opinion now, in books and articles on the career of Billy Wilder, casts Brackett as second fiddle in the writing team. This shift—based on hearsay and fueled by auteurist wish fulfillment—has occurred in recent decades as a parallel to director worship. Prior to the 1960s, those who thought about screenwriting at all would have looked on such an appraisal as strangely contrarian.

It's important to emphasize that in the instance of Brackett and Wilder virtually all critical opinion has come from outside: neither man took credit for anything more than working hard to entertain. A certain old-school gentlemanliness made boasting taboo, just as it forbade referring to oneself as an "artist."

Apart from writing, Charles Brackett's contribution to the team in his role as producer of such Brackettandwilder monuments as *The Lost Weekend, A Foreign Affair,* and *Sunset Boulevard* often slips by unnoticed, one reason being that producer doesn't equal auteur. A second reason: critics, film historians, and the public understand more clearly the director's work than the producer's. For convenience, if not in reality, a picture belongs exclusively to its director, though a powerful producer who regards the aesthetic bottom line on a par with the financial guarantees the director's artistic freedom.

Today Brackett the producer arouses even less interest than Brackett the writer. And Brackett the writer exists in the long shadow of Billy Wilder, for this is the Age of the Director. It does not detract from Wilder, however, to even the writing score and give back to Brackett at least fifty percent of the credit, rather than the twenty or thirty percent tacitly, condescendingly assigned by the Wilder claque.

But not by Wilder himself. He has never suggested that Brackett was anything less than the perfect partner. Indeed, he once summed up Brackett's great influence on his own writing: "He spoke excellent English. He was a very classy guy, a couple of pegs above the ordinary Hollywood writer. He was very patient with me, but he also insisted on my English becoming less ridiculous than it was then. I went to [Brackett's] good school—it lifted my street English a few pegs." Their partnership blended the best of each man's talent, resulting in pictures whose brilliance outshines the work that either man achieved without the other.

In a later chapter, as plaintiff against Wilder and his second longtime partner, I.A.L. Diamond, I will submit damning evidence that Diamond's influence ruined Billy Wilder. Here, arguing for the defense, I present the case for Brackett's invaluable mastery.

———

Born in 1943, James Larmore Jr. was six years old at the time of *Sunset Boulevard*. He spent long stretches of his childhood and youth with his grandfather, observing him at work throughout the fifties and until his retirement after *State Fair* in 1962. (Charles Brackett died in 1969.)

Larmore, at age seven, went to Paramount with his grandfather one day for a particular purpose. He explained what happened:

I was terrified of gunfire on the screen, and of loud explosions. Chaz would often take me to the movies on Saturday afternoon. Because of my phobia, however, I would always ask, "Is there shooting?" and he would have to reassure me.

I happened to be in the looping room when they were working on the scene where Norma Desmond shoots Joe Gillis and he falls into the pool. The projectionist first showed the whole scene without any sound. So I had that impression, as if it were a silent movie. Then—I suppose Chaz gave a signal—the projectionist rolled the scene with sound track added. She fired the shots—and I didn't flinch. From then on, I had no terror of gunfire or explosions in the movies. *Sunset Boulevard* cured my fear, probably by conditioning me for the shots before they happened.

Although the myth of Wilder and Brackett had them goofing off much of the day and scribbling unforgettable dialogue only when they had nothing better to do, reality shows bursts of hard work 24/7, with odd hours snatched for social life and always followed by still longer hours of busy pencils on yellow legal pads.

"The reason Billy became a director and Chaz a producer is because they were writers who wanted to maintain control of their work on the screen," Larmore said. "Billy is noted for talking about the importance of writing. And that's what they were both about: good writing."

When Wilder meets up with a serious interviewer, he typically spends more time talking about writing scripts than shooting them. Cinematically restrained, his pictures rely on screenplays and the right actors to bring dialogue to life rather than camera pyrotechnics or showy editing room brilliance. He attracts the ear of the audience first, knowing that the eye will follow. Marta Eggerth, the star of a German film that Wilder wrote, said, "In Billy's American films I can spot the music even in his dialogue." (Surely she meant *their* dialogue.)

I said to James Larmore that both his grandfather and Billy Wilder seemed to do a great deal of thoughtful work at home, away from the distractions of the office.

He replied,

I don't know about Billy but Chaz was always at work on the actual writing. I think they worked on things on their own a lot, as well as working together in the office. My grandfather was constantly reworking different scenes from current scripts.

He worked at home all the time with legal pads and Blackhawk pencils. Sometimes he would disappear to take a nap, but even then I used to find him writing instead of napping. Maybe he needed a nap because he was an insomniac. Sometimes when he couldn't sleep he'd get up and write all night. He wrote lying down, or semi-reclining either in a chair or on a bed.

James Larmore's recollections italicize Brackett's industry, which no one doubts. Proving the artistry of his collaboration with Wilder, however, requires less anecdotal evidence. That, unfortunately, verges on the impossible since no one alive had a ringside seat except Billy Wilder, and he doesn't discuss it. Two exhibits, however, may shed light on Charles Brackett's role in the affair.

The first is *American Colony*, Brackett's fourth novel. Published in 1929, it's a fashionable story of Jazz Age expats in France à la Fitzgerald. An equally appropriate title would have been *Brittle Is the Night*. The novel opens with a vaguely homoerotic scene between two men on the Riviera. They, like most of the characters, belong self-consciously to the Lost Generation.

Jack, who is swimming, returns to the yawl and tells Ted, stretched in the sun, "Hand me my pants." Ted coyly picks up the trousers with his toes. Then Jack surveys himself, admires his sunburn, which is "not quite up to Ted's but the white streak from navel to mid-thigh showed what progress the rest of his body had made."

" 'Admiring yourself?' Ted called. 'Oh, my dear!' ... With a bad masculine imitation of a feminine handkerchief wave Ted went to the other side of the yawl."

The important observation here has little to do with the quality of Brackett's prose. But the rhythm of that half-bitchy exchange between two men, for example, evokes the exchange between Joe Gillis and the repo men early in *Sunset Boulevard.*

GILLIS

Why should I give you the keys?

MAN NO. ONE

Because the company's played ball with you long enough. Because you're three payments behind. And because we've got a court order. Now come on—the keys.

MAN NO. TWO

Or do you want us to jack it up and haul it away?

GILLIS

Relax, fans. The car isn't here.

Or the very next scene in the picture, Joe Gillis in Sheldrake's office at Paramount. Fred Clark, as Sheldrake, bears little resemblance to stereotypical studio brass as portrayed in movies about Hollywood. Rather, he's the kind of sardonic, wasp-tongued male often portrayed by Clifton Webb and George Sanders. Indeed, Clifton Webb plays just that kind of man in *Titanic* (1953), produced and cowritten by Brackett. In the Wilder pictures before and after Brackett, there's no real equivalent of this character type.

I'm not the first one to note that Brackett's novels bear the influence of Fitzgerald. Jeffrey Meyers, editor of a recent edition of the *Sunset Boule-*

vard screenplay, draws explicit parallels. "Charles Brackett, a friend of Scott Fitzgerald, quotes a phrase from Fitzgerald's notebooks when Joe says of himself: 'He always wanted a pool. Well, in the end he got a pool—only the price turned out to be a little high.'"

Meyers supports his assertion with this footnote: "See F. Scott Fitzgerald, *The Crack-Up*, ed. Edmund Wilson, p. 165: 'I have asked a lot of my emotions.... The price was high.... It was the extra I had. Now it has gone.'" Meyers adds that "the unexpurgated edition of the *Notebooks* (1978) reveals that the author Fitzgerald satirizes in the first entry under 'Literary,' p. 175, is Charles Brackett."

Meyers also points out an even more striking Fitzgerald influence, viz. *The Great Gatsby*, published in 1925. "At the end of that novel, when Wilson, mistakenly thinking that Gatsby has killed Wilson's wife in a car accident, shoots him in the pool, Fitzgerald writes: '[Gatsby] paid a high price for living too long with a single dream.'"

I leave the dissertation to an enterprising doctoral candidate. It's an intriguing hint, however: a man gets shot and dies floating facedown in a pool. A young Midwesterner narrates the story after the hero's death, and that narration is *The Great Gatsby*. Did Jay Gatsby and the narrator of his story somehow merge twenty-five years later in the character Joe Gillis?

Billy Wilder wrote very little on his own in English. The rhythms of his prose, however, run through various transcripts of speeches and lectures given over the years. Here's Wilder verbatim from an American Film Institute Seminar with Billy Wilder in 1978: "Narration or no narration, you better get a hook into the audience right away. They are restless. The kid wants to go and pee, the aunt forgot the popcorn, you yourself don't feel so good, and you're worried is the car going to be stolen—and you've got to find something which makes them forget the popcorn and tell the kids to shut up—'You can pee later, or pee in your pants'—you need the hook."

Billy Wilder's syntax in conversation and in interviews is not the syntax of a Wilder picture—not *Sunset Boulevard*, not any other one. Rather, the language in a Wilder film, and its flow, belong mainly to Brackett, to Diamond, or to any other collaborator in Wilder's career. The wit, the verve, and probably much of the plot no doubt come routinely out of Wilder's mouth.

None of this detracts a syllable from Wilder. It shows his good sense in letting his greatest characters, who are Americans, sound American. (In view of Stroheim's implacable personality, one assumes that Max von Mayerling's dialogue and line readings come largely from Stroheim himself.)

If there were a perfume called *Sunset Boulevard*, it could be said to waft through Charles Brackett's novels. In *American Colony* a minor character drives an Isotta-Fraschini. One character has "a sensitive face . . . like an old dress that had been turned and turned to have something decent to show the world." The hard-boiled tone sounds a bit like Joe Gillis's voice-over description of Norma Desmond's script: "Sometimes it's interesting to see just how bad bad writing can be. This promised to go the limit."

In a later novel, *Entirely Surrounded*, published in 1934, a number of bitchy exchanges might be called Wilderesque, suggesting that Brackett, too, possessed a soupçon of "bad taste"—too "bad," in fact, to pass any Hollywood censor at the time.

A character named Agnes says of someone in her social circle, "Why couldn't she be left some business venture by which she might make money and which would involve the possibility of romance?"

" 'A corner on the contraceptive market,' Mr. Hulbert suggested happily."

Later in the novel two characters discuss how they would raise a son with homosexual tendencies. " 'I'd insist on rigorous athletic training, have a fencing instructor, a boxing instructor—'

" 'And after you'd spent all that nice money,' Daisy Lester said, wistfully, 'one day you'd come home and find him trimming your hats.' "

James Larmore Jr. said of Billy Wilder: "He brought a certain irreverence that sometimes rankled my grandfather, I think, but nowadays people who write about my grandfather or make documentaries about

Billy say that Chaz was too genteel to want to do the things Billy got involved in."

Such people perhaps mistake good manners for prudery. Opinions might change if they read Brackett's novels. They are urbane, edgy stories, impatient with bourgeois values, dark, and yes, cynical. They also have a surprising number of homosexual characters.

Perhaps Brackett, despite his avuncular looks and his Republican milieu, saw the world as not such a genteel place, meaning that not all the darkness came from Wilder. In his writing, however, Brackett trimmed the fat from his vision to avoid excess, just as Wilder, in his best pictures, controlled his own directorial "bad taste" and "cynicism"—at least during his years with Brackett. Only after the split up did Wilder's self-indulgence take over.

A glimpse of Brackett's lighter wit turns up in a letter to Gloria Swanson on December 9, 1950, after he had left Paramount for 20th Century–Fox. Although Oscar nominations were a couple of months ahead, the strongest contenders seemed obvious.

"Gloria, my darling," he wrote,

How great to get a letter from you. *Sunset Boulevard* and *All About Eve* being squared off against each other for 1950 honors, I feel a little as though I were slipping out this letter from the stronghold of the enemy. And I'm going to add to the treachery by whispering that I think *Sunset* a much better performance than Miss D's . . .

I haven't yet told you how infinitely I enjoyed the whole business of the Command Performance, and the photographs of you and the Queen [i.e., Elizabeth the Queen Mother, consort of George VI and mother of Elizabeth II] with the Queen sweet and dumpy and you slim and distinguished . . .

The only way to prove very much at all about the Brackett–Wilder collaboration is by analyzing their films. That's the evidence that counts—the rich result of their twelve years together. And those pictures are skyscrapers. By contrast (and with several high-rise exceptions) the ones

Wilder made post-Brackett conform to standard studio building code: they're bungalows, storefronts, cabins, warehouses . . . and toward the end, the property is condemned.

One autumn day in 1949, after *Sunset Boulevard* was in the can but months before its release, Charles Brackett and Billy Wilder met as usual in their office. According to Brackett, "Billy smiled that sweet smile of his at me and said, 'You know, Charlie, after this, I don't think we should work together anymore. I think it would be better for both of us if we just split up.' "

Those words left Brackett speechless. They left him shattered. Years later, not long before his death, he told his friend Garson Kanin, "Billy got right into the business of the day, and we said no more about it. But it was such an unexpected blow, I thought I'd never recover from it. And, in fact, I don't think I ever have."

Neither man commented publicly at the time. At the age of ninety Wilder gave an oblique explanation: "It's like a box of matches. You pick up the match and strike it against the box, and there's always fire, but then one day there is just one small corner of that abrasive paper left for you to strike the match on. It was not there anymore. The match wasn't striking."

On October 30, 1950, two months after the release of *Sunset Boulevard*, Louella Parsons reported in the *Los Angeles Examiner* that Charles Brackett had resigned from Paramount the day before. Brackett quit, according to Parsons and other journalists, after an argument with Sam Briskin, head of production. She wrote that "Briskin, whom I was unable to reach at his Palm Springs home, is reported to have objected to the writer-producer's recent two-day trip to New York to speak before the Motion Picture Advertisers Association on behalf of the Academy. Briskin claimed that the trip delayed studio production.

" 'I am not in the habit of giving anyone an accounting of my comings or goings,' Brackett is reported to have told Briskin when he walked out.

"However, yesterday's argument was only one of many previous upsets. I understand Brackett and the studio heads haven't been seeing eye to eye for several months."

Brackett went immediately to Darryl F. Zanuck and 20th Century–Fox, where he produced and cowrote a number of pictures including *Niagara, The Virgin Queen, The King and I,* and *Journey to the Center of the Earth.*

In the early sixties, after twelve years at Fox, the post-Zanuck studio canceled his contract on a technicality. Billy Wilder called a press conference and made the following statement: "In view of the treatment accorded Charles Brackett . . . I cannot imagine any self-respecting artist, whether director, writer, actor, producer, or musician, going to work for 20th Century–Fox under its present administration."

His words caused anger and embarrassment at Fox. The studio telephoned Wilder to offer their version, but he retracted nothing. In spite of his defection from "the happiest marriage in Hollywood," he remained an honorable spouse to the end.

chapter 5

Who Is Gloria Swanson?

*W*hen twenty-year-old Nancy Olson, a contract player at Paramount, got word from the studio in 1949 that her next assignment was *Sunset Boulevard* with William Holden, she assumed she was to play Norma Desmond. Fifty years later Olson laughs at herself, pleading self-defense: "After all, I had just done a picture with Bill Holden called *Canadian Pacific*. Why shouldn't I play the lead opposite him this time?"

When Paramount informed her that the director was Billy Wilder, she realized this would be a sizeable picture. But since she still hadn't seen the script, her misapprehension continued. Then she found out who was really to play the lead opposite Holden. Her reaction: "Who the heck is Gloria Swanson?"

Olson admits she was probably "the most naive girl" in Hollywood. "Please!" she says, rolling her eyes. "I was a doctor's daughter from Milwaukee. Press agents and columnists dubbed me 'Wholesome Olson.' Do you know how inexperienced I was? The studio would call and say, 'We'd like you to come Thursday afternoon at two o'clock to read with a new young man we're interested in for a screen test.' I'd say, 'Oh, I can't possibly make it; I have an exam at UCLA.' And Paramount was paying me seven hundred dollars a week!"

William Holden knew the significance of *Sunset Boulevard* and of Billy Wilder. Having been in pictures since 1939, Holden also recalled that Gloria Swanson used to be big. But right up until two weeks before the cameras rolled, he had no idea that he would costar with her in this potent story of the ghosts of Hollywood past. Only a year or so later did it dawn on Holden that the picture had repositioned his floundering career. It took a decade, perhaps two decades, for him to realize that *Sunset Boulevard* had conferred on him, as on everyone connected with it, the seal of screen immortality.

Holden was nobody's original choice for antihero Joe Gillis. First crack at the role went to Montgomery Clift, who was widely considered the most beautiful male face in town. And his career was on fire. He had done three top films in a row: Fred Zinnemann's *The Search*, Howard Hawks's *Red River* (both 1948), and William Wyler's *The Heiress* (1949). Clift jumped at the chance to play the out-of-work screenwriter who swerves off Sunset Boulevard and into the spidery hands of mantrap Norma Desmond.

Then Clift broke his contract. In the spring of 1949, a couple of weeks before he was due on the set, Clift phoned from Berlin, where he was finishing up his fourth picture, *The Big Lift*, to declare himself out. "I don't like it," he told agent Herman Citron. "I'm not gonna do it."

Clift's official reason for reneging, as stated to Billy Wilder in a second transatlantic telephone call, was this: "I don't think I could be convincing making love to a woman twice my age."

"Bullshit!" Wilder yelled over the primitive, crackling phone connection. "If you're any kind of actor you can be convincing making love to *any* woman!" Later Wilder said, "Very strange for a New York actor, whose audience consisted of elderly women!"

Wilder was no doubt privy at the time to the rumor that has circulated ever since: that Jazz Age singer Libby Holman, Clift's inamorata and mentor since 1942, made him turn down *Sunset Boulevard* because she was convinced the story was about her. To be sure, the parallels are striking. Holman, some fifteen years older than Clift, liked young, pretty, androgynous men (and slightly older women). She had been a big star of Broadway and supper clubs in the 1920s, until booze, drugs, and recklessness helped push her out of the spotlight. There had also been half-hearted attempts at a comeback. Theatre critic Brooks Atkinson once called Holman "a dark purple menace"—an epithet that surely fits Norma Desmond, as well.

But the biggest story about Libby Holman was the mysterious death of her young, pretty husband in 1932. Tobacco heir Zachary Smith Reynolds, whom she had married the previous year when he was nineteen and she was either twenty-five or twenty-seven, was shot to death on July 6, 1932 in a bedroom of his family estate in Winston-Salem, North Carolina. Holman was indicted for murder, although she and others in the house that night vigorously maintained that Reynolds committed suicide. Holman was later cleared, but the lingering aroma of gunsmoke—erotic, tragic, or a strange mix of both—saturated the rest of her life. It was said that Holman kept young, bisexual Montgomery Clift on a long leash. If so, she snapped it taut and brought him to heel the day she read his new script from Paramount.

Charles Brackett knew Libby Holman, and he knew her strange story, for in the twenties they moved in the same Jazz Age circles. (In Brackett's novel *Entirely Surrounded*, a character named *Smith* Wetherby also shoots himself.)

A line from *Sunset Boulevard*—"Madame is the greatest star of them all"—sums up the career of Gloria Swanson. Or so it might have done at one time, just not in 1949. By then she was twenty-five years past her zenith, and young Nancy Olson's unfamiliarity with the Swanson legend was typical in the "new" Hollywood—that is, the crowd that had ruled the industry since sound arrived in 1927. Never at home in Hollywood, Swanson stuck around as long as she could stand it, then moved east. Not because she couldn't make the changeover—she quickly starred in half a dozen talkies—but rather because she didn't much like the parts offered her. And so in 1938 she decamped to New York and stayed there the rest of her life.

Ever since *Sunset Boulevard* came out picture people, journalists, and movie fans have tried to cast Gloria Swanson as an offscreen Norma

Desmond. The sotto voce speculation runs something like this: Silent-movie fame, six husbands, countless lovers, power, money . . . the loss of all that must have left her not only a health-food fanatic but also a little cracked.

Anything but, and the way to rile Swanson was to suggest otherwise. She was, after all, a sensible Midwesterner, raised in Chicago, and after Hollywood she lived lavishly at 920 Fifth Avenue, at the corner of Seventy-third Street and a couple of blocks from Henry Clay Frick's mansion. At the time of *Sunset Boulevard* she had a TV show, she painted and sculpted, designed women's fashions, and she wasn't half bad as an inventor and amateur scientist.

Though she had quit school after the ninth grade to make pictures, Swanson acquired a broad education bolstered by an extensive library. Raymond Daum, Swanson's friend for many years before her death in 1983, recalls her first editions of James Joyce, among many others. Swanson herself said, "I was hungry for knowledge. So I started at the age of seventeen, just getting my hands on books. I'd rather read a book than go to any ball."

Daum adds that she "surrounded herself with people who could teach her." According to him, Swanson entertained Richard Byrd, the polar explorer; she gave a tea party for the wives of astronauts; she invited doctors and statesmen and thinkers to come to her home and talk. An unlikely guest was the Rev. Billy Graham, with whom she seems to have discussed motion pictures but not religion.

All these projects and activities, and keeping up to date—surely Gloria Swanson offscreen was the antithesis of the character that made her immortal. Certainly she wanted it that way, for she didn't like to think otherwise.

And yet, as we'll see, Norma Desmond wouldn't leave Swanson alone. Perhaps Brackett and Wilder had inadvertently created a vampiric presence who took hold forever. Or maybe it was Swanson who couldn't turn loose of Norma Desmond. After all, this character had released her from long obscurity into the limelight of her alma mater, Paramount Pictures. Norma Desmond had made her big again.

The story of Gloria Swanson vs. Norma Desmond is a drama in

itself, simultaneously matter-of-fact and creepy, quotidian and over the top. And not unprecedented. Such ambiguous bonding often takes place when actors play indelible roles. Bela Lugosi, for instance, loathed his eternal Dracula typecasting, dreaming instead of romantic leads. Vivien Leigh outdistanced Scarlett O'Hara but not Blanche DuBois, who imprisoned her personally and professionally. A sunnier example is Bette Davis, who said of Margo Channing in *All About Eve*, "I had to work hard to remember I was playing a part."

Whatever the meaning of Swanson as Norma Desmond—and of Norma Desmond as Swanson—their relationship redoubled. Eventually their union grew more complex than that of actress to character. As in mathematics, where congruent triangles coincide exactly when superimposed, so in Hollywood, where these two great stars came to resemble twin personalities in the same celluloid skin.

Gloria Swanson, in 1948, was old news in Hollywood. Her last picture, *Father Takes a Wife*, released in 1941, was as deservedly forgotten as her first, made in 1915 and clumsily titled *The Fable of Elvira and Farina and the Meal Ticket*. In New York, however, her star still flickered, for she had blossomed in the new medium of television. The number of TV sets in New York City had jumped from 17,000 in early 1947 to 300,000 a year later. Viewers gobbled up everything offered, making the city a frantic hub not only of network programming, but of local shows, as well.

The Gloria Swanson Hour, a weekly show devoted to shopping, cookery, new products, and goings-on about town, got a big publicity buildup in local papers. Swanson even appeared on the cover of the first issue of *TV Guide* when it was still a fledgling publication distributed only in metropolitan New York.

In the fall of 1948, as her six-month contract with WPIX drew to a close, Swanson was hospitalized for surgery. Her employers presented a television to watch during recuperation—in those days hospital rooms were equipped only with radios—and she turned it on. Until then, she had been too busy starring on TV to look at it. Now, for the first time, she watched the thing. She was appalled. "That's awful," she said about one program after another. "It looked cheap and thrown together, too crude."

Even before leaving the hospital, Swanson, whose image had once been so huge, made up her mind against the small screen. She dictated to her secretary a letter of resignation.

In her memoirs, Swanson wrote: "An hour and a half after that letter was delivered, the phone rang. It was the casting director from Paramount in Hollywood. He said they wanted me to go out there and have a screen test."

Swanson, of course, was miffed. The perfect retort would have been the Norma Desmond line, "Without me there wouldn't be any Paramount Studio!" but those matchless words from the script belonged to her future. Swanson answered instead, "I've made two dozen pictures for Paramount. Why would they need to test me?"

What the casting director could not say, without being both tacky and tactless, was that the studio needed an actress who looked sufficiently old to star in Wilder's new picture. Besides that, some at Paramount wondered whether Swanson had any screen presence left, and a test was the way to find out. When she informed the casting director that she was still a hospital patient, he escaped the need for candor. They discussed her health and he agreed to phone after her recovery. Years later, Swanson wrote: "After *Father Takes a Wife* I was no longer optimistic about comebacks."

At that point in her 1980 autobiography, *Swanson on Swanson*, she echoed a poignant line from *Sunset Boulevard*: "The calls from Paramount continued." In the film, it's not DeMille phoning Norma Desmond, but a studio underling who wants her car, not her, for a picture. In the case of Swanson, however, it was the producer and cowriter, Charles Brackett, who called to offer her a crack at a major role in a major picture. When she asked about the director, he told her it was Billy Wilder.

A flashback to 1934: The last time Swanson and Billy Wilder crossed paths she was still a big star, though her career after the 1920s had begun to sag. Wilder, then an unknown refugee who still spelled his name

"Billie," was one of eight writers who worked on a Swanson film called *Music in the Air*. For this he received his first American screen credit. The director was Joe May, Wilder's old friend whom we now recall as a broken recluse dependent on charity.

Neither Wilder nor Swanson seemed to remember one another very well from that picture. Indeed, it's likely they said no more than "How do you do?" while working on it. Asked in extreme old age if *Music in the Air* brought back any memories, Wilder said, "None. Except I remembered Gloria Swanson later for *Sunset Boulevard.*" Based on a Broadway musical by Jerome Kern and Oscar Hammerstein II, the film didn't live up to its promise. Variously described as "wretched," "tepidly old-fashioned," and "predictable," it did nothing for anyone who worked on it. One of Wilder's biographers sums up the experience in purple prose that seems to capture the dispiriting experience: "Wilder saw Gloria Swanson on the lot, her pride and desperation wrapped around her like a tattered ermine robe."

By 1948, Joe May was a sad case, Billy Wilder had become one of Hollywood's top writer-directors, and Swanson's tattered ermine robe, though metaphorical, was valued at exactly $350—her weekly salary for *The Gloria Swanson Hour*. Suddenly, however, with that phone call from Charles Brackett, her wilting career got an injection of rocket fuel. He offered her a suite at the Beverly Hills Hotel and, provided the screen test pleased all parties, a salary of $50,000 for *Sunset Boulevard*.

Gloria's mother, Adelaide, was in Swanson's apartment the day of the fateful phone call. "Mother, we've had a dreadful Christmas," Gloria said. "How would you like to make up for it and go to Beverly Hills with me for a few weeks?"

There's a glitch in Swanson's chronology. She puts her surgery just before Christmas. Apparently, from the statement to her mother— "We've had a dreadful Christmas"—she remained hospitalized on December 25, or either she was recently discharged. The call from Charles Brackett, according to her account, would have come between Christmas and the New Year. And yet, among her papers in the vast Swanson Collection at the University of Texas at Austin, I came across this telegram from Brackett to Swanson, dated September 4, 1948: "Plane delayed will telephone on arrival in New York at about 11:30. Hope you can change our engagement to luncheon. Apologetically, Charles Brackett."

It's unlike the precise, exacting Swanson to fall four months wide of the mark, especially since she had an excellent memory even in old age, and also because she saved every document, every scrap of correspondence throughout most of her life. In case of memory lapse, she also had two others helping with her memoirs, Raymond Daum, her archivist, and Wayne Lawson, now the literary editor of *Vanity Fair*, who did most of the actual writing.

Whether Paramount phoned in September or December is not of surpassing significance, except for what it reveals about Brackett and Wilder's casting choices. Charles Brackett's telegram on September 4 indicates that he had something important to say to Swanson, important enough for him to fly to New York to say it. (It's possible, of course, that he combined the Swanson visit with other studio business in the city.) Since they had no reason for a meeting other than to discuss *Sunset Boulevard*, this suggests that Brackett and Wilder ruled out Mae West, Mary Pickford, and Pola Negri early on, perhaps before they actually wrote a line of dialogue. Neither man ever mentioned showing a script to their three prospective Normas. No doubt they merely told the story to these disdainful divas.

The Saturday Evening Post, in a two-part article on Swanson in July 1950, shortly before *Sunset Boulevard* was released, states that Paramount phoned her "on September third." The writer continues, "Miss Swanson, thinking it was a bit part, said she might be able to leave her program for two weeks." When she heard the offer in its entirety, however, "she said she would be in Hollywood by the first of the year."

The same magazine article quotes Charles Brackett: "Nobody else was considered for the part. We knew no time would be wasted getting into the story as soon as Swanson appeared on the screen. Youngsters who never saw her would immediately accept her as an old-time movie queen. Older fans would identify with the characterization and get a bigger emotional wallop from the story." His statement, though not literally true, nonetheless said it all. In the beginning, Brackett and Wilder created Norma Desmond from the rib of Gloria Swanson.

Despite her no-nonsense approach to life, Swanson must have dreaded the ghosts awaiting her in Hollywood. Some, having died, had indeed lost corporeal form, and these included two of her ex-husbands, the actor Wallace Beery and Herbert K. Somborn, who, in the twenties married Gloria and also built the Brown Derby. Others were the living ghosts of diminished stars and devalued moviemakers. A bit of archaeological rummaging in her memory resurrected the ghost of young Los Angeles, little more than a country town when Swanson first arrived and now a somewhat sinister world city in the sunshine. And hovering everywhere, the ghost of her earlier self, sure to be encountered at all the wrong moments.

If it were possible to condense the Swanson legend, the vignette would go something like this: A few years after stepping off the train in Hollywood as a teenager, Gloria Swanson became one of the archetypes always to be associated with the development of motion pictures. The others are Charlie Chaplin, Mary Pickford, Douglas Fairbanks, Rudolph Valentino, and Greta Garbo. She earned a million dollars a year in the days when most of it was take-home pay and it would buy the world. Swanson's worldwide fans considered her the embodiment of impeccable luxury and sophistication, not only for her opulent film roles but also for the spendthrift lavishness of her private life.

At the apex of her fame she traveled to France to film *Madame Sans-Gêne* (1925), and came home with a third husband who bestowed on her the title Marquise de la Falaise de la Coudraye. (The marriage ended, and all copies of the film later vanished.) When Gloria and the Marquis sailed into New York, "her billing was the largest ever seen on Times Square up to that time. Her name in electric lights occupied the whole front of the Rivoli Theatre, with the stars and stripes and French tricolor flying above."

Their progress by rail across the country resembled a festive version of President Lincoln's funeral cortege sixty years earlier. In many towns along the way, school let out so that the children, escorted by teachers and parents, could see Royalty roll by in a private train. Fanatical fans prostrated themselves, fainted, flung flowers in riotous devotion.

In Hollywood two brass bands heralded her visit. Gloria and her spouse saw "troops of policemen on horseback, Sid Grauman's theatre usherettes on white ponies, a red carpet ten yards wide, and a huge platform decorated with flowers and bunting and signs of welcome." Swanson, somewhat amused by the dazzling kitsch, later wrote that "the faces on that platform were like the Last Judgment—everyone I'd worked with or known in Hollywood. Mary Pickford, Douglas Fairbanks, Charlie Chaplin, Joe Schenck, Norma Talmadge, and D. W. Griffith were there in a very conspicuous bloc. They were after me to join their company, United Artists. Paramount had rounded up its most famous faces for the welcome, most notably Mr. DeMille and Rudy Valentino." This ballyhoo yielded to a parade, led by a platoon of motorcycle cops, which progressed up Sunset Boulevard to the Swanson villa in Beverly Hills.

This was done in utter seriousness, though today it sounds like an operetta scenario for Jeanette MacDonald and Nelson Eddy. Nothing, of course, could top such a froufrou party, and Swanson's inevitable decline set in at once.

Her films suffered from anemia for three years, until *Queen Kelly* in 1928. With her big-shot lover Joseph Kennedy dispensing Gloria's money, they hired Erich von Stroheim, who was even more extravagant than Swanson. Eventually she instructed Kennedy to fire him. Down the drain whoosed her career, Stroheim's, and close to a million dollars of Swanson's money. The picture wasn't released in the U.S., and did only piddling business abroad. The magnificent ruin of it, available on video, shows brilliant work by Swanson, Stroheim, and everyone else involved.

She had fight left in her, and later in 1928 she soared in *Sadie Thompson*. After that she drifted. By 1948, Gloria Swanson was a past without a future. At the age of fifty, she had devolved from the great silver screen to the thirteen-inch home set, and those wonderful people out there in the dark now kept the lights on, talked back, munched frozen dinners, washed them down with beer and, in place of tears and laughter, emitted loud, satisfied burps.

Hollywood was a dangerous place for a fifty-year-old woman. Especially dangerous for a former queen who now must answer to arrogant minions, for they knew how to grind a legend into pulp. At times Gloria Swanson felt temptation like an undertow, pulling her back toward the safe fortress on Fifth Avenue where she ruled as a garrulous, high-living chatelaine. In New York, she belonged; in Hollywood, she had felt like an exile even when she reigned.

Surveying the Chateau Swanson on the eve of her departure, Gloria beheld a happy domain. Despite a chronic shortage of dough, she wasn't exactly down to her last mink. In fact, she had a roomful, including the four full-length furs she had bought the previous decade for a trip to Switzerland. "I thought I might be cold," Swanson explained logically to a visitor. Acquisition of those four brought her total to eighteen—and that was years earlier. Since she never deaccessioned the wardrobe and constantly had it retooled, she probably owned two dozen or so—mink, chinchilla, sable—by the first snow of 1948.

Even in lean times, Swanson's apparel budget was $7,000 a year. As president of Forever Young, her dress business, Swanson considered it a company expense. After all, a celebrity who designs women's fashions must maintain her image as a fashion plate. A reporter who called on Swanson at the time of *Sunset Boulevard* described the vast full-room closet that Swanson called her "store." Formerly a dressing room ten by fifteen feet, "it is filled from floor to ceiling with shelves and double-tiered racks, and is large enough to accommodate only her winter or summer clothes and accessories. Out-of-season apparel is kept in a separate storeroom in the building. Her current wardrobe includes about three hundred dresses and suits, one hundred pairs of shoes, three cases of gloves, and five long shelves of hats. She rarely wears a hat as it comes from the milliner. It doesn't satisfy her until she has added her own individual touches."

Not long ago, during a conversation with Swanson's friend Raymond Daum, I said, "You visited Swanson countless times at 920 Fifth Avenue. I wonder if you'll take me on a memory tour of the place?"

"I went there for the first time in 1956," he said. "Ginger Rogers put me in touch with a friend of hers, the publicist Earl Blackwell. One day he called and said, 'I want you to take a friend of mine to a cocktail party. The lady is Gloria Swanson.' I couldn't believe it. I said to myself, Why, she has to be dead.

"That name was really out of the past, although I had seen *Sunset Boulevard* just six years earlier. We always thought she was older than she was. Anyway, I took her to the party and when we got there she said, 'Don't eat any of this food. It's the worst thing in the world. Just nibble a pretzel and I'll cook dinner for you later.'"

Daum remembers a Swanson dinner of brown rice and steamed vegetables. She told him, "If you want to get drunk you'll have to do it with these little splits of champagne. That's all I allow in my fridge."

Raymond Daum became a regular at Swanson's home, first as a friend and later as her archivist and "man of affairs," the unofficial title he uses to describe keeping her big, busy life in order.

"Her apartment was a maisonette," Daum says,

because it was on the ground floor. By the way, Igor Stravinsky and his wife had one of the big apartments upstairs. You entered Gloria's from Seventy-third Street. You came into a foyer and to the left was the dining room. She later turned that into an office. That's where I holed up.

So you take a left and there's the dining room. Off the foyer you have this large—she called it "the White Room." It was almost a solarium. She turned that into a living room, with a piano. The other large room next to it was the library. Beautiful—very French, with a plan of Paris hanging above the leather couch. It was beautifully furnished in period furniture, and her portrait—one of her portraits—was there, then off of that room was the bar and a tiny dining area.

That led off to her little garden with a fountain. It had a wall around it, very well protected.

When you come back into the foyer you take a right, and walk down a long corridor. You pass the guest bedroom on the left, then at the very end is Gloria's suite. She has a large bath whose windows look out on the garden.

Now, we backtrack down the corridor and to the right is the kitchen, with her maid's quarters adjacent. Several small rooms for the maid.

You see, there were other maids' quarters on a different floor, but those were used originally to house maids for the entire building. Gloria rented several of those maids' rooms for her dress business, and also for storage of her own wardrobe—racks and racks of clothes. To get up there you took the freight elevator to the top floor of the building, about the thirteenth or fourteenth. In later years she talked about adding a bath to her business area on the top floor and turning part of it into a small apartment. I would have lived up there, but I never did.

Swanson's home, unlike many such showplaces, looked lived in. No one ever mistook it for the period rooms at the Metropolitan Museum. Two photo spreads that appeared in the *New York Sunday News*—the first in 1961, the second in 1966—show informal rooms that reflect the taste of Gloria Swanson, not of a decorator. Perhaps intentionally, Swanson herself upstages every object in her home.

A visitor in 1950 counted seventeen family pictures in the living room: Swanson's elder daughter, also named Gloria; her adopted son, Joseph; her second daughter, Michelle; and her grandchildren. The same visitor looked at the family Bible, where Swanson "recorded the birth dates of her own and her daughter's children" and also kept telegrams announcing the arrival of each grandchild.

All of this opulence and material security, along with the comfort of sentimental mementoes, receded as Swanson and her mother, Adelaide, chugged across America toward Hollywood in their first-class compartment. In 1949 the trip still took five days, but how different from a quarter century earlier when, as the Marquise de la Falaise de la Coudraye, she had commanded the rails. This time, instead of a triumphal entry into Hollywood, Swanson must come in through the back door, as it were.

Like an insignificant starlet, she had to take a test. Never mind that the studio had her in mind for a very A-list picture. She was nobody's marquise now.

California was celebrating the centennial of the 1849 Gold Rush when Swanson's train pulled into Union Station. Arriving at Paramount, she found the studio in the grip of centennial fever, although the connection remained opaque. They couldn't even claim Chaplin's *The Gold Rush* (1925), which belonged to United Artists. All the same, the studio realized there was publicity in them thar hills.

Over the famous entrance gate Swanson saw "a tremendous sign, in the form of a comet, displaying pictures of past and present stars. The size of these pictures, ranging from the head to the tail of the device, ostensibly was determined by each performer's importance."

Gloria peered at the ostentatious comet. Where was she? Since she had left Paramount twenty-three years earlier, she searched the smaller likenesses in the tail of the thing. Not there. Oh well, why should they remember her? After all, she was merely one of the biggest stars the town had produced. Curious to see who the studio considered big enough to be prominently pictured in the comet's head, she gazed up and saw her own profile. She was a figurehead in every sense of the word.

Swanson glowed with gratitude. They hadn't forgotten her, and after *Sunset Boulevard* she'd make another picture, and another. . . . Just then Bill Meiklejohn, the studio's chief casting director, joined her. "How do you like it, Gloria?" he beamed.

"Oh Bill, I don't know what to say, it's—"

"Baby, am I glad to see you!" he exclaimed. "You took me off a helluva spot. If I'd put Crosby's picture on the front end of that comet, Hope would've blown his top, and Crosby would've had a fit if Hope was up there. Stanwyck or Hutton would've scratched my eyes out if one got top billing over the other. You turned out to be a real lifesaver."

"That's how I knew I was home," Swanson later told an interviewer as she recounted this ironic little misunderstanding. "Right back in the jungle, up to my ears in the old rat race."

The notion of a screen test still bothered Swanson. She asked her old pal George Cukor whether she should refuse after all. He advised against it, pointing out that Brackett and Wilder were "the brightest things at Paramount. If they ask you to do ten screen tests, do them." William Powell, Clifton Webb, Allan Dwan, and other friends also urged her not to jeopardize working with Paramount's wonder boys.

The next day Swanson met with Wilder and Brackett. Perhaps expecting rigid Teutonic orderliness on the part of Wilder, she got a shock. When she asked to see a copy of the script, he informed her in his charming accent, between puffs of smoke, that they had only a few pages.

Turning to the distinguished Charles Brackett, she heard: "We're working on it, Gloria, but we haven't quite decided how the picture ends."

"Well, what's it about?" she inquired.

They reeled off the bare bones of the plot and ended by revealing that there was a murder in it.

"Who murders whom?" asked the curious Swanson.

"We honestly aren't sure yet," said Billy. Changing the subject to avoid further cross-questioning, he handed her three pages of script, gave her an elfish grin, and said, "That'll be plenty for the test. We just want to have a look at you."

The name of the "blond young man," as Swanson called him, who filmed the screen test with her has been lost to history. Otherwise, he would surely enjoy footnote immortality. Swanson passed the test, of course. In it she spoke several lines from the scene where Norma Desmond maintains that she is still the greatest.

Contracts were signed and hands shaken. Swanson spent the next few days in reunions with Adolph Zukor and other relics of Paramount's infancy. She posed for press pictures with him and studio barons high and low, meanwhile settling in with Mother for a stay of several months.

A few days later Brackett and Wilder had news for Swanson, but they couldn't decide how to break it. Tact was required, and finesse, to avoid a possible star walkout.

Finally they found the courage to tell her: Montgomery Clift declined to play romantic scenes with a woman her age. And . . . and, "Would you mind doing another screen test? Now Gloria, it's not for you, it's for William Holden. You know, our new Joe Gillis? Well, he's thirty-one and he's afraid that he'll look too old for you. He thinks you look so young. Now hold on, we might have to age you with makeup, ha ha, just a little, because you don't look a day over—"

A frown line bisected the Swanson brow. "But women of fifty who take care of themselves today don't look old," she declared. "Can't you use makeup on Mr. Holden instead, to make him look more youthful?"

Whatever they really thought about that second screen test, Wilder and Brackett didn't push their luck. Holden regressed to twenty-five, and Swanson, who even in her teens had looked as glamorously mature as a matron of forty, stayed as young as she was.

Or did she? Wally Westmore, head of Paramount's makeup department, described in detail how to add years to an actor. Among Swanson's papers I came across a fragment of some long-ago press release, titled "How Wally Westmore Aged Gloria Swanson for Her Role in *Sunset Boulevard*." Oddly, he discusses only general techniques without mentioning Swanson in particular: "Aging is accomplished by subtle shading and highlighting of features. Shading under the eyes creates the illusion of [words missing]. We also shade the lines from exterior of nostrils to mouth, creating a deeper line than normally exists. We also accentuate the lines between the brows. In all cases we accentuate the face line by highlighting alongside of the line. Following this principle we shade over the eyes and between the bridge of the nose and eye. We shade a good deal darker in the corner close to the nose (between the eye and nose) so that the eye appears more deeply set."

It's possible that Westmore was describing how he aged Swanson for the beauty regimen scenes, where she worries about looking physically and emotionally worn out. If Swanson had undergone the makeup department's aging process for all scenes, she surely would have boasted that she (unlike most actresses) looked so young at fifty that her youth required a disguise. The press release sounds so impersonal that it's also possible it applies not to Swanson alone but to actors generally.

Karl Silvera

In studio-era Hollywood, department heads routinely got screen credit for work actually done by other members of their respective departments—music, art direction, costumes, make-up. Such was the case in *Sunset Boulevard*, where Wally Westmore received sole credit for "Makeup Supervision." But two others in the department—Karl Silvera and Frank Thayer—applied makeup to the cast every day during filming, beginning at about six o'clock in the morning.

When I asked Silvera about the studio practice of crediting only a department head, he said—without apparent irony— "Wally got credit for everything I did for thirteen years." Silvera said he made up "Erich, Nancy, Bill, and sometimes Gloria." On days when he didn't work on Swanson's face, Frank Thayer did.

Silvera recalls that Gloria Swanson looked younger than fifty. Asked how he made her up on a typical work day, he explained, "I'd apply the base makeup to get the uniform color, then I did the shading if shading was needed, and then rouge, powder, eye makeup, and finally lipstick." He said that Billy Wilder often instructed him to give Swanson and others in the cast a certain facial surface for a particular scene. According to Silvera, "Billy was very definite in what he wanted. He had his own ideas, and I consider him one of the most talented men I ever worked with."

As for others in the cast, Silvera recalls Nancy Olson as "a very pretty young lady" who required only "a simple base, a little eye makeup, and some rouge." William Holden got "just straight base makeup and sometimes not even that—he didn't want to wear any if he could avoid it." Erich von Stroheim "was jazzed up a little to give him more mystique, as you would shade a painting. We wanted his eyes to look deep set and mysterious."

Silvera began his career as a makeup artist in 1936. He spent thirteen years at Paramount and seventeen years at Warner Bros. Later he worked in television, on *The Munsters* from 1964–1966 and on *Falcon Crest* for six years before his retirement in 1987.

As part of the Paramount troupe, Silvera worked in a minor capacity on *Samson and Delilah* just prior to *Sunset Boulevard*—"I helped out on beards and character work," he said.

Miss Swanson is ageless: the myth proved useful. In 1952, following her triumph in *Sunset Boulevard*, Swanson appeared in a series of print ads for Jergens face cream. Each one featured a photo of Gloria glamorized to perfection, and over it, in large print, a rhetorical question: "Will you look as young as Gloria Swanson on your 52nd birthday?" and "Will you look as exciting as Gloria Swanson at 52?" and also "Will you look as young as Gloria Swanson the Spring you're 53?" The smaller copy underneath one such ad informed the public that "When Gloria Swanson was filming *Sunset Boulevard*, makeup men had to paint wrinkles on her face to make her look middle-aged. What was her secret?" The answer, of course, was Jergens face cream.

Whether it was Jergens or a higher-priced spread remains a secret. A titillating rumor made the rounds in New York years ago that Swanson kept a smooth face by applying semen to it. That seems doubtful; if such were the case, all Hollywood would look like the Gerber baby.

While shooting *Sunset Boulevard*, Swanson and her mother lived for a time at 1131 Horn Avenue, Apartment 10. (In her book she wrote, "I rented a house on Mulholland Drive," but this seems a false memory. It contradicts her address on the Paramount roster, and Swanson's younger daughter, Michelle Farmer-Amon, also confirms the Horn Avenue address. Later, when seventeen-year-old Michelle flew from New York to join her mother and grandmother in Los Angeles in the spring of 1949, they all lived at 8540 Hedges Place, a house that Swanson rented from actor Kurt Kreuger.)

It was in the apartment on Horn Avenue that Swanson first stepped out of her own identity and put on the persona of Norma Desmond. Swanson's daughter laughed as she told me, "Oh, when my mother came home from the studio in the evening, my grandmother would joke, 'Here comes Norma Desmond.'" When I asked Michelle to elaborate she said, "It's because my mother got under the skin of Norma Desmond and she didn't leave it until the end of the film. So my grandmother called her Norma."

I asked, "Did she, as Norma Desmond, become difficult to live with?" Michelle roared with laughter. "No more difficult than she was normally!" Then, in fairness to her mother, she added, "Part of being difficult meant she was difficult with herself. She was a hard worker. She learned her lines before everybody else, I'm sure; she was very professional about that. She was always on time at the studio because it was her job."

For a dyed-in-the-wool pro like Swanson, it must have been maddening not to know exactly what movie she was filming. Who wouldn't become difficult? Yet it's literally true that, right up to the last day on the set, and even beyond, *Sunset Boulevard* was an unwieldy, nontransparent block of ad hoc story and mutating dialogue. The most definite thing about the project was its indefiniteness. Swanson said later, "They didn't know what they were going to do with it from day to day. I had only twenty-six pages when I went on the set for the first time."

Michelle recalls her mother's travails in detail: "Originally her role in *Sunset Boulevard* was supposed to be much less important. It sounds silly now when you see the film, but it's true. Every day Billy Wilder would rewrite the lines, so she'd have to learn them again. At night she would memorize her dialogue at home, then at the studio in the morning all the lines changed. They would bring new pages of script to her dressing room and she would sit there and memorize them. I was there on the set. I remember it."

To Thine Own Script Be True

One day while doing research among Gloria Swanson's papers at the University of Texas at Austin, I asked to see her copy of the *Sunset Boulevard* script. I was dismayed to hear: "That won't be possible because it's in a special exhibition."

Fortunately, that exhibition was in the Harry Ransom Humanities Research Center, which owns the Swanson papers. I enlisted the help of Carol Henderson, a member of the staff, who accompanied me downstairs to the lobby where a number of treasures from the collection had been mounted in locked display cases. By chance—or design?—the script of *Sunset Boulevard* stood proudly beside a Shakespeare first folio. While two security guards watched, I put on special gloves to turn pages of the relic.

Swanson made few changes or annotations, since she received this bound copy only when the picture had wrapped. On one page, the line "I'm a star" was crossed out in ink and replaced by "No one leaves a star." The handwriting didn't resemble Swanson's; perhaps these few corrections were made by a studio secretary.

Finishing my examination, I removed the gloves and a guard re-locked the display case. "I don't get it," he said. "Gloria Swanson beside Shakespeare? Why are they together?"

The short answer is, "During the past century movies have become, for much of the world, the epitome of culture." The long answer—how this happened, and why, and whether *Sunset Boulevard* will endure as the cinematic equivalent of a first folio—requires many books, and at least another century.

A tantalizing possibility that Swanson never addressed directly is this: Did she write, or rewrite, a significant part of Norma Desmond's dialogue? Hints of such phantom collaboration surfaced in my conversation with Cecilia Presley, granddaughter of Cecil B. DeMille, who said: "Gloria Swanson sent him a telegram asking if he would play himself in the picture. She signed it 'Young Fellow,' which had been his name for her thirty years earlier when they made pictures together. By 1949, however, it had slipped his mind. When he got the telegram, he was disgruntled by the long-ago nickname which he couldn't place. Then someone on his staff reminded him, and he lit up."

Presley speculates that casting DeMille as himself might have been part of Swanson's strategy to "soften and humanize" Norma Desmond, since she found the character unsympathetic as originally written. To be sure, most of *Sunset Boulevard's* tender moments occur in the scene between Norma and DeMille. And the poignance of their scene wasn't there in earlier versions of the script.

For example, pages dated April 26, 1949, one week into filming, indicate an exchange between DeMille and Norma Desmond that is considerably more matter-of-fact than what we see onscreen. There DeMille does not welcome Norma with the words, "It's good to see you," as he does in the final version. Norma's tears when the old-time extras and crew members recognize her don't exist in that earlier version, nor does this touching exchange when Norma brushes those tears from her eyes:

DEMILLE

What's the matter, dear?

NORMA

Nothing. I just didn't realize what it would be like to come back to the old studio. I had no idea how much I'd missed it.

DEMILLE

We've missed you, too, dear.

NORMA

We'll be working again, won't we, Chief? We'll make our greatest picture.

DEMILLE

That's what I want to talk to you about.

This same scene in the earlier version depicts Norma Desmond as unpleasantly hard, and minus the vulnerability that subsequently added greatness to the character of this fallen star. Perhaps at Swanson's behest, the following was deleted from Norma's dialogue: "Can't you see them standing at the box office? Lines that stretch for blocks!" What she tells DeMille in the picture is, "Oh, I don't care about the money. I just want to work again. You don't know what it means to know that you want me."

Another telling omission is a speech that Brackett and Wilder originally had Norma deliver to Gillis in the backseat of the Isotta-Fraschini as they drive away from Paramount. Referring to DeMille, she was to have said, "He's a shrewd old fox. He can smell box office. Only I'm going to outfox him a little. This isn't going to be C. B. DeMille's *Salome*. It's going to be Norma Desmond's *Salome*, a Norma Desmond production, starring Norma Desmond. . . . Home, Max." So mean-spirited are those lines that if they had remained in the script they would have strangled our sympathy for pitiable, ruinous Norma Desmond.

It's impossible to prove that Gloria Swanson suggested this or that change, or whether Wilder and Brackett came to view Norma with more compassion as they beheld her incarnation in the Swanson flesh. It seems likely, however, that the writers would have listened to Swanson, since she, from day one, knew Norma Desmond better than the two men who created her ever would. Indeed, Norma Desmond was the dark side of Swanson. (When *Sunset Boulevard* came out, one reviewer made the perceptive comment that Norma's dialogue "is the purple prose of subtitles.")

Gloria Swanson's telegram to DeMille, if it exists, would perhaps lie among his papers at Brigham Young University. But since those papers fill more than a thousand boxes, the possibility of locating it seems remote.

When I mentioned to Swanson's daughter Michelle what DeMille's granddaughter told me about the telegram, she said, "I have a vague memory of something like that." Next I asked if she recalled whether her mother actually made suggestions regarding certain Norma Desmond lines of dialogue. "She did, I'm sure she did," was the answer. "You see, I can remember her being upset about certain lines. Since they changed her dialogue every day, and thus the personality of Norma Desmond, she was unhappy that she had played the character one way in the beginning, which was, perhaps, a scene from the end of the script, and a different way later on when they filmed a scene from the beginning."

Here's what Raymond Daum, Swanson's friend and confidant, has to say. "Gloria told me that in the mornings Billy Wilder and Charles Brackett would come to her dressing room. The three of them would go over the script. One or the other of them would ask, 'Now, what would Norma say?' and Gloria would tell them. If lines they had written the night before didn't strike her as befitting Norma's style or vocal rhythms, she would inform Brackett and Wilder, 'No, I don't think Norma would say that.' Then Gloria would add to, or subtract from, what Brackett and Wilder had written. I got the impression that she contributed an enormous amount."

Swanson also talked about Wilder and Brackett's original unsympathetic characterization of Norma Desmond. Daum says, "I'm not sure the idea of visiting DeMille on the set was hers. It's possible that Wilder, or he and Brackett together, thought that up as a way of making Norma Desmond more vulnerable. She pleaded with them to make Norma sympathetic."

A Swanson colleague from her later years takes a sceptical view of her supposed contributions. "She liked to take credit. She was capable of exaggerations like, 'I designed the dresses and Edith Head helped' or 'I wrote half that script.'"

Certainly the Swanson ego never suffered from underdevelopment. Nevertheless, I'm skeptical of that colleague's scepticism. Swanson never boasted to an interviewer that she contributed a single line of dialogue; she only discussed the matter with close friends. Nor does she hint in her autobiography that she did anything more than act the role of Norma

Desmond. Had she wished to snatch a bit of scriptwriting glory, opportunity was there.

We also know that Billy Wilder was open to suggestions from his cast. "The script is there," he said, "and if something better occurs, I'm the first to accept it—from an actor, an electrician, from the script girl, or even from the producer, which is rare enough."

Wilder also said that "one of the best ideas in the picture came from Erich von Stroheim, although it arrived too late for me to develop it fully, but it's there all the same. I'm referring to the fan letters that still arrive for Norma Desmond—written by Max." Although amenable to some ideas, Wilder had his limits. When Stroheim pressed to have his character, Max, shown laundering Norma's underwear—and more lovingly than a cloying suds commercial on TV—Wilder said no.

Charles Brackett, in a 1951 letter to Swanson consoling her for her loss of the Best Actress Oscar to Judy Holliday, suggested the considerable influence she exerted in shaping Norma Desmond: "I remember you that first day, saying, 'But I've got to know more about her—is she really nuts? Is her arrogance genuine, or is she faking it? What's the line of the part?' To this you got no answer, as we too were feeling our way, and only reached our final conclusion through you."

No one doubts that most of the script came from Wilder and Brackett, with the occasional assist from Marshman. Whatever grace notes cast members might have added, the witty irony of the scattershot Brackett-andwilder approach is that ultimately they shaped *Sunset Boulevard* into the most coherent of films. It's all of a piece, minus loose ends and with mere microscopic incongruities. Not only does the picture adhere to a strict three-act structure, it also advances with Mozartian ease. (Cinematographer, editor, art directors, and others are also responsible for its graceful flow.) This classical balance of form works in counterpoint to the lurid, gothic content, as though the ragtag band of gypsies from *Il Trovatore* had pitched camp in the Pantheon.

chapter 6

"The Cameras Have Arrived"

Sunset Boulevard left a paper trail more complete than that of many other major films. Reading these documents, it's instructive to find contractual expectations spelled out in vast (and sometimes puzzling) detail. Less edifying are the long worksheets with columns of figures for hundreds of employees and for thousands of hours of production time. These, in fact, soon numb the brain. Yet these myriad legal files and accounting ledgers do yield certain insights about *Sunset Boulevard* and about studio-era filmmaking in general. For example:

Swanson's compensation was "$50,000, $5,000 per week for 10 weeks—next two succeeding weeks to be 'free'" ("free" meaning that Swanson was to be available for publicity, retakes, etc.). The studio agreed to pay her train fare, "first class, including Pullman, from New York to Los Angeles, for commencement of Artist's services, and provided Artist shall return to New York within 30 days following completion of services and shall have accepted no other motion picture engagements in Los Angeles or its environs."

Erich von Stroheim received "first-class transportation from Paris and reasonable living expense for Artist and one other person while en route," as well as return transportation to Paris. He was to be paid $5,000 per week for seven weeks, with the additional stipend of "one million French Francs upon execution of agreement and an additional 500,000 French Francs per week, payable weekly during seven-week period."

Hedda Hopper signed on for $5,000 per week, with a one-week guar-antee. Cecil B. DeMille was paid a flat rate of $10,000, while Nancy Olson, under contract to Paramount, received $5,000 per picture. As for the Waxworks, Buster Keaton got $1,000 for one day's work, Anna Q. Nilsson $200 for the same amount of time, and H.B. Warner, who worked "⅙ + ⅖ day," received a total of $1,250.

Montgomery Clift's salary, according to an estimate sheet, was to have been $60,000. His replacement, William Holden, saved the studio a neat sum, for Holden commanded a mere $30,000. That's because he was not yet considered a first-rate screen presence. When Wilder chose him to play Joe Gillis, Holden was finishing up a picture called *Father Is a Bachelor* at Columbia.

An illustration of his status at the time comes from another Para-mount estimate sheet: "...based on Holden's Columbia finishing April 11, 1949. On this basis there is a 1-day layoff for Holden (April 12) before starting on *Sunset Boulevard* April 13, 1949. If Holden's Columbia pic. finishes April 13 (2 days behind schedule), the additional cost will be $4,000. This allows a 1-day layoff for Holden (April 14) before starting *Sunset Boulevard* on April 15, 1949." In other words, he was studio chattel who got time off only when he couldn't be used.

Wilder's opinion of Holden at the time was a notch higher than the financial estimator's at Paramount: "He photographed like an actor who could possibly have a brain in his head." Later, Wilder revised his opinion upward. He and Holden became friends for life. Holden said that Wilder opened the world of culture and travel for him.

Nancy Olson, who made four pictures with Holden, assesses her friend and costar in these poignant terms: "Bill was the perfect person for Joe Gillis at the perfect moment in life. His career was beginning to slide. He was playing roles like the husband in *Apartment for Peggy* where the picture was about Peggy and not about him. Low-budget, churned-out films. He was already drinking too much, and he was just a little frayed around the edges."

———————

Finally, on April 18, 1949, the cameras rolled. Several writers have stated that Billy Wilder shot his films in sequence, but such linear filmmaking has always been virtually impossible. What these writers mean, probably, is that for the sake of realism, Wilder preferred to shoot early scenes first and later scenes toward the end of production.

He also preferred shooting day scenes during the day and night scenes at night. According to Nancy Olson, "The scene in Sheldrake's office was shot during the day, and the scene where Norma goes to Paramount to visit DeMille. One of our office scenes, Bill Holden's and mine, takes place in daylight and Billy shot it in daylight. Another scene with Joe Gillis and Betty Schaeffer that takes place at night was filmed at night. And my arrival at Norma's house—the arrival was done at night, but the interiors of her house Billy shot during the day."

Nancy Olson's first scene in the film—when she expresses misgivings about the script Joe Gillis is trying to sell to Sheldrake, the producer— was also her first scene for Wilder. (She had appeared in only one other movie, *Canadian Pacific*, released in 1949.) "That first scene was the hardest one in the picture for me," Olson recalls. "Why? Because I was a question mark. I could have been fired the next day. Billy could simply have said, 'Nancy's not going to work out.'

"So, to cover my nervousness and insecurity, I prepared for it with extra drive. I wanted the lines to come tripping off my tongue. I think I did that first scene with exactly the right energy, because Billy was thrilled with it."

Pausing to reconsider, Olson decides that a later scene involving a long take was perhaps her most difficult, though for a different reason. About a month and a half into shooting, the day came for Olson and Holden to play their love scene. In the story, they're writing a script at night in her cubicle in the readers' department at Paramount. And that's where Wilder shot it.

Shooting at night for verisimilitude, Wilder had Holden and Olson rehearse the scene. She remembers that "Billy smiled during rehearsal, so I felt I was on the right track." Olson points out that union rules required the studio to serve dinner for everyone involved in after-hours shooting.

"So there was a party atmosphere," she says. "Audrey was there—the future Mrs. Wilder—and Bill's wife, Ardis, was also there. Do you know what I called her? 'Mrs. Holden!' That's how callow I was. Anyway, suddenly I was no longer on a closed set, which is what we were used to working on. I felt very unprotected because I was about to play this tender, intimate love scene, which included the embrace and the kiss."

As Olson describes the studio atmosphere, it sounds like pagan revels in *Samson and Delilah*, which was finishing up production on a nearby sound stage: "Everyone was down there drinking martinis, and eating dinner, laughing and talking—it was a big party. I thought, Well, I'm being tested. Trial by fire."

The shooting script opens the scene this way: "Start on a LONG SHOT. THE BOOM MOVES FORWARD to the only two lights. They are the door and window of Betty Schaeffer's cubicle. Betty sits at the desk, typing. Gillis . . . is pacing the floor."

These memories of merrymaking juxtaposed with her big love scene make Olson more animated. Her rising voice and widening eyes belie the cool, measured Betty Schaeffer—a performance which won an Academy Award nomination as Best Supporting Actress for 1950. "Okay," she continues, standing up to "direct" the scene in her elegant sitting room in Beverly Hills. "Bill was there, I'm here, they're all down there, the camera's over there on a boom, and now Bill and I rehearse but we don't actually embrace. Bill says, 'Nancy, I'll take you here, and then you move and we'll just kiss, okay?' I said okay.

"Then Billy came over to us. He said, 'Now Nancy, now Bill—please do not break the embrace until I say cut. I'm going to let you go on for a little while, because it's going to be a montage into the next shot. So just keep kissing each other. It will seem a long time, but trust me, this is what I want.' "

Olson interjects an aside: "What I'm about to tell you is so typical of Billy Wilder on the set."

Back to Paramount, 1949, and she's about to kiss Bill Holden. "So we play the scene. We get to the embrace, and we kiss . . . kiss . . . and kiss. Not a word from Billy Wilder, not a word that even sounds like 'cut.' That kiss must have gone on for thirty seconds or longer. I was ready to say 'Uhhhhmmmmm uhhhmmm.'" Olson laughs, then drops to a stage whisper: "All of a sudden, down below, this female voice says [and Olson shrieks it out in angry-parrot tones], 'Cut! Cut that out! Cut!' And it was— Mrs. Holden!"

Ed Sikov, a recent Wilder biographer who interviewed neither Billy Wilder nor Nancy Olson, recounts a version of this incident in which he implies that the kiss was all too real, that Ardis Holden (whose screen name was Brenda Marshall) just happened to drop by, and ended up in a jealous snit. "Mrs. Holden," he writes, "didn't find the joke very funny." Olson hoots at such a spin.

"It was a prank, of course it was!" she insists. "A Billy Wilder prank. Ardis was in on it, and so was everyone else—except me. For one thing, Bill Holden was not seductive with me. I appreciate that, because I had enough on my plate. I was very straitlaced."

An Olson jump cut to 1995: "I was back at Paramount to do a TV special. Right back there on the balcony in the readers' department where Betty Schaeffer and Joe Gillis worked on their script and also fell in love. That building houses *Star Trek* now, and they were shooting an episode. Word got around that I was talking about the balcony scene in *Sunset Boulevard*, and Trekkies started pouring out to watch. I felt like Norma Desmond! But no one came up to say hello. No one asked for my autograph. They just stood at a distance and gaped as though I were some new animal in the zoo. I expected someone to say, 'Oh yes, she does have a white tail, you know.' When I left I waved them a Norma Desmond good-bye."

Who's That Lady?

According to the fan magazine *Silver Screen* for August 1949, Ardis Holden appears briefly in *Sunset Boulevard*. In that account Mrs. Holden had a lunch date with Bill one day. Arriving at the sound stage where the morning's filming took place, she read a disconcerting sign: KEEP OUT! ONLY ACTORS WORKING IN SUN-SET BOULEVARD ALLOWED ON THIS SET. When Holden emerged, his wife asked him to take her inside. And he did—as an extra in the studio scene where Norma Desmond returns to Paramount.

True or false? Neither of her names—Brenda Marshall, Ardis Holden—appears in any cast list. Nor have I ever spotted her in a crowd scene. I'm even more skeptical reading her supposed statement to *Silver Screen*: "When a woman's in love, there's always a way."

Of course there was a director's chair, with *Wilder* stamped on it, but if someone had removed it Billy wouldn't have noticed. "I never sat down there for longer than three minutes," he said, "and sometimes not even once."

Probably the most kinetic director in Hollywood, Wilder reminded Gloria Swanson of Toscanini conducting an orchestra. "He has such authority," she recalled, "but he conducts in a very light, delicate, polite manner—and also madly irreverent."

Whatever brutal jibes and nasty remarks Wilder made over the years, his actors were spared. No one in the cast of *Sunset Boulevard* ever criticized his behavior, and despite famous clashes with Marilyn Monroe on *Some Like It Hot* and Humphrey Bogart on *Sabrina*, actors usually finished a Wilder picture wanting to work with him again. One of his biographers captured him in director's mode: "However despondent or fatigued he might be feeling, Wilder never showed it to his actors. He was a fountain of energy, of ideas and enthusiasm, of persiflage and sarcastic banter, of compliments and anecdotes, and he seemed to blossom when he stood by the camera, a hat perched on his head, a cigarette between his lips, a slight crouch as he empathized physically with each actor, shouting, 'Go . . . hit it . . . roll 'em.'"

Before the camera rolled, rehearsals had nudged actors closer to Wilder's plan. In the case of Nancy Olson, "the assistant director would come to my dressing room and we'd go over the scene. Not that he directed at all; he only read with me. The purpose was to get a tone of the scene."

If Olson's line reading wasn't all the assistant director thought Wilder might wish, he'd look at Olson as if to say, "Really? Is that how it's going to be?" She would laugh and say, "Well, let's try it again."

The next step was blocking the scene through the camera. This is the part of filmmaking you rarely see in movies about making movies because it's tedious and time consuming. Blocking entails all the glamour of waiting in line at the supermarket.

According to Olson, Wilder would say, "Now, Nancy, let's have you come through that door." He might suggest: "Let's see, just walk through it." Olson would walk in the way she thought Betty Schaeffer would walk, then perhaps lean over the desk, pick up an object and look at it. "Billy would say, 'That's fine' or 'No, we can't do that, the camera can't go that far. So try it over here.'"

After the general blocking, and before the camera actually turned, Wilder would lead the actors through one or two rehearsals that prefigured the actual scene. This final couple of rehearsals might be considered camera ready.

Gerd Oswald

Charles C. Coleman was assistant director on *Sunset Boulevard*. Second assistant director, or "second," was Gerd Oswald, who later became a director in his own right—*A Kiss Before Dying* (1956), *Bunny O'Hare* (1971).

Born in Berlin in 1916, Oswald grew up in the world of German silent pictures, for his father was director and producer

Richard Oswald. Both Oswalds came to Hollywood in 1938. Interviewed in 1979, ten years before his death, Gerd Oswald said, "In the days when I started there, I guess that was 1941 or 1942, Paramount was really *the* class studio in every respect."

Recalling *Sunset Boulevard*, he said: "Everybody, Swanson and Von Stroheim and H. B. Warner, some of the old-timers, they all fell back in that milieu [of silent pictures]. It was sort of a strange feeling, working on that movie."

Oswald had known Stroheim since youth. He called him "a marvelous, marvelous man. A bit of a dreamer, full of tales. I looked him up in Paris every time I'd go back to Europe. I was extremely fond of him."

Of Billy Wilder, Oswald said: "You can't get really too close to him. Even though I knew him through my father, I remember him when we both met in Vienna many years ago when I was ten years old. But when I worked with him at Paramount on both *Sunset Boulevard* and *A Foreign Affair* [as second assistant director], I didn't have that close feeling that he'd known me since I was a kid. It was like he'd met me in this hemisphere."

It's surprising to learn that Wilder, with his eye for detail and his emphasis on characterization, rarely *directed* actors in the usual sense of the word. Swanson said, "He never gave a line reading to me, and I never saw him give one to another actor. And he never showed me how to do a scene. He would discuss a character but he expected you to know how to play it, speak the words."

Swanson recalled a day early in the shooting when Bill Holden told Wilder that "he needed to know more about Gillis in order to fill out the character, that the script was incomplete and unclear and therefore frustrating for him as an actor." Wilder looked at his leading man. "How much do you know about Bill Holden?" was Billy's Zen-like response. He wouldn't say another word. To judge by Holden's performance, he looked into the heart of Holden and dared to face the truth.

Nor did Nancy Olson get special help, even though she was new to the business. I asked her about the scene near the end of *Sunset Boulevard* when her character, Betty Schaeffer, comes to the Desmond house to rescue Joe Gillis, and he refuses to leave with her. As he is about to escort her out of the wrought iron gates he says, "I can't look at you anymore, Joe." Then, in a gesture reminiscent of Renaissance paintings that depict Adam and Eve expelled from the Garden of Eden, Betty turns away and covers her face with her arm. In the next shot, Joe Gillis ushers Betty out of the Gates of Paradise—or in this case Purgatory, since it's the Desmond house she's quitting.

Because Wilder is a passionate art collector, and this is one of the most conspicuous painterly touches in *Sunset Boulevard*, I expected to learn that it was his idea. But Olson says, "It was a spontaneous gesture on my part. Billy never said to me, 'Nancy, put your arm up and turn away from him.'" She adds, "When I did that scene it touched me fantastically. I didn't have a clue as to how it should be played, and I got practically no direction. Actually, Billy wanted me to have tears in that scene. He asked if I wanted something blown into my eyes. Well, we tried that and it really didn't work, so maybe I used that gesture instead of tears."

Surprised that an inexperienced actress of twenty could come up with some of the nuances in Olson's performance, I asked her, "Didn't he tell you anything specific that he wanted in a scene?"

"No," she answered, "he never did. I remember the scene where Bill Holden and I walked on the back lot, where I turned my head and said the line about having my nose fixed. What Billy did was, he created an atmosphere of being relaxed." Olson's lively patter slowed as she echoed Wilder's method of creating such an atmosphere for her and Holden: "Now, we're just going to take a walk, Nancy, we're just going to talk and be together."

The line about the nose job comes as Olson and Holden stroll up the New York street, a generic and much used set on the Paramount back lot. Telling him about herself and how she came to work in the readers' department, Betty Schaeffer says, "I had ten years of dramatic lessons, diction, dancing. Then the studio made a test. Well, they didn't like my nose—it slanted this way a little. So I went to a doctor and had it fixed. They made more tests, and they were crazy about my nose—only they didn't like my acting."

"I got letters for years, by the way," Olson confides. "They all wanted to know, Who did your nose?" She laughs. "That's the one good thing I was born with, my nose, and then in *Sunset Boulevard* I had to tell the world that somebody else made it. Anyway, Billy liked that scene, he thought it worked well for Bill and me."

Billy Wilder was up to three packs of cigarettes a day in 1949, and if he wasn't puffing a cigarette he was lighting a cigar. One reason, perhaps, for the unstoppable nervous energy was that, as filming progressed, he and Brackett and Marshman needed to stay one jump ahead of production. Wilder's strain was the greatest, because after the next day's pages were written he also had to direct them. He told an interviewer, "Many people in Hollywood have the impression that I improvise on the set, working from only a rough scenario. Actually, what is not on paper by morning will never be on film in the evening. Can you imagine me down on the stages trying to think of dialogue on the spur of the moment while the stars and a highly paid crew stand and wait? My scripts never are finished, but that is quite different to shooting if off the cuff. Up to the last minute, up to the morning of the tear-soaked Olivetti, my collaborator and I are improving the script to our own satisfaction."

When Swanson wrote her autobiography thirty years after *Sunset Boulevard*, she omitted an impromptu tribute paid her the first day she reported for work. Was the omission owing to modesty, or to an eerie echo of Norma Desmond's return to Paramount that Swanson didn't care to dwell on? According to a witness, "Veteran extras and technicians crowded around her, clamoring for a smile of recognition. People who didn't know she was still alive came from adjacent sets to gape at a legendary personality in the flesh. When she stepped before the camera for her first take, a strange silence descended on the vast studio. She was the old professional, taking charge of the situation with stylish competence."

Though she left it out of her book, Swanson had touched on the incident years earlier. Speaking with John Kobal in 1964, she said, "When I walked on that film set, the whole crew . . . I've known them all their lives . . . they hadn't seen me . . . it was like the prodigal had returned. There was such an atmosphere of camaraderie, it made everything so easy. I had every bit of help you can imagine." According to Kobal, "Wilder saw this and incorporated it into the script to become Norma Desmond's moving visit to the DeMille set."

Swanson soon had a chance to show her appreciation for the rousing welcome. When the schedule required a number of cast and crew members to work through a weekend, night and day, Swanson surprised her tired colleagues by ordering twelve large cakes and hosting an impromptu party.

chapter 7

The Bedroom of Norma Desmond

imes city desk? Hedda Hopper speaking. I'm talking from the bedroom of Norma Desmond. Don't bother with a rewrite man, take it direct. Ready?—As day breaks over the murder house, Norma Desmond, famous star of yesteryear, is in a state of complete mental shock.

Norma Desmond's house—and the Babylonian too-muchness of it—is one of the most famous shelters in film history, ranking with Tara, Manderley, and that Victorian pile behind the Bates Motel. How appropriate, given Norma's delusions, that her place didn't really exist. Or rather, it existed only in fragments, and they were scattered all over Los Angeles.

The actual house, used for exterior shots only, stood at 4201 Wilshire between Irving and Lorraine boulevards at the intersection of Crenshaw. Built between 1919 and 1924 by William O. Jenkins, who owned sugar plantations in Mexico, the mansion was rarely occupied. The Jenkins family lived in it for just one year before returning to Mexico. In 1936 J. Paul Getty bought the derelect house, according to some accounts, as a home for a former wife. In any case, the house stood empty, looked after by a couple who acted as caretakers, until its demolition in 1957.

Good Palazzo Keeping

Elaine St. James, a syndicated columnist and author of *Simplify Your Life: 100 Ways to Slow Down and Enjoy the Things that Really Matter*, urges her readers to "throw out the car phone," "stop buying clothes that have to be dry-cleaned," and "learn to say no." Reading her commonsense column one day, I had the whimsical notion of asking this simplicity expert what advice she would offer Norma Desmond for uncluttering a cobwebbed life.

St. James said, "I have a couple of thoughts I'll run by you, recognizing from the outset that Norma is never going to simplify her life. You could perhaps suggest that she hold her own garage sale and never go to someone else's. I like to think she has just bought her third book on how to get organized and she can't find it anywhere. She should definitely resist the temptation to move to a bigger house. She realizes it's time to clean things out because the fish in her acquarium have been dead for a week."

"As well as the monkey," I added.

"The monkey, too."

I asked, "Do you think he died from clutter?"

"Yes, an overdose of clutter. And of course, Norma did, too! Too much stuff, too many men. The basic rule is to practice moderation in all things, but Norma would not understand the concept."

"Should Norma Desmond throw out everything she hasn't used in the past quarter century?" I inquired.

"Absolutely. And stay out of the mall—not that she has ever been to one. She should never, ever window shop. Or, she could pretend that the Joneses have the simplest, least-cluttered house on the block and try to keep up with them. Although I'm not sure Norma knows where her block is."

To postwar sensibilities the house looked sinister because of age and heft. In that split-level era when a suburban box was the dream of every nuclear family, an old palazzo like Norma's held value only for the land it occupied, which invited development. And that's exactly what happened to the Getty place, with depressing results. On the actual grounds of the Getty/Desmond house stands a monstrous structure called the Harbor Building. Gross and totalitarian, it epitomizes the style I call "California Stalinist."

One drizzly morning in Los Angeles I parked on Irving Boulevard and walked around Norma Desmond's old neighborhood, or at least this split-off part of it, since the supposed grounds of her estate lay six or seven miles west, toward the end of Sunset Boulevard in Holmby Hills. The house that Norma shared, in a sense, with the unhappy Gettys had vanished without a trace.

Near this northeast corner of Irving and Wilshire, however, stands another old house that might pass for Norma Desmond's in a pinch. Just your basic $4.5 million Italianate minimansion, it has aged well, and it's properly forbidding. Strolling several times up and down the sidewalk, half expecting to be nailed for loitering, I gawked until I imagined the house began to gawk back.

What a shame that in the fifties the Getty place seemed not worth saving. Had it endured a few years longer it might well have dazzled the pages of glossy magazines, for newspaper accounts of the time make it sound worthy of Charles Foster Kane. Two weeks before the house was destroyed in 1957, the *Los Angeles Times* reported that the walls, thirteen and a half inches thick, were still up though much else had been removed: "Gone are the costly interior panelings which once adorned them. Gone, too, are the imported tiles which covered the walls and ceilings of bathrooms and kitchens [and] . . . the floor of complicated parquetry and the black walnut staircase winding up from the formal entry. Still there, however, is the bank-type walk-in vault. It is where the library used to be. It is about ten feet square, a massive cubicle with walls of concrete and steel thick enough for a battle line pillbox."

John Meehan, who shared the 1950 Academy Award for Art Direction-Set Decoration (Black-and-White) with Hans Dreier, Sam

Comer, and Ray Moyer for *Sunset Boulevard*, said that his wife discovered the Getty house and suggested it as the home of Norma Desmond. Since there was no swimming pool at the location, Paramount dug one, with the stipulation that this and all improvements be removed after filming to avoid a property tax increase.

Although Brackett and Wilder dreamed up the shot of Joe Gillis's body floating facedown on the pool's surface, it was John Meehan who devised the way to shoot it. Meehan later recalled Wilder's telling him, "Baby, the shot I want is a fish's viewpoint." Meehan remembered a magazine article he had read at his barber's a few days earlier—how a fisherman looks to a fish. Next day he returned to the barber's and pawed through stacks of magazines without finding the article. Left holding the bag, Meehan rummaged the studio prop department for an aquarium, plastic dolls, and a mirror.

After filling the aquarium, he sank the small mirror to the bottom and floated a doll on the water's surface. Imagining his eyes as the camera, Meehan peered into the water and focused on the mirror, which captured the doll's wavy image. After several trial setups he ascertained the angle from water to air in which the scene above him was as clear as the one below—about forty-eight degrees. The scene in the finder showed that the shot was upside down and in reverse—a glitch which the optical department could fix.

Meehan then set up the actual shot. At the bottom of a portable process tank he placed an eight-by-six-foot dance rehearsal mirror. After sinking the tank to the bottom of the pool, he backed the police and news photographers with a muslin canopy which, photographed in black and white, would mimic the dawn sky. That done, cinematographer John F. Seitz was able to light the scene effectively in a short time. With the camera set up alongside the pool, Seitz pointed it down at the mirror on the bottom of the tank and filmed Holden's bobbing reflection. According to Meehan, the shot "turned out to be a simple, inexpensive way to get through-water or underwater shots" by obviating "the use of expensive underwater equipment."

For the benefit of future filmmakers, Meehan noted that "the water must, as usual, be well filtered for clarity and kept at a low temperature of about forty degrees" because "at higher temperatures the natural gases that build up in the water cut down the light transmission." No one, however, explained how long Holden, facedown in the water, kept his eyes open for the shot. Nor what measures were taken to prevent hypothermia. (When *Sunset Boulevard* was released, the joke around Hollywood was that a screenwriter either winds up *with* a pool, or *in* one.)

"Portable property"—a Dickens phrase in *Great Expectations*—takes on new meaning when used to describe the remainder of Norma Desmond's estate. Lower-story interiors were built as sets on Stage 9 at Paramount, while the upper hall and Norma's bedroom were constructed several buildings away, on Stage 5.

Did any bedroom ever look more sleep deprived? You can't help thinking that if Norma had changed the décor and opened a window she might have avoided a breakdown. Her bedroom is like some Peacock Throne of the Id—a courtesan's boudoir designed for everything but slumber. To furnish it, the art directors and set decorators seem to have plundered not only Paramount's vast prop department but also the European rococo and half the stately homes of Bel-Air and Beverly Hills.

A cloying Cupid flutters at the foot of "that bed like a gilded rowboat," as Gillis calls it. In every direction there's one too many of each object—chandeliers, mirrors, fringed lamps, pillows on the bed. Gillis sums it up as "all satin and ruffles . . . the perfect setting for a silent movie queen."

There are far more than one too many of the ubiquitous Norma Desmond photos, not only in the bedroom but throughout the house. Their excess functions on several levels. That multitude of eyes monitors every movement, heightening the claustrophobia of the Desmond compound. The image glut underlines Norma's desperate egotism, while reinforcing her mad delusion that she, at fifty, still looks young enough to play the nubile Salome.

Is there also a classical allusion lurking in the subtext? Argus, a monster in Greek mythology, had a hundred eyes, only some of which slept while the rest kept wide-open vigil. In 1950, a headline in the studio publication *Paramount News* announced, "100 Swanson Photos Appear in *Sunset.*" In fact, according to the article, more than a hundred Swanson likenesses were used, including "oil paintings, caricatures, sketches, old glamour portraits, scenes from past pictures, groups of personalities from bygone days." The bulk of these pictures came from Swanson, with others loaned by DeMille and still others pulled from the studio's photo files. (A few years ago Meryl Streep posed à la Norma Desmond for *Vanity Fair*. Supine across a satin sofa with photos of herself bedecking every adjacent surface, she looks too self-satisfied to be anyone in Hollywood except Meryl Streep.)

Proust, one of Wilder's favorite novelists, had already spelled out what a more introspective Norma Desmond might have said about her own room: "My bedroom became the fixed point on which my melancholy and anxious thoughts were centred."

The fateful driveway that Gillis careens into when a tire blows was part of the Janss home at 10060 Sunset Boulevard. The address we see stenciled on the curb when the film opens—10086—didn't exist, then or now. (Several retakes of the drive were shot months later in Griffith Park.) Gillis's temporary digs in the room over Norma's garage were equally schizo: interiors on Stage 5, stairs and other exteriors at a garage on the Getty property.

Every time I'm in Los Angeles I drive the length of Sunset Boulevard, from its inauspicious beginning downtown to the jumping-off place in Pacific Palisades. In Holmby Hills I slow down to look for 10086, hoping some prankster might have slapped the number on a curb if only to help sell star maps. It's not there, of course, but even on bright, sunny days I feel a frisson as I come close. No matter that eucalyptus trees, Technicolor parterres, and pampered, controlled vegetation paint the roadsides in benign variegation. If you look closely you'll see a shadowy entrance to an obscure drive that just might be *hers*. That's when I speed up. It's no place for a blowout, not for Joe Gillis and certainly not for me.

Schwab's Drug Store

From *Gone Hollywood* by Christopher Finch and Linda Rosen-krantz: "Schwab's Drug Store was the natural successor to the drugstore that Sam Kress had opened in 1918 at the intersection of Hollywood and Cahuenga boulevards. This had been a popular hangout for extras and small-time actors in the silent era. Because Kress was willing to cash checks and extend credit, so many would-be Western stars congregated on the premises that his establishment gave birth to the term 'drugstore cowboy.'

"Schwab's was operated by the four Schwab brothers—Jack, Leon, Bernard, and Marvin—and their formidable mother, who also owned a drugstore downtown. When they opened in Hollywood—taking over a failing enterprise next to a Reuben's market on Sunset and brightening it up with a new soda fountain and a pinball room in the back—Leon made the rounds of the nearby studios to drum up business. He can hardly have imagined how successful he would be. Among the earliest patrons were Charlie Chaplin and Harold Lloyd, both pinball addicts, and with customers of this stature, the crowds soon followed. What made Schwab's so special, however, was the fact that it was the opposite of exclusive, attracting people from all ranks of the film industry. Credit was virtually automatic, and starving bit players could always be sure of a free meal.... Agents and managers conducted business there, packing the phone booths, and Schwab's also served as informal real estate office, providing an exchange for information on everything from cheap apartments to Beverly Hills mansions.

"Although it is not true that Lana Turner was discovered there, she did frequent the place, as did Ida Lupino, Olivia de Havilland, Orson Welles, and Rita Hayworth.... The lineup of celebrities led Sidney Skolsky—who virtually used it as an office—to nickname the drugstore 'the Schwabadero.' Sometimes, when the fountain was busy, stars would mix shakes or man the cash register. And until pinball machines were banned, they often took part in noisy contests, with enthusiastic sections packing the back room."

For purposes of the film, pieces of Hollywood and the rest of Los Angeles were assembled as if from a kit. The parking lot we see William Holden pull out of, thus initiating the chase scene—repo men in pursuit of Gillis—was the lot and bootblack stand near the El Capitan Theatre close by Hollywood and Vine. The actual chase took place on several streets, including the Sunset Strip, Sunset Boulevard west of the Strip, and Stone Canyon Drive. The shopping excursion—Joe and Norma in the car en route to his sartorial makeover—was shot on Lindenhurst Drive in Beverly Hills, while the actual scene was filmed in the Men's Shop of Bullocks' Department Store on Wilshire.

Gillis traveled to the actual Bel-Air Golf Course in pursuit of his agent, played by Lloyd Gough. Wilder, considering the real Schwab's Drug Store impractical, had the interior duplicated on the Paramount lot. But Schwab's from the outside was really Schwab's.

Are You Now, Or Have You Ever Been?

The following item appeared in the *New York Herald-Tribune* on May 16, 1951:

Film Inquiry Hears 4 Today

Washington, May 15 (AP)—The House Committee on Un-American Activities announced today it will hear four more Hollywood witnesses tomorrow when it resumes its investigation of Communist influences in motion pictures. Committee Counsel Frank Tavenner Jr. named them as screen writer Leonardo Bercovici, Alvin Hamer, and Lloyd Gough, actors, and Bea Winters, former agency secretary.

Two days later the *New York Times* reported that "Lloyd Gough, a screen actor, became the seventeenth witness in the current Hollywood investigation to refuse to answer any questions concerning present or past affiliation with the Communist party . . . Mr. Gough, suave and at times apparently amused by the proceedings, claimed the protection of the Fifth Amendment to the Constitution against giving testimony that might tend to incriminate him, as others had done. He refused to say whether he was now or had been a member of the Communist party. . . . Asked whether he was now or ever had been a member of the Elks or the Knights of Columbus, he said no."

That question about the Elks or the Knights of Columbus tells as much about the meanness of the House Committee on Un-American Activities, and about its needling pettiness, as an issue of the *Congressional Record* during the McCarthy hearings. Had the committee—and the era—been merely mean and petty, the damage would have been less severe.

Lloyd Gough seems to have held up his side in the pitched battle. He was asked by Representative Charles E. Potter, a Michigan Republican and a badly crippled veteran of World War II, whether he would enter military service in the event of another war. According to the *New York Times*, "Mr. Gough retorted that, as the Joint Chiefs of Staff and others had stated that this country would not be ready for war for two years or more, 'it seems you are sending me back to the firing line too early.'"

Conveniently overlooked, among such hypothetical probing, was Gough's very real military service a few years earlier. An infantryman during the war, he had won the Bronze Star for his bravery in the Normandy invasion.

Among Gough's other all-American credentials was his performance as Thomas Jefferson in the play *Declaration*, produced in Los Angeles by the Actors Lab in 1948. The play dealt with the Alien and Sedition Acts of 1798, repressive measures opposed by Jefferson because he believed they violated the First Amendment's guarantee of freedom of speech and the press and were an invasion of the rights of the states. By the logic of the Un-American Activities Committee, however, such a Jeffersonian stance qualified as reason for alarm; perhaps Gough's part in the play helped color him Red. The same year that he was hauled before the committee, Gough costarred in *Storm Warning* with an actor who, when he became president, caused no anxiety from a Jeffersonian stance: Ronald Reagan.

Gough's career suffered because of the blacklist. Not until the 1960s did he reemerge, when he worked frequently in television and appeared in such films as *Tony Rome, Madigan,* and *The Great White Hope*. Vindication of a sort arrived in 1976, when Gough appeared in *The Front*, which dealt with blacklisting in the McCarthy era. The picture was written by blacklisted Walter Bernstein, produced and directed by blacklisted Martin Ritt, and in the credits after each actor's name—Zero Mostel, John Randolph, Lloyd Gough, Joshua Shelley, Herschel Bernardi— appeared the date on which he was blacklisted.

Lloyd Gough died in 1984 at the age of seventy-seven.

One location used in the film later attracted a cult of locals and out of towners. It's the Alto Nido Apartments at 1851 North Ivar Avenue, where Joe Gillis lived before Norma captured him. *Discover Hollywood*, published by the Hollywood Arts Council, lists the site under "Places of Interest." It's also mentioned in the *Insight Guide to Southern California*, which adds that "Marie Dressler lived in a Spanish-style house at number 1850." And a friend of mine who works in the neighborhood reports that he sometimes strolls by during lunch hour and "has erotic thoughts about William Holden in his bathrobe, maybe wearing nothing under it."

No surprise, really, that the Alto Nido should become a shrine. After all, cinematographer John Seitz shot some of his most bravura footage right there. The screenplay details the beginning as "Slow dissolve to: Hollywood, seen from the Hilltop at Ivar & Franklin Streets." In the scene, Holden's voice-over begins, "I was living in an apartment house above Franklin and Ivar." Before the dissolve ends the camera is tracking backward up Ivar. The screenplay continues, "Camera pans toward the Alto Nido, an ugly Moorish structure of stucco about four stories high. Camera moves toward an open window on the third floor, where we look in on Joe Gillis' apartment."

The script's straightforward language doesn't convey the emotions aroused by that ominous, voyeuristic shot. With its serpentine glide, the camera italicizes this man's unsuspecting vulnerability. Joe Gillis, there at the typewriter in his robe, is marked. He's even more vulnerable because of what he's wearing, or not wearing. My friend, quoted above, finds him erotic in a bathrobe, with the possibility of nakedness underneath. If Holden had on slacks and shirt, he'd be less sexy and also less susceptible to fate. But surprised by the all-seeing camera, and defenseless, Joe Gillis is about to be raped—by destiny, in the shape of Norma's gun.

Ten years after *Sunset Boulevard*, Hitchcock opened *Psycho* with an even more voyeuristic shot as the camera stares into the hotel room where Janet Leigh and John Gavin are ending their midday tryst. Did Hitchcock the voyeur perhaps invent this through-the-window shot? Certainly he used it early on, in *The Lady Vanishes* (1938) and *Shadow of a Doubt* (1943).

If Gloria Swanson's mother, Adelaide, had had any say-so, it would have been *she* and not Norma Desmond who seduced William Holden.

"My mother adored Bill," Swanson said. "She came to the set just to watch him." A few years later Adelaide, still infatuated, bought stock in Wilder's *Stalag 17* because Holden was the star. We can imagine Adelaide's ecstasy, both amorous and financial, when her heartthrob won the Oscar as Best Actor of 1953.

Queen Kelly, Swanson's disastrous 1928 film that was never released in the United States, gained a few moments of belated immortality via *Sunset Boulevard*, for that's the silent picture Norma Desmond projects for Joe Gillis. Ironically, that recognition takes place in a talking picture, and the *Sunset* credits do not acknowledge the silent footage.

Over twenty years after *Queen Kelly* was abandoned, it was still encrusted with bad luck. Gloria Swanson, who had produced it, granted Paramount the right to use the clip in *Sunset Boulevard*. A legal document executed on June 7, 1949, and signed by Swanson, stated in part, "I hereby represent and warrant that I am the sole and exclusive owner of the motion picture photoplay entitled *Queen Kelly*." Two weeks later Billy Wilder received this telegram from Walter Futter of Somerville, Massachusetts: "A publicity item published here states you are interested in footage from *Queen Kelly*. I own this negative and all rights having bought same from Miss Swanson some years ago."

It's unclear who Walter Futter was, though he might have been associated with Joseph Kennedy. Since Kennedy and Swanson were intimately involved—financially and personally—at the time of *Queen Kelly*, and since Futter resided in a Boston suburb, we may assume a link.

Following Futter's telegram, Paramount investigated and found that he was indeed more than just a crackpot claimant. On July 7, 1949, C. J. Scollard, of Paramount's New York office, wrote to Gloria Swanson that the last royalty checks on *Queen Kelly* were drawn between 1936 to 1938. Scollard continued, "It is quite possible that the bank might have loaned Futter the money to buy whatever he bought from you. . . . It seems to me the important thing to get is the contract you made with Futter. That will disclose the rights you conveyed to him and the rights you retained."

Swanson does not mention Futter's name in her book. When I

inquired at the John F. Kennedy Library in Boston I received no help in ascertaining Futter's possible connection with Joseph Kennedy. In fact, my query couldn't have met with a chillier response if I had inquired about the relationship between Marilyn Monroe and JFK. After a moment of fumbling hesitation, an archivist informed me that such information pertaining to Mr. Kennedy was sealed. And then hung up.

Since the *Queen Kelly* clip ultimately appeared in *Sunset Boulevard*, however, Swanson apparently owned the negative after all.

chapter 8

That's Why the Lady Has a Chimp

$\mathcal{E}$ ven in the raffish milieu of a Hollywood studio, Gloria Swanson considered herself a lady. An up-to-date lady, of course, meaning she could laugh at the occasional off-color story, but a lady whose Victorian residue recoiled from bald-faced vulgarity. On the set with Billy Wilder, Swanson often found her broad-mindedness tested.

Wilder relished crossing the line. He surely knew he could jolt Swanson with his puckish aggression. Since the *Sunset Boulevard* script contained little that was overtly shocking, Wilder loaded the film with raunchy suggestions. Why, for instance, is Max so complaisant in procuring a young gigolo for Norma Desmond, his ex-wife? Does he perhaps watch through those glory-hole doors with the locks gouged out? Again, Max's servile presence in the Desmond house suggests his pleasure in subjection to the dominatrix. There's even a Wilder wink toward necrophilia when Norma, a wannabe Salome, oozes desire for the head of John the Baptist on a tray, "kissing his cold, dead lips."

Bestiality, one of the few sexual possibilities still looked on as shocking, must have tickled Wilder to no end half a century ago. It had been tried around Hollywood, at least according to those Babylonish rumors, but Wilder surely pioneered in onscreen depiction of cross-species romance. To the literal-minded such an assertion is hogwash, since you don't *see* Norma and the chimp smooching or making goo-goo eyes. To Wilder, of course, such subtlety made the broken taboo funnier: those who got the joke wouldn't dare let on. Aiming at the lowest Freudian denominator, Wilder had Norma Desmond eulogize the dead beast with this zinger: "He always liked fires and poking at them with a stick."

The dead chimpanzee cost twenty-five dollars for two days. Although the corpse resembles a wax replica, Swanson referred to it as "stuffed." The tab for the chimp's small white coffin came to one hundred and fifty dollars.

The Loved One

When the art director asked Billy Wilder for guidance on the interment of Norma Desmond's pet, Wilder answered: "Just make it an everyday funeral for the average Hollywood monkey." The reason Joe Gillis gains entree to Norma's house is because she and Max mistake him for the undertaker. Gillis: "Later on, just for comedy relief, the real guy arrived with a baby coffin. It was all done with great dignity. He must have been a very important chimp. The great grandson of King Kong, maybe."

The pet undertaker, seen for a few seconds in long shot, appeared in 1,100 films during his long career. Today nobody knows his name.

Franklyn Farnum (1876–1961) started out as a chorus boy in Boston in 1906. He starred in light opera and musical comedies on Broadway before moving to Hollywood in 1914. There, in early two-reel westerns, his name carried the kind of magic associated with Tom Mix and William S. Hart. During that time, a billboard with his face on it dominated Times Square.

But "Smiling Franklyn Farnum," as he was known at the height of his fame, took a different road than Norma Desmond. When stardom passed him by he sought jobs as an extra—over a thousand such—and served for several years as president of the Screen Extras Guild. According to some sources he appeard in *Samson and Delilah* and *All About Eve*.

Filming the monkey scenes early on, Wilder waited to catch Swanson offguard. Then he would remind her: "Remember, Gloria, that Norma is having an affair with the monkey." Next time: "Don't forget, the monkey is your lover." A few takes later, when the dead monkey's dark, hairy arm drops limply off his bier: "Well, there goes your last lover. You wore him out." Preparing to shoot the scene where Max and Norma bury the monkey: "Remember, please, that your lover is in the garden."

At first Swanson smiled. Then she laughed politely, because she adored Billy Wilder and found most of his jokes hilarious. But then one day he used *that word*. In a moment of directorial abandon, he instructed, "Now, one more time, Gloria, and show us what you feel. After all, Norma Desmond was fucking the monkey."

At that, Gloria Swanson's smile vanished and her face froze into a look of stunned horror.

She, of course, never commented on Norma's supposed affair, but for Wilder the joke stayed fresh. In the 1980s he told an interviewer, "Somebody asked me recently if that monkey really was the ex-lover of Norma Desmond, and if William Holden took its place. I said, 'Yes, of course, that's exactly right, but look, I was very discreet. I used a little chimpanzee and not a *huge* orangutan.' "

According to another source, Wilder's simian sex joke climaxed in the nineties. At an opening-night party in Beverly Hills for Andrew Lloyd Webber's musical version of *Sunset Boulevard*, "everyone was being very civil and polite until one woman asked, 'Billy, why does the show open with this, this monkey?' " Wilder's deadpan reply: "Don't you understand? Norma Desmond was fucking the monkey before Joe Gillis came along." Standing within earshot was Nancy Reagan, "who looked like she was about to pass out."

Paramount at its apex has been characterized as the studio with "European-flavored stories, directors, and stars, and a product aimed at the readers of sophisticated, high-society magazines." Billy Wilder helped erode the studio's high-mindedness, and even before *Sunset Boulevard*'s release lesser hands had grabbed the monkey joke. In Paramount's *My Friend Irma Goes West*, filmed after *Sunset Boulevard* but released in July 1950, a month before Wilder's film, Corinne Calvet plays a Hollywood star whose "traveling companion" is Pierre, a chimp in a matching leopard print outfit who kisses Calvet wetly on the cheek. (The monkey, by the way, is the best actor in this Martin and Lewis comedy.)

From Paramount the monkey tide spread, making those animals highly employable in such pictures as Fox's *Monkey Business* (1952) and *Bedtime for Bonzo* at Universal, about a professor (Ronald Reagan) who treats a chimp as his child for a heredity experiment. A 1952 sequel, *Bonzo Goes to College*, was made without Reagan.

The point of this digression on monkeys in the movies is that while average screenwriters and directors used them for easy comedy, it was a typical Wilder touch to cast a *dead* chimp for hollow laughter and the pathos of the macabre.

Once Joe Gillis has settled in as gigolo to Norma Desmond, he finds little to occupy him after performing his official duties. In voice-over he says, "Whenever she suspected I was getting bored, she would put on a live show for me: the Norma Desmond Follies. Her first number was always the Mack Sennett bathing beauty."

Norma Desmond's back story had her as one of Sennett's bathing beauties ("I can still see myself in the line: Marie Prevost, Mabel Normand ... Mabel was always stepping on my feet"), but Gloria Swanson never was. It annoyed her that journalists and fans got it wrong, blithely assuming that, because she had posed for publicity stills wearing one of the typical bathing girl costumes of the day, she had also been a seaside chorus girl.

"I was never a bathing girl in my life," Swanson said. "I did light comedies for Sennett. I never worked with a low comedian until my last picture for Sennett, and that's why I left him." Swanson's irritation came from her belief that, since she had been a featured player with Sennett, she was demeaned by being mistaken for one more pretty face in an outmoded swimsuit.

Swanson's bathing girl imitation is good, but her Chaplin soars to brilliance. What more potent symbol of silent Hollywood was there for her to imitate than Chaplin, the first twentieth-century superstar? As film historian Gerald Mast points out, "Chaplin's face, figure, and icons (bowler hat, cane, shoes, moustache) became more familiar to more people than any previous face and figure in history."

Chaplin and Swanson went back very far. In 1914, when fifteen-year-old Gloria was starting her film career at the Essanay Studio in Chicago, Chaplin arrived from California. He was to make some short pictures, and Essanay gave him carte blanche among their girls as he searched for a comic partner. Decades later Swanson wrote, "He picked me and spent one morning trying to get me to work up routines with him. These all involved kicking each other in the pants, running into things, and falling over each other. He kept laughing and making his eyes twinkle and talking in a light, gentle voice and encouraging me to let myself go and be silly. He reminded me of a pixie from some other world altogether, and for the life of me I couldn't get the feel of his frisky little skits."

Feeling "like a cow trying to dance with a toy poodle," Swanson told Chaplin she didn't see the humor in the things he was asking her to do. The next morning Gloria was told that "Mr. Chaplin felt I didn't have a strong enough comic sense to be in his pictures." Swanson, independent and not to be trifled with, was "absolutely delighted and considered his rejection a real compliment." She had no intention of losing her dignity, even for a part in a picture. "I would have been mortified," she said, "if anybody I knew had ever seen me get kicked in the pants or hit with a revolving plank by an odd sprite in a hobo outfit."

By the time she filmed *Manhandled* in 1924, Swanson's own face and figure had become nearly as familiar as Chaplin's. Rehearsing a party scene for director Allan Dwan, Swanson took a black derby from one of the crew and put it on. "Then," she recalled, "I grabbed a cane from somebody and started wobbling around in an impersonation of Chaplin.

People laughed and clapped, and Allan said to keep it in. The next day we got a more accurate Chaplin costume for me and shot the whole sequence in an afternoon."

When the time came to film Norma Desmond's impersonations in *Sunset Boulevard*, Wilder and Brackett suggested Douglas Fairbanks. Swanson countered, "Why don't I do the Chaplin thing I did in *Manhandled?*"

Wilder agreed, and the wardrobe department sent in fifty derbies for Swanson to choose from. Next day, when she walked in wearing the one she had picked, "Billy Wilder and the whole crew were wearing the forty-nine that were left over." But Wilder hadn't finished his joke. "Two days later," Swanson said, "when we shot a scene of Norma and Max burying Norma's pet chimpanzee, Mr. Wilder directed me to remove the Spanish shawl covering the chimp in the white coffin, and when I did so, the stuffed monkey was also wearing a derby."

Swanson considered her Chaplin imitation in *Manhandled* "far better than the one in *Sunset Boulevard* because I looked more like Chaplin, my face was rounder and in those days I had puppy fat. It wasn't an elongated face as it is now." (Swanson was speaking in 1964.) Chaplin apparently agreed. Swanson once showed him a photograph of herself impersonating him in *Manhandled*, and he thought it was—Charlie Chaplin!

chapter 9

"Ten Thousand Midnights Ago"

For *Sunset Boulevard*, Wilder assembled one of the strangest casts ever to appear in a top studio picture. Not that any one actor is strikingly odd. Rather, the peculiarity results from seeing them all together in the same film and knowing that each actor either *is* the character he or she plays, or easily could be. How many other directors would have intuited the quirky fineness of this ensemble? Still another Wilder touch: the audacity to typecast and, at the same time, to cast the very same actors against type.

Except for Hedda Hopper, whose typecasting only exaggerates her pushy persona. She plays "Hedda Hopper," a gossip columnist who's even brassier than the real H. H. Wilder and Brackett enticed both Hopper and her rival, Louella Parsons, to appear in the picture. According to Hedda, writing in 1952, "Louella and I have been offered a fistful of money to appear on radio and in pictures together. I always accept; she always declines...I appeared [in *Sunset Boulevard*], and for months she didn't mention the picture or the name of its star in her column."

Wilder gives a funny description of his hoped-for scene with the two gossip columnists: "I had in mind not only Hedda on the phone, but downstairs Louella in the ladies' room on another one, saying, 'Get off that phone, you bitch. Let me talk!' Then they both get on the phone saying, 'Get me the copy desk. No, wait a minute—hang on. Hang up, I was on that phone first! Now, Louella, I'm gonna come down and I'm gonna—' 'Shut up, Hedda, I've had it with you!'"

Wilder's lines, and his line readings of the two parts, illustrate his penchant for bitchy slapstick. This vignette might also be read as a displaced sample of the famously raucous Wilder and Brackett collaboration.

Hedda told a slightly different version. She said that Brackett and Wilder extended the first invitation to her, and she immediately "began scheming a scene in which Louella and I would rush for a telephone. Then I would trip and say sweetly, 'After you, Louella.' When she got her invitation and was told I had already been signed, she stormed: 'Get her off. I won't be in it if she is.' When Wilder and Brackett didn't accede to her demand, Louella refused to appear."

After filming her *Sunset Boulevard* cameo, Hedda wrote in her column: "I spent the day sitting on a bed that originally belonged to Gaby Deslys, the Parisian star. I hope some of her glamour rubbed off on me, but I doubt it." Hedda also reported this exchange with Wilder: "'I must have been lousy, Billy. You never mentioned my performance.' Said he, 'I was afraid to. I intended sending you a note and some flowers tomorrow.' 'I'd rather have your words now, and you can skip the flowers,' said I. I got the compliment, but, oh boy, did I have to beg for it."

It's hard to infer from this what Wilder really thought. Did he perhaps find Hedda too garish, or would his note have complimented her on being the perfect vulture?

Gloria Swanson, who according to close friends possessed an amazing talent for "artificial graciousness," i.e., the ability to loathe a person and still be charming to her face, made no secret of her dislike for Hedda Hopper. In private she said: "That bitch, I can't stand her." Dickson Hughes, a longtime associate of Swanson's, recalls a party at the Waldorf-Astoria where the two confronted one another. "They were extremely polite, but the air was electric with lovely vitriol."

Another Hollywood columnist, Sidney Skolsky, appeared in the picture but landed on the proverbial cutting room floor. In the script, Gillis encounters Skolsky when he goes to Schwab's early on to make phone calls. Skolsky asks, "Got anything for the column?" and Gillis replies sardonically, "Sure. Just sold an original for a hundred grand. *The Life of the Warner Brothers.* Starring the Ritz Brothers. Playing opposite the Andrews Sisters." To which Skolsky responds with his trademark motto, "But don't get me wrong—I love Hollywood."

According to Wilder, the scene was cut because "Sidney Skolsky was not very good." Perhaps Wilder felt free to make the cut because Skolsky wielded far less power than his despotic colleagues, Hedda and Louella. Wilder later claimed that Skolsky "proceeded to knock the picture, he just hated it because I cut him out."

One of the most famous cameos in film history is Cecil B. DeMille playing himself in *Sunset Boulevard*. He's onscreen for only a few minutes, yet he seems to command star billing. That's because, playing his own legend, he's perfectly cast. It's also because he brings with him a chunk of his monumental career—not only the *Samson and Delilah* set where Norma Desmond visits him, but forty previous years of filmmaking. In terms of the script, DeMille's career is the counterpoint to Norma's, for he has endured. He's the story's one lasting success.

We learn early on that Norma, like Gloria Swanson, made "a lot of pictures" with DeMille. (Later she puts the total at twelve; Swanson herself starred in six DeMille pictures between 1919 and 1921.) The reason for DeMille's stature in *Sunset Boulevard*, however, owes less to his august career than to his generosity: he plays the only character with an uncorrupted heart. Sensing disaster for the star he helped create, DeMille tries to forestall it. In his compassionate regard for Norma Desmond he seems more humane than any hero in a DeMille epic.

And that was the whole point. Speaking with Cecilia Presley, DeMille's granddaughter, I said that DeMille probably brought more warmth and kindness to his role in *Sunset Boulevard* than any actor portraying an old-time director could have. She replied, "That was Grandfather. That was the man I knew so well." She concedes, however, that on the set of his own films he could sometimes be quite different. Adding a comment on his attire—green corduroy suit and brown puttees—she said: "In *Sunset Boulevard* he's wearing the clothes he always wore on the set. The reason for the boots was because of bad ankles. Boots gave him support."

Billy Wilder sounds genuinely fond of DeMille: "He was absolutely marvelous. Wonderful to work with, well prepared, cooperative. Politically we did not see eye to eye, but he came to mind right off when we thought of her going back to the studio. DeMille was important in that vignette of old-timers not wanting to hurt each other, not saying, 'Oh, fuck off, who the hell needs you?'"

When the veteran director asked for a script change, Wilder complied. Originally the screenplay called for him to greet Norma Desmond with these words: "I haven't seen you since Lindbergh landed in Paris and we danced on the nightclub table." DeMille explained his objection to that speech: "I never go to nightclubs. And if I did I wouldn't dance on a table, even if Lindbergh flew to Paris twice. And if I did dance, it would be with Mrs. DeMille." The dialogue was changed so that Norma says, "Last time I saw you was someplace very gay. I remember waving to you. I was dancing on a table." DeMille's rejoinder is this: "A lot of people were. Lindbergh had just landed in Paris."

When DeMille's scenes were finished, Wilder patted C. B. on the back and said, "Very good, my boy. Leave your name with my secretary. I may have a small part for you in my next picture."

Wilder's compliments do not mean that he admired the bloated DeMille product of later years. While writing *Stalag 17* Billy got a phone call from C. B., who invited him to a screening of his latest epic. Wilder squirmed through the endless circus spectacle. When the lights finally came on Billy jumped up and bowed. "Cecil," he said, "you have made *The Greatest Show on Earth.*" The elderly director beamed and inclined his head in theatrical modesty. "Thank you, Billy," he replied, thinking Wilder had said, "You have made the greatest show on earth."

It seems unfair to judge DeMille solely on his big-top behemoth or the Holy Land histrionics of *Samson and Delilah* (1949) and *The Ten Commandments* (1956). After all, he made more than fifty silent pictures and most of them need no apologies. *Male and Female* (1919), for instance, with Gloria Swanson, shows DeMille's sensibility as exuberant, sensuous, and not entirely taken in by his own voluptuous hokum. Several of his early talking pictures—*The Sign of the Cross* (1932), *Cleopatra* (1934), *The Crusades* (1935)—hold up because of their visual sophistication. It's too bad these films weren't silent, for the dialogue in a DeMille picture always capsizes it. Largely crowd-pleasing kitsch, the lines sometimes soar into the camp stratosphere, as when Samson (Victor Mature) calls Delilah (Hedy Lamarr) a "Philistine gutter rat" or Edward G. Robinson, in *The Ten Commandments,* declaims in the rhetoric of High Hollywood Hebrew, "Joshua will always be grateful to you, my little mud flower."

It's appropriate in all sorts of ways that *Samson and Delilah* flits across the filmscape of *Sunset Boulevard.* According to Wilder, DeMille's picture had just wrapped when he started shooting his own. The sets were still up.

What a stroke of luck that it was an outré DeMille epic, and not, say, William Wyler's *The Heiress,* that lay so conviently to hand on a Paramount sound stage, for *Samson and Delilah* chimes with Norma Desmond's exotic view of life, her vanished silent-picture world, her gigantic career, and the ludicrous comeback vehicle she's dreamed up, starring herself as teenage Salome. Wilder's visual allusion to *Samson and Delilah* amounts to a sardonic comment on Hollywood follies past and present, for DeMille's opus could belong to any era of filmmaking. It comments on the crazy continuity of the movies and the fickleness of Hollywood fate: Norma Desmond, to judge by the *Queen Kelly* clip, was a screen artist and is now passé, while DeMille has long outlasted his artistic betters— Griffith, Stroheim, Keaton. Wilder's elliptical inclusion of *Samson and Delilah*—it's never identified by title in *Sunset Boulevard*—is like Charles Ives adding a snatch of "Oh, Suzanna" to one of his symphonies.

Other connections stitch the two films together. Hans Dreier, art director of *Samson and Delilah,* was also art director (with John Meehan) of *Sunset Boulevard.* On DeMille's picture Dreier pulled out all the biblical stops: it's overstuffed with serpent gods, spears, helmets, and breast plates, plush litters hauled by slaves, harps, jeweled ewers, and richly appointed tents with fringe on top. In the pagan temple stands a monolithic statue of Dagon; a miniature replica of the statue turns up at the New Year's Eve party in *Sunset Boulevard.* There the chubby idol rests on a stand beside the telephone where two blonde starlets erupt in fits of lascivious giggles.

"No man leaves Delilah," fumes Hedy Lamarr, and we hear an echo of her pronuciamento in *Sunset Boulevard* when Norma Desmond says, "No one ever leaves a star."

For their work on *Samson and Delilah*, Edith Head and four other designers won the 1950 Oscar for Best Costume Design on a color picture. Head also designed the costumes for *Sunset Boulevard*, but wasn't nominated in the black-and-white category for that picture. Instead, she and Charles LeMaire were nominated, and won, for the costumes they designed for *All About Eve*.

Despite her Oscar, however, Head didn't like *Samson and Delilah*. "It is not a film of which I'm proud," she said. "I don't even have fond memories of it." Here's why: "I never thought I did good work for DeMille. I was always part of a team; he never let me do a film on my own for him. I always had to do what that conceited old goat wanted, whether he was correct or not. He never did an authentic costume picture in his entire career, and in my opinion that made him a damn liar as well as an egotist."

As chief of Paramount's costume department and probably the most famous designer in Hollywood, Edith Head wielded power, though not sufficient to defy a director of DeMille's standing. And so her revenge was subtle: she plucked a feather from DeMille and presented it to Norma Desmond.

It all started with the most talked about item in *Samson and Delilah*, the cape made of peacock feathers worn by Hedy Lamarr. When stories circulated that this was the same cape worn by Gloria Swanson in the lions den in *Male and Female*, DeMille was furious. Afraid the public might believe he had used a leftover from an earlier epic, DeMille told the *New York Times* that he had personally followed molting peacocks around his ten-thousand-acre ranch, "catching feathers as they dropped and saving only the best for Delilah's cape."

Edith hooted when she heard that. "Of course he didn't go out and gather dirty bird feathers," she said. "My own staff helped collect them and bring them in. We sorted by size, color, and brillance. It took days. A leftover indeed! DeMille never used anything that was left over from something else; he was too egotistical for that." (Long ago he had angered Edith by telling her, when she brought costume sketches for his approval, "I think my four-year-old daughter could do better than these. Try again.")

Mindful of DeMille's aversion to recycled finery, Edith designed a hat for Norma Desmond to wear when she calls on him at the studio. Rimmed in white fur, the hat has one graceful but unexpected embellishment. . . . And so when Gloria Swanson played the scene with Cecil B. DeMille, the focal point of her chapeau was a peacock feather from Delilah's cape. Long and slender, it bobbed and almost got tangled in a microphone, and Edith Head loved telling the story of how she used a DeMille leftover right under the nose—within tickling distance, in fact—of the "conceited old goat."

Producer A. C. Lyles recalls watching DeMille and Swanson during the filming of *Sunset Boulevard*. "He was a stickler about actors hitting their mark. But then Billy Wilder did a couple of takes and DeMille never quite hit his mark. We all smiled to ourselves. Not to take anything away from him as an actor—we just found it endearing."

Phil Koury, a reporter from the *New York Times*, wrote a full account of the director directed. "This is a new and strange world for me," said DeMille, who was sixty-eight at the time.

According to Koury,

There were four scenes, each requiring two hours and an average of seven takes. Throughout this wordless combat between two techniques of film direction, DeMille radiated kindness and fatherly concern, with Wilder demonstrating a momumental sense of management to the crowd of curious that jammed Stage Five for the occasion.

All is set and the camera grinds as DeMille rehearses this make-believe scene from *Samson and Delilah*, probably just as he had reheared it some months earlier in reality for his own camera. An assistant tells DeMille that Norma Desmond is on her way to see him. Then the assistant adds, "She must be a million years old." DeMille replies, "I hate to think where that puts me. I could be her father."

Wilder moves in. "Just what we wanted, Mr. DeMille, exactly. But may we do it again?"

DeMille smiles. "Yes, I know. I registered surprise too soon."

Another try. This time the fault is in repetition. The word "terribly" is in the conversation twice in quick succession. In the next take the word is gone entirely. This time DeMille substitutes "awfully" and the assistant, forgetting "terribly," says "very."

Once more, DeMille begins to look around, grinning. "This is the fifth take. Am I that bad?"

Wilder moves about with amazing swiftness, assuring the performers all is going beautifully.

The sixth try. The assistant did not move quickly enough and the camera beat him to the spot.

Once more, "Very good, very good," exclaims Wilder. "Once again, please." DeMille looks about him, smiling softly. "I don't suppose Paramount will pick up my option after this."

Twice more the scene is tried. Wilder, apparently satisfied, instructs the cameraman to print three of the takes.

Wilder's verdict on the experience: "Mr. DeMille was too courteous to make suggestions, and I was too afraid."

Acting in *Sunset Boulevard* was not DeMille's first appearance onscreen, though it was his most substantial. Since playing a card dealer in his own early picture, *The Squaw Man*, in 1914, he had done cameos in some half dozen films, often playing himself. During the fifties, he also appeared uncredited in *Son of Paleface* (1952) and in *The Buster Keaton Story* (1957).

One reason other filmmakers invited DeMille to play himself was because of his formidable presence. Though understated and held in abeyance, his power never wavered. Had he lived in a later era he might have run for president as the Republican candidate, for he possessed charisma, avuncular charm, and conservative credentials at a time when Ronald Reagan was still a Democrat.

Nowhere did DeMille seem more in command than on his daily journey to the studio. During most of his career he lived in the Laughlin Park area, which lies between Los Feliz Boulevard and Franklin Avenue and a couple of miles from Paramount. In the thirties his street was actually renamed DeMille Drive.

From the moment of leaving his splendid house, DeMille rode through the streets like a reigning monarch. The instant he headed his car down the winding private roadway from his home a call went out from his secretary in residence, Gladys Rosson, to the studio: "Mr. DeMille is on the way." His studio staff duly alerted, they flew about making ready their executive's papers, files, scripts, and paraphernalia. If he had sent advance word that he wished to see one or the other of them, that underling was expected to be seated in the bungalow outside DeMille's office awaiting his arrival.

The great man's progress from garage to office was unimpeded save for the occasional traffic light, and arriving at Paramount he expected to find the street door to the bungalow propped open. Close by stood an assistant ready to seize DeMille's valise as the titanic presence emerged from his solid and dignified car.

Yet despite such pageantry and imperious demands, DeMille also had qualities of a lovable old dear. Ann del Valle, who worked as his secretary from the time of *The Ten Commandments*, told me that Florence Cole, his head secretary at the studio for some forty years, filed letters sent to DeMille according to a detail he might remember and ask for. For example, said Mrs. del Valle, "a minister from Omaha was filed under 'Five Grandchildren' because Mr. DeMille remembered that one thing."

As an example of DeMille's generosity of spirit, Mrs. del Valle added that "Gloria Swanson remained close to Cecil B. DeMille to the end of time. If she stopped by without an appointment, Florence Cole always waved her into his office without an announcement."

A. C. Lyles recalls similar warmth between the pair. "It was wonderful," he says, "to see the affection and the respect DeMille gave Gloria Swanson offcamera while they were making *Sunset Boulevard*. He certainly did it oncamera, but he was also gallant with her all the time." That leads Lyles to another memory, this one from the midthirties when he was a teenager working for Adolph Zukor: "Gloria Swanson would come to Paramount, and I would meet her at the gate. I would take her to Mr. Zukor's office. Then Zukor would call DeMille, he would come over, and the three of them would sit and talk about the old days."

"The old days"—those melancholy words express one of *Sunset Boulevard*'s main themes.

Enter the Waxworks—Buster Keaton, Anna Q. Nilsson, and H.B. Warner. Like Swanson, this time-worn trio had known enormous celebrity in silent pictures. Keaton, along with Chaplin, was one of the first great film artists. Nilsson (the Q. stands for "Querentia") made her first film, *Molly Pitcher*, in 1911, and was later billed as "the first Swedish movie star." (If Norma Desmond had said that her bridge table friend was "greater than Garbo," she wouldn't have been entirely wrong.) H.B. Warner started out in 1914 and is best remembered for playing Christ in DeMille's *King of Kings* in 1927. At the end of the crucifixion scene, which was filmed on Christmas Eve of 1926, many of the thousand-plus extras, with cast and crew, faced the three crosses and wept. Others fell to their knees as the organ that DeMille had brought to the set pealed out the music of Bach.

But that was long ago, especially in midcentury Hollywood. The Waxworks is a rather cruel allusion not only to Madame Tussaud's but also to a German expressionist film of 1924, the horror-fantasy *Das Wachsfigurenkabinett*, which Wilder would have seen as a young man.

Keaton said his brief appearence at the card table in *Sunset Boulevard* was "like old home week." Certainly his cameo was almost silent; in close-up, he utters the word "pass" two times. Nilsson speaks three words and Warner one. Their monosyllables buttress Norma's assertion that "we didn't need dialogue. We had *faces*."

And those three faces, still striking though collapsed, might be seen as gargoyles guarding the parapets of Norma Desmond, or as a warning chorus midway through the tragedy. The warning, of course, goes unheeded.

What strange destinies led those three from the nineteenth century into modern Hollywood, where old creatures of their sort languished in disrepute. Having transgressed the flame and flesh of youth, they survived as ruins in the middle of gleaming newness. As such, they were consigned to the dustbins of studio history, like those thousands of cans of silent film disintegrating in dark vaults. These exiles from the old days, and many others like them, flickered faintly as star leavings fallen from the heights, reduced to mere scraps of glamour.

Buster Keaton dared never to smile, a revolutionary approach to show-biz comedy, where audience acceptance might be gauged by the winsomeness of teeth and dimples. Born into a family of big-tent medicine show performers in 1895 during a stint in Piqua, Kansas, the boy was christened Joseph Keaton. At the time of Keaton's birth, Harry Houdini was performing magic in the tent with the elder Keatons. They all lived in the same boardinghouse.

At the age of six months, baby Joseph tumbled down a flight of stairs. He squealed and squawked, but apart from the noise he came through the fall with aplomb. Houdini was impressed. "What a buster!" he exclaimed, and voilà, the stage name.

By the age of three Buster Keaton had full-time employment as the Human Mop in a cockamamie routine dreamed up by his father, who literally swept the floor with the outstretched body of his tyke. Was it avant-garde comedy or child abuse? The kid soon had his revenge, for by his sixth birthday he had nabbed first billing. The family having switched from medicine show to vaudeville, the act was renamed "Buster, assisted by Joe and Myra Keaton."

Buster became an accomplished acrobat who never smiled when his old man tossed him around. "When I was seven," he said, "I was smart enough to see that the more sober I looked, the bigger the laughs."

Acrobats and booze don't mix, and by 1917 Buster's father was hitting the bottle. He endangered them all. The act broke up; Buster forsook the stage for movies. Fatty Arbuckle directed Keaton's debut film, a two-reeler called *The Butcher Boy* (1917).

The years from 1920 to 1927 brought glory to Keaton. A legendary time in filmmaking, the twenties up to the advent of talking pictures were the apex of Buster's career. A list of his principal films during that period evokes the brilliance and originality of his art: *One Week, Our Hospitality, Sherlock Jr., The Navigator, Seven Chances, Go West, Battling Butler, The General, College, Steamboat Bill Jr., The Cameraman.*

When critics and comedians pour praise on Keaton, or label him "the greatest of all clowns," as Orson Welles did, they have these films in mind. Along with Chaplin, possibly surpassing him, Buster Keaton looms as a genius, the Molière of early pictures. Film historian David Robinson made perhaps the most cogent assessment of Keaton's art: "He is a sort of poet; and as a poet, in the end the deeper secrets of his charm and humour will elude us."

With his poetry came familiar demons: alcoholism, breakdowns, shattered marriages, professional humiliation. He appeared in dozens of films in his long slide, pictures whose titles sound stupidly funny until you stop to think what Keaton might have done if he hadn't needed quick cash: *Pest from the West, Pardon My Berth Marks, The Taming of the Snood, How to Stuff a Wild Bikini.*

In 1952 Keaton appeared with Chaplin in *Limelight,* a film whose Chaplinesque self-adoration diminishes the greatness of both men. One day, between takes, they had a revealing offscreen conversation. "Do you look at television, Charlie?" asked Keaton.

"Good heavens, no," said Chaplin. "The idea of actors letting themselves be shown on that lousy, stinking little screen!"

Keaton, on the other hand, appeared many times on TV, from *The Ed Wynn Show* in 1949 to *Candid Camera* and *Here's Lucy,* not to mention the commercials that made him financially secure. These TV appearances, which amount to a minor second career, were shown in 1996 in a retrospective at the Museum of Television and Radio in New York.

Billy Wilder said, "When I was a student in Vienna I adored Buster Keaton and had seen every Keaton film." Wilder, a bridge addict, invited Keaton to appear at Norma Desmond's bridge table as one of the Waxworks. "The beauty was not only that I finally encountered him," Billy said, "but that he was also one of the great amateur bridge players. Look, I would have taken him even if he never had played cards. I wanted his face."

When the old-timers were assembled on the set, Keaton looked at the others, especially Swanson, whom he had not seen since he was married to silent-screen actress Natalie Talmadge in the twenties. In what Swanson called his "unmatchable deadpan," he muttered, "Waxworks is right." The others howled with laughter.

Later Swanson said that Buster "looked ravaged, as indeed he had been, by alcohol."

The bridge game took two days to shoot. "Just watch what Buster does with the cards," Wilder told the others. "See how he picks them up and holds them, how he takes the tricks." Wilder found Keaton "an absolute delight to work with."

Buster Keaton, seventy years old, died on February 1, 1966, the same day as another visitor to Norma Desmond's house on Sunset Boulevard—Hedda Hopper.

A few years later, Keaton's name occasioned a classic pun. When Aristotle Onassis was considering the purchase of Keaton's former home in Los Angeles, a photographer took a picture of Onassis in front of the property. When the photo appeared in the *New York Daily News*, it was captioned, "Aristotle Contemplating the Home of Buster."

The phrase "accident prone" might have been invented as an epithet for Anna Q. Nilsson. She was born in a small town in Sweden in 1888 and came to the United States on a visit around 1910. Intending to stay only a few weeks, she had the happy accident, in New York, of meeting a photographer who fancied her blondeness. Soon she saw herself on magazine covers and illustrators hired her to model for their story art. Movies came next, leading to accident number two: her American visit lasted the rest of her life.

After her film debut in 1911 she made scores of silents for the Kalem Company in New York. In Hollywood, Nilsson became one of the first blonde beauties of the screen. In 1923 she played a monkey woman in DeMille's *Adam's Rib*, advertised as "a tale of the youngest flapper and the oldest sin." The same year she read a novel about a young woman who masqueraded as a man. Nilsson set her heart on playing the trouser role, even though, as she recalled, "DeMille and [Jesse L.] Lasky both tried to laugh me out of it." The film was *Ponjola* (1923).

Her studio colleagues, seeing her long blonde hair cut off at the roots for the boy role, recoiled in shock. "Why didn't you use a wig?" they demanded. For fun, she sometimes played the boy offcamera. At a luncheon, Nilsson's masculine prettiness and her mannish body language fooled an old friend. Anna made a pass at the woman and got slapped. Shooting *Ponjola* footage on a ship off the California coast, Nilsson went into the ladies' room and was forcibly ejected by a burly steward.

In 1928, after signing a new contract with RKO, she went on vacation to the High Sierras for a rest between pictures. While there she was thrown from a rampaging horse and broke a hip. The injury kept her bedridden in a cast for two years. "They said I'd never walk again," Nilsson told an interviewer in 1953. "It took me seven years but I did it. Threw away steel braces, then crutches, and saw most of the world while I was doing it."

From the time of the riding accident, luck wasn't on her side. "Funny thing," she said. "I had been insured for some amazing amount, a million dollars I think, by the studio in the event that something happened to me while I was working. But I wasn't at work. I was on vacation."

Those years of infirmity ended her career in starring roles, although some later speculated that her strong accent would have interefered with work in talkies. In 1941 a column reported that "Anna Q. Nilsson is back in motion pictures again, playing her first featured role since that spring in 1928 when her screen career was halted by a horse that fell on her. She's shooting *The Great Man's Lady* with Barbara Stanwyck and Joel McCrea. She plays an important character, a woman reporter from Washington."

In 1943 she slipped on an icy New York sidewalk and wound up in another hospital with a broken vertebra.

On April 13, 1947, the *Los Angeles Times* reported on her preparations for *The Farmer's Daughter*, starring Loretta Young. According to the paper, this was "Miss Nilsson's 'comeback' (she hates the word) picture." That familiar attitude, and the familiar phrase, which Gloria Swanson later spat out when William Holden mentioned her *comeback*: "I hate that word! It's a return. A return to the millions of people who have never forgiven me for deserting the screen."

After finishing *The Farmer's Daughter*, Nilsson was driving down Wilshire Boulevard when she rammed into the back of another car. Her injuries, though not serious, nevertheless forced her once again to stop work. The man she hit, a real estate broker, charged the actress with negligence and sued her for $25,583. She denied the charge, and denied also that the other driver had been seriously injured. In 1948 she paid $1,250 to settle the lawsuit.

Nilsson turned up in another, more famous, *Adam's Rib* in 1949, this one George Cukor's. She did a few cameos in later pictures, the last one being *Seven Brides for Seven Brothers* in 1954. Around that time she smiled when an interviewer asked her to recall the silent era. "Ah," she said, "we used to have such fun. Those were wonderful days. Wonderful."

In February 1973 the *Hollywood Reporter* ran this jaunty item in one of its columns: "Drop a cheery note to veteran film queen Anna Q. Nilsson at Loma Linda Hospital, where she's being treated for an accidental fall at her Sun City home. Would you believe that no one, but no one, at the hospital had the faintest idea who she was till they found the phone number of our sheet's Jess Hoaglin in her handbag and gave a quick buzz? Such is fickle fame!"

Nilsson did not recover. She died in February 1974 after a one-year hospitalization. An attending nurse attributed the death to the infirmities of old age. Her obituary in *Variety* included the information that "old-timers recall the blonde actress as the first resident of Malibu, which was later to become a film colony on the beach. She built a small house, and lived there for several years."

Henry Wilcoxon

When Cecil B. DeMille gets word that Norma Desmond is on her way to Stage 18, he is in the midst of rehearsing a scene from *Samson and Delilah*. DeMille gives these directions: "Harry Wilcoxon, draw your sword and raise that drape with it. Samson's lying unconscious over here."

Henry (Harry) Wilcoxon (1905–1984) appeared not only in *Sunset Boulevard*'s *Samson and Delilah*, but in the real one, also.

And in other DeMille pictures, as well, including *Cleopatra, The Crusades, The Greatest Show on Earth,* and *The Ten Commandments.* Although his name suggests a forgotten idol of silent pictures, Wilcoxon made his first picture in 1931 in England. According to Gerd Oswald, second assistant director on *Sunset Boulevard,* "Wilcoxon could do no wrong with DeMille. As a matter of fact, you had to go through Wilcoxon to get to DeMille."

Writing about the Waxworks, Gloria Swanson recalled that when they reunited for *Sunset Boulevard,* "Anna looked splendid, but H.B. Warner appeared brittle, almost transparent, when he showed up." One reason, no doubt, was his age, for at seventy-three he was older than anyone else in the cast.

Warner's family had been well known on the British stage for several generations when he was born in 1876. He was christened Henry Byron Charles Stewart Warner Lickford. At six he made his stage debut, left the theatre to study medicine at University College, London, then returned to the stage. In 1905 he emigrated to the United States where he worked as a leading man in popular dramas before starting his film career in 1914. In 1923 Warner starred with Gloria Swanson in *Zaza.*

His association with the role of Christ remained with him throughout his life. Years later a minister told Warner: "I saw you in *King of Kings* as a child and now, every time I speak of Jesus, it is your face I see."

In 1936 Frank Capra used Warner for the first time, in *Mr. Deeds Goes to Town.* After that, Capra cast "that fine actor of courtly grace," as he described Warner in his autobiography, again and again. Warner was nominated for an Oscar as Best Supporting Actor for his performance as Chang in Capra's *Lost Horizon* (1937).

Television critic Jim McPherson, writing of his dislike for Capra's treacly classic *It's a Wonderful Life,* praised Warner for giving perhaps the only unsugared performance in the film: "If I were ever to sit through the thing again, it would be solely to reenjoy the contribution of stage-and-screen veteran H. B. Warner's wonderful work as the tormented alcoholic druggist Mr. Gower."

After *Sunset Boulevard*, Warner made a few fleeting appearances in pictures. As a favor to the man who made him world famous, he came out of retirement a final time to do a small role in DeMille's *The Ten Commandments*. Two years later, in 1958, he died a few days before Christmas. The *Los Angeles Examiner* ran an obituary with this heading: "Stars He Worked With Absent at Warner Rites."

The story began, "None of the stars who appeared with veteran actor H. B. Warner in scores of motion pictures came to bid him farewell yesterday at his quiet funeral services. Only about 20 friends sat solemnly in the chapel of Pierce Brothers Hollywood Mortuary while the Rev. Kermit Castcanos of All Saints Episcopal Church in Beverly Hills conducted the services for the 83-year-old actor who once portrayed Jesus Christ.

"Although none of the celebrities with whom Warner worked during his long career came to the funeral, many sent floral wreaths."

Fame trickles down into odd cracks and corners. Gore Vidal, in his 1968 novel *Myra Breckinridge*, gives his heroine these mock-nostalgic lines: "One must be thankful for those strips of celluloid which still endure to remind us that once there were gods and goddesses in our midst and Metro-Goldwyn-Mayer (where I now sit) preserved their shadows for all time! Could the actual Christ have possessed a fraction of the radiance and the mystery of H. B. Warner in the first *King of Kings* or revealed, even on the cross, so much as a shadow of the moonstruck Nemi-agony of Jeffrey Hunter in the second *King of Kings*, that astonishing creation of Nicholas Ray?"

chapter 10

" All Right, Mr. De Mille, I'm Ready for My Close-up "

ohn F. Seitz, Wilder's cinematographer, was another old-timer. Starting out in 1917, he had, like Gloria Swanson (and also like Norma Desmond), worked with Rudolph Valentino. One of Seitz's early successes was *The Four Horsemen of the Apocalypse* in 1921, the film that made Valentino a star.

The question "What does a cinematographer do?" has a hundred answers. One of the better ones is this: He paints with light. Preferable to such a Q&A approach, however, are stylistic examples of *how* he wields his camera and *what* he paints. Always, of course, the cinematographer's first consideration is his raw material, light. It comes in two grades: natural and artificial.

One reason *Sunset Boulevard* is a great film is because of its pictorialism and the way those images move on the screen. Seitz used the camera as a precision instrument to engrave on the film complementary textures of waxy rot and polished foreboding. His camera rarely calls attention to itself, though it's always on the go, looking around and peering into corners and tracking in closer, then tracking out. A busy camera indeed, whose restrained mobility prevents visual dead spots in *Sunset Boulevard*.

Even Seitz's bravura shots are understated, as for example the camera's introduction of Norma Desmond. What a way to make an entrance! Speaking her first line—"You there, why are you so late?"—she is framed between two columns on the balcony of her palazzo. In front of the

columns hangs a slatted bamboo shade that half hides this peculiar crea-
ture. Large, dark glasses make Norma mysterious, ominous. The camera
starts a slow zoom toward her, then it stops—wary, sensing peril. This
hesitation, which foreshadows events to come, contrasts with Joe Gillis
who, rushing headlong to the altar of Norma Desmond, proffers himself
to a lethal fate.

A leading cameraman in both the silent and the sound eras, Seitz
photographed three other Wilder films in the forties: *Five Graves to Cairo*,
Double Indemnity, and *The Lost Weekend*.

According to film historian Tom Stempel, "The forties were really
Seitz's heyday." In addition to his work for Wilder and other directors, he
shot three pictures for Preston Sturges: *Sullivan's Travels* (1941), *The Miracle
of Morgan's Creek*, and *Hail the Conquering Hero* (both 1944).

Stempel points out visual parallels in the films that Seitz photographed for Sturges and those he did for Wilder:

> Particularly in *Sullivan's Travels* he brings together both the light and
> the dark. Certain scenes—in the trailer, for instance—are very
> bright, and others, such as the chain gang sequences, are very dark.
> And he makes them all fit into one picture. Then, in both *Double
> Indemnity* and *Sunset Boulevard*, Seitz does something that has always
> impressed me. Both are films noirs, and he finesses the fact that
> both are set in the sunniest of locales, Los Angeles. As he did with
> Sturges, he brings together the light and the dark in the same film,
> without any seams showing. And in *Sunset Boulevard* he brings
> together the realistic lighting of Joe Gillis out in the real world
> with the gothic look of Norma's mansion. Again, with no seams
> showing.

In 1971, seven years before his death, Seitz told an interviewer, "Do
you remember how foggy it was last June? Well, we had weather like that
during *Sunset Boulevard*. We had to have daylight and sun for a number of
scenes, like when Norma Desmond takes Joe Gillis out to buy the proper
clothes. So we'd drop everything else as soon as there was a peep of sun.
We'd go and try to get the shots."

Seitz continued, "You know, I've noticed that anyone who ever worked at UFA hated to shoot in the middle of the day. And I do, too. The least interesting time of the day is noon. That's because everything is so bright. Freddy Zinnemann was the same way. Billy Wilder, too, they all were who came from UFA."

In the early days of motion pictures, the cinematographer actually operated the camera and lit the set. By the time of *Sunset Boulevard*, however, a camera operator—in this instance, Otto Pierce—actually ran the camera. Technically, John F. Seitz was director of photography. In that capacity, he functioned rather like a conductor who supervises musicians to assure a fine performance. Maestro Seitz, however, didn't stick around until the fat lady sang.

According to Wilder, Seitz "hated to watch actors act." Wilder would choose camera setups, then he would ask Seitz, "What do you think?" If Seitz came up with "something better or a little variant," Wilder would accede. Seitz would then light the scene—and clear out.

Wilder, rarely nonplussed, still seemed puzzled years later when he discussed Seitz's odd aversion: "When I said, 'action,' he would go into a corner of the stage, *facing the wall*. He would scratch his head through his wide-brimmed hat. He couldn't stand it. Could not stand actors. He did that on every picture I made with him. At rehearsal he would watch a little bit, but then for the takes he could not stand to watch actors act."

While the director of photography faced the wall and scratched his head, the camera operator executed those perfect shots that Seitz and Wilder had dreamed up. A curious phobia for a cinematographer, though obviously no handicap to his genius.

Nancy Olson, as one of those dreaded actors, never got to know John F. Seitz. But she did hear a rumor. Recalling the shoot, she said, "I never saw him do it, but this is what I heard. I remember someone telling me that when they started in the morning at Norma Desmond's house, he would take some dust and throw it in the air."

I asked Olson if she knew where in the picture a viewer might spot dusty surfaces or motes floating in the air. "I never saw him do it," she said. "But supposedly, when he wanted a murky kind of shot he would scatter dust to achieve the right atmosphere. Find out—it's very interesting."

Next I asked Billy Wilder. "That was true in another picture," he said, "in a picture called *Double Indemnity*. That was a creepy house in the Valley. I just had the cameraman try it with dust and he did it."

I asked if that also happened later when they made *Sunset Boulevard*. "There he did it, too, a little bit," said Wilder.

When asked if he could recall in which scenes Seitz scattered the dust, Wilder replied, "I don't. That I don't know."

Speaking to Cameron Crowe a couple of years earlier for *Conversations with Wilder*, their collaborative book, Billy Wilder recalled that on *Double Indemnity*, "John Seitz took some magnesium and he kind of made it into dust and then he blew it up there, and that's when we were shooting, before it settled." Wilder told an earlier interviewer that "Seitz made some shreddings for me and they photographed like motes in sunbeams."

The obvious result of Seitz's handiwork in *Sunset Boulevard* is the scene where Gloria Swanson stands in the light of the projector while watching herself in *Queen Kelly*. That overwrought scene could serve as visual illustration of a line from T. S. Eliot's "The Wasteland": "I will show you fear in a handful of dust." Less specifically, the whole of Desmondland embodies a line from another poet, Thomas Hardy, for the place seems "strewn with years-deep dust."

Finally I posed the dust question to Swanson's younger daughter, Michelle Farmer-Amon, and she gave me the kind of no-nonsense answer that shows her to be her mother's daughter in every sense of the word. "I doubt it very much," she said. "Knowing my mother, who was an ecologist, I doubt that she would have enjoyed having dust sprinkled about. They might have done it behind her back. But I'm certain that she wasn't aware of it."

No one involved in the picture knew, of course, that they were filming a classic, yet the buzz was highly favorable. According to the *Hollywood*

Reporter not long after the picture wrapped, "for months reports have come out of Paramount about the extraordinary performance of Gloria Swanson in the role of the faded star."

On the set, too, *Sunset Boulevard* generated its own heat. Nancy Olson, though a newcomer, realized she could learn much from watching such high-calibre work, and so she came to the set even on days when she wasn't called. She was there, for example, when they filmed the tango scene. "It was mesmerizing," Olson recalls. "There was such a *mood* created on the set, and the music, and Bill, and Gloria."

The tango scene also contained a multilevel in-joke. In the script, Norma Desmond says to Joe Gillis, "You know, this floor used to be wood but I had it changed. Valentino said there's nothing like tile for a tango." It's entirely possible Valentino really said it—not to Norma Desmond but to Gloria Swanson, for they made one film together. That was *Beyond the Rocks* in 1922, and in it they danced a tango.

Described as "a glamorous, clothes-and-jewel-bedrenched love story which set off their mutual electric chemistry to perfection," *Beyond the Rocks* takes its title from a scene in which Swanson tips over in a rowboat "beyond the rocks" and is rescued by Valentino. In her book Swanson doesn't comment on Valentino's signature dance; instead she describes her outfit: "For the tango sequence, the wardrode department made me a gold-beaded and embroidered lace evening gown so shimmering and beautiful that moviegoers talked about it for the next year. I also wore a king's ransom in velvet, silk ruffles, sable, and chinchilla, all dripping from shoulders to floor with over a million dollars' worth of jewels."

John F. Seitz was part of the Valentino in-joke. According to an article in *American Cinematographer* at the time of *Sunset Boulevard*, he used a "dance dolly—a small platform on wheels—placed immediately in front of and attached to the camera which, in turn, was also mounted on a moveable platform. Men behind the camera moved both the camera platform and the dolly, thus permitting a shot of the dancers making a complete three hundred-and-sixty-degree turn around the room."

That idea was far from new. Seitz had "first introduced it when he filmed Rudolph Valentino and Alice Terry dancing the tango in *The Four Horsemen of the Apocalypse* back in 1921."

To judge by photographs taken on the set, Wilder knew what he wanted in the dance sequence. Rehearsing the tango with Swanson, he looks professionally detached, but she rests her head on his shoulder, eyes closed, just as she did in the actual take with Holden. And why not? Wilder, as a young blade in Berlin, hired himself out to dance with older ladies. His biographers label him a gigolo, claiming that those evenings didn't end with dinner. Wilder refutes such charges; he recently said, "I was not the best dancer, but I had the best *dialogue* with the ladies I was dancing with." His denials are not altogether convincing, however, perhaps because one wants him to have lived the role of a Weimar Joe Gillis.

"As inexperienced as I was," says Nancy Olson, "I sensed part of what was going on in *Sunset Boulevard*. Even I realized they might not get away with it, because they were telling the story of how Hollywood makes promises it doesn't keep. Hollywood had promised young Norma Desmond she would be immortal."

And then abandoned her. The hopes and fears, the ruthless dreams and unkept promises of Hollywood's first half century came together in celluloid apotheosis the day Gloria Swanson turned into Salome on the stairs.

"Yes! I was there," Olson exclaims. "In fact, I think Billy Wilder wanted a big crowd that day. Hedda Hopper, of course—she appears in the sequence, but I had the feeling she would have been there anyway. It was a mob scene, reporters and photographers, and Billy was directing everybody—but Erich von Stroheim was also directing Norma Desmond for the newsreel cameras. Bill Holden was there, too, by the way, even though he was "dead" and supposedly floating in the pool. Who wouldn't come back from the dead to watch *that?*"

The final sequence of *Sunset Boulevard* took two days to film. Hedda Hopper claimed she "spent the first day sitting on a bed." She meant, of course, Norma Desmond's bed with the ornate Cupid at the foot. Underneath that Cupid, according to Hopper, stood Erich von Stroheim. The two of them watched as Norma was questioned by the homicide squad and police reporters.

Michelle, Swanson's teenaged daughter, watched from the sidelines. Recalling a technical problem, she explains that "the staircase curved slightly. My mother, being very professional, did not want to glance down to see where she was putting her feet. She felt that would break character for Norma Desmond. She very intentionally never looked down. She had tiny feet, so I suppose she didn't risk missing a stair step."

Swanson herself said, "Billy Wilder wanted me to come down on the inside of the stairway where the steps were narrowest. On high heels I would have tripped for sure, so I played the scene barefoot. I imagined a steel ramrod in me from head to toe holding me together and I descended as in a trance."

Nancy Olson calls the staircase scene "a moment of high drama." Her memory of it seems as fresh as yesterday: "It was as if you really were in Norma Desmond's house, and she had gone mad, and now this incredibly famous star who had just murdered her lover was about to come down the stairs! What dramatic event shall I compare it to? It was like—" and here Olson's voice plummets to a stage whisper "—the president is about to come down the stairs at the White House and *resign from office!*" She laughs at her own theatricality. "What I mean, of course, is that the air was charged. Something momentous was about to take place."

Gloria Swanson: "I hated to have the picture end. None had ever challenged or engrossed me more."

Michelle adds, "At the end of the scene, when Mother spoke her final line, 'All right, Mr. DeMille, I'm ready for my close-up' and Billy Wilder called, 'Print it!,' those members of the cast and crew already standing burst into applause. Everyone applauded—extras on the stairs and at the foot of the stairs, camera crew, lighting men, William Holden, Von Stroheim, Nancy Olson, Hedda Hopper—they all clapped on and on. Everyone else—people not already standing, and those at the far ends of the set—also applauded loudly, and every one of them rose to their feet to give her a long ovation."

Swanson broke into tears. Later she said, "I had a party planned for this last day, but then and there the cast and crew gave me one instead, right on the set. Everyone was in a great state of emotion, and Mother and Michelle and I said that night in our rented house that there were only three of us in it now, meaning that Norma Desmond had taken her leave."

Billy Wilder, as always, had the last word, or in this case the last image. As Norma Desmond walks into the lens as though to embrace "those wonderful people out there in the dark," the shot dissolves into a fuzzy, overexposed image. Light engulfs Norma, as if she were emerging from the tunnel in a near-death experience. For once, even Wilder lost control for a moment. "The focus gets thrown out by the focus carrier," he said. "I left the camera running. I didn't know where to cut."

chapter 11

Chiffon, Velvet, Chinchilla, Tulle, Brocade, Taffeta, Ermine, and Leopard-Printed Crêpe

That's a partial list of the fabrics and furs used for Swanson's wardrobe in *Sunset Boulevard*.

The words themselves sound exotic and a bit outrageous to twenty-first-century ears. Indeed, in 1950 these fabrics already seemed both chichi and passé. As such, they converged with the surreal and abnormal microclimates of Norma Desmond's environment.

Edith Head, who ran Paramount's costume department, was the ideal choice, and the expected one, to fashion the wardrobe of a forgotten star who thinks she's still big. Edith had glimpsed the past before it was passé. In 1923, as a teenager, she took a job at Paramount as a sketch artist. At that time Gloria Swanson reigned as studio royalty, and three years later, in 1926, when Gloria returned from France with her new husband and a new title—Marquise de la Falaise de la Coudraye—she was welcomed like Cleopatra in Rome. The studio handed out hundreds of roses and ordered the staff—young Edith included—to toss them worshipfully as the marquis and marquise emerged from their Rolls-Royce.

Years later Edith recalled that the couple's limousine was "leopard lined"—just like Norma Desmond's Isotta-Fraschini. This crafty detail reveals that Edith was part of *Sunset Boulevard*'s elaborate self-referential in-joke, which pressed every button of Hollywood history. She, like everybody on the picture, seems to have worked in every conceivable detail from yesteryear at Paramount.

Although someone other than Edith upholstered the interior of Norma Desmond's automobile in leopard to echo Swanson's Rolls-Royce, Edith also got mileage from it. She made sure that leopard print, so redolent of silent-era glamour, became the predominant motif of Norma Desmond's wardrobe: Norma matches her automobile in both fabric and antiquity. These leopard spots were also a gibe at Pola Negri, Swanson's putative rival at Paramount, and the pet leopard she walked on a leash. No wonder Swanson felt enormous attraction to the role of Norma Desmond, for she was portraying not only the archetype of silent siren but also a version of her earlier self.

At the time Edith was flinging roses at Gloria, the two women also enjoyed a more intimate connection, although unknown to Swanson. The young Edith, when she wasn't sketching in the costume department, was given the task of washing out Gloria Swanson's hosiery after a day on the set. Although Edith caught occasional glimpses of the glittering star, they were not introduced until *Sunset Boulevard*.

"I was apprehensive about working with Gloria," Edith said later. "I had dressed a great number of stars, but in my mind Gloria represented the greatest from the days when I was walking around with stars in my eyes."

They met for the first time in the Wilder and Brackett office at Paramount. Edith wondered if Swanson would like her; months later the designer learned "that she had requested me." Wilder told Edith Head that "he wanted Gloria to convey a feeling of the past, but he didn't want her to re-create it. He didn't want anything ridiculous or laughable." Director and designer agreed that Norma Desmond, though trapped in her silent movie days, still kept up with the present, at least in clothes, hair styles, and makeup.

Head translated Wilder's words into the language of fashion: "What Billy was telling me was that he wanted me to find some way of combining Jazz Age clothes with the [late forties] New Look. I knew it could be done, but actually doing it was one of the greatest challenges of my entire career."

Edith went about her difficult assignment by creating costumes for Norma Desmond that looked contemporary and yet conveyed a feeling "that they weren't exactly from the current era, despite the fact that they were obviously fine, new clothes worn by a woman of wealth and style to whom image meant a great deal."

In psychological terms, Norma's outfits function simultaneously as case history and diagnosis. As such, they all point in the same direction: prognosis negative. And though Wilder sought to avoid the overtly absurd, he had no way of knowing that a few years later the concept of camp would sabotage his restraint.

When we make her acquaintance Norma seems almost to have escaped from the zoo. She's got up in sweeping, floor-length house pajamas (also called a hostess gown) trimmed in leopard print, a matching leopard turban, dark glasses, and pounds of jewelery on her left arm. Her couture resembles some gerontological version of Frederick's of Hollywood crossed with Audubon. This rara avis undulates her spidery arms, stiffens her fingers into talons, opens her eyes and then narrows them to slits, as if they were visual gills.

Fashion writer Patty Fox views the Desmond wardrobe somewhat less exuberantly. She said, "The clothes, the enlarged shapes of the jewelery—it was all to create drama, and drama makes a presence. I don't think her clothes were overly dramatic, because of Gloria Swanson herself, who was both businesswoman and drama queen. In *Sunset Boulevard* the fashion supported the nature of the character."

Norma Desmond's day seems to include the entire complicated cycle of the "well-dressed woman," as adapted by Hollywood movies from ladies of the haute bourgeoisie. Around the house Norma moults from dressing gown to morning frock, from afternoon *tailleur* into cocktail gown and then evening clothes, all with spectacularly gaudy accessories. For evening, she has a negligée collection suitable for regular and holiday use, including Best Dressed New Year's Eve suicide attempt. This parade of glamour garments resembles a surreal mix of costumes for Myra Breckinridge, Lady Macbeth, and the boys in *Priscilla, Queen of the Desert*. "Because Norma Desmond was an actress who had become lost in her own imagination," Edith said, "I tried to make her look as if she was always impersonating someone."

Before Norma cuts her wrists to the sweet strains of "Auld Lang Syne," she's wearing a bizarre birdlike outfit that looks like a drag queen's version of the Queen of Sheba, or a mad Fabergé egg. In the script it's described as "a diamanté evening dress, very high style, with long black gloves and a headdress of paradise feathers."

For less theatrical scenes, did Edith Head perhaps get ideas from Erté about dressing Norma Desmond? At the bridge table with the Wax-works, for instance, she wears a flashy art deco outfit in silver and lumi-nous black that's suitable for framing.

Where Norma goes, leopard is sure to follow. Reclining on a chaise longue by the refurbished pool, she's dolled up in leopard resort wear with matching wedgies. At first glance Joe Gillis's swimsuit matches her outfit. On closer inspection, however, you realize that it clashes with Leopard Norma: his trunks are patterned in black and white arabesques rather than spots.

For the final sequence in *Sunset Boulevard*, when Norma descends the staircase after her crime of passion, Edith once more blurred the lines between the midcentury present and the Jazz Age: "I defined her wide waist only slightly, recalling the shapelessness of the 1920s, rather than giving her that whittled hourglass silhouette that characterized the early 1950s."

Head's description sounds rather conservative. In reality, however, Norma's Salome garb is a froufrou, diaphanous cape over a strapless gown, with flashing mirrored disks in her hair that resemble giant sequins. And bracelets that outjangle a cell phone. This ensemble is per-haps even more extravagant than it was meant to be. It's the sort of span-gled drapery that Mama Rose might have picked out for Gypsy Rose Lee.

It's important to realize that Gloria Swanson herself was in on the joke. In fact, Edith designed *with* Swanson as well as *for* her. "I found her not only easy to work with but particularly helpful because she had so many costumes already planned in her mind," Edith said. "She was recre-ating a past that she knew and I didn't." And unlike Norma Desmond, Gloria could laugh at herself.

A legendary clotheshorse, Swanson was savvy about costumes. She had worked with great Hollywood designers of the past, and her dress company, Forever Young, remained a viable enterprise in New York. Other comments by Edith Head hint at the women's close collaboration:

"Gloria showed me how she would be moving in each scene and she was careful to point out the difference between how she would have done things in the early days of Hollywood and how they were being done in 1950. She didn't want me to be confused. She was very aware of the nuances that were in this role."

Head prepared and discarded sketches, then she and Swanson considered and rejected countless bolts of fabric, shoes, accessories, and jewelery, analyzing both their dramatic and photographic qualities. In collaboration, they strove to communicate "the wearer's preoccupation with a time when movie stars wore costumes off as well as on the screen."

A flash forward: In 1974, twenty-four years after *Sunset Boulevard*, Gloria Swanson returned to Paramount once more to narrate a television documentary about the studio's greatest movies. For the film, she asked to wear a remake of the black velvet and white ermine suit that Edith Head had designed for Norma Desmond when *she* returns to Paramount to visit DeMille. Not only had the ensemble vanished, but no one could locate a peacock feather to decorate the new ermine toque made for her. Swanson was aghast. "Imagine," she said, "not one single white peacock feather in all Hollywood!"

An interviewer once asked Edith Head, "Why do you feel that clothes make the woman?"

Edith answered, "They also make the man. You see, a naked man or woman in the bathtub hasn't much identity. They are a body with certain hair. However, you can translate any man or woman through the medium of clothes into practically anything you want."

Translating Gloria Swanson into Norma Desmond might be compared with adapting a text from seventeenth-century British English into modern American. At first it looks easy, though the translator soon finds herself in quicksand. By contrast, Edith's sartorial job with the men of *Sunset Boulevard* might be likened to changing Canadian English into American: straightforward, with few pitfalls.

William Holden possessed the knack of wearing clothes elegantly, whether the clothes were elegant or not. He lacked the self-conscious posturing of a model; instead, he exploited clothes like a second set of emotions. (That's one reason he was a better choice than Montgomery Clift to play Joe Gillis. Clift always wore clothes as if they scratched.)

During the first half hour of *Sunset Boulevard*, Gillis wears a seedy outfit meant to italicize penury. The jacket and pants, obviously off the rack, fit his body only approximately. The shirt, flimsy and shapeless, seems cut from an early bolt of polyester. Nor, apparently, does Gillis own a change of clothes, since he's still in this outfit long after taking up with Norma. Her comment, "That's a dreadful shirt you're wearing," prompts her to take him shopping at Bullock's on Wilshire Boulevard. (If only Joe Gillis had remembered Thoreau's injunction: "Beware of all enterprises that require new clothes.")

Following Joe's sartorial makeover, a subtle change occurs not only in his wardrobe but also in his face: the expression becomes more confident, less frayed. After the shopping spree Joe looks spruced up in well-tailored suits and masculine overcoats that emphasize his build. In his New Year's Eve tuxedo he really does resemble Valentino, thereby reinforcing Norma's delusions and her grip on the vanished past.

In the dialogue there is one allusion to women's clothes—Gillis's voice-over mention of Norma's veil en route to Paramount—but numerous references to men's. And appropriately so, since Joe is the sex object here. Examples: the Bullock's salesman, with an insinuating inflection: "Well, as long as the lady's paying for it, why not take the vicuna?" Artie Green, when Joe arrives at the party wearing the coat: "Judas H. Priest, who did you borrow that from? Adolphe Menjou?" Joe to Betty Schaeffer when she tells him to get his things together and leave Norma's house: "All my things? All my eighteen suits, all my custom-made shoes and the six dozen shirts, and the cuff links and the platinum key chains, and the cigarette cases?"

When it came to other men in the cast, Edith made Lloyd Gough, as Joe's agent, look baggily outdated in a Depression-era golfing outfit. Since she always had a reason for the way she dressed a character, it's easy to read this garb as Edith's oblique scorn of Hollywood agents—with the complicity, no doubt, of Billy Wilder.

Erich von Stroheim, as Max, is not out of uniform during the picture, befitting his personal myth and his many film roles as military officers. As for DeMille, Edith had no say-so in her enemy's *Sunset Boulevard* costume. He wore his own clothes.

And so did Nancy Olson. Though obviously not one of the guys, her outfits are second only to Lloyd Gough's for drabness. "Billy Wilder wanted me to be superplain. I needed nothing more than my own home wardrobe. Billy selected some of my oldest dresses, which I had worn in school."

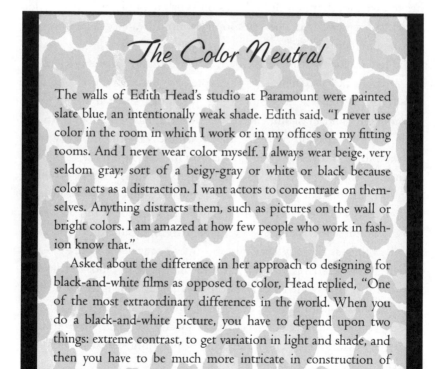

The Color Neutral

The walls of Edith Head's studio at Paramount were painted slate blue, an intentionally weak shade. Edith said, "I never use color in the room in which I work or in my offices or my fitting rooms. And I never wear color myself. I always wear beige, very seldom gray; sort of a beigy-gray or white or black because color acts as a distraction. I want actors to concentrate on themselves. Anything distracts them, such as pictures on the wall or bright colors. I am amazed at how few people who work in fashion know that."

Asked about the difference in her approach to designing for black-and-white films as opposed to color, Head replied, "One of the most extraordinary differences in the world. When you do a black-and-white picture, you have to depend upon two things: extreme contrast, to get variation in light and shade, and then you have to be much more intricate in construction of clothes and much more elaborate in accessories, decoration, embroidery, and things of that sort.

"Our costuming in earlier days was much more, we used to call it—photographic. We didn't use *dead* black or *dead* white; we used off-black and off-white. But we used a great deal of contrast. And also our clothes were elaborate. While a simple color dress would look beautiful today in a color film, for black and white we used to have more embroidery, more fur. For black-and-white pictures you must have more of everything and it's much more difficult."

Stars got along well with Edith Head. Most seemed genuinely fond of her, though if they hadn't been it would have behooved them to pretend. They had heard a statement she once made: "You know, I could take anybody in this room and make them look ten pounds thinner, or ten pounds fatter. I've done that." And of course, Edith also knew who had real breasts and who had the mock.

Two of Norma Desmond's most eccentric accessories were not designed by Edith Head. The first, her lorgnette, was an outré touch not because it was so rare at the time but because only dowagers used lorgnettes onscreen; certainly not a fifty-year-old glamour puss, faded or not. As an affectation, it jumps out at you even as Norma tries to conceal it.

Norma's other accoutrement is one of the great Hollywood hand props of any era. ("Hand props" are those handled by actors, as distinct from fixed "set props.") This one defines Norma Desmond as far-out, and it intrigues viewers, most of whom have never beheld anything like it. It's the item Holden refers to midway through the movie when he says, in voice-over: "I felt caught, like a cigarette in that contraption on her finger."

Tracing the origin of that contraption proved elusive, like the quest for a Stone Age artifact. The object itself, happily, required little search: it's in Box Number 324.4 of the Gloria Swanson Collection at the University of Texas. While doing research there, I mentioned to the curator that I was unable to find anything substantive on the cigarette holder. Ten minutes later the "contraption" was hooked around my finger.

There was a moment of intoxication as I brushed up against a legend. A nonsmoker, I wanted to rush outside and light up.

Instead I traced the item on a sheet of yellow paper. Later, measuring my trace work, I was surprised to find that the holder is only three and a half inches long. Made of silver, now tarnished, it's catalogued and filed along with Swanson's inventions. Assuming that because Swanson, in the twenties, invented and received patents for other tobacco accessories—a "match-holding cigarette container" and a "combined cigarette and match package"—she must also have invented this, I felt frustrated to discover no patent number or other documentation for the cigarette holder. As it turns out, the holder wasn't a Swanson invention.

Later I asked Billy Wilder about the object, and here's what he told me. "It was used by the wife of Dore Schary, who was the head of Metro, and she always sported this kind of a cigarette holder. I think it was a New York fad in the twenties, but this was taken over by Swanson. I gave it to Swanson."

My next informant, Jill Robinson, is a writer who lives in London. The daughter of Dore Schary and Miriam Svet Schary, she gave me this account: "I think it was Marlene Dietrich who gave one of those holders to my mother. You see, my mother's face was partially paralyzed from a childhood accident, and Marlene thought using this kind of holder might make it easier for her to smoke cigarettes."

Intrigued, I pressed Jill Robinson for total recall. She speculated that the fad began in Europe during the Belle Epoque. "Ladies at the time weren't really supposed to smoke," she said, "and in society you wore gloves. This holder would keep the cigarette from soiling them."

I said that Norma Desmond has a very distinct way of crooking her finger when she uses the contraption.

"That's exactly what my mother did," Robinson laughed. "She was always poking people in the eye with it, especially us when we were children. She had a collection of those cigarette holders. She must have had eight or ten. I have the remaining one, and it's beautiful."

I've spotted this same kind of holder in three other films. In *Dr. Monica* (1934), it's used by a character who resembles Louella Parsons. She's older than the other women in the picture, all of whom smoke constantly but without holders. This suggests that the contraption, like a lorgnette, was an accoutrement for mature women. But in *My Friend Irma Goes West* (1950), it's young Corinne Calvet who smokes her cigarette in a Norma Desmond holder. In the Turkish-Italian film *Steam: The Turkish Bath*, released in the U.S. in 1999, another young woman uses a similar holder, although the character has inherited it from an elderly relative in Istanbul.

Gloria Swanson herself, despite her devotion to otherwise healthy living, stopped smoking only late in life. In the 1970s she sometimes held a carnation in her hand on television talk shows in lieu of a cigarette.

chapter 12

If It's a Paramount Picture, It's the Best Show in Town*

S unset Boulevard, a glossary of visual, verbal, and film history in-jokes, can be read as a 110-minute punch line. That's because the art direction, along with the script, seems calculated to titillate. Every frame tips you off that this ribald, grotesque story is *really* about . . . and just when you think you've got it, suddenly you realize that the joke's on you, too. After all, the fact that you're watching implicates you as one of "those wonderful people out there in the dark."

Now, of course, the jokes in *Sunset Boulevard* add up to camp humor, but in 1950 all Hollywood must have squirmed. Their taste, like Norma Desmond's, was only as secure as their latest contract. How long before someone dug up the bodies to make a picture called "North Bristol Avenue" or "Bellagio Road"? The chilling fact hit home: Norma Desmond was *everyone's* neighbor.

If William Randolph Hearst ever saw *Sunset Boulevard* he may well have pondered a lawsuit, because Desmondland is a reduced version of Hearst Castle. The greatest star of them all shared with Citizen Hearst—and Citizen Kane—a fondness for the mishmash Mediterranean gothic-baroque.

If Mae West saw the picture, it's possible she left the theatre relieved that they didn't call it "570 North Rossmore," for Norma's decor resem-

---

*The studio's motto.

bled Mae's own. In both cases, the "set" had been designed to reflect the leading lady. The difference was a matter of hue: Norma Desmond lived in noir, Mae West in surroundings of kitschy gilded white and frilly pink.

These chiaroscuro-loving ladies shared the same interior decorator, Hans Dreier.

Mae West occupied an apartment at the Ravenswood on North Rossmore from her arrival in Hollywood in 1932 until her death in 1980. By the midthirties her heaving bosom and raunchy scripts had created such a furor that the Hays Office wanted to run her out of town. Paramount, in a rather limp gesture of moral rearmament, attempted to sanitize her image without crippling her dynamic draw at the box office. Seeking to reposition Mae in the media as safely domestic, the studio sent Hans Dreier up to see her. As head of the studio's art department, he could do the trick if anyone could.

Dreier, surely with tongue in cheek, ordered "white-and-gold furniture of a style best described as early French Candy Box. The living room featured polar bear rugs, a long, fringed sofa, and a white-and-gold baby grand piano." Mae basked in Dreier's piece of work. "You'll notice the furniture is more white than gold," she informed a gaping journalist. "Out here we're artistic, but restrained. I like restraint—if it doesn't go too far."

Mae slept—if at all—in a gilt swan bed. The swan's great sculpted tail feathers formed the headboard; at the foot, his downy gold neck began. It rose several feet in a graceful erotic curve, then swooped down into a tumescent head with extended beak or, as Mae might have put it, "pecker up." The bed had made a sensational appearance in her play *Diamond Lil.*

How could Wilder and Brackett *not* have thought of Mae West when writing, and casting, *Sunset Boulevard*? And after she turned them down for the starring role, they must have crowed when Hans Dreier presented sketches for the bedroom of Norma Desmond—"that room of hers," Joe Gillis calls it, "all satin and ruffles. . . . The perfect setting for a silent-movie queen."

If Dreier hadn't been head of Paramount's art department he might have landed the job anyway, for he had art directed not only Mae's apartment but also a couple of her films. For *Belle of the Nineties* (1934), Dreier and set designer Bernard Herzbrun created Ace Lamont's Sensation

House, a sumptuous New Orleans gaming palace where Mae's character, Ruby Carter, both lives and performs. "Its appointments included a marble staircase, gold-framed paintings (one of them looked more like an 'Old Mistress' than an Old Master), and a nude statue on which Ruby strikes a match." In this film and in all her others, Mae West is as tough and pitiless with men as Norma Desmond is. One difference, of course, is that Mae has a heart. Another is that she doesn't shoot. The gun is always in *his* pocket.

Convenience and convention designate *Sunset Boulevard* as Billy Wilder's film. Hollywood taxonomy then branches toward stars and supporting cast, on to the writing, and eventually to art direction, music, editing, costume design, and all those other "minor" categories which, in recent years, have bloated the Oscar ceremonies almost beyond endurance. In the studio era, however, these men and women had no faces. As for names, those usually appeared in small type on a single title card in the end credits. Sometimes they didn't appear at all, but who cared? By then everyone had left the theatre anyway.

Until the sixties, when academic film study and encyclopedic critics such as Pauline Kael started to spotlight the masters of studio craft, few outside the industry understood those curious categories. Could anyone besides members of a craft union detail the workday of an art director? A set decorator? To confuse matters more, there were editors and also sound editors on a picture, sometimes a film editor but other times an editorial supervisor or an editorial advisor. Even directors were largely ignored until recent decades. No one ever put Billy Wilder, George Cukor, or Alfred Hitchcock on the cover of *Photoplay*.

Eventually, however, as scholars and worshipful amateurs parsed the filmmaking process to the bone, hundreds of artisans and technical experts developed a following. It's not rare to stumble on a coterie (or a website) devoted to those who "handcrafted" the movies during the studio era. Books and articles on them appear regularly. Perhaps because contemporary stars have become less starlike, attention has shifted increasingly to those beyond camera range.

To some extent this has always been true. Art director Paul Iribe, for example, in *The Affairs of Anatol* (1921) corrected C.B. DeMille's vulgar streak with such dazzling and intoxicating results that several art critics wrote about the picture in serious journals.

Hans Dreier might be said to have toned up rather than to have corrected Billy Wilder's supposed "bad taste" in the thirteen pictures they worked on together (seven of them directed by Wilder, the other six cowritten by him). But that statement only holds if you accept the outmoded party line about Wilder as the exemplar of bad taste. Even at face value that premise is a bit absurd, since "bad taste"—in quotes or out— has always fueled Hollywood. My own revisionist critique is this: that Wilder's vulgarity took over only after *Sunset Boulevard*, when he no longer collaborated with Charles Brackett, Hans Dreier, and other discriminating stalwarts in the Paramount establishment. But more on that later.

Dreier, like Wilder, started out at UFA and retained a large measure of that studio's expressionism in his later work. Born in Germany in 1885 and trained as an architect, he worked on building projects for the German imperial government in the Cameroons, West Africa. In 1919, after his release from the army, Dreier made minor contributions to thirty-four films during his four years at UFA. Joining Paramount in 1923, he was promoted to supervising art director in 1932 and headed the studio's art department until his retirement in the early fifties. Dreier died in 1966.

Tall, straight, and Nordic-looking, Hans Dreier ran Paramount's art department like a Prussian fortress. According to younger colleague Robert Clatworthy (*Touch of Evil, Psycho*), Dreier was "absolutely charming" away from work and "a taskmaster" who "changed faces the minute he walked in the office. Then it was punctuality, discipline." A studio press release in 1935 dubbed Dreier the "generalissimo of Paramount's art department."

An interviewer once asked Dreier if he, and other art directors, promoted a certain studio "look" in their pictures. "No," he answered, "the art director is responsible for creating the reality of the backgrounds against which the characters in the story move." In other words, no one ever sat down and decided that Paramount pictures would look like this, Warner Bros. pictures like that, and so on. Yet sharp-eyed viewers do perceive a Paramount visual style as different from the style of Warner Bros. or Fox as a Monet from a Cézanne, or a Cézanne from a Toulouse-Lautrec.

Paramount art direction is typically described as having a "sophisticated, polished, and witty elegance" and "an opulence of surface," as being "gilded, luminous, as rich and brocaded as Renaissance tapestry." To the extent that such generalizations indeed sum up the visual content of the studio's films, much credit is due Hans Dreier. And the directors he worked with, for prior to Wilder he worked on ten Lubitsch films, including *Trouble in Paradise* (1932) and *Design for Living* (1933). Dreier also made a dozen pictures with Joseph von Sternberg, the most famous one being, in terms of visual splendor, *The Scarlet Empress* (1934).

Dreier won his first Academy Award for Mitchell Leisen's *Frenchman's Creek* (1944). Then one laden night in March 1951 he received his second and third Oscars: for DeMille's *Samson and Delilah* (the color award) and moments later for *Sunset Boulevard* (black-and-white). All of these awards were shared, the first with Ernst Fegte, the second with Walter Tyler, and the third with John Meehan. To complicate matters, Sam Comer and Ray Moyer also won Oscars for Best Set Decoration on *Samson and Delilah* and *Sunset Boulevard*. The reason for such shared recompense is, in simplest terms, that art direction and set decoration are even more intertwined than the other collaborations on a film. The closest we can come to pinpointing who did what on *Sunset Boulevard* is to say that the sets were probably conceived and produced by John Meehan, with Dreier closely supervising.

Their collective brilliance in designing the film is evident in the first shot: "Sunset Blvd." stenciled on the curb. Then Joe Gillis's meagre apartment, with unmade bed and apparently no chair, since he sits on the edge of the bed to type his scripts. The room and all in it evoke unattractive bohemian penury. With grim irony, this bedroom of a Hollywood never-was prefigures the bedroom of a has-been.

It's a few miles, and psychological light years, from there to the grandiose creepiness of Norma Desmond's house and its funeral parlor overtones: the monkey corpse draped in a shawl, a child's coffin for the burial, a lugubrious pipe organ, and burning candles sufficient to fill up a Spanish mission church. The abode of spectres, it reeks of sex and melancholy.

To make it that way, Dreier and Meehan hadn't far to look, for Paramount's bulging warehouse was an empire of fantastic accumulations. For years Dreier and the studio's other art directors had stockpiled antiques, curios, rare fabrics, and objets d'art. What they had not yet acquired was built as needed by studio craftsmen or bought from antiquaries. According to A. C. Lyles, "You couldn't tell studio-made from genuine antiques." He adds, "When a picture went on location, members of the art department would scour the countryside, visiting antique shops in the area. Anything that looked useful for future productions they shipped back to the studio. I've been on locations when the art director would buy crates of antique furniture, clothing, props of every kind."

The day came when all of these sets were struck and their extravagant furnishings returned to storage. Exit Dreier.

By mid-June of 1949 principal photography was completed. A short time later Franz Waxman viewed the *Sunset Boulevard* workprint and jotted his first notes for the score. When he laid down his pen toward the end of summer, he had composed a masterful drama in music equal to the film's writing, direction, cinematography, and editing. But Waxman's score goes beyond dutiful complement to the picture's visual and verbal discourse. Though married emotionally and technologically to *Sunset Boulevard*, Waxman's music is also autonomous. In fact, the concert hall and audio recordings show it as larger than even Waxman himself perhaps realized.

One might call Franz Waxman's *Sunset Boulevard* score a sonata in noir. The stentorian first three notes set the tone: they sound both defiant and dirgelike. The fourth note surges out of the depths and into a tense cascade of strings and strident brass; in seconds you hear foreshadowing musical cues as distinctive as Bernard Herrmann's in *Psycho*.

Throughout the film snatches of jazz punctuate the score, as when Gillis makes his first stop at Schwab's to call his agent from a pay phone.

These alternate with bluesy strains, suggesting overripeness and rot in Hollywood's dark corners. Stravinskyian throbs and thrusts underline apprehension, as in the chase scene when repo men pursue Gillis down Sunset Boulevard until he wheels into Norma Desmond's driveway with a blowout.

When Gillis first walks through the gates of Desmondland we hear harp music. Is this rapturous sound perhaps Waxman's musical red herring, an ironic miscue to make Joe's eventual violent death more shocking?

In addition to Waxman's own compositions, *Sunset Boulevard* contains a generous amount of source music—that is, nonunderscore by other composers. Erich von Stroheim pumps that hoary standard of horror-film fare, Bach's Toccata and Fugue in D Minor, on the wheezing organ. After Norma slaps Gillis, he stalks out and hails a cab to the boisterous New Year's Eve party at his friend Artie's. There Jay Livingston and Ray Evans, both seated at the piano, are performing "Buttons and Bows," a big hit at the time that they had actually composed. The jaunty song is fresh, youthful, contemporary, like the partygoers packed into Artie's small apartment. This party and this song remind Gillis of everything missing from Norma's lugubrious palazzo.

"Stop That Playing, Max!"

The script is very specific: "A pair of hands in white gloves, playing the organ. PULL BACK: They belong to Max von Mayerling. He is sitting erect, his bull neck taut as a wrestler's as he fights out somber chord after somber chord." The music, however, is not specified. When the day came to shoot the scene, Billy Wilder may well have flashed on half a dozen previous films for his grandiose choice, Bach's Toccata and Fugue in D Minor. In *Dr. Jekyll and Mr. Hyde* (1932), hands (presumably those of Frederic March) play the piece under the opening credits. In *The Black Cat* (1934), Boris Karloff plays the piece on an organ. Bela Lugosi ditto in *The Raven* (1935). In *Mad Love* (1935), Peter Lorre plays the organ, although not the Toccata and Fugue. Lorre is, however, a bald, somewhat sinister, German-accented actor pumping the organ. And Lorre and Wilder had been roommates for a while in their early days in Hollywood. Max, enraptured by the music he's playing, suddenly seems less sinister and more humane. But even Bach hasn't the power to calm the savage beast in Norma Desmond, who screams: "Stop that playing, Max!"

The musty musicians hired for Norma Desmond's New Year's Eve party keep playing long after she has retired upstairs to her suicide attempt. When Gillis rushes back to her bedside, the sentimental strains of a 1920s waltz, "Charmaine," drift up from below. "Auld Lang Syne" starts just after Norma, lying in bed with bandaged wrists, tells Gillis, "I'll do it again." The nickelodeon music we hear when Norma performs her Mack Sennett bathing beauty number for Gillis is "Over the Waves." And while Gillis and Betty Schaeffer, on the back lot at night, take what Waxman designated as "The Studio Stroll," the ingenious composer included a disguised quote from the signature tune of Paramount's "Eyes and Ears of the World" newsreels.

Born in Königshütte, Germany, in 1906, Waxman (who later modified the spelling of his name from the original Wachsmann) defied his father, an industrialist who wanted the youth to become a banker. For young Franz, however, melody spoke louder than money. After a couple of years as a teller he quit the bank, set out for Dresden and further study at the local music academy. In 1923, during the best of times and the worst of times for the Weimar Republic, Waxman arrived in Berlin. To pay tuition at the conservatory he played piano in cafes. Recall the world of

Cabaret for a stylized glimpse of Waxman's Berlin, and Wilder's, a city soon to attempt the murder of its most talented residents.

Beginning in the late twenties, Waxman arranged and orchestrated films at UFA. In 1930 he orchestrated and conducted Frederick Hollander's score for Marlene Dietrich's breakthrough picture, *The Blue Angel.* Other pictures followed and then suddenly his career, like his life, was in danger. Early in 1934 a gang of Nazi thugs beat up Waxman on a street in Berlin. He and his fiancée left Germany in great haste. Destination: Paris.

Countless other refugees, including Waxman's friend Billy Wilder, arrived in France about the same time. Wilder and Waxman had met at UFA in the early thirties. In Berlin they worked on two pictures together—Wilder as writer, Waxman as composer—before fleeing Germany. In Paris Waxman composed the score for Billy Wilder's first assignment as a fledgling director, *Mauvaise Graine* (1934).

Nicholas Christopher, in his book *Somewhere in the Night*, makes the point that Hollywood film noir was influenced not only by German expressionist films but also by "the so-called French poetic realism of the late thirties." Citing a number of refugee directors who stopped in Paris en route to Hollywood, Christopher notes that they "were not only exposed to the poetic realism films, but directed a good many themselves."

Although *Mauvaise Graine* doesn't exactly qualify as French poetic realism, it is a screen poem. The story is about a ring of Parisian car thieves, but the real subject is moviemaking. The camera—ever in motion, always feasting on Paris—can't resist framing compositions of cars, streets, buildings, faces. Even if you didn't know that Wilder was a nimble dancer, you'd guess it from the rhythm of his debut film.

An opening credit reads, "Musique de Waxman," and as always this composer is in step with his director. Waxman's score is mainly French fox-trot tunes that modulate into darker tone colors as the crime story progresses. (*Mauvaise Graine* obviously influenced Godard's *Breathless*. Ironically, it's Godard's 1959 film that has dated while Wilder's bursts with freshness and youth.)

Later, in Hollywood, Wilder and Waxman worked together on five pictures. Franz Waxman didn't say a lot about his score for *Sunset Boulevard*: he was too busy writing music to talk about music. In all, he worked on the scores of 144 films, including *The Bride of Frankenstein* in 1935. He is the only composer ever to have won two Oscars in successive years: for *Sunset Boulevard* in 1950 and for *A Place in the Sun* the following year.

Waxman did, however, say this much about the music he composed for *Sunset Boulevard*:

> The main theme is one of a tango character, which stems from a scene in which Gloria Swanson makes reference to the early days of Hollywood and the tango dancing of Rudolph Valentino. This is the atmosphere in which she still lives in 1950 and I took this little bit of characterization as inspiration for the musical theme. As we see the hero packing to leave her home, the music underneath is the same as in the main title, only much slower, much heavier, much more foreboding of the tragic things to come. As he leaves the house she runs frantically after him. At this time the tango theme repeats itself in twisted and tortured harmonies until the fatal shot is heard. Then as we discover her in the grotesque pose, her mind already half-gone, we hear a faint oboe solo in a theme as disjointed as her mind is at this moment.

Many years later, Billy Wilder recalled: "The final scene was written to Richard Strauss's 'The Dance of the Seven Veils.' I had that record on, and we would rehearse to that record. I had that in mind and Waxman did that [i.e., composed a pastiche of it]. We couldn't use Strauss because it would have cost a fortune. It would also have been an insult to Waxman, with whom I made many pictures."

Long after Waxman's death in 1967, his old friend Wilder paid him this compliment: "I had my favorite composers, they were Franz Waxman and Miklós Rózsa. They provided my best scores. They knew my work, knew it intuitively."

Wilder apparently believed that editor Doane Harrison also knew his work intuitively, since they worked together on twenty-three pictures over three decades. Even before Wilder directed his first Hollywood film, he and Harrison were colleagues. Beginning with *Midnight* in 1939, which Brackett and Wilder wrote and Mitchell Leisen directed, through *The Fortune Cookie* (1966), which Harrison coproduced, Wilder's work usually has Harrison's name in the credits. Usually that credit reads "editor." Other times Harrison is "editorial advisor" or "associate producer." On *Sunset Boulevard* he worked with another editor, Arthur P. Schmidt, whom Wilder used on several subsequent pictures, including *Some Like It Hot.* (The *Sunset Boulevard* credits list Harrison as "editing supervisor" and Schmidt as "editor.")

In an interview Wilder once said, "I worked with a very good cutter, Doane Harrison, from whom I learned a great deal. He was much more of a help to me than the cameraman. When I became a director from a writer my technical knowledge was very meagre."

In valuable early lessons, Harrison taught Wilder how to preplan each shot as part of a total editing scheme. The results: Time and money saved, and few protection shots required. (The term "protection shot," also called "coverage," refers to footage shot from various setups and angles that may be needed for editing a sequence in the cutting room.)

In a sense Harrison functioned both as mentor and assistant director, since "he was always nearby to consult on what shots were needed to complete the day's shoot." With his editor both on the set and an active participant in the filming, Wilder was able to say, "When I'm finished with a picture, there's very little celluloid left on the cutting room floor." By helping Wilder avoid unnecessary shots, Harrison enabled him to make pictures in the simplest way possible; in Wilder's reductive words, "I just shoot the way I think it's going to look."

Many directors considered this efficient method both unorthodox and undesirable. For one thing, director and editor often viewed one another as competitors, if not outright antagonists, since a director's work might be assembled in the editing room in ways he found abhorrent. Many directors—including Hitchcock, John Ford, and Joseph L. Mankiewicz—in effect cut their films as they shot, meaning they printed a minimum number of takes in order to exert greater control over their work. With relatively few takes of any given scene, an intrusive editor—

or worse, an omnipotent producer—had little choice but to accept the picture as conceived by its director.

Described as "a lanky, stoop-shouldered, laconic man" who "didn't look very healthy," Harrison started as a film cutter in the early twenties and spent most of his career at Paramount. His death in 1968, at the age of seventy-four, meant both personal and professional loss for Billy Wilder.

Harrison's contribution to *Sunset Boulevard*—and it's virtually impossible to label it precisely—surely helped make the picture a seamless, balanced, measured work of art. Specifically, it's likely that Harrison's eye, and his rhythmic instincts, did much to ensure that no scene goes on too long and that no scene is truncated; that we view the actors from a number of different camera angles in various locales; and that the painful story is told swiftly, without overemphasis, and from the proper aesthetic distance.

chapter 13

Fiasco

You've never seen the original opening of *Sunset Boulevard*, nor have I. Virtually no one has. Billy Wilder wants us never to see it. It's the sequence that nearly ruined him.

The familiar opening is this: after the first shot—"Sunset Blvd." stenciled on a curbstone—the camera leaves the curb and moves east. The gray asphalt of the street fills the frame as speed accelerates and credit titles appear in the same stenciled lettering. The camera pans up and you see two oncoming police motorcycles, followed by three speeding cars from the homocide squad.

That, however, is not the opening sequence Wilder and Brackett first had in mind. What they wrote, and filmed, following the credit titles was a pan to the rear end of a moving vehicle. Their script, finally completed just as filming ended, designated the vehicle as a black hearse.

The camera pans higher to show the word "coroner" on the hearse. A series of shots follows it through the streets to the L.A. County Morgue. Inside the building, a medium shot of a corpse covered by a sheet. The feet are naked. On the left big toe of the corpse, in ordinary handwriting, a linen tag reads:

Joseph Gillis
Homicide
5/17/49

An attendant wheels the corpse into a huge, windowless room. Along the walls are some two dozen covered corpses. The attendant pushes Gillis into a vacant space. Beyond him, the feet of the other corpses stretch from under their sheets: men's feet, women's feet, some white and some black, all with linen tags dangling from the left big toe.

In voice-over, a man speaks: "Don't be scared. There's a lot of us here. It's all right." Gillis answers, "I'm not scared." A ghostly conversation follows as a fat man asks Gillis how he died. Gillis demurs. The fat man informs Gillis that he himself died of a heart attack. Finally Gillis says, "Me, I drowned." A boy chimes in, "So did I." Another man, designated in the script as a "Negro," joins the conversation. A woman speaks words of comfort to the boy, who worries that his parents won't find him.

The spectral chat goes on for four pages in the script. When the fat man catches on that Gillis has Hollywood connections, he asks, "You in the movies?" and Gillis gives him a capsule bio that ends with the line, "I was having a tough time making a living." The fat man retorts, "It's your dying I was asking about."

From that point Gillis's narrative, and the footage, become more or less as they are in the release print of *Sunset Boulevard*. From the morgue, a dissolve to the hilltop at Ivar and Franklin. The camera moves through the window into Gillis's apartment, the buzzer sounds, and two repo men stand at his door, demanding car keys. Brackett and Wilder never considered ending the picture any way other than with Norma Desmond's close-up.

Larry Blake

Larry Blake (1914–1982) made his film debut in 1937 in *The Road Back*, a sequel to the 1930 antiwar picture *All Quiet on the Western Front*. He served in the navy during World War II, sank into heavy drinking, and joined Alcoholics Anonymous in 1946. The following year he and another actor founded the first AA group for motion picture people, using a small building near Paramount that they rented with the help of Howard Hughes.

One day in 1949 Blake, en route to audition for the part of first finance man in *Sunset Boulevard*, took a wrong turn in a studio corridor. He stopped a little guy in black-framed glasses. "I'm trying to find Billy Wilder's office," Blake said.

"Go down there and turn left and it's the second door on your right," the man told him. Then he added, "You must be reading for his new picture."

"Yeah," Blake said. "I've been in the movie business since 1937 and I've never heard of this guy Wilder. He must be somebody's relative or something." They both laughed. The stranger said, "Good luck."

Blake entered Wilder's outer office to find a roomful of actors there for the same reason. Five minutes later the inner office door opened and the little guy in black-framed glasses stepped out. Spotting Larry Blake, the man said, "He has the job, thank you very much, gentlemen." The guy in glasses was Billy Wilder.

After playing the repo man in black hat who does the talking, Blake worked steadily in dozens of bit parts and supporting roles. He appeared in *High Noon* (1952), *Angel Face* (1953), *Earth vs. the Flying Saucers* (1956), *Elmer Gantry* (1960), and Billy Wilder's *The Front Page* in 1974. Larry Blake's last film was *Time After Time* (1979).

Although the camera passes but once though a window, characters frequently pass through gates in *Sunset Boulevard*—the gates of Desmondland, or the gates of Paramount. In real life, it might well have been Billy Wilder who made his exit if preview audiences had had any say in the matter. They despised *Sunset Boulevard*.

Wilder has told the story many times and he makes it funny, though it must have been horrible when it took place.

Because of the touchy subject matter, Paramount sought a venue far from Hollywood to preview the picture. Evanston, Illinois, seemed distant enough. After the opening credits, when the story moved down Sunset Boulevard and into the L.A. County Morgue, the audience stunned Billy Wilder. Years later he recalled, "When the morgue label was tied on Mr. Holden's toe, they started to scream with laughter. In the mood of hilarity I walked out of the preview, very depressed."

Also in the preview audience were eight or ten executives from Paramount—"Just enough to fire me," Wilder said later. Shocked and distraught, he tried to move out of earshot of the cruel laughter. "So there were some steps leading down to the toilets," Wilder said, "and I'm sitting there on the fourth step. I'm sick to my stomach, and there's a lady passing me by. She's got a big picture hat and she's going down to the ladies' room. She sees me sitting there and she turns around and she says, 'Have you ever seen shit like this in your life?' I said, 'Never! Never! Never!' "

Years later Wilder called his original opening of *Sunset Boulevard* "a weird kind of framing sequence containing some of the best material I've ever shot."

No audience has seen the morgue sequence since 1949, although Wilder did save the footage. When Sherry Lansing, head of Paramount, approached him about including the deleted sequence as an addendum to the DVD version of *Sunset Boulevard*, the answer was no. (Although Wilder sometimes claims to hold the missing sequence, he told director Cameron Crowe, "I don't know who has it now.")

That strange discourse in the original opening may have derived from Thornton Wilder's *Our Town*, which opened on Broadway in 1938. If Brackett and Wilder didn't know it from the stage, they would have seen the film version in 1940, with William Holden in the cast. *Our Town* owed a debt to *Spoon River Anthology*, a volume of verse epitaphs by Edgar Lee Masters, which remained popular for years after its publication in 1915. Charles Brackett would have known this quintessentially American work, Wilder probably not. Whatever the source of Brackett and Wilder's own poetic epitaphs, however, preview audiences reacted with relentless mirth.

A second preview was held in Poughkeepsie, New York—"Where they're not used to such things," in Wilder's droll words. "Same goddamn reaction," said Wilder. Nor did they like it at the preview in Great Neck, Long Island. In fact, the response there was even worse. Paramount postponed release of the film for months. Rumors buzzed that *Sunset Boulevard* might be shelved. Wilder made changes, chiefly the substitution of Gillis's floating body for that conversation in the morgue. Years later, the director still seemed miffed by the changes forced on him by those first benighted audiences: "So we chopped it off and the narrator's voice begins by saying, 'Yes, this is Sunset Boulevard.' It was announced coldly, like the opening of a supermarket."

Franz Waxman designated the original opening sequence "Conversing Corpses" on his score. After Wilder deleted the sequence, Waxman made minor changes so that he could recycle the morgue music in the revised opening.

Those catastrophic previews took place late in 1949. At Paramount's insistence, Wilder tinkered with the film for the next six months, never forgetting the high stakes. By midsummer of 1950 the picture previewed again, this time in theatres around Los Angeles. Jack Stevenson, who was affiliated with the Paramount Film Distributing Company in San Francisco, wrote to Gloria Swanson: "There have been several sneak previews of *Sunset Boulevard* and it is really creating quite a sensation."

In July 1950 the picture previewed once more in the Midwest. This time audience reaction, though decidedly mixed, came closer to the mark. Gloria Swanson saved some of the preview cards from a screening at the Fisher Theatre in Detroit. The cards are headed like this:

HOLLYWOOD PREVIEW
"SUNSET BOULEVARD"
starring
Gloria Swanson and John Lund [sic]
Thursday, July 6th, 1950

John Lund's name must be a printing error. In a way, it's an outlandish symbol of the blind faith studios put in the opinions of preview audiences. Both the folly and the wisdom of heeding these judgments become clear from the comments made about *Sunset Boulevard*. Although many of these amateur critiques sound ignorant and silly, studio personnel analyzed such jottings as if they were the Torah, the Holy Gospels, and *Variety* reduced to a few lines in pencil. Of the cards Swanson saved, only one person put a query beside the name John Lund. Indeed, several cards referred to John Lund's excellent acting. (Gloria Swanson seems to have attended this preview; a couple of cards imply her presence.) Roughly seventy-five percent of those who filled out cards reacted favorably to Swanson and to the picture.

"The rude awaking [sic]" was the gnomic opinion of one Reed Carrington after his exposure to Norma Desmond and company. "I think this picture was lousy," wrote a Stuart Gorelick. "Although Miss Swanson's acting was superb, I did not like the plot."

"Exceptional and wonderful acting as would be expected of both Swanson and Von Stroheim. In fact whole cast was excellent," was the opinion of Mrs. William F. Golden. Another lady, Dorothy B. Nichols, would have preferred an operatic climax à la Tosca: "Gorgeous picture—fine acting—phony finish—why not have her jump over the balustrade and clear everything up."

"Good acting but I didn't like it," opined hard-to-please Mrs. W. Smart. The full-bodied response of Mrs. Robert C. Hanson reveals her as a perceptive viewer: "The hurt in my throat for the nostalgia of bygone days—simply stupendous, beautifully done."

Film historian Jeanine Basinger reminds us what it was like to see *Sunset Boulevard* when it was new: "For many in the audience, it was an extraordinary blurring of fact and fiction, since for them it had been less than twenty-five years since it had all been real. When Norma's bridge group meets, and the other players include Anna Q. Nilsson, Buster Keaton, and H. B. Warner, older people in the audience gasped. I know, I was there, ushering, watching it numerous times."

chapter 14

The Whole Audience Stood Up and Cheered

On the morning of Thursday, August 10, 1950, a sixteen-year-old boy named Miles Kreuger, who lived on the Upper West Side of Manhattan, got up at four o'clock to go to the movies. This youngster was perhaps one of the few young people in New York who knew anything about silent pictures. Not only was he aware of the silents and their stars, he loved those dramas and comedies where they didn't need words. When the Museum of Modern Art's film department screened a picture from the teens or twenties, Miles watched with all the fascinated avidity of Norma Desmond beholding herself in the silent clip in *Sunset Boulevard*. As a matter of fact he had, on several occasions at the museum, watched a Gloria Swanson silent picture with Swanson herself in the audience. Once he attended a screening of *Sadie Thompson* when both Swanson and her costar Raoul Walsh showed up.

Having met Gloria Swanson and talked with her, he was thrilled to learn that this great silent star had made a new picture.

On that warm summer morning the boy dropped a dime in the subway turnstile at Ninety-first Street and Broadway (a station now as defunct as the ten-cent fare) and arrived at Radio City Music Hall by six o'clock—four and a half hours before the doors opened. He was, of course, the first one on line and the first patron to buy a ticket for the world premiere of *Sunset Boulevard*.

Miles Kreuger still has that ticket stub. "Not long after that," he told me recently, "others began to arrive and soon the line stretched around the block. That surprised me, because it didn't seem to me the kind of picture that would attract such a huge crowd." The teenage Miles found it a good augury, however, that so many other picturegoers wanted to see Hollywood's unexpected tribute to silent films. "For you see," he added, "in the few years that had transpired since the end of the silent era in the late twenties, silent movies had become as archaic as hieroglyphics."

I asked Miles about the composition of that first-time audience, but he said he recalls very little. "I sat in the front row, so I didn't even see the audience. I was immersed in the film. It served as my answer to wide screen before wide screen existed."

Sitting in row one at Radio City proved not to be the neck-wrenching trauma it might be in smaller theatres. That's because the music hall's large stage occupied considerable space between the audience and the screen. Nevertheless, Miles recalls it as "a chilling experience because of those images, those faces, glowering down."

It's not surprising to learn that he stayed for the second performance. "During the stage show I decided to try the least desirable seat in the house. I moved to the last row of the third balcony. From there the movie looked like a flickering postage stamp." At some point in the afternoon he phoned his mother to tell her he wouldn't be home for dinner. "It's too exciting, so I'll just eat candy bars."

Like a hypnotist or a shrink, I asked Miles to regress to the age of sixteen and describe the impact *Sunset Boulevard* had on him. "Oh," he replied, "I haven't changed; I'm still sixteen. What did I think of it? It struck me as a modern-day fairy tale and I thought of Norma Desmond as a wicked witch who lives in a strange castle separated from the outside world, and she captures the handsome young prince."

Other boyish impressions retained by the man: "I was taken by the brilliance of the script. By the time I left Radio City that day I had memorized half the dialogue." (He stayed for a third performance, which let out shortly after 6:00 P.M.) "I thought it would be fun to live in that house. And I understood who Norma Desmond was because I knew who Gloria Swanson was. I'm not sure I knew about Hollywood has-beens or comebacks, for I don't believe I had a good sense of the passage of time. Remember, when I was growing up in the forties we didn't have new movie stars very often. From the time I was born Clark Gable was the top. He, Myrna Loy, Gary Cooper, Barbara Stanwyck—they formed an unchanging cadre. When someone new did come along—Gregory Peck, Dana Andrews—I didn't think of them as comparable stars."

It's a wonder young Miles Kreuger got home at all that day, for the Radio City Music Hall playbill reads like an entire season's offerings at lesser venues. (Indeed, it was possible at one time to purchase season tickets for Radio City.)

Between screenings of *Sunset Boulevard* during a typical week of its run, every audience at the "Showplace of the Nation" would have heard a short opening concert played on the music hall's grand organ. Next, and equally splendid no doubt, the Music Hall Symphony Orchestra played Liszt's "Grand Fantasy." Then came a five-part stage extravaganza happily called "On the Bright Side," as if in ironic contrast to Billy Wilder's dark masterpiece. The first part of this show, "Beaux Arts Ball," featured the Music Hall Glee Club. After that the Rockettes, choreographed to matchless precision, kicked their famous legs in a showpiece called "Colorama."

When at last applause died down, the music hall's resident dancers, singers, and actors joined together in a series of vignettes purporting to portray "Greenwich Village." The final sketch in the stage show, "Valse des Fleurs," combined the terpsichorean talents of the Rockettes and the Music Hall Corps de Ballet with the music of Tchaikovsky. From organ prelude to final pas de deux, the spectacle went on for some forty-five minutes.

After this protracted spell on the bright side, house lights faded and the Paramount logo flashed across the screen of Radio City Music Hall. Gone was Liszt, gone the Rockettes. Franz Waxman's adrenaline chords jolted the picture to a slam-bang start that contradicted the picture's very title: a floating dead man in a pool declared that it was five o'clock in the morning in Los Angeles, California.

On Sunset Boulevard sirens shrilled in the distance. The audience tensed in wary alert. A phalanx of policemen sped closer and veered left onto a derelict estate. Out of the deep, one gazed up at William Holden's watery crucifixion.

All across that theatre of seven thousand seats, night had fallen. Brightness was extinguished by a moral sunset, which began at dawn in a big white elephant of a house and deepened, at last, into a close-up of Hollywood's Götterdämmerung.

Norma Desmond Had a Point

Had you strolled around New York on the day *Sunset Boulevard* opened you might not have chosen to see it, despite the blandishments of Radio City Music Hall. Competition was formidable, in quantity at least, and instead of the music hall you might have picked the Roxy, another legendary movie palace. There Elia Kazan's *Panic in the Streets* was on, starring Richard Widmark, Kirk Douglas, and Barbara Bel Geddes. As a fringe benefit you would have heard popular vocalist Frances Langford sing, and after that a frilly stage show called "Summer Carnival" would have detained you from the sizzling New York streets.

Playing at the Capitol, *A Lady Without a Passport* starred Hedy Lamarr and John Hodiak. This melodrama was fetchingly advertised with a come-on line bannered above the Lamarr legs and cleavage: "That Delilah girl is on the loose." Performing on stage was Pearl Bailey, "Star of Screen, Radio, and Records."

Elsewhere in Manhattan: Dean Martin and Jerry Lewis in *My Friend Irma Goes West*, Fred Astaire and Vera-Ellen in *Three Little Words*, Claudette Colbert and Robert Ryan starring in *The Secret Fury*, *Destination Moon* with John Archer and Warner Anderson, James Stewart and Shelley Winters in *Winchester '73*, Margaret Sullavan as the lead in *No Sad Songs for Me*, Robert Mitchum in *The Story of G.I. Joe*. In addition to these rather unexceptional offerings, several classic films were playing, either as first runs or in revival, among them *City Lights, The Third Man, Bicycle Thief,* and *Passport to Pimlico.*

Going over this list, it's hard to argue with Norma Desmond. New York theatres proved her point: the pictures had indeed gotten small.

The day after *Sunset Boulevard* opened at the music hall, it was reviewed not by the lead critic of the *New York Times,* but rather by an underling who mysteriously signed himself T. M. P. This person, whose writing outshone the pompous prose of *Times* critic Bosley Crowther, praised the screenwriters for their "powerful story of the ambitions and frustrations that combine to make life in the cardboard city so fascinating to the out-side world." The reviewer also judged it "inconceivable that anyone other than Gloria Swanson might have been considered for the role" and con-cluded by calling *Sunset Boulevard* "a great motion picture."

Other New York reviewers agreed. From the *Herald-Tribune:* "Charles Brackett and Billy Wilder have slashed open Hollywood in a brilliantly moody melodrama." The *Journal-American* raved, calling it "a great picture of a great story of a great star. . . . It elevates Gloria Swanson, a fine actress, to heights she never before has attained. Few, indeed, are the actresses who have." The *Post* called it "a major work of Hollywood art."

A week later the *New Yorker* panned *Sunset Boulevard.* In one of the few negative reviews, the unsigned critic tagged it "a pretentious slice of Roquefort" and conceded only that the picture "has some engrossing scenes" and "contains the germ of a good idea."

Further afield, *Variety* gave the picture a favorable review that ended with a mild caveat: "This is a picture worthy of special exhibitor effort, for it will need extra work to realize its greatest drawing potentialities." the *Hollywood Reporter,* although never noted for the profundity of its cri-tiques, carried an unsigned review that today seems not only perceptive but eerily prophetic: "[This review] will be studied years hence when the pundits of the screen set themselves the task of analyzing the durability and greatness of *Sunset Boulevard,* [which] will be brought back again and again in revivals, in art houses, in schools and in studio projection rooms as a lesson in the art and science of the screen."

In the liberal Catholic weekly *Commonweal,* reviewer Philip T. Hartung also predicted enduring regard for the film. Imagining a time when the triumph of television might turn Hollywood into a ghost town, he speculated that "then the Library of Congress will be glad to have in its archives a print of *Sunset Boulevard.*" The *Christian Century* warned its audience of moderate-to-liberal Protestant readers that "morbid characterizations of unadmirable people make this a *most unpleasant but very effective* film." Lauding the film's "great lady" who "spans another decade with her magic," *Good Housekeeping* adjured, "Let no youngster ask, 'Who was Gloria Swanson?' " (Which was, of course, exactly the question they did ask.)

In the November 1950 issue of *Sight and Sound* James Agee wrote a five-page essay on *Sunset Boulevard* that is generally considered the first critical discussion of the Hollywood-on-Hollywood film as a distinct genre. Of all film critics of his time, Agee probably loved movies the most. In addition to film reviews, Agee also wrote screenplays (*The African Queen, The Night of the Hunter*). Although his prose seems rather stiff and dated now, his perceptions remain up to date.

Owing to Brackett and Wilder's severe eulogy of silent pictures and silent stars, Agee found that "the silent era, and art, are granted a kind of barbarous grandeur and intensity." He took a minority view that in *Sunset Boulevard* silent-picture art and artists "are also a good deal hammier than they actually were at their best." (True, Norma Desmond is hammy, but she's patterned after the more flamboyant silent vamps, not a restrained actress like Lillian Gish. Swanson herself, in silent pictures, was much less operatic than Norma.)

Agee pointed out that "the lost people [i.e., Norma, Max, the Waxworks] are given splendor, recklessness, an aura of awe; the contemporaries [Joe, Betty Schaeffer, Artie, Sheldrake] by comparison are small, smart, safe-playing, incapable of any kind of grandeur, good or bad." Although Agee felt that Brackett and Wilder "fail to make much of the powerful tragic pos-

sibilities which are inherent in their story," they were nevertheless "beautifully equipped to do the cold, exact, adroit, sardonic job they have done."

Many important studio films opened in New York weeks before their
Hollywood openings. Nevertheless, the splashy affair at a glamorous Los
Angeles picture palace such as Grauman's Chinese or the Pantages was
widely considered *the* premiere. In popular movie mythology, initial New
York showings amounted to little more than glorified previews. The East
was foreplay. Hollywood climaxed with screaming fans, searchlights, lim-
ousines, the glamour and the gowns.

In the case of *Sunset Boulevard*, the irony is exquisite. Paramount's decision to avoid a showy Hollywood premiere for the definitive movie about
Hollywood belongs in a script by Charles Brackett and Billy Wilder. They
did not, of course, make the decision, though they did cooperate.

Beginning in January 1950, a special screening campaign started up.
Paramount's publicity department altered its usual practice of showing a
new picture to accommodate requests—for example, from the press,
from industry officials, special interest groups, and the like. Rather, preview screenings of *Sunset Boulevard* stretched out over a period of some
eight months. By August, twenty-one such previews had taken place. To
maintain arousal, the publicity department also established waiting lists.
When a particular list reached seventy-five or a hundred important
names, a screening was finally held.

According to the *Hollywood Reporter*, many of those twenty-one screenings "were virtual premieres as a result of the list of stars who attended."

This innovative screening schedule worked. Word of mouth redoubled and the names Swanson, Wilder, Brackett, Holden, Stroheim, et al.,
popped up daily in the gossip columns. Long before its release, *Sunset
Boulevard* became the most talked about picture of 1950. Whether intentional or not, the Paramount ploy of delayed gratification also served as
damage control. For *Sunset Boulevard* was nitroglycerin, and like that
explosive liquid, the picture demanded cautious handling. The studio
knew that crowd hysteria or sudden heat could blast the guilty parties
into Desmondesque obscurity.

Louis B. Mayer and his minions at MGM launched a preemptive strike.

Swanson recalled that early in 1950 "on the evening of the first big screening in Hollywood, Louis B. Mayer had a dinner party for about twenty people. From there we went to the Paramount screening room, where the audience of three hundred people seemed to include everyone in motion pictures." According to Swanson, these studio previews usually were "morbidly restrained, devoid of the slightest overt reaction." The reason: no one dared betray an incorrect response by clapping too loudly, or by withholding requisite applause. Like a bejeweled politburo, the timorous elite awaited reaction from the high muck-a-mucks.

That night was different. "The whole audience stood up and cheered," said Swanson. "People clustered around me, and I had trouble moving up the aisle."

Edith Head was there, and this is what she reported: "Gloria made a grand entrance wearing a floor-length silver lamé dress. As everyone watched the film, the screening room was silent. The credits rolled, the screen went black, and still there was silence. Then there was thunderous applause. A few people walked out, murmuring that the film would be the ruination of Hollywood, but the rest swarmed around Swanson and Wilder."

"I could read in all their eyes a single message of elation," said Swanson. "If she can do it, why should we be terrified?" Swanson's ambiguity is perhaps intentional. *If she can do it* may mean all of these: survive a Hollywood career, make a comeback, grow old gracefully, and still look fabulous in silver lamé when one is a grandmother over fifty.

Barbara Stanwyck joined the swarm around Gloria Swanson, while Louis B. Mayer stalked out with his entourage, muttering rancorous epithets.

Stanwyck, so self-possessed onscreen, "had tears streaming down her face as she pushed her way up to congratulate Gloria." When at last she reached Swanson, they embraced. Then Stanwyck dropped theatrically to her knees and kissed the hem of Gloria's dress. Edith Head also wanted to hug Gloria, but "there were so many people around that I couldn't get near her." Billy Wilder, commenting later on Stanwyck's beau geste, called it "one of those ridiculous adulation things."

Preoccupied with worship, Swanson didn't see Louis B. Mayer's contorted face or hear his vile pronouncements, for by the time Stanwyck had finished genuflecting he had reached the foyer and other acolytes surged toward Swanson. She was imprisoned by her triumph.

Despite the accolades of newer stars, Swanson wanted to find her old friend Mary Pickford, who was reportedly in the audience. "Where's Mary?" she asked.

"She can't show herself, Gloria," someone said. "She's overcome. We all are."

Billy Haines, the star of silent pictures and early talkies who left the screen in the midthirties to become a prominent interior decorator, escorted Joan Crawford to the Paramount screening. He adored *Sunset Boulevard*, and when someone complained that old-time stars were never as loony as Norma Desmond, nor silent-film mansions as ostentatious as hers, Haines defended Wilder's interpretation. "Bebe Daniels, Norma Shearer, and Pola Negri all had homes with ugly interiors like that," he said. "I went through that period with all of them. Gold lace shawls draped over pianos and fancy vases filled with pussy willow. Our homes gave off the odor of milk and ashes." (Haines, in his decorating career, had helped to change that style so radically that by 1950 it was universally perceived as hideous.)

Who's Afraid of Norma Desmond?

As part of its advertising campaign, Paramount solicited quotes from a number of famous stars, most of them women. Curiously, all of the actresses polled were younger than Norma Desmond. Only Humphrey Bogart (and perhaps, in a stretch, Joan Crawford) was Norma's contemporary—and Gloria Swanson's.

Joan Fontaine, 33: "The praise which all of Hollywood has heaped on Gloria Swanson, Billy Wilder, and Charles Brackett for *Sunset Boulevard* is richly deserved. This picture is a distinguished and engrossing product of filmmaking. I am sure it will be highly successful."

Loretta Young, 37: "Take my advice. For an unforgettable experience hurry to *Sunset Boulevard.* That's it, my friend."

Gale Storm, 28: "I think *Sunset Boulevard* is one of the greats of motion picture history."

Joan Crawford, 46: "Seeing *Sunset Boulevard* is a thrilling experience which I will never forget."

Gene Tierney, 30: "I think it's the most wonderful picture I've ever seen."

Barbara Stanwyck, 43: "Gloria Swanson and William Holden in *Sunset Boulevard* join the all-time greats of motion picture history."

Humphrey Bogart, 51: "One of the great pictures of 1950 or any other year. Gloria Swanson's performance is brilliant and exciting."

Greta Garbo, 45, was miffed by Norma's line, "There just aren't any faces like that anymore. Maybe one—Garbo." After seeing the picture, Garbo commented to a friend, "I thought Billy Wilder was a friend of mine." Her remark suggests that she misconstrued the line as referring to the past.

Mae Murray, 65, a silent star whose career faltered even before the advent of talkies, had this to say after watching Swanson's over-the-top performance as Norma Desmond: "None of us floozies was *that* nuts."

Almost fifty years later, in the American Film Institute's televised salute to those films on its 100 Best list, Cher, 53, sounded as though she were being interviewed for *This Old House*: "I could not stop looking at Gloria Swanson's home. I just thought, I want that, I want some part of that, I'm not sure what it is but I like that house." Whoopi Goldberg, 50, said, "Her madness at the end of that film is so succinct. It's not crazy mad—it's a very quiet, misty madness."

Billy Wilder, having kissed Swanson good night and congratulated her once more, left the theatre to drive home. In the lobby he passed a clutch of men who seemed transfixed by the red-faced orator in their midst. Snippets of the man's imprecations hit Billy's ear: ". . . that lowdown scum Wilder . . . immoral bastards who come here and . . ."

Moving closer, he saw Louis B. Mayer, his host at dinner a few hours earlier, cocooned by a chorus of yes-men. At that moment Mayer spied Wilder. "You befouled your own nest," screamed the paterfamilias of MGM. "You should be kicked out of this country, tarred and feathered, goddamn foreigner son of a bitch."

Wilder, seldom speechless, was so stunned that he lost his wit. A master of the stinging riposte, he could think of no clever rejoinder. Instead he walked up to Mayer and said flatly, "I directed the picture. Why don't you go fuck yourself?"

And walked away. The Metro yes-men were aghast, Wilder remembered years later. "They were horrified, turning to His Majesty."

A royal command performance of *Sunset Boulevard* was held at the Empire Theatre, London, on October 30, 1950, at "8.0 prompt," according to a pair of tickets that Gloria Swanson saved. Had they been purchased, these tickets would have gone for twenty-six pounds, five shillings—roughly a hundred dollars, "in aid of the Cinematograph Trade Benevolent Fund."

A few days earlier the *Daily Herald* had run this item: "Gloria Swanson is staying at the Savoy Hotel to prepare herself before appearing before the King and Queen at the Royal Film Command Performance next Monday."

When *Boulevard du Crépuscule* opened at the Paramount Theatre in Paris on April 18, 1951, Swanson was unable to attend the gala premiere. She was appearing on Broadway with José Ferrer in a revival of *Twentieth Century*. Erich von Stroheim and his longtime companion, Denise Vernac, did attend, however, traveling the short distance from their home outside of Paris. Other luminaries at the gala included Baron van Botzeler, ambassador of the Netherlands in France, and Elsa Schiaparelli, the couturiere. The event was held under the patronage of the president of the French Republic, and presided over by David Bruce, American ambassador to France. Ironically, considering the opening and closing scenes of *Sunset Boulevard*, the Paris Police Orchestra of one hundred instruments played American and French songs from the stage of the theatre. Soon after the premiere, the picture opened in four other Paris cinemas.

In Germany, Paramount staged a contest for best German title. Of the thousand entries received, the winning one was submitted by Manfred Conrad, a student in Düsseldorf. He won a hundred and fifty marks for *Boulevard der Dämmerung*, which literally means "Twilight Boulevard." Elsewhere the picture was known as *Crepúsculo dos Deuses* (Portuguese), *Viale del Tramonto* (Italian), and *Jainkoen Ilunsentia* (Basque).

When *El Crepúsculo de los Dioses* reached Cuba, a young woman wearing a Gloria Swanson mask was hired to drive a 1951 Pontiac convertible through the streets of Havana. This bit of magical realism plugged not only *Sunset Boulevard*, but the twenty-fifth anniversary of Pontiac, as well. According to press reports, the ersatz Cuban Swanson "spent every afternoon for a week traveling the streets of downtown Havana, and on many occasions literally stopped traffic."

In Lima, Peru, the welcome was less festive. Deemed strictly adult fare, *Sunset Boulevard* was forbidden to youths under twenty-one.

Although *Sunset Boulevard* was a succès d'estime and also a popular hit with urban audiences in the United States and abroad, it was not a financial blockbuster. No doubt the picture's psychological landscape struck middle America as too lugubrious. Then, too, the perceived unwholesomeness of the situation—dominant aging woman, submissive young man, intergenerational sex for money, a monkey grave where the backyard barbecue ought to be—seemed guaranteed to tax the broadmindedness of all but the most tolerant. (*Samson and Delilah*, on the other hand, became the number one box office hit of 1950. A kinky tale in its own right, it gleamed nonetheless with biblical rectitude.)

When *Sunset Boulevard* ended its seven-week run at Radio City Music Hall at the end of September 1950, *Variety* reported that its total gross there was "around $1,020,000." That figure boosted it to the rank of "sixth biggest-grossing picture ever at the Hall." Alas for Paramount,

Radio City in this instance proved as atypical of America as was New York City itself. *Variety* explained why: "While *Sunset* is breaking records in major cities, it is doing below average in a number of minor openings. Feeling by Par execs is that it is a pic that must be keyed by publicity and exploitation and that it is impossible, no matter how big a job is done, to reach through the sticks. Par is attempting to counteract this by preparing new ads to be used by small-town houses."

Long before *Sunset Boulevard's* opening in either major cities or the sticks, Gloria Swanson had pushed herself to the verge of exhaustion on a cross-country publicity tour that took her to thirty-three cities in thirteen weeks. Swanson's tour was ostensibly to beat media drums for *The Heiress*, Paramount's 1949 release starring Olivia de Havilland and Montgomery Clift, who had ungraciously refused the role of Joe Gillis.

It seems peculiar today that Swanson should wear herself out for a picture she wasn't involved in. Curious, too, that she was simultaneously plugging *Sunset Boulevard*, which no one outside the industry would see for months. And yet studio publicity junkets were often organized that way.

Using an ingenious version of joint accounting, a studio would send out one or more stars like Swanson to build up good will for a new picture already in release. Frequently this sort of tour was deemed beneficial for a film that lacked built-in audience appeal, as *The Heiress* was in spite of its artistic merits. While on the road, stars were of course expected to fuel word of mouth for their own forthcoming films, as Swanson certainly did. She seems not to have devoted very much attention to *The Heiress*, nor was she expected to. Rather, in interviews, personal appearances, hospital and orphanage visits, luncheons with exhibitors, and the like, Swanson's job was to talk about herself, her work, the studio, and especially her new picture, which finally went into release just as her tour wound down. The first item in her job description: spread glamour—for which she earned a thousand dollars a week.

Swanson later explained in her memoirs why such an upbeat tour seemed crucial at that moment:

Paramount and all the other studios were pouring money and effort at a great rate into counteracting the bad publicity caused by the eruptions of scandal in the early months of 1950. The first of these was the nationwide uproar created by Oscar-winning Ingrid Bergman's giving birth to an illegitimate child, whose father was Roberto Rossellini, the Italian film director. Americans everywhere went purple at the thought that the good girl, the saint, the nun of pictures, should flaunt her adultery in their faces, and the studios were spending millions to prove that all Hollywood wasn't bad. The second source of fearful scandal was Senator Joseph McCarthy, who announced in Washington that he had lists of Communists all over America bent on the overthrow of our government. Hollywood was trembling. I personally admire Ingrid Bergman enormously for having gone ahead and had her baby . . . I also doubted that there were Communists hiding behind every corporation desk and director's chair. But while I spoke what I felt to my friends, I managed briefly to be a good-will ambassador for the industry, now that I had so recently, like a prodigal, returned to it, as if from the dead.

Because those studio junkets haven't been widely written about, Swanson's is worth lingering over. Since she saved everything—not only itineraries and correspondence but train tickets and receipts from dry-cleaning establishments—it's easy to track her from Boston to Philadelphia, on to Atlanta, Memphis, New Orleans, Des Moines, Salt Lake City, Seattle, San Francisco, and the twenty-four cities in between.

Swanson, like most VIPs of the time, traveled by train. I quote screenwriter Anita Loos to contrast those first-class journeys with the unseductive present-day appointments of Amtrak: "Compartments glittered with polished mahogany, shiny brass, and red brocade; the seats flaunted antimacassars of heavy lace. Gazing out on drab railroad tracks or the flat plains of Kansas doubled one's pleasure in the impeccable service and gourmet food. The maître d'hôtel would come to the compartment to announce he'd acquired some trout caught that morning in an icy mountain stream of Colorado or that the guinea hen had hung for just the proper time.

"There was always a steady stream of celebrities; a screen star with her entourage of husband, lover, manager, agent, hairdresser, or maid." (Swanson, after five divorces, was between men on this tour.)

Arriving in a new city, Gloria had scant time to languish in her deluxe hotel suite. The media, then as now, swarmed insatiably, as though they had never forgiven her for deserting Hollywood. Every TV station on her tour route seems to have run a Swanson feature. The same for radio and newspapers. Often the radio show would be recorded for later broadcast; in such cases, the interview followed a script prepared in advance by Paramount's publicity department. At one point Swanson asked the studio for script revisions since, as she wrote, "We should try to say something that hasn't been said 'by the yard' on every program—'glamorous' and 'queen' have been done to death."

The script began with the commentator's introduction:

Today we have a famous person as a surprise. For those of you who have seen and heard this actress she needs no introduction, and for those of you who have not let me say only this—that were the history to be written of the silent motion picture industry and talking pictures you could not write it without writing the history of this actress' life . . .

GS: Thank you very much. Goodness! You've been very generous and kind to me.

COMMENTATOR: Gloria Swanson has made a wonderful come-back.

GS: Comeback! (In the voice of Norma Desmond) I *hate* that word. It is a return . . . a return to the millions of people who have never forgiven me for deserting the screen.

COMMENTATOR: Hey, wait a minute, I didn't mean—

GS: (laughing) That's a line from the picture, *Sunset Boulevard*, and that was the voice of Norma Desmond. That's the part I play. (She goes on to tell a bit about her part and the picture.)

COMMENTATOR: Why was it called *Sunset Boulevard*?

GS: That's simple. Because Norma Desmond lived in an enormous house of the twenties on one of the landmarks of Hollywood, Sunset Boulevard. A lot of famous stars have lived on Sunset Boulevard—even I.

The latter statement rings with radio poetic license, but surely Swanson was entitled to a bit of harmless mendacity. She must have felt whipped by endless repetitions of this script, by tired epithets like "glamorous" and "queen," and by bizarre questions from the public. Among her countless souvenirs is a bunch of handwritten cards submitted at one of her personal appearances on this exhausting trek.

It's unclear where these questions were submitted; perhaps after a screening of *Sunset Boulevard*, possibly—in a primitive version of the call-in show—by members of the audience at a live radio interview. By turns ludicrous, poignant, surreal, the questions combine the celebrity obsessions of *The Day of the Locust* and *Vanity Fair*'s "Proust Questionnaire," with a dash of "Dear Abby" thrown in. (Gloria's long-suffering answers can only be guessed at.)

"Miss Swanson, did you tour Yellowstone Park in 1912? I was sure I saw you and your husband, the late Wallace Berry [sic], at one of the hotels."

"What is your favorite sport, and what kind of dog do you think is the best pet for a small child?"

"Would you mind telling me if you are older or younger than Mary Pickford?"

"Could you please advise me where would be the best location for a small grocery and notion store?"

"Do you think Rudolph Valentino was the greatest lover on screen or has someone outdone him?"

"I am here to contact someone who was in silent pictures as I have a special question to ask. You may know my girlfriend. Thank you." (This one in quavery nineteenth-century handwriting.)

"I live in a very modest home but I often wonder if a great personality like yourself would come and eat just one ordinary good meal?"

Added to these encounters was studio-assigned homework. Swanson, already on the road, received a letter in which an executive included a long list of branch managers and division chiefs of Paramount's sales force. He had marked a check beside the name of each man on the list who was in the business in silent days. "These men," he wrote, "the same as I, are more than pleased to find you back on the screen and they are anxious to do everything they can to promote your position." He suggested that she write each man a personal note, "thanking him for the job he is going to do for you in selling *Sunset Boulevard.*" He urged her to remind those with check marks "that both you and they worked together previously in the silent film days."

Swanson dutifully composed four different versions, all dated May 22, 1950. These notes, a seductive mix of sincerity and noblesse oblige, might almost have been written by Norma Desmond—or by Max for Norma. One letter began, "I believe you used to 'know me when'—when everything in life was easier." Further along she wrote, "Going back to Paramount was like going home."

Another one started out, "I have learned via the grapevine that you used to sell my pictures in the 'old days.'" Still another opening line: "I understand you are one of the old-timers—well, so am I." And another: "'They' tell me I have another career ahead of me because of *Sunset Boulevard.* Well, I know what you did for me in the past, so I am looking to you to do all you can in the future."

Later, after the picture opened, Gloria wrote equally gracious letters to those who plugged and reviewed it. A typical one, to Kate Cameron of the *New York Daily News:* "If I were to start enumerating my thanks for all the nice things you've written about me during my career, I'd just run out of paper, that's all. So let's take up with *Sunset Boulevard* and things just prior to it and, of all things, your superb review of the film itself."

There came a day, however, when charm and graciousness fled. Queenliness departed along with glamour, leaving Gloria Swanson crumpled in a raw-nerved heap. Desperate and depleted, she wrote a long letter to Max Youngstein of Paramount's New York office. Excerpts reveal a woman on the verge:

Since going over the past four weeks schedule, I have noticed that I have worked every weekend, either Saturday or Sunday, and though it was my understanding I was not to work nights, as well as daytimes, I have done so on the average of four to five evenings a week, even though I have averaged three and four appointments during the day as well.

This past week I have seriously thought of giving up the whole thing because, having once had a nervous breakdown, I know the symptoms and, believe me, lately I have had them more than once.

This is not a letter for the sheer purpose of griping or complaining but to call to your attention what must be done from here on, only because I know I cannot take this grind much longer.

Max Youngstein's reply does not overflow with the milk of human kindness. Behind his businesslike phrases you can almost hear him chomp a cigar as he barks, "Lady, you're gettin' paid a grand a week!" In his letter he reminded her, "Certainly you realize that all of the work we have lined up for you has been for the mutual benefit of Gloria Swanson and Paramount Pictures." He continued, with a whiff of sarcasm, "The results to date have been impressive, but they will not be worthwhile if they result in a nervous breakdown." Further along he corrected Swanson: "I, frankly, do not recall that I ever stated that you would not be working nights." He ended: "I assure you that we can keep the whole thing under control if all parties keep their good sense."

In the end, however, "all parties" triumphed. *Sunset Boulevard* reaped a bumper harvest of publicity and enthusiastic reviews. A bit later the Academy of Motion Picture Arts and Sciences laureled it with an impressive number of nominations.

As for Swanson, she did make her comeback. In that unprecedented return she echoed the silent-era greatness of the star "Gloria Swanson." Her performance in *Sunset Boulevard* also quoted—or misquoted—the actual Gloria Swanson, although sans quotation marks. We will see presently how Norma Desmond made Swanson immortal—and almost demolished her in the process. For the moment, however, Swanson is poised to make another picture, and another one after that . . . the old team, Gloria Swanson and Paramount, together again.

The period from early 1949, when she accepted the role of Norma Desmond, to 1951, when the accolades began to wane, proved to be her professional apotheosis. Many years earlier she had been acclaimed for star appeal, glamour, fashions and furs, upscale marriages, and good acting. Now she was honored for *great* acting . . . and for durability. Even the studio, at times a cruel taskmaster, bestowed a figurative kiss to the hem of Swanson's garment.

In a burst of late-summer magnanimity, Paramount's publicity department made her an honorary member in recognition of her outstanding contribution to the *Sunset Boulevard* campaign. *Variety* reported that Swanson "also was given a gold key to the publicity department as an added token of the group's appreciation. The tribute marked the first time anyone has been named an honorary member of the department."

chapter 15

And the Winner <u>Isn't</u> Gloria Swanson

A headline in the *Los Angeles Examiner* on October 1, 1950, sums up Hollywood's reaction to the star of *Sunset Boulevard*: "Gloria Swanson's Magnificent Comeback—'20s Siren Still Glamour Queen."

The article led with: "When a star is born—that's news. But when a star is reborn at the age of 52—that's a miracle."

And when she's tapped as a Best Actress nominee, that's another miracle. The nominees, and the awards, for 1950 in fact recognized an unaccustomed amount of talent along with the usual quotient of mediocrity. Two films destined to become classics—*All About Eve* and *Sunset Boulevard*—received fourteen and eleven nominations, respectively.

It's a famous aberration of Oscar history that both pictures, released the same year, competed in several categories and in a sense canceled one another out. *All About Eve* won in six categories; in several of these it zapped *Sunset Boulevard*, which, without the strong competition of *Eve*, would probably have triumphed over other, weaker entries. Both films were nominated as Best Picture; *Eve* won. (The other nominated films were *Born Yesterday*, *Father of the Bride*, and *King Solomon's Mines*.) George Sanders beat Erich von Stroheim for Best Supporting Actor; Joseph L. Mankiewicz, and not Billy Wilder, took home the award for Best Director.

In the Best Supporting Actress category, Celeste Holm and Thelma Ritter were both nominated for *Eve*, along with Nancy Olson for *Sunset Boulevard*. The other contenders were Hope Emerson for *Caged* and

Josephine Hull for *Harvey*. Well over half a century later, it still seems faintly unfair that Hull won.

William Holden, without Best Actor competition from *Eve*, nevertheless lost to José Ferrer for his showy performance in *Cyrano de Bergerac*. Both *Sunset Boulevard* and *All About Eve* lost the Best Cinematography (Black-and-White) award to *The Third Man*, and neither won for Best Film Editing, though both were nominated; the winner was *King Solomon's Mines*.

Sunset Boulevard, despite its eleven nominations, won in only three categories: Best Original Story and Best Screenplay (as distinct from Best Adapted Screenplay, which Joseph L. Mankiewicz won for *All About Eve*); Best Art Direction-Set Decoration (Black-and-White); and Best Scoring of a Dramatic or Comedy Picture. In these latter two categories, *Sunset Boulevard* was chosen over *Eve*.

Surely the greatest irony of 1950, perhaps of Academy Awards history, was the list of nominees for Best Actress. Rarely has there been such a lineup. In the running along with Swanson were Bette Davis and Anne Baxter, both nominated for *All About Eve*; Judy Holliday for *Born Yesterday*; and Eleanor Parker for *Caged*. It's fairly certain that Davis and Baxter annihilated one another's chances. Even if Anne Baxter had run as Best Supporting Actress—the category where she belonged—Bette Davis and Swanson might well have knocked one another out of the ring.

Or perhaps not. It would have been better for one of them to win, and one lose, than for both to lose. The ideal solution, of course, would have been a tie, but that was practically unheard of. It had happened only once in a major category, in the awards for 1931–32 when Swanson's ex-husband Wallace Beery in *The Champ* and Frederic March in *Dr. Jekyll and Mr. Hyde* both won as Best Actor. In 1968 it would happen again when Barbra Streisand won Best Actress for *Funny Girl* and Katharine Hepburn for *The Lion in Winter*.

The sad reality of 1950 still haunts that abundant year, for two of the greatest performances in movies—Bette Davis as Margo Channing, Gloria Swanson as Norma Desmond—went uncrowned. The winner was Judy Holliday, a smaller star, in a smaller picture, *Born Yesterday*.

———

When the 1950 Academy Award nominations were announced on February 12, 1951, both stars of a current Broadway play were among the nominees. José Ferrer and Gloria Swanson were costarring in a revival of the Ben Hecht and Charles MacArthur comedy, *Twentieth Century*. A New York newspaper pointed out an amusing coincidence: in one scene of the play Swanson's character Lily Garland proudly displays to Ferrer an Oscar she has won. He inquires sarcastically, "What did you get that for, bowling?" After the nominations were announced, audiences at *Twentieth Century* whistled, shouted, and almost stopped the show every time Ferrer asked Swanson that question.

Swanson's fifty-second birthday fell on March 27, two days before the Academy Awards. She and Ferrer were unable to leave the play and fly to Hollywood, so he decided to throw a combined birthday and Oscar party. By March 29—Oscar night—the guest list had jumped to nearly three hundred, including the other Academy Award nominees who were in New York: Celeste Holm, Thelma Ritter, Sam Jaffe, George Cukor, and Judy Holliday. With so many of its nominated members in the East, the Academy arranged a radio hookup between New York and Hollywood. That way, winners on the East Coast could address the Hollywood audience and also the nationwide audience tuned in to the broadcast. (Awards night had been a radio event since 1945. It was first televised in 1953.)

The awards ceremony, held at the RKO Pantages Theatre on Hollywood Boulevard, began at 8:00 P.M. It was 11:00 P.M. in New York, and plays were letting out. At the Cafe La Zambra a high-spirited party was getting under way. Reporters, photographers, and a host of Broadway actors made no attempt to control the outbreak of Oscar fever.

Early in the evening in Hollywood Charles Brackett, president of the Academy of Motion Picture Arts and Sciences, delivered a solemn speech in which he addressed such timely topics as "the Russian land grab" and "young American blood spilled in Korea." Hearing him that night as he read from notes about the world situation while seldom looking at the audience, one might have guessed his Republican politics but not his urbane brillance. His genius seemed momentarily eclipsed by the Red scare. But then, academy presidents often look like scared rabbits.

The Hollywood audience—including nominee Nancy Olson, who recalls feeling fatalistic but not nervous—applauded Brackett's speech. Far away in "liberal" New York, however, the reception was somewhat cool. Several of those at La Zambra had already been fingered by the House Un-American Activities Committee, including the host, José Ferrer. The long, spectral shadow of Joseph McCarthy would soon fall across Judy Holliday, as well.

As the evening progressed, the awards increased in importance and prestige. After various technical Oscars, Arlene Dahl and Lex Barker (married to one another at the time) presented the award for Best Art Direction-Set Decoration (Black-and-White). The winners—for *Sunset Boulevard*—were Hans Dreier, John Meehan, Sam Comer, and Ray Moyer.

In New York, those partygoers who managed to hear the announcement above the noise applauded. Someone told Gloria the news, which pleased her. She did not take it as a portent, however, since she didn't expect to win. "I had somehow known in my bones from the beginning that I wouldn't," she said later.

In those days the Academy Awards lasted roughly as long as the average movie: about two hours. Not until much later did the evening evolve into an overstuffed multiplex of interminable comedy, gushy gratitude, open-vault montages of film history, and a vaudeville of clownish fashions. And so, on that evening in late March of 1951, Marilyn Monroe, Debbie Reynolds, Marlene Dietrich, and a number of other stars and starlets read the nominees and handed out awards. The audience heard brief speeches or a mere "thank-you" as the proceedings followed a brisk agenda.

Gene Kelly presented the award for Best Scoring of a Musical—*Annie Get Your Gun*—and then he also presented the award for Best Scoring of a Dramatic or Comedy Picture. The winner, Franz Waxman for *Sunset Boulevard*, spoke for half a minute. His English carried only a light German accent.

In New York, intermittent calls for quiet went unheard or were ignored as the din continued. Shouts, laughter, barmen's orders—then someone ran up to Sam Jaffee's table with a piece of news lost in the raucous babble of La Zambra: nominated for his supporting role in *The Asphalt Jungle*, he had just lost to George Sanders.

The evening had reached an aroused frenzy. The press quickly asked the remaining New York nominees to sit together at a well-lit table in the center of the room.

Swanson, among her theatre colleagues, looked every inch the movie star. She wore a sleeveless black dress with halter top, a beaded hat with tall feathers, long black kid gloves, and a white fur jacket. At the behest of the "media types," as she called them—men, for the most part, "with microphones or note pads in their hands or with cameras strapped around their necks"—she left her mother, Adelaide, and her teenage daughter, Michelle, and moved to a large table in the middle of La Zambra. Judy Holliday approached from another direction. When they spotted one another they laughed, then shook hands. It was their first face-to-face encounter.

Gloria sat down on José Ferrer's left, Judy on his right. George Cukor took the seat beside Gloria, and Celeste Holm seated herself on Cukor's other side. "George and I were old friends," Swanson said later, "but as the director of *Born Yesterday* he was certainly rooting for Judy Holliday, his star."

A nervous hush now gripped the restaurant. With the volume turned up, radio voices from Hollywood drowned out the tinkle of glasses and the rattle of plates and cutlery. Dean Jagger's voice came over the airwaves: "The award for Best Supporting Actress goes to . . ." He opened the envelope, looked at the card, and announced, "Josephine Hull for *Harvey*." Many years later Swanson recalled that immediately after this surprise, "Celeste Holm moved back to her original table" while the others stayed put. Did Holm decamp to rejoin a companion, or to gnash her teeth?

"What a sleazy affair," George Cukor whispered to Gloria. "Are you going to make a speech if you get it?"

"Heavens, no," Swanson answered, "but they pestered me right up until three days ago for a written statement." Then Cukor smiled past Swanson at Judy Holliday, who smiled back nervously. (One of those "pestering" Swanson was Billy Wilder, who sent her this telegram on

March 23: "Dear Gloria: I understand you will be unable to attend Academy Awards. The studio informs me that I am to accept your award if you should win. Please let me know what you want me to say but make it short as my delivery is sincere but decidedly amateurish. Good luck to you we are all keeping our fingers crossed.")

Tension tightened in the room. They heard the nominees for Best Actor: "Louis Calhern in *The Magnificent Yankee,* José Ferrer in *Cyrano de Bergerac,* William Holden in *Sunset Boulevard,* James Stewart in *Harvey,* Spencer Tracy in *Father of the Bride.*" Many others, in New York and in Hollywood, shared Swanson's thoughts: "Joe Ferrer couldn't possibly win, because he had been pointed out as a Communist sympathizer in the hearings being conducted in Washington under Senator McCarthy and had been subpoenaed to appear before the House Un-American Activities Committee in a month. No matter how wonderful his performance was, too many members of the Academy would vote against him just on account of that."

When Ferrer won, Swanson let out a war whoop. So did Judy Holliday. As Helen Hayes accepted his Oscar on the stage of the Pantages Theatre, those three hundred gathered at La Zambra rose, cheered, and clapped wildly. Radio technicians with mikes rushed to the table for his acceptance speech. "Hello, ladies and gentlemen, three thousand miles away," he began, "and hello Helen Hayes." Ferrer continued, "This award means more to me than an honor to an actor. I consider it a vote of confidence and an act of faith and, believe me, I'll not let you down." He expressed gratitude "from the bottom of my heart."

As he sat down again a reporter asked if he had intended a political reference in his speech. "You're goddamned right I did!" he shouted above the pandemonium. "I meant it as a rebuke to all the people who tried to affect the voting by referring to things that are A, beside the point, and B, untrue."

Someone plunked the fake Oscar from *Twentieth Century* on the table where Ferrer, Swanson, and the other nominees remained. For the press, what a fantastic photo op! They asked Swanson and Holliday to kiss Ferrer on either cheek as flashbulbs popped. Then they cajoled the actresses to reach for the Oscar in a fake battle. "Judy and I were both acutely embarrassed to go along with the galumphing horseplay," Swanson said. But, as she pointed out, "it couldn't go on for long because the next fraught moment had come."

Then as now, if one picked *the* climactic moment of the Academy Awards it would surely be the announcement of Best Actress. Broderick Crawford read the nominees. "And the winner *is*...Judy Holliday in *Born Yesterday!*"

Ethel Barrymore accepted the award in Hollywood. Seventy-one at the time, she swept magestically onstage, bowed like the true First Lady of the American Stage (who on earth bestowed that epithet upon Helen Hayes?), and made a lovely speech that sounded like all of Theatre rolled into twenty-five words or less. Barrymore was magnificent—the award should have been hers to keep.

As it turned out, Ethel Barrymore's acceptance speech on behalf of Judy Holliday was the only one heard in Hollywood or elsewhere. A sound engineer at the ABC radio network forgot to pull the proper switch, and Judy's speech reached no further than the next table at La Zambra.

Thirty years later, in her memoirs, Gloria said flatly about her Oscar loss: "I honestly didn't care." Here is her account of the moments following the announcement from Hollywood that Judy Holliday had just won the Academy Award as Best Actress of 1950:

> Judy was overcome. She stood up and turned this way and that and couldn't speak. I said, "Judy, darling," and reached for her. She looked lost, as if she didn't recognize anyone. She was laughing and crying at the same time, and everyone was applauding her. Her father and her husband rushed up to her, and George Cukor went and stood beside her. We were all talking at once and a hundred flashbulbs were going off, blinding us.
>
> I hadn't thought I would be greatly affected one way or another, and I wasn't. I knew Hollywood too well. . . . The simple truth of the matter was, I just happened to be the sort of person who couldn't be motivated by competition or prizes . . . I realized, however, that the people around me were expecting me to react differ-

ently. Even in the people I knew there was a barely perceptible change. Joe [Ferrer] turned and gave me a big consolation hug. Michelle came and stood protectively at my side, drying her pretty eyes at regular intervals. Judy Holliday, when she dared to look at me at all, seemed to be pleading for forgiveness.

Swanson considered the press "far less subtle." They asked in funereal tones: "Would you care to make a statement?" They reminded her that she had been nominated the very first year of the Academy Awards, for *Sadie Thompson* in 1927–28, and nominated again for her first talkie, *The Trespasser* in 1929–30. Both times she lost, though reporters didn't remind her of that. But surely, they seemed to imply, after a third loss you must be—devastated. "It slowly dawned on me," said Swanson, "that they were unconsciously asking for . . . a mad scene."

George Cukor invited Gloria to join him and a contingent from La Zambra for supper nearby. She declined, saying she was tired, and beckoned to her mother and her daughter. On the ride uptown Adelaide and Michelle must have reminded her of the spectral pair, doctor and asylum nurse, who come for Blanche DuBois at the end of *A Streetcar Named Desire*. Overprotective, they treated her gingerly, as though at any moment the chauffeur might need to turn the car around and head for Bellvue.

Alone in her bedroom that night, Gloria Swanson, as if awakened from a long and troubled dream, realized what had come over them all. Everyone, everyone but her, had seen it already. Now she herself gazed upon the Doppelgänger who had joined her in the spotlight. Like the title figure in *The Masque of the Red Death*, this intruder "held illimitable dominion over all." With perfect clarity Gloria Swanson beheld her evil twin. "She was just about ten feet tall, and her name was Norma Desmond."

At the end of *The Oscar* (1966), a rancid movie about the bastards of Hollywood, Stephen Boyd is poised to accept the Academy Award for Best Actor. He's so certain of his chances that, as nominees are read out, he stands up. He takes a step toward the aisle, ready to dash onstage and acknowledge the revival of his gasping career.

"And the winner is Frank Sinatra!" Hearing that, Boyd falls back, crumples into his seat with the campiest of stricken looks on his face, and starts the most grudging, wooden clapping—his way of depicting tragedy.

Although the scene is spectacularly cheap, it tells a nasty truth about Oscar losers: they're soreheads. And if they're really not, people say they are anyway.

Rumors have gone around for years that Gloria Swanson made a waspish remark to Judy Holliday when the younger actress won the Oscar. One of Holliday's biographers, Will Holtzman, tells it like this:

> As the nominees were recited for Best Actress, Swanson leaned over to Judy and whispered, "One of us is about to be very happy." Judy smiled nervously. A moment later Judy was named the winner and the lightbulbs popped and the reporters shouted questions as she tried to make her way to the microphone.... Half crying, half laughing, Judy came back to the table dazed. Swanson called, "Judy, darling," and again whispered something. This time there was no smile; Judy's jaw dropped, her eyes burned.
>
> The first thing Judy did when she got home was call [her friend Yetta Cohn] ... Judy mentioned Swanson. "After I came back from the microphone, Gloria Swanson waved me over."
>
> "No kidding," Yetta said excitedly. "What did she say?"
>
> "She snapped at me, 'Why couldn't you have waited till next year?'"

Garson Kanin, who was there that night, said that Judy Holliday repeated to him Swanson's prediction, "One of us is about to be very happy." Kanin, who wrote *Born Yesterday* for Broadway and watched Judy "creating the character before our eyes," was a close friend of hers. She didn't mention an unpleasant Swanson remark to him. In that case: Oh Desmond, where is thy sting?

Another Holliday biographer, Gary Carey, has it both ways. He portrays Swanson sweeping into La Zambra "as though Cecil B. DeMille had whispered in her ear that the cameras were rolling and, yes, it was finally time for her close-up. . . . The photographers had flashbulbs only for Gloria. Once the tumult had subsided, Swanson settled down next to Judy and bared her heart. [She] freely admitted that she was rooting for herself. This is probably my last chance, she confided. . . . Holliday was not at all offended by Swanson's candor—she was touched and a bit shocked that this woman, after so many husbands and lovers and a fabulous career, should need an Oscar so urgently."

According to Carey, when Judy won the Oscar, "Ferrer and Swanson cooed and hovered in the background." Yet another source has Swanson saying to Holliday, jovially and without rancor, "Darling, why couldn't you have waited till next year?" Press reports from 1951 quote Swanson on her loss: "Well, this just means the old warhorse has got to go back to work."

When I asked Swanson's longtime friend Raymond Daum about these contradictory reports, he declared, "No, that's not Gloria's personality or her style. Whatever she said to Judy Holliday she would have said jokingly. Gloria was gracious. She would never deliberately hurt someone." Then he laughed and added enigmatically, "Unless they were under her spell."

Several other friends agree that Swanson would have spoken only kind words at such a time. I heard one dissenting voice. According to a close friend who requested anonymity, "If Gloria could have slipped her hands around Judy's neck she would have strangled her." In later years this friend queried Swanson about Oscar night, 1951. Gloria demurred: "Well, I had to be civilized, you know."

Charles Brackett, as producer and cowriter of *Sunset Boulevard*, naturally felt the sting of Swanson's rejection. As president of the Academy, he was expected to remain neutral. He didn't.

In a letter to Swanson dated April 5, 1951, Brackett wrote: "You know how dearly I was hoping that [presenter] Ralph Bunch would pull your name out of that envelope, but I also hope you know how unimportant I think that final tinsel on the big Christmas tree of your achievement. In the hearts of everybody, you'd gotten it the year before, when you'd have walked away with it had the picture had a 1949 release. Never forget that a great many of our members had seen *Sunset* not in early 1950, but in late '49. All sense of timeliness was gone."

Far away in Hollywood, more ambiguity.

Billy Wilder attended the Oscar ceremony at the Pantages Theatre, and so did Joseph L. Mankiewicz. Along with their other nominations, both men were up for Best Director. (Along with Cukor for *Born Yesterday*, John Huston for *The Asphalt Jungle*, and Carol Reed for *The Third Man*.)

Wilder and Mankiewicz were friends, and also friendly rivals. Friendship and rivalry skirmish in a story that Wilder told Mankiewicz's son Christopher. I quote from a recent conversation I had with Christopher Mankiewicz.

> On Oscar night in 1951 my father had won an award for best screenplay adapted from something else, and Wilder, Brackett, and Marshman had won for best original screenplay. The next award, ready to be announced, was for best director, and so my father and Billy were both asked to remain backstage in case one of them should be the next winner.
>
> Billy said he and my father got into this conversation and my father was absolutely effusive in his praise, saying what an honor it was even to be nominated with somebody as great as Billy, how he had always admired Billy and considered him one of the greatest directors of all time.
>
> Now Billy, of course, is known as, shall we say, a raconteur. As for the veracity of all this—my father denied it ever happened. But in any case, Billy relished telling how my father was in the midst of crowning him with love and admiration when all of a sudden they announced: "And the winner is Joseph L. Mankiewicz for *All About Eve!*"
>
> Billy said, "Your father almost threw me to the ground as he jumped over my body to race out on the stage and accept his Oscar. I lay there thinking: A moment ago I was the greatest thing that ever happened, now I'm a piece of shit."

Christopher Mankiewicz adds, "I think the part about pushing him down is exaggerated. My father always questioned Billy's taste, always felt there was a kind of vulgarity about Billy that he didn't agree with. But I think that's the only thing he didn't like about Billy."

Whatever the degree of Wilder's fabrication, both men agreed at all points on one of their fellow laureates. Earlier in the evening Louis B. Mayer had received an honorary statuette "for distinguished service to the motion picture industry." In view of Mayer's loathing for Wilder and his picture, irony filled the room like carbon monoxide when Charles Brackett, producer of *Sunset Boulevard*, presented the award to Mayer, calling him "one of our most distinguished citizens in Hollywood."

Mayer's great works, as enumerated that night, included his role in founding the Motion Picture Academy and his inauguration of the star system. He received a big hand. "This is truly an experience," he said, holding his award to his chest. "This fills me with humility and great responsibility in the years to come."

Those years, however, were not to come—at least not for Louis B. Mayer. A few months later he was kicked out of MGM and replaced by former chief of production Dore Schary.

On Oscar night rumors already buzzed that Metro's parent company, Loew's, Inc., considered Mayer's departure overdue. And so it required only a pair of ears, and not second sight, to perceive behind the rousing applause not just a fair measure of genuine warmth for the sentimental old tyrant, but also vindication and relief.

After the Oscar ceremony MGM gave a party at the Beverly Hills Hotel. Top executives of the studio attended, including heir presumptive Dore Schary. So did Metro's stars, producers, and directors. At the party, Schary stayed on one side of the room and Mayer stayed on the other. A few months later Joseph L. Mankiewicz left Darryl F. Zanuck's 20th Century–Fox and moved back to MGM, where he had spent a long and unhappy stretch of his early career. This time, Mankiewicz occupied the cream-colored office left vacant by Louis B. Mayer.

Zanuck also won a special honor on Oscar night. He received the Irving G. Thalberg Memorial Award. Perhaps he felt particularly deserving after his row with one of Billy Wilder's cast members from *Sunset Boulevard*. A few days earlier Zanuck had phoned Charles Brackett to urge him, as president of the Academy, not to seat Hedda Hopper on the aisle at the Pantages Theatre. She had alarmed several of Hollywood's more liberal denizens by threatening to stand up, unfurl an American flag, and stomp out if the "pinko commie" José Ferrer won an Oscar.

Brackett, alarmed by this diplomatic crisis, in turn spoke to Hedda. She denied all. She did lament to Brackett, however, that she wished she *had* cooked up such a scheme, since it would have been a good gag.

Was everybody miserable that night?

When William Holden and his wife, Ardis, arrived at the Pantages Theatre, they looked like the poster couple for marital bliss. Holden's handsome face had no Brandoesque subtext of threat or androgyny. Ardis, since marrying Bill in 1941, had made a few pictures under her screen name Brenda Marshall; now, as though heeding the great American summons to postwar women, she had become a housewife.

Ardis Holden's face had the chiseled bone structure and finely etched features of a minor beauty. From one angle she resembled a less masculine Jane Russell; from another, a brunette Dina Merrill. It's understandable, from today's vantage point, why Ardis didn't go far in Hollywood: she didn't fill a niche. Too clean-cut for "girls with experience" roles, she at the same time appeared a bit too knowing for the virgin next door.

Bill and Ardis sat beside Billy Wilder and Audrey Wilder, who was also a former actress. At the end of the evening, when Paramount left almost empty-handed in spite of its impressive nominations, the Holdens and the Wilders dutifully attended the studio's post-Oscar party at Mocambo on Sunset Strip.

On arrival at the nightclub, and when necessary throughout the evening, Holden managed a loser's smile for photographers. Billy Wilder's face told a different story, though perhaps Audrey alone could decipher it. Since his expression has always mixed pain and pleasure with a perpetual look of astonishment, Wilder might have suffered from the disappointment. On the other hand, he may well have relished the joke.

He tried to comfort Holden. "It was a miscarriage of justice, Bill," said Wilder. "You really should have won tonight."

"Oh, I don't think so," Ardis remarked with the hidden poison of a brown recluse spider. "José Ferrer was much better than Bill." Even the Wilders, who had heard it all, hadn't heard this kind of brutality. (Holden's costar, Nancy Olson, describes Ardis as "an icy woman.")

Holden, whose life had begun already to assume the lineaments of *The Lost Weekend*, stared at his wife in thirsty shock. When that long gaping moment ended, he poured himself another drink.

And Ardis was relentless. Three years later, on March 25, 1954, she and Bill arrived at the Pantages Theatre on another Oscar night. Once again he was nominated, this time for Wilder's *Stalag 17*. Strong competition put Holden at a disadvantage, so that he didn't expect to win. But he did.

The rest of the evening sounds like a pathetic scene from *The Star*, a 1952 *Sunset Boulevard* rip-off. In it Bette Davis plays an Oscar-winning actress who has fallen on evil days. At one point, in her cups, she clutches the statuette and says, "Come on, Oscar! Let's you and me get drunk." After the ceremony the Holdens drove to the home of their close friends Paul and Ruth Clemens. As the two couples sat in the comfortable den, they drank brandy and dissected the evening's events.

"I still can't believe it," Bill Holden said. He gazed at the golden Oscar standing in front of him on the coffee table.

"Well, you know, Bill," Ardis said blandly, as though commenting on the weather, "you really didn't get the award for *Stalag*. They gave it to you for *Sunset Boulevard*."

Holden lowered his eyes and ground his teeth, as he always did in moments of stifled anger. He was still seething when they arrived home. He missed the driveway, hit the brick post, and tore a fender off his Cadillac. When Bill awoke the next morning, he was sitting in his favorite leather chair in the den, still wearing his tuxedo, the Oscar in his lap.

Once, between Oscar-night devastations, a reporter came to interview the Holdens at home. "Mrs. Holden, what's it like to be married to such a handsome man?" the reporter panted. Ardis stared at her husband. Finally she answered, "Oh, do you really think he's that handsome?"

The bitterness of Oscar losers (and their spouses) grows from some poisoned root of the ego. How could it fail to flourish when top awards—

acting, directing, writing, producing—all are chosen by the most subjective criteria and then trumpeted by Hollywood and the world as if some ultimate, objective standard were used to winnow artistic talent? In fact, winners and losers often reflect no more than a whim—or a grudge.

Even a sensible midwestern prairie woman like Gloria Swanson wasn't immune to the toxins of Oscar loss. Invidious creepers sprouted in the garden of her heart. Despite her disclaimers after losing to Judy Holliday, she must have had grinding moments when, like Norma Desmond, she gnashed her teeth in snarling contempt of Hollywood and "those imbeciles! They took the idols and smashed them. And who have they got now? Some nobodies."

Swanson's friend Raymond Daum believes, based on many conversations with her over the years, that Gloria suffered sharply from the Academy's misreckoning. "She was never properly acknowledged by that business," he said "and it hurt her deeply." Near the end of her life, when the Academy sought to acquire her papers, she said no. Instead, Swanson sold the vast and valuable collection to the University of Texas at Austin.

No doubt Swanson did realize, on the night of March 29, 1951, that her last chance at the award had now gone by. She already had a consolation prize of sorts, however. At the end of filming *Sunset Boulevard* she had received a cigarette box with these words engraved on it:

To Proclaim That
GLORIA SWANSON
Is the Greatest Star of Them All
And the Idol of
Cast, Staff, and Crew
of
"Sunset Boulevard"
June 20, 1949

She kept the cigarette box on her coffee table in the library at 920 Fifth Avenue, and she would sometimes hold it up before her closest friends and proclaim, "*That* is my Oscar!"

$\mathcal{I}$'ve Got Nobody Floating in My Pool

O verseas, *Sunset Boulevard* garnered a number of awards. At the Danish Film Critics' Festival it won the equivalent of a Danish Oscar as best American picture released in Denmark during the 1950–51 season. In Finland, the picture received an award from the nation's film journalists. *Elle*, the French magazine, chose Swanson as best foreign actress of 1950. The Film Journalists Guild of Italy chose her for a similar award. Writing in Milan's daily newspaper *La Stampa*, a critic called *Sunset Boulevard*—titled *Viale del Tramonto* in Italian—"without a doubt one of the finest films ever produced in any country." The film also received awards in Mexico, Brazil, and several other countries.

Meanwhile, Hollywood's Foreign Correspondents Association had already recognized Swanson by giving her its Golden Globe for "the Best Dramatic Performance of 1950 by an Actress." (When this award was auctioned by Christie's in 2000 it sold for $25,850, more than twice its presale estimate. At the same auction, Marlon Brando's overcoat from *The Godfather* fetched $20,000 and Miles Davis's trumpet $70,500.)

Worldwide accolades, however, could not save *Sunset Boulevard* from a long period of obscurity. After its first run in large American cities, then in cities abroad, the picture trickled down to smaller venues: from suburban movie houses to unspectacular theatres like the one memorialized in *The Last Picture Show*, and finally to drive-ins, where it played on double and triple bills. Then it disappeared.

Miles Kreuger, the eager sixteen-year-old we met when *Sunset Boulevard* opened at Radio City, was a man in his late twenties before the picture reappeared. After attending Bard College, Kreuger returned to Manhattan where, during the fifties, he witnessed the demolition of several of his favorite New York movie houses: the Empire in 1953, the Paramount, the Capitol, then the Roxy in 1960.

Following such calamitous loss, fortune suddenly changed again. Though nothing could bring back the splendor of those lost temples, one man—Dan Talbot—dedicated himself to recapturing the magic images that once had made them sacrosanct. Miles Kreuger witnessed the revival; once more, he was first in line. In his words,

Dan Talbot bought the Yorktown Theatre on the Upper West Side in 1960, changed its name to the New Yorker, and ran it somewhat along the lines of the Museum of Modern Art's film programming. That is, in series, with retrospectives and program notes for each feature. The only difference being that Dan's was commercial, the museum's was not.

In addition to program notes for every film, feature schedules were printed well in advance. He charged a nickel for the notes. He invited me to write some, and wait till you hear who also wrote for him: Jules Pfeiffer, Jack Kerouac, Peter Bogdanovich. I lived on Ninety-third Street, close enough to walk to Eighty-eighth and Broadway, where the theatre was. By the way, the New Yorker makes an appearance in *Annie Hall*.

Swanson saved among her papers a long, densely printed sheet of notes—the one for the program commencing August 10, 1960. The main attraction was *Sunset Boulevard*, followed by two Buster Keaton shorts, *The Boat* and *The Playhouse*. Annotations for all three were written by Peter Bogdanovich, identified in his bio line as "the New Yorker Theatre's critic in residence."

Twenty-one at the time, Bogdanovich seems to have grasped the totality of *Sunset Boulevard*. In his lengthy analysis he details "the amazing influence that the movies have had on every generation since 1910." He contrasts the overblown world of silent pictures and silent stars with the "painfully naturalistic" talkies, especially the kind of pictures written by Joe Gillis and Betty Schaeffer. In a long paragraph devoted to the influence of *Citizen Kane* on *Sunset Boulevard*, he emphasizes that "Wilder, employing a similar technique, achieves a similarly sharp effect, but ultimately it is his effect, not Welles'."

Swanson Drops in on Norma Desmond

Dan Talbot, who ran the New Yorker Theatre on the Upper West Side of Manhattan from 1960 to 1973, was standing in the lobby one night in August 1960 while *Sunset Boulevard* played on his screen. Glancing toward the street, Talbot saw a chauffeur-driven Rolls-Royce pull up and stop. The next thing he knew Gloria Swanson and a friend—"a young stud," Talbot recalls—swept into the homey old barn of a theatre. "She wore a sexy, tight-fitting dress," Talbot recalls, "and she looked great."

Swanson, unlike Norma Desmond, *could* tear herself away from one of her old pictures. She didn't linger. Talbot recalls that he and Swanson chatted for "maybe twenty minutes" and then she left. Since she remained at the back of the auditorium, no one in the audience guessed that an eminence had been so near.

Booking *Sunset Boulevard* into the New Yorker had been a chore. When Talbot phoned Paramount's New York distribution office he was told the studio owned no prints of the picture. That was probably true. *Sunset Boulevard* hadn't been shown for nearly ten years. The negative, of course, lay safe in a studio vault, but during the 1950s television and hundreds of new movies a year left little demand for revivals.

Dan Talbot phoned another exhibitor, Pauline Kael, who ran the Cinema Guild twin theatres in Berkeley, California. He knew Kael from her occasional magazine articles on movies, although in 1960 her days as a critic lay ahead. She happened to know that a print of *Sunset Boulevard* did exist in a Paramount storage warehouse in Texas. When Talbot confronted the studio's New York executives with this information they reacted with suprise. Soon they tracked down the print and Talbot booked it for a week in August.

"It was hugely successful," he recalled, "and instead of one week it played for three. That was the only print in the country, and it actually looked pretty good." Not long after that Paramount struck additional prints and *Sunset Boulevard* began showing around the country. These revivals, and television, helped to make Billy Wilder's masterpiece as familiar to millions as it always had been to connoisseurs.

Throughout that ten-year span from August 10, 1950, when *Sunset Boulevard* opened at Radio City, to August 10, 1960, when the New Yorker Theatre revived it, Gloria Swanson tried to wave good-bye to Norma Desmond. Like Chaplin slipping out of a sticky spot, Swanson fudged and fidgeted, smiled, grimaced, bowed, wriggled free, tipped her hat, and sidled off without a backward glance.

And Norma Desmond, defying each Houdini move, clung like a virus. Swanson's good-byes boomeranged as Norma's hellos. Norma Desmond stalked and overshadowed, camouflaged every other Swanson film role, and ultimately, in a great ironic coup, appropriated Swanson's identity. For, at the end of her days, Gloria Swanson, like Norma, succumbed to ill-fated love for a mouth-watering guy less than half her age. Like Joe Gillis, this man was a mediocre screenwriter said to have capitalized on his romance with an old-time movie star. A little later we'll learn of her sad delusion. But first, Swanson's thirty-three-year struggle to oust the succubus, Norma Desmond.

To search for Norma Desmond's backstory, or that of any fictional character, amounts to pure folly. Where was she born? Who were the husbands after Max von Mayerling? Did the studios shun her when talkies arrived, or did Norma's own temperamental bullheadedness do her in? It's diverting to ask these questions. Try to answer them with a straight face, however, and you'll come off as risible, like those solemn academics satirized in a mock monograph, *How Many Children Had Lady Macbeth?*

To speculate on Brackett and Wilder's sources for Norma Desmond is another matter. No doubt they often thought of Gloria Swanson, so that Norma Desmond's backstory is much like Swanson's, though filtered through the fourth dimension. They also thought—at least in naming their irrepressible diva—of drug-addicted, scandal-plagued silent stars Norma Talmadge and Mabel Normand, along with murdered silent-film director William Desmond Taylor.

Norma Desmond has no real antecedents in the movies themselves. Although she resembles every star, and her story symbolizes fleeting fame, she arrived through some back door in the joint writing establishment of Brackettandwilder.

Perhaps one ancestor in Norma Desmond's family tree is Larry Renault, the imperiously obnoxious washed-up movie star played by John Barrymore in *Dinner at Eight* (1933). So engorged is his ego that he studiously commits suicide under a floor lamp so that he will be discovered with his profile looking its matinee-idol best. Larry Renault, however, lacks the fallen nobility of Norma Desmond. We believe she was not only big, but adored by millions, and with reason: on the screen, at least, she had great feeling. We suspect that apart from her demanding nature she once had good qualities offscreen, as well. DeMille claims that "as a lovely little girl of seventeen" Norma possessed "more courage and wit and heart than ever came together in one youngster."

It's fitting that yet another male character prefigures Norma Desmond. After all, she's more than a tough broad; she's downright butch. ("I said sit down," she snarls at Joe Gillis. He sits.) If Norma's dark side owes something to John Barrymore's Larry Renault, the lighter streaks of camp in her chiaroscuro soul recall another Barrymore character: the outrageous, egotistical, arm-waving Broadway producer-director Oscar Jaffee in *Twentieth Century* (1934).

To characterize Oscar Jaffee, Barrymore uses pyrotechnics of the nineteenth-century stage—highly mannered, overdone acting à la Sir Henry Irving. (Swanson does the same with bravura conventions of silent-screen melodrama.) Bits of dialogue in *Sunset Boulevard* also echo the Ben Hecht–Charles MacArthur script of *Twentieth Century*. "I don't like anyone chewing gum on the stage. Spit it out, please," demands Oscar Jaffee. (Norma to Joe Gillis: "And must you chew gum?") When Jaffee hits on the ludicrous notion of staging the Oberammergau Passion Play for his paramour, Lily Garland, he sounds as loony as Norma framing Salome. "Fits her like a glove," declares Jaffee. "What a Magdalene she'll make. I'm going to have Judas strangle himself on her hair."

Like Norma, Oscar Jaffee knows the horoscope. "I was born under the sign of Sagitarius—that's the archer," he explains as he strikes a fey arrow-shooting pose. (Norma to Joe: "I like Sagitarians. You can trust them.")

One role barely contains Oscar Jaffee; he spills over into impersonations, both male and female. So does Norma Desmond: Chaplin, a Mack Sennett bathing beauty, even hints of Salome. Like all manipulative egomaniacs, Jaffee threatens suicide to get his way; Norma ditto.

There's even a gondola bed in *Twentieth Century*, with a cloying Cupid perched on the foot. A dead ringer for Norma's bed, here it belongs to Lily Garland (Carole Lombard), who appears halfway through the picture in a Desmondesque leopard outfit. You can't help feeling, though, that if Barrymore could have gotten away with wearing leopard he would have—he's that flamboyant.

The next entry in this parade of masculine floats is Gustav von Aschenbach, from Thomas Mann's *Death in Venice*. Written in 1912 and first translated into English in 1929, the novella was readily available to both Wilder and Brackett. How closely did they read?

Both *Death in Venice* and *Sunset Boulevard* unfold in opulent surroundings of suffocating, high-priced gaudiness. Aschenbach and Norma Desmond, both artists of the same age, doom themselves in pursuit of young male flesh. The strange, overwrought artificiality of Venice matches up with Hollywood.

Aschenbach's poignant ambition is to make a love comeback, as it were. Norma Desmond wants the same, although, befitting an actress, she gives her career a slight edge. Age haunts them. Toward the end of the story, Aschenbach "left the beach, walked back to the hotel, and took the elevator up to his floor. Inside his room he lingered at the mirror for a long time, studying his gray hair, his pinched and tired face."

Time for a makeover. In *Death in Venice* and in *Sunset Boulevard*, big set-piece scenes document the rejuvenation of face and body. "An army of beauty experts" invaded Norma's house, according to Joe, and "she went through a merciless series of treatments." Much of this we see.

In the novella a rather queeny barber grooms Aschenbach into a grotesque imitation of youth.

> Like someone who cannot stop, who cannot do enough, he moved more and more briskly from one challenge to the next. Aschenbach, resting comfortably, unable to resist . . . studied his reflection, and he saw that his eyebrows arched more evenly and decisively, his eyes were elongated, their glow brought out by a slight application on the lids. Farther down, he saw a delicate carmine awakening on what had been brownish and leathery; his lips, anemic only a moment before, swelled in a raspberry tint; his crow's-feet and the furrows of his cheeks and mouth had vanished under cream and a youthful bloom. . . . At last the makeup man was satisfied and showed it, as his kind do, by abjectly thanking the person he had served.
>
> "Some insignificant assistance," he said, adding a final detail to Aschenbach's appearance. "Now the signore will have no qualms about falling in love."

The irony, of course, is heavier than the makeup. What these measures accomplish is the sad transformation of a distinguished frog prince into a boy-chasing faux beauty queen.

Hollywood being a citadel of unreality, it's appropriate that *Sunset Boulevard* should pulse to fairy-tale rhythms. Miles Kreuger felt the palpitations that day in 1950 when he saw the first show at Radio City. At sixteen, he hadn't traveled far from childhood. Although the pulse beats are submerged, think of castles, unwary innocents trapped by ogres, young lovers separated. . . . Think of *Beauty and the Beast*.

Cocteau's film came out in 1946, and it's possible it influenced Hans Dreier's art direction more than it influenced writing or direction. The Beast's castle, in its attractive repulsion, isn't so much more fantastic than Norma Desmond's palazzo. In the Cocteau film those sconces that are live human arms holding lighted candles in the Beast's mausoleum-like halls could be seen as surreal omens of Norma's shrine to her burned-out fame.

It's repo men who set both plots in motion. In L.A. they're after Joe Gillis's car. In rural France it's the family farm they threaten to snatch from Beauty's father. When the Beast first appears to Beauty and demands, "Where are you going?" he roars with Desmondesque authority, like Norma speaking to Gillis for the first time: "You there, why are you so late?" (Beauty fainted dead away, but real men don't pass out.)

Several times, the Beast shapes his paws into desperate, needy Norma Desmond curls. His stylized speech and ugly handsomeness match up with Norma Desmond's, just as Joe Gillis's ravishing good looks amount to (male) Beauty. Certainly this monstrous Beast in his elaborate setting is more appealing than the film's "normal" characters—again like Norma Desmond. Garbo's famous plea after she saw the Cocteau film—"Give me back my beast"—echoes what many of us wish for at the end of *Sunset Boulevard*.

Some commentators read Norma Desmond as a latter-day vampire, a category that privileges androgyny over female masculinity. The critic Lucy Fischer, writing about *Sunset Boulevard* in Janet Todd's anthology *Women and Film*, explores the "pernicious image that underlies Gillis's conception of the aging Norma Desmond." Fischer's Norma Desmond might have crept out of the pages of Bram Stoker or Anne Rice: "Norma is seen initially . . . as mysterious silhouette behind a slatted shade or screen. When she is finally glimpsed, she is dressed in black, lurking in a dark shadow, exuding an ominous presence. Norma Desmond is like Dracula or Nosferatu, waiting to ensnare her next unsuspecting victim. Hence our suspicion when Norma suggests that Joe move into the mansion with her, and our terror when we learn that Max has made up the bedroom for him before he has agreed to stay."

Fischer's clues to bloodsucking include Norma's dark glasses and the "sinister wire holder" for her cigarettes. Norma's ghoulish feeding on her old movies implies slitting the veins of her own youthful persona. "Undead," writes Fischer, is the best word to characterize Norma Desmond, "who is technically alive yet mired in a state of suspended animation."

We'd better think twice before saying "Give me back my beast" at the end of *this* picture, for Lucy Fischer sees Norma Desmond's final close-up as "a direct and threatening advance on the audience."

Even more chilling, it was Gloria Swanson's advance on herself. Because her performance was ne plus ultra, *Sunset Boulevard* killed Swanson's screen career. She made only three pictures in the remaining thirty-three years of her life.

In *Three for Bedroom C* (1952), a piece of toxic fluff, Swanson played well-adjusted, single-parent movie star Ann Haven—in other words, Norma Desmond Lite. Next she starred with Vittorio De Sica and Brigitte Bardot in *Nero's Mistress*, which Swanson herself described as "so bad that six years elapsed between the shooting in Italy in 1956 and the picture's release in a dubbed version in the United States in 1962." In *Airport 1975* (1974), Swanson played herself. In it she caricatures both Gloria Swanson and Norma Desmond, adding the only charm to this dull disaster. (Swanson to a fellow passenger on the ill-fated 747: "Young man, you think this thing won't fly? In 1917 I was flying in something wilder than this. You know who the pilot was? Cecil B. DeMille. We flew from Hollywood nonstop to Pasadena.")

The films she turned down seem as bad as the ones she made. Director Mitchell Leisen wanted her to play the doctor's wife in his 1951 picture *Darling, How Could You?* Once more, Paramount demanded a screen test. Swanson refused on the very plausible grounds that *Sunset Boulevard* had proven her capabilities.

As early as Oscar night 1951 Swanson had glimpsed Norma Desmond lurking beside her. During her years of obscurity, the public had forgotten Gloria Swanson. "In order to spring back to them in one leap," Swanson said later, "I had had to have a bigger-than-life part. I had found it, all right. In fact, my present danger seemed to lie in the fact that I had played the part too well."

Although she didn't win the Academy Award, Swanson convinced the world of what she called "that corniest of all theatrical cliches—that on very rare occasions the actor actually becomes the part. Barrymore *is* Hamlet. Garbo *is* Camille. Swanson *is* Norma Desmond."

Three decades later, when she wrote her autobiography, Swanson devoted only a dozen pages to the role that made her immortal. Not that she had anything against the picture, or Wilder, or her costars. The aftertaste was bitter because Hollywood had typecast her forever as Norma Desmond. "More and more scripts arrived at my door," Swanson wrote, "that were awful imitations of *Sunset Boulevard*, all featuring a deranged superstar crashing toward tragedy." (One such script may well have been *The Star*, a camp high point—meaning a low point—in Bette Davis's career. In this back room paraphrase of *Sunset Boulevard*, Davis plays Margaret Elliott, a down-at-heels, middle-aged actress desperate to land a part in *The Fateful Winter*—as an eighteen-year-old! "You don't know what it means to stand in front of the camera again," says Bette.)

Endless unpleasing offers led to Swanson's resolve: "I didn't want to spend the rest of my life, until I couldn't remember lines any longer or read cue cards, playing Norma Desmond over and over again." As a result of that decision, Swanson's reputation became fossilized. Since few people watched silent films, and even fewer saw *Three for Bedroom C* or *Nero's Mistress*, the moviegoing public perceived Swanson's career as having stopped, like Miss Havisham's clock, in 1950. True, it had stopped at

high noon, but careers must keep on ticking. As it turned out, the joke-
ster who quipped that the moral of *Sunset Boulevard* was "Sic Transit Gloria Swanson" hit it on the head.

Norma Desmond's Little Instruction Book

That's a fetching title for a book of wisdom on sale near the cash
register, but author Willie Jolley called his inspirational volume
A Setback Is a Setup for a Comeback. Identified on the dust jacket as
"America's leading motivational speaker/singer combination,"
Jolley offers a twelve-step plan for comebacks of every sort. If
you, like Norma Desmond, *hate that word,* call it a "return," as she
did, and still hope for the author's promised results.

This book would not find a place here except for a couple of
details. The first is that word, "comeback," which, having
become relatively unused in general discourse, has come to be
associated with Herself.

Willie Jolley might not agree. Though his chapters begin
with uplifting quotations—by Helen Keller, Vince Lombardi,
and Maya Angelou—there's not a peep about Norma Desmond,
Gloria Swanson, Billy Wilder, or *Sunset Boulevard.* Is there, however, an oblique tribute to them in the chapter where the seventh
of the twelve steps toward comeback is revealed? It is titled
"Take Action: You Can Have Lights, You Can Have Cameras,
but Nothing Happens Until You Take Action."

Aha! So Jolley has watched her descending the staircase in a
state of complete mental shock. But since he takes the parallel
no further, perhaps he has been swayed only at great remove by
the strange aroma of Norma Desmond.

With all this in mind, and in case I'm invited to appear on *Oprah*, I jotted my own half dozen steps for making a comeback using principles deduced from the extravagant psychology of Norma Desmond.

1. Don't settle for less than DeMille. In practical terms, start big, stay big; take your ideas and complaints to the top. If your P.C. blows up, insist that Bill Gates come and fix it.
2. Aging is for wimps; stay as young as you were. Ladies: Unplug that biological clock. Gents: "I'm too young for Viagra."
3. Stay on good terms with your exes. Better still, put 'em to work. They're the best help you'll find.
4. Be a control freak. Do not hesitate to tell lovers and associates to stop chewing gum, buy a new shirt, empty your ashtray.
5. If things don't go to suit you, a suicide attempt is an excellent means of empowerment.
6. Fight gun control. Call, write, or e-mail the NRA and tell them that you support a star's right to bear arms. Take advantage of Saturday night specials, especially on major holidays.

By the 1960s Swanson could kid Norma Desmond. Or was laughter her final garlic to fling at the blood drinker? When she appeared on stage or TV, Swanson would tell the director, "If you hear one intonation or see one mannerism of Norma Desmond, for goodness sake, come and tell me—or smack me!"

She told an interviewer in 1964, "I've got nobody floating in my pool. I don't have a pool, for that matter, but there are some bathtubs around here [she made a swift gesture in the direction of other rooms in her New York apartment] and nobody is floating facedown in them as far as I know!" The sympathetic interviewer, as though joining her side in battle, wrote that "Gloria could play Norma Desmond, but Norma could never have played Gloria Swanson."

In London about that time, Kevin Brownlow witnessed a Swanson scene that made its way into *The Parade's Gone By*, his homage to the era of silent pictures: "The ageless Gloria Swanson, magnificently attired in a flowing diaphanous gown, lay back on a couch in the Carlton Tower Hotel. The television executive, transfixed by her clear blue eyes, expressed astonishment that this heroine of his youth should retain all her magic.

" 'The story of *Sunset Boulevard*—how much of it was your story?' he asked.

" 'All of it, dear,' said Miss Swanson, adopting a Norma Desmond drawl. 'I really *am* the greatest star of them all. But I hide away from people. I live in the past. And if you take a quick look in the bathroom, you'll find a body floating facedownward right now.' "

In 1966 Swanson dropped in on Chaplin at Pinewood Studios in London, where he was directing Marlon Brando and Sophia Loren in *The Countess from Hong Kong*. Like so many incidents from her life after 1950, this one assumed the gestalt of *Sunset Boulevard*. Once more, Kevin Brownlow looked at Gloria Swanson and caught a glimpse of Norma Desmond.

When Gloria's chauffer drove up to the gate at Pinewood, "the sergeant on duty saluted smartly" and said, "Good afternoon, Miss Swanson." Then he directed the chauffeur to the sound stage where Chaplin was at work.

She sighed with relief and said, "Thank heaven for that. I thought I was going to have to play a *Sunset Boulevard* scene to get in." Brownlow adds that since Swanson wanted the visit to be informal, she had not let Chaplin know she was on her way. "Let's just arrive and see what happens," she said. Gloria Swanson had not observed Chaplin on a movie set since 1915 in Chicago, when she was hired—and soon dismissed for lack of comic flair—from one of his early films. The picture was *His New Job*.

In Bronlow's words, "The set was crowded with seated, inactive technicians. It was quiet and orderly, but with an air of expectation, like the moments before a boxing match. The ringside spectators turned and stared as Gloria Swanson entered. From the lighted area of the otherwise dark, hangarlike stage, a stout figure appeared, in a gray hat, a gray jacket, and green-tinted glasses. He grinned that unmistakable Chaplin grin, and held out his arms."

"Fifty years!" cried Gloria Swanson. They embraced.

"Do you remember when you kicked me twelve times in the derriere, and then threw me out?" she asked. "Back in 1915, at Essanay?"

"Ah, yes," replied Chaplin. "Well, I always thought you'd make a better *dramatic* actress."

Swanson, of course, didn't spend her years visiting other people's sets. She stayed busy: her family, her lovers, theatrical appearances in New York and out of town, her various business ventures, as well as painting and sculpture. And though the big screen no longer needed her, the little screen did. She appeared often on television, where she made at least one semiclassic, *Killer Bees*, in 1974. As Madame von Bohlen—with a German accent to match her name—Swanson played the iron-willed matriarch of a California wine-growing family. But this was no *Falcon Crest*, for Madame, gilding the Napa grape, also exerts a strange power over a colony of bees thriving in her vineyard. It's pure movie of the week, though if you see it you probably won't forget Swanson's farewell to her drones: "Widersehen, dahlings."

Meanwhile, all those post-*Sunset*, weirdo-recluse roles that Swanson disdained went to Joan Crawford, Bette Davis, Tallulah Bankhead, and other legends willing to overlook the fact that pictures had gotten small, and lousy.

chapter 17

Boulevard!

Gloria Swanson considered herself among those with psychic pow-
ers, and she was definitely musical, so it's not surprising that she
foresaw *Sunset Boulevard*'s Broadway potential. In fact, the year Andrew
Lloyd Webber, in London, reached the age of five, Swanson in Los Angeles hired a composing team to craft a musical theatre version of the film.
In a sense, she was following the same impulse as those who deluged her
for years with scripts she deplored that were "awful imitations of *Sunset
Boulevard*." But show business would be a thin enterprise indeed if previous hits—and misses—were not regularly recobbled.

Swanson's eye for the genuine set her apart from that host of producers who beseeched her to play sham Norma Desmonds. Since the real
Norma had taken up residence in the Swanson spotlight, why not take
advantage of her ambiguous presence?

Swanson's original ticket to Desmondland, however, was not written
round trip. The attempt to backtrack flung her smack-dab into the
Wicked Witch of Melrose Avenue, a.k.a. Paramount Pictures, and this
time the studio wanted none of Swanson—not even her car. Worse still,
on the day of catastrophe there was no sweet old DeMille to cushion
the blow.

In December 1953, Dickson Hughes and Richard Stapley, two young composers in Los Angeles, were hard at work on a show called *About Time*. They had constructed this revue so that it resembled *Time* magazine—that is, in tone and structure the musical numbers evoked the news weekly.

For all that, the lady editor of this imaginary musical magazine wasn't based on *Time* publisher Henry Luce, nor even on his wife, the colorful Clare Booth—a couple that Dorothy Parker once labeled "Arsenic and Old Luce." Instead, Hughes and Stapley modeled their editor on Fleur Cowles, one of the very few top female magazine editors of the time. Cowles, whom Dickson Hughes describes as "a Helen Gurley Brown ahead of her time," edited *Flair*, which he calls "a glitzy, marvelous magazine with all kinds of fold-outs and wonderful visual effects. It was a *Vanity Fair*-type publication." The composers thought of Gloria Swanson for the lead.

Swanson, meanwhile, had appeared on Broadway a couple of years earlier in *Nina*, a play that flopped. Even by 1953, her wounds hadn't healed. All the same, when Hughes and Stapley approached her with *About Time* she invited them for a meeting there in Los Angeles, where she happened to be visiting from New York.

"She was immediately friendly," Dickson Hughes recalled almost fifty years later. "No reserve, no star attitude." During that first evening the three spent together, Swanson listened to songs and other material from *About Time*, and according to Hughes, "she saw some merit in what we had written." But, still bruised from the critical drubbing of *Nina*, Swanson proclaimed: "I just will not ever do another Broadway show. Well, not unless somebody writes a musical adaptation of *Sunset Boulevard*."

Such a show had never occurred to the composers. But what an idea! "From that point on," said Hughes, "the evening turned into a party, and we weren't even drinking. When we left Swanson, we were as excited as she was.

"Next morning when we got up, Stapley and I went to work on the show. He had a great idea: a number based on her next-to-last line in the film, '... those wonderful people out there in the dark.' I sat down at the piano and started noodling. He would hum along and say, 'No, no, take it this way, go down there on the melody.' In less than an hour's time we had the whole kernel of the number set."

They phoned Gloria Swanson. "What do you think of this?" Hughes asked, and played the number for her over the phone. She said, "Come up here immediately!"

A bit later Hughes and Stapley arrived at the house where Swanson was a guest. Following her suggestions, they made a few changes and then about 4:30 in the afternoon she called an old friend, D. A. Doran, a top executive at Paramount who also was a lawyer.

"'D. A., this is Gloria. I want you to hear something.'" Hughes laughs, recalling Swanson's delirious enthusiasm. "She put the phone close to me at the piano, and I did the song. I could hear Doran's voice, like Looney Tunes gabble, saying, "Gloria, what is this?" When Hughes came to the end of the song, Swanson took over. 'D. A., isn't that brilliant?'"

"Very interesting," he answered. "What is it?"

She told him nonstop about the two brilliant young men and the marvelous idea of a Broadway show based on *Sunset Boulevard*—"And what do I need to do to get the rights?"

Accustomed to star turns, Doran said, "Well, gee, Gloria, I don't know but I can certainly look into it. I'll talk to a few people and get back to you."

"I'm not sure whether he called her or she called him a few days later," Hughes says, "but in her impatience she probably called him, one of those wonderful movie star moments like, *Well now, what's happening over there?* I wasn't present when the call was made, but Gloria told me, 'It looks wonderful! D. A. says we'll have no problems at all, just go ahead and do it.'" Hughes mentions a one-year option given by Paramount, which may well have been oral and not written—in which case it wasn't worth the paper it wasn't written on. (Among Swanson's papers I found no official agreement between her and the studio. I did locate correspondence among various parties detailing a *proposed* option agreement.)

Hughes refers to "a letter granting the option," which might be considered legally binding although still risky for the party seeking rights, viz. Swanson. He says, "Paramount stipulated as one of the requirements that the studio would have the right to assess the material as it was created." Red flag number one.

Swanson's trust, the casual option arrangements, and the studio's obvious advantage send a chill up the spine of anyone acquainted with the legal workings of show business. For a savvy businesswoman, Swanson made a big mistake. Even in 1953, before the country had learned to stop worrying and love litigation, her naive enthusiasm amounted to something grotesque: Norma Desmond in a Mickey Rooney–Judy Garland putting-on-a-show-in-the-backyard fever dream. Call it "Nightmare Over Sunset."

The nightmare stayed rosy-hued for years, at least from Swanson's point of view. She saw the glittering lights of a theatre marquee, nothing more. In the depths of Paramount, however, a spectre was haunting Gloria Swanson. It was the spectre of denial.

On March 29, 1954, Swanson, back in New York, sent a letter to Adolph Zukor, whom she had known since the first day she entered the gates of Paramount. "Dear Mr. Zukor," she wrote, "It is my desire to buy a print of *Sunset Boulevard* from Paramount, and I am hoping you can make this possible." She explained why, then went on, "Sometime when you are in New York I would be very happy if you and your wife would come by on a Saturday or Sunday and have a cup of tea with me; this is about the only time I have to catch up with old friends and it seems such a pity we have not done this. Kind regards to you and your wife, Affectionately, [signed] Gloria."

When the letter reached eighty-one-year-old Zukor, he handed it to an underling who scribbled across the bottom of Gloria's page: "Suggest you send to Frank Freeman for guidance as to nature of reply."

Red flag number two is stapled to Swanson's letter. It's a handwritten note to Zukor from studio vice president Freeman: "We absolutely do not sell 16 M prints of our Pictures. In some instances by contrast we have agreed to give a 16 M print to an actor or actress, and sometimes to a producer or director, but we are doing everything in our power to stop this—the *abuse* is something alarming." Presumably, Swanson's request for a print was denied in less abrupt language.

Dickson Hughes and Richard Stapley, meanwhile, worked under the cloudless sky of inspiration. As stipulated by Paramount, the studio was to assess the material as the composers created it. Therefore, when they had committed a couple of numbers to paper in first-draft form, Hughes and Stapley trekked to Paramount. There they performed the songs before the head of the music department and also for a young production assistant, Alan J. Pakula, who later became a well-known director. "We did the songs," says Hughes, "they were well received, the officials at Paramount seemed most enthusiastic, and the word came down from the studio: 'Go ahead. Finish the project.'" Their visit to Paramount took place early in 1954.

Time passes. This demanding adaptation occupies the two composers even though they have lives apart from *Sunset Boulevard*. Since they are not full-time employees of Gloria Swanson, their livelihoods come from elsewhere. Dickson Hughes, for instance, pursues a career as a singer and pianist. He's appearing at Johnny Frenchman's, a fashionable and popular bar-restaurant on the ocean side of the Pacific Coast Highway near Topanga Canyon.

Hughes said that about a year later, in 1955, when the *Sunset Boulevard* option was nearing expiration, Swanson had interested two or three New York producers in the project. Even more encouraging, an English producer had tentatively planned an out-of-London tour for the show.

Swanson hired the law firm of Gang, Kopp, and Tyre to negotiate with Paramount Pictures on her behalf. A letter dated January 27, 1955, from Hermione K. Brown, of the law firm, to Gloria Swanson sets forth the studio's terms for acquiring an option for stage rights to *Sunset Boulevard*. To summarize the contents of that long letter: 1) Option rights: $2,500 cash as a nonreturnable advance against royalties; 2) Royalties: 2½ percent of the box office gross receipts; 3) Option term: until April 1, 1956; 4) With respect to rights in the play: if not produced on Broadway on or before April 1, 1956 as a first-class production, all rights become Paramount's property including all rights in the book of the play; if play is produced, Paramount expects to acquire all motion picture rights in the stage production as part of its deal; 5) Paramount will agree not to reissue film in the U.S. or to release it for TV for a period from beginning of option to two years after the opening of the show on Broadway; 6) Paramount wants right of approval of the producer and the librettist. Since the score has already been written and heard, the studio will approve the composers.

Paramount obviously had the upper hand in these negotiations. The studio, in possession of something Swanson desperately wanted, no doubt perceived her willingness to meet its far-reaching demands. Recognizing the publicity value of a successful Broadway show, Paramount seemed mildly interested in Swanson's project—provided she take all risks and make all concessions. The terms outlined above clearly indicate that the studio's interests would not be compromised.

Swanson failed to realize that she was a tiny David facing the Melrose Avenue Goliath—and she didn't even have a slingshot. Meanwhile, as patron of the project, she paid stipends to Hughes and Stapley for their work. She also paid lawyers and assumed incidental expenses.

Early in 1955, Swanson wrote to Erich von Stroheim, who lived in France, asking him to come to New York and play Max in her musical. In his reply, dated April 30, Stroheim sounds cautiously sanguine: "Your idea seems to be very good, provided that the adaptation is not going to be a completely different story in which the adaptors have systematically and religiously cut out all the outstanding good scenes and substituted them by little stinkos of their own! The changes you have indicated in your letter are decidedly for the better, particularly as far as they concern a certain Max von Mayerling! All I hope is that you won't have a ballet or a variety show put in place of that heartbreaking scene between you and Bill when you are dancing together all alone. Whether I would like to play my little part? What a superfluous question!"

Even if Swanson's musical had been produced, it's unlikely that the impossible old genius, and Swanson's sometime nemesis, would actually have appeared in it. In 1956 he began to suffer pain in his back. The diagnosis was cancer. Erich von Stroheim died on May 12, 1957.

During one of our conversations, I asked Dickson Hughes, "In those days before videos, and with *Sunset Boulevard* unavailable otherwise, how were you able to remember exactly the scenes and lines from the picture as you worked on the adaptation?"

He said, "I think Richard Stapley and I pulled it out of the air from memory. We did have Swanson's shooting script to work from, however. I had of course seen the picture in L.A. when it was first released, and I never forgot it. But it didn't occur to me that it could have songs added. *Sunset Boulevard* was already a perfect work."

I asked how he and Stapley collaborated, whether one wrote words and the other music. "Oh no," he answered, "we worked together. I was really the principal creator. He was the idea person, and also he occasionally made some good critical assessments. So we gave ourselves credit as 'Music and lyrics by Dickson Hughes and Richard Stapley.' We never differentiated who did what."

Forty years later, when Andrew Lloyd Webber transformed *Sunset Boulevard* into a musical, he and lyricists Don Black and Christopher Hampton kept the film's structure. They also retained much of the dialogue.

Hughes and Stapley, on the other hand, reconfigured the story. For example, their show opens with Norma Desmond rehearsing for her comeback film. Hughes summarizes the opening like this: "She's tired and overwrought. She says, 'I cannot rehearse anymore, Max. Oh Max, tell me what it'll be like after my picture is finished.'

"In his role as protector, Max tries to soothe her. He describes what the first day back at the studio will be like. That sends Norma into an entirely different mood and she starts to sing her fantasy. When that section is over, she says to Max, 'Now tell me what it will be like at the premiere.'"

At that point Dickson Hughes sang Norma Desmond's aria for me: "Suddenly bright glare is all I can see/ But I know that right there, and smiling at me/ Are the ones who silently give me that magical spark/ Those wonderful people out there in the dark."

Then Hughes revealed a surprising detail: "The idea of opening like this came from José Ferrer. He said the show needed a moment at the very beginning that tells us precisely who this character, Norma

Desmond, is. Not just a crazy lady in dark glasses, but someone we really do identify with." Ferrer's suggestion came when Swanson and Hughes spent the evening with him and his wife at the time, Rosemary Clooney. According to Hughes, "Gloria wanted José Ferrer to direct the Broadway production."

But we're jumping ahead. Back to Los Angeles, where the composers worked at the show during much of 1954—until Richard Stapley vanished. Ending his personal and professional relationship with Dickson Hughes, he moved to Europe and the two composers did not meet again for many years.

At this point Hughes became the sole composer. He and Swanson continued working on the show, although sporadically. After all, he lived in Malibu and she in New York. "There was no particular dramatic decision to put the show aside," Hughes says. "Gloria pursued it, but not full-time. Her life stayed full and busy, although when she encountered producers and potential backers she told them about the musical *Sunset Boulevard.* But it remained largely on hold from 1955 to 1957. Gloria and I didn't see one another often, though once or twice when she was in L.A. she came out to visit me in Malibu." He adds that from the time the proposed English production fell through, "I had no regular income from her at all."

Norma Desmond was recalled to life by Steve Allen, the host of NBC's Sunday night variety hour that competed for ratings with *The Ed Sullivan Show* on CBS.

Swanson phoned Hughes one day in November 1957 to tell him she was to appear on *The Steve Allen Show* singing "Those Wonderful People Out There in the Dark." She said, "Will you come to New York and supervise the staging of the number?" He was soon on his way, with NBC picking up the tab.

Hughes and Swanson, and the actor playing Max, soon had the musical number on its feet. In rehearsal, however, Swanson realized that Max wasn't getting his lines right. "He hadn't had time to really prepare," says Hughes. "I felt bad for him but he just wasn't making it. Finally Gloria, with her movie star temperament, told the producer, 'He's all wrong and Dickson knows the lines, so why don't we have him say them offcamera?' And she had Max fired." (Although Hughes had the looks of a heart-throb, union rules kept him out of sight.)

By this time *Sunset Boulevard*, the musical, bore the glitzier title *Boulevard!* That choice was Swanson's. Dickson Hughes wanted to call the show *Starring Norma Desmond*, a title he still considers more glamorous. Steve Allen, introducing Swanson on the air, used neither. Hughes can repeat the announcement verbatim: "Tonight we're honored to have this great star of silent films and the movies of today sing a song from her forth-coming production, a musical version of *Sunset Boulevard* by Dickson Hughes and Richard Stapley."

A clip from the show reveals Swanson's voice as well trained. In the bygone style of singing show tunes operatically, she sounds somewhat like Irene Dunne, Kitty Carlisle, and all those other movie sopranos of the thirties. When Swanson sings, "The people who matter, the people who care . . . those wonderful people out there in the dark," you believe she really is Norma Desmond *rediviva*.

So did many others, including important Broadway producers. Among these, Hughes names Robert Fryer and Lawrence Carr, Robert Griffith and Harold Prince.

Swanson kept Paramount abreast of this encouraging East Coast buzz. On December 1, 1957, she wrote to D. A. Doran:

> Now that I have succeeded in interesting several top-flight produc-ers in *Sunset Boulevard* as a musical play, the time has come for us to enter into a written agreement to protect me on the original idea . . . and arranging for production and financing. The produc-ers I refer to, as having approached me, include Fryer and Carr, David Merrick, and several others I know would be acceptable to Paramount.
>
> The agreement as worded would give me a formal option of one year in which the play can be prepared for Broadway, just to be safe, although Fryer and Carr are talking about an October opening.
>
> The interest [created by *The Steve Allen Show*] has been unbeliev-

able.... By now I have worked out plans for the entire enterprise, including financing. In order to get this far, however, I have had to spend a considerable amount of time and money, primarily on the composers.... The time is ripe for us to move ahead at top speed. Since this is a costly matter to me, would you please, D. A., let me hear from you at once about the contract.

Swanson's letter betrays an undertone of anxiety, even at a moment when optimism seemed most warranted. She added a P.S. to D. A. Doran: "Enclosing extra copy in case you think this letter will be helpful to the New York office." Swanson's tone of hat-in-hand, anything-to-please doesn't suit her; one wants her to demand, not to entreat. From this point on in her dealings with Paramount, she sounds like one of the hundred neediest theatrical cases.

A few days later Swanson sent D. A. Doran a tape recording of the song she sang on *The Steve Allen Show*. An accompanying note enthused, "If only you get the same thrill I got hearing it played." She informed him that she was sending, under separate cover, "a draft of the first act of the musical." Another P.S. suggests Swanson's mounting desperation: "D. A., is it not possible for Paramount to give me a simple paper saying that no matter whom you deal with as a producer, you will protect my interest, making sure that I get something out of the producer's share of any producer you deal with. I would love to have you phone me after you get this letter (my private number is REgent 4-7228), or send me a wire telling me when you will have time to speak to me on the phone."

Although impatient with Paramount and anxious over the studio's tepid reactions to her big plans, Swanson nevertheless made a grand gesture. She imported Dickson Hughes to New York.

Between phone calls from Harold Prince and David Merrick, Swanson urged Hughes to join her. After all, they had a show to do. As she gazed from the safety of 920 Fifth Avenue in the treacherous direction of Broadway, Swanson saw green lights the size of emeralds and never a flash of jungle red. Even the amber light of caution—why no response from D. A. Doran?—winked conspiratorially at *her*, *HER*, *Glo-*

ria Desmond, Norma Swanson. Those idiots! Without her there wouldn't be any Paramount Studio!

"I came back to California, packed everything up, and moved to New York. Gloria was very helpful to me. She gave me furniture out of a storage room in her apartment." In Manhattan, Dickson Hughes took jobs singing and playing in supper clubs, as he had done in Los Angeles.

Then good news. Robert Fryer and Lawrence Carr soon became the de facto producers of *Boulevard!* Many details of their relationship with Gloria Swanson are unclear, although Hughes refers to the year 1958 as "the Fryer and Carr period." He says, "It looked very much as if they were going to produce the show. Gloria and I met every day. We continued to shape, polish, change, and rework the whole project."

Asked to specify Swanson's contribution to the show, as distinct from his own, Hughes puts it this way: "She was adding certain elements to Norma's character that were not in the film. She decided that Norma should not be rich, that it would make the things she did for Joe Gillis much more heart-rending if she was pawning her jewelry to finance her grand gestures. That she added. In the picture she was limitlessly rich."

Hughes adds an intriguing detail that Swanson told him during their collaboration. "She said she had big arguments with Billy Wilder about that point. Norma Desmond would have seemed much more sympathetic in the film if she had made sacrifices for this young man rather than just peeling money off the top."

In addition, says Hughes, "to make Max more believable and understandable—not just a weird, aloof foreign element—but to make him warmer and more accessible as a character, we added lines to explain why he had given up his own career to make a star of her. Also, more on how he became her protector and finally her servant."

I asked Hughes if Swanson contributed any tunes or lyrics. "No, no, that part was all mine," he said.

Would she sing a song as soon as you composed it? "Sure. Oh, it was an exciting time for both of us."

Did Swanson ever say, "I can't sing this, it's too high?" Or too low?

"No, I knew what her range was and so I stuck to notes that she could reach. Sometimes, at the piano, I'd do a run-through of a number and I'd say, 'Now maybe this can be changed; this lyric is not right so let me work on it some more.' After two or three times of hearing it that way, I'd say, 'Well, I think we've got it nailed here.' Then I'd sing it through. Usually she'd stand behind me and look over my shoulder, reading from the lead sheet that I'd written out."

Did Swanson read music? "Well, she had a great ear. And she had already heard the melodies several times. She'd kind of hum along, sing lightly. It was just a working session, you know, so she wasn't performing."

What kind of piano did Swanson have in her apartment on Fifth Avenue? "A grand. It was in this huge room that she used as her studio. In it she kept her artist's equipment, including a standard for doing sculpture in clay. In the studio she also had stereo equipment, recording equipment, all of that. The room had a fireplace, and often we'd have cocktails in there."

According to Hughes, it was Swanson's friend Gus Schirmer who brought the producers Robert Fryer and Lawrence Carr to her. Gus Schirmer, an agent, was the son of Gustave Schirmer, heir to the music publishing firm. Years earlier Schirmer *père* and Swanson had been lovers; they remained friends. Hughes recalls that Gus Schirmer Jr. acted as their agent for *Boulevard!*, although without a formal agreement.

Fryer and Carr, by the late fifties, had become important figures in the New York theatre scene. In 1956 they produced *Auntie Mame,* starring Rosalind Russell, which ran through 1958. Earlier Fryer had produced *Wonderful Town,* also with Russell; later he and Carr produced *Mame,* which ran from 1966 to 1970. Their serious interest in *Boulevard!* suggests the show's commercial appeal.

Swanson, meanwhile, had hired Steven Weinrib, a theatrical attorney, to handle her negotiations with Fryer and Carr. He had also become involved in her one-sided appeals to Paramount, which seem to have produced little more than continued "personal reassurances" from D. A. Doran on the telephone: "Gloria, don't worry, it's all okay, everything's fine."

In the autumn of 1958 Swanson traveled to London on *Boulevard!* business. On her return to New York she no doubt felt frustrated by mounting obstacles to her dream show, including a contretemps with her ostensible producers. Home for just a few days, she wrote to Fryer and Carr on October 3:

> Since my return from Europe, I have been shocked to learn that Dick Hughes and I have been given an undeserved reputation about town of being "difficult to deal with." I have been told that you cited this as your reason for giving up *Sunset Boulevard*.
>
> You must have short memories, so may I point out that we, Dick and I, without any signed option, willingly and happily made *every change* in the book and score suggested by you, your ex-director and "our" agent. Further, we gave innumerable auditions for you, Mr. Shubert and [his] associate.... More, I even stood on an empty stage so that you could be satisfied that my voice could be heard in the last row of the last balcony. Do you know any other actress who would have done this for you? After all, I have sung before. I have a hunch that even Judy Holliday, with no voice at all, wasn't even asked to do this. Besides, why should she—she uses microphones, as do the professional singers Lena Horne and Abbe Lane.
>
> Had you been honest in discussions of *Sunset Boulevard*, you would have said that you couldn't make up your minds after months and months of stalling—that you fought among yourselves (more wasted time)—and that finally you asked for a clause that would have turned the book, music and lyrics over to others without first giving us the opportunity to make your changes....

A letter on October 10 signed by Robert Fryer protests her angry accusations: "I read with great distress your letter of October 3. Someone has been maligning us completely to you. I will take any oath you want that I have never said anything derogatory about either you or Dick. I have only the highest praise for both of you. The idea of your being 'difficult to deal with' is preposterous. One could not find more cooperative people than both of you."

Dickson Hughes accepts Fryer's claim of innocence. "There was really no dispute, and I'm sure they did not badmouth us. You know how this business is, and how people talk. Gloria, being such a major star, had had confrontations with various people in the film industry. She had enemies."

Whether Fryer and Carr badmouthed Swanson and Hughes seems beside the point. Swanson's letter sets forth greater cause for anger: they have stalled, wasted time, and sought to wrest artistic control from her. Worst of all, perhaps, they have put her through the Broadway version of a screen test by standing her on an empty stage to audition for her own show. Fryer, in his letter, refutes none of these charges.

One day in February 1959 Swanson phoned Dickson Hughes at his apartment on East Fifty-eighth Street. "Are you sitting down?" she said.

"I will—if I should," he answered.

"It's over."

On February 12 she had sent a telegram to D. A. Doran informing him that Chappell Music Company, publisher of Rogers and Hammerstein, the Gershwins, Cole Porter, et al., "thinks highly enough of *Sunset* score to want to publish same." She signed the telegram "Love, Gloria." She also informed him (and others at Paramount) of interest by the St. Louis Municipal Opera in staging her show, with the added possibility of a regional tour.

Her next communiqué from Paramount came from Russell Holman, a lawyer in the studio's New York office. It's unclear whether he phoned Swanson or sent a wire. He might just as well have taped a note to a rock and flung it through her window.

Swanson's reply to Holman, dated February 16, tells all:

Now that I am out of shock, could you have possibly really meant that you had no intention of a deal going through with Fryer and Carr? And that when I did the *Steve Allen Show* . . . you regarded this as a whim of mine?

Please, Russell, you must surely realize that *Sunset Boulevard* has had four years of work put on it, to say nothing of my personal expense of $20,000. That is why it is hard for me to believe that you had no intention all along the line. I naturally do not expect an answer to this letter, but I do think you ought to know that there are such things as moral obligations, or at least there used to be. . . .

Forgive the harshness of this letter but because you, too, have probably had deep disappointments in your life, I hope you will understand mine, as one human being to another, leaving the entire motion picture business out of it.

Holman's reply, dated February 20, might, with a few adjustments, have been delivered from the Kremlin to a cold war neighbor, had any satellite state dared complain.

I am, of course, very sorry to have caused you shock and disappointment. Paramount's intentions are thoroughly honorable and have been throughout the long period—four years, according to your letter—during which you discussed intermittently with certain of our executives your hopes of effecting an arrangement . . . for a production of a stage musical based on *Sunset Boulevard*.

. . . Our executives are firmly of the opinion that in order to secure the maximum revenue from this reissue that it would be damaging for the property to be offered to the entertainment public in another form such as a stage musical.

"I was devastated. Crushed," says Dickson Hughes. "But I tried to put it behind me. I had to get on with my life."

To do so was perhaps less daunting for a young composer at the start of his career than for a woman of sixty. For Hughes, the Swanson years had been a carousel of rewarding work, bonhomie, and occasional hilarity. Though their efforts ended in a cul-de-sac, Hughes, turning back, could regard a boulevard of memories with his own private movie star, a high-maintainance, Fifth Avenue-dwelling, health-food-addicted Auntie Mame.

And, had he consulted a fortune-teller that cold day in February of 1959, Dickson Hughes might have heard a startling prediction. For indeed, their *Boulevard!* diverged but Swanson kept on it, never relinquishing hope. Eventually her wish, or a fragment of it, was granted, though in an oddly left-handed way—and only after death had separated her from the realization of all dreams.

Dickson Hughes traveled another road, a road that led, following a long flight of years, to *Swanson on Sunset*, a show he wrote about—writing a show with Gloria Swanson!

Hughes naturally saved all his music and lyrics from *Boulevard!* Over the years he was musical director in various stock companies, he performed in clubs, and worked in industrial show business in New York—i.e., he wrote songs, jingles, and entire shows for clients presenting new products. He also developed a concert-lecture called *The American Musical and How It Got That Way*, which he still performs. In 1983 he moved back to California.

Fast forward to December 1993, and the opening of Andrew Lloyd Webber's musical, *Sunset Boulevard* in Los Angeles. Round about that time an item appeared in a drama column of the *Los Angeles Times*. The squib, supplied by a publicist named Alan Eichler, mentioned that Lloyd Webber was not the first to set *Sunset Boulevard* to music. The item briefly outlined the Swanson *Sunset*. "I was stunned that anybody still alive had heard of this," says Hughes. "I looked him up in the phone book and gave him a call."

A few days later they met for lunch at the Greenery, on Santa Monica Boulevard. "We were there for hours," recalls Hughes. "After he heard my long story he said, 'That's fascinating. Why don't you use this as the book for a musical memoir? Since it happened to you, no one can challenge your rights to the material. Add to that the songs you created for your version of *Sunset Boulevard*.'"

Hughes proceeded eagerly with his musical about writing a musical. It opened in 1994 at a nightclub, the Hollywood Roosevelt Cinegrill, and went on to a successful run. Hughes performed at the piano, stepping downstage to play his younger self in dramatic scenes. Richard Leibell played his partner, Richard Stapley. Laurie Franks, in a demanding role, portrayed not only Gloria Swanson, but also Swanson playing Norma Desmond.

Swanson on Sunset opens with footage from Swanson's appearance on *The Steve Allen Show*. Shortly after that, someone utters these disheartening words to Laurie Franks: "They'll never turn *Sunset Boulevard* into a musical." The irony is especially fine considering that this is the *third* musical version of the film: Swanson's abortive effort, then Andrew Lloyd Webber's hit, and finally this postmodern play about a play that did not happen—and then did.

One might easily use *Swanson on Sunset*, with its catalogue of mix-and-match sources, as a tidy paradigm of deconstruction. Holding up a mirror to the film, and to musical versions of it, this show dismantles the entire structure of *Sunset Boulevard*. *Swanson on Sunset* unbuttons its original source, turns the garment inside out, rips the seams, dyes it, and refashions a virtual costume into an ironic lesson: "How You Can Write a Musical," and also how you never should. Dickson Hughes, inverting the aesthetic hierarchy of a classic Hollywood film, privileges failure—his and Swanson's—to show the arbitrary nature of a work of art. In his hands, *Sunset Boulevard* has come undone; Billy Wilder's picture, stripped of a center, now has countless centers. Meaning that the long shot, the fade-out, and the rejected take are as valid as the close-up.

The comic side of Dickson Hughes's Swanson years often involved a fancy car.

Near the time of the Hughes–Swanson collaboration, Swanson had a rich boyfriend named Lewis Bredin who, according to Hughes, "was madly devoted to her and helped her foot some of the bills"—including, presumably, the costs of *Boulevard!* For her birthday one year he gave her a Rolls-Royce. When I asked Hughes if Swanson drove it through the crowded streets of Manhattan, he said, "Oh no, she had a driver." In a deadpan tone he added, "I used it once to move from one apartment to another, which Gloria didn't know about."

I badgered him for details. "Let's see," he drawled, savoring my delight, "a luggage rack on top of the Rolls, with a mattress."

I said, "I certainly hope your move took place on the East Side, for maximum elegance."

"Oh yes, of course, the Upper East Side, naturally."

I said it sounded like *The Beverly Hillbillies* on Park Avenue. "That's the way it looked," he said. "I thought, if the landlord of this building sees a Rolls-Royce pull up with furniture on top, well—"

A year or so later, Swanson's Rolls turned up in Los Angeles so that she could use it while in town. In the summer of 1957, Gloria phoned Dickson Hughes to say, "I've got to go to New York. I want the car there, but I'll have to pay an outrageous price to have it driven back." Hughes recalls that "she burbled on and on about the cost of it all."

Since he happened to be between jobs, he suggested: "I'd be delighted to drive it to New York, stay there a few days, and have you fly me back home." Swanson chimed in grandly, "Well, if you're going to drive then I'll make the trip with you."

"Now you know," Hughes said in a droll tone, "she had a fixation about her diet. She ate strictly organic foods. When we went to dinner parties she took her own sandwich, typically seven-grain bread with almond butter and raisins. She'd slip it to the maid when we arrived. When dinner was served, this little sandwich would appear on her plate at the elegant table."

"Did everyone pretend not to notice?" I inquired.

"Once in a while someone would say, 'Gloria, what are *you* eating? We don't seem to have any of that.'"

Naturally, before setting out across the country Swanson outfitted the Rolls like a Bedouin provisioning his camel. Hughes:

She had two wonderful hampers specially constructed of flexible plastic. They held ice, which refrigerated our food supply. These hampers fitted into the trunk of the Rolls. During the day, we stopped at roadside tables and spread out our organic picnic. We had sandwiches, hard-boiled eggs, goat's milk—nothing from cows—fresh fruits, raisins, and nuts of all kinds.

We took turns driving. Gloria was an excellent driver. When I was at the wheel she read, and sometimes she'd take out her drawing pad and sketch a scene that caught her eye.

During our six days on the road we seldom ate in restaurants. But once we did stop at a greasy spoon somewhere in Indiana or Ohio. It was a dreadful experience, as going to a restaurant with her usually was. The first thing that happened, the waitress sashayed over with a filthy dishrag to mop the table—right in front of us. She said [he uses a Carol Burnett voice], "Well, what'll you have?"

Gloria said indignantly, "I do wish you could have done that earlier!" The waitress, of course, had no idea that this was a great Hollywood star. I'm sure she hadn't seen our automobile pull up in front. Then it got worse. Gloria glanced at the menu and said, outraged, "Look at this! Look at what people eat!" It was the usual greasy spoon menu of pork and beans, burgers, bacon and eggs. Gloria took great pains to dissect every item and tell what was wrong with each one.

The waitress was trying not to hear all of this, but she couldn't escape it. Then she got nervous. She rattled around behind the counter, but she still heard every word. You see, when Gloria was on a tear she made no effort to modulate her volume.

What did she order?

"Oh, nothing, of course. She said, 'Bring me a cup of very hot water.' And she used her own tea bag."

One night in Ohio they stopped at a tourist home. Hughes, as usual, signed his own name in the register, then put her down as "Mrs. Davey" (using the surname of her fifth husband, long gone by this point). The proprietress gave him a knowing look and said, "The bridal suite is available. It's on the top floor, and I think you and Mrs. Davey will be very comfortable there." When they went up to look at it, they discovered what Hughes calls "the worst possible combination of elements—artificial flowers, lots of pink tulle, swags over the bed—unbelievable." He made a nimble escape by saying, "You can let Mrs. Davey have this room and I'll take the one down on the second floor."

When he joined Gloria a bit later for their nightcap—vodka and organic apple juice—they laughed their heads off. Hughes is still laughing when he tells me, "In the morning she came to my room, knocked, and lectured me as though it were my fault: 'Never, ever do that to me again.'" They laughed some more, pulled themselves together, and hit the road.

But Swanson wasn't amused the day they went to see some of her early talkies at the Museum of Modern Art. At the outset her mood bordered on the reverent.

In the early sixties, with *Boulevard!* in the past, she and Hughes discussed other projects they might pursue. He suggested an album with her singing familiar songs she introduced in her first sound films, particularly "Love (Your Spell Is Everywhere)"—a song so closely associated with Gloria Swanson that orchestras in nightclubs and restaurants would play it when she entered. (A trivia note: This is the song's correct title, although it's universally known by the first line of the song: "Love Your Magic Spell Is Everywhere.")

Swanson liked the idea of an album. She told Hughes, "If we're to do that I'll call the Museum of Modern Art film department and arrange showings of those pictures where I sing." A few days later the two set off for private screenings of movies that few people consider worthy of Swanson—or worthy of adoration. "I was interested," says Hughes, "only in the song segments. I certainly didn't want to sit through the interminable unfolding of those dreadful, dated films."

Since the museum's screening room had no technical equipment for transferring the songs onto tape, Hughes brought Swanson's portable Ampex reel-to-reel system. They set it up down front, near the screen. When the film rolled, he waited until she called out, "The song's coming up," then he dashed down the aisle and clicked on the tape recorder.

"It was still early afternoon," Hughes recalls, "so I was kind of fascinated to see how she had photographed thirty years earlier, under that strange pasty makeup, with obviously artificial eyebrows—I thought she looked far more beautiful now."

They watched *The Trespasser*, the 1929 film in which she introduced her signature song. "But the rest of *The Trespasser* was trespassing against me," groaned Hughes. "As it wore on I leaned over and said, 'Now, is there another musical moment in this one?' She snapped, 'No, but you've got to watch it!'"

Gloria in retrograde, Norma Desmond ascendant.

Hughes leaned back and tried to stay awake. "The next one," he says, "was something silly like *Molly* or *Polly*—who knows. Anyway, it started and it was awful. A couple of times I whispered tactfully, 'Now, don't forget to tell me when the songs are coming on.' She said, 'Oh, I will, I will.' A moment later she squeezed my arm and said, 'Okay.' I started down the aisle to turn on the tape recorder and out of the black came this demand: 'Watch this!' Not, 'Are you doing okay?' or 'Is it working?' That silly movie had nothing to do with the reason we were there, except to her, of course."

Hughes crawled back to his seat and began surreptitiously to observe her from the corner of his eye. "I watched Gloria watching herself onscreen. Her facial expressions were exactly like Norma Desmond's, watching *Queen Kelly* with Joe Gillis. She was enraptured and captivated by what she saw on the screen from twenty-five or thirty years earlier. Totally swept away."

An awesome story with a thundering punch line: "There in the Museum of Modern Art, she gripped my arm exactly the way Norma Desmond grips Gillis in *Sunset Boulevard*."

When Gloria was Gloria, however, Hughes found her easy to get on with. Though she was his patroness, she never patronized. "It was strictly friendship right from the beginning," he vows. "She respected what she chose to view as my talent. The only time she ever raised her voice came that day when I paid more attention to the tape recorder than to her image on the screen. That really pissed her off."

Swanson never accepted the fact that phase two of her greatest role, with music added, was not to be. Sometime in the sixties, according to Dickson Hughes, he and Swanson got together once more to make a demo tape of songs from the show. "She believed that if we only had a first-rate presentation tape, *Boulevard!* might be reborn," he says. "So we made one in the apartment of a friend of ours, Bob Austin, who lived at

400 East Fifty-ninth Street. He had magnificent home stereo equipment and a grand piano."

Swanson, thrilled with the tape and full of lingering hope for a production, never stopped playing it. According to Hughes, "She used to get it out almost every time she had guests for cocktails or for dinner. She played it for everyone. And people grew excited along with her. I mean, she kept it alive in her head, in her emotions." And yet, perhaps because of teardrops hitting the page, she never mentioned the show in the five hundred pages of her autobiography.

chapter 18

"Funny How Gentle People Get with You Once You're Dead"

*W*e last saw William Holden floating not in Norma Desmond's pool but rather in a pool of vitriol spewed out by his wife, Ardis, on Oscar night. In the years after Holden played Joe Gillis, destiny wrote a surprise ending that not even Billy Wilder would have thought of: William Holden's was the most *Sunset Boulevard* life of all. The years, like Paramount, cast him as Joe Gillis.

In the context of the film, Holden's Gillis hates being Norma Desmond's gigolo. He suffers guilty pangs. In terms of Hollywood morality, censorship division, the gigolo must die in the end, like other screen undesirables: bad girls, loose women, homosexuals, criminals, and an array of nonconformists. The one false note of *Sunset Boulevard* occurs when Betty Schaeffer comes to rescue Joe from Norma's clutches and he refuses to leave. Why?

Gillis considers himself too evil for good Betty Schaeffer—who doesn't give a damn that he's been screwing the old dame if only he will come away with her. She says, "Joe, I haven't heard any of this. I never got those telephone calls. I've never been in this house. Now get your things together and let's get out of here." But Joe, like long-suffering wives in films of the forties and fifties, must sacrifice his own happiness for that of . . . who?

Not Norma; he's leaving her anyway. Not Betty, who will be miserable without him. The only remote nobility in Joe's misplaced decision is to spare his friend Artie Green the heartbreak of a broken engagement. But it's obvious to us, and surely to Joe as well, that Betty does not love Artie. He constantly irritates her. And no wonder. He's the kind of schmuck who plagues most of Wilder's late films, from about 1960 to the end.

The reasons for Joe's self-sacrifice are so pure they stink. They're psychologically bogus. Surely Wilder, Brackett, and D. M. Marshman wrote the scene only to placate the gaggle of Mrs. Grundys at the Production Code office. It's aesthetically correct only in terms of fundamentalist storytelling: Because Norma Desmond, as overbearing female, coopts the tradional male role, then weaker Joe Gillis, as female surrogate, must pay the price for his carnal sins. In other words, female desire must be punished, and if there's no female handy, a declawed male will do.

In some peculiar way, however, the story of Joe Gillis is also the story of William Holden. For Holden, too, seems to have believed himself unworthy of being loved. A possible key to his guilt is a statement he once made: "I'm a whore. All actors are whores. We sell our bodies to the highest bidder. I had practice being a whore. When I was a young actor starting out in Hollywood, I used to service actresses who were older than me."

For a conservative, straight-arrow Midwestener who was William Beedle before he became Bill Holden, that confession is a stick of dynamite. No doubt a thousand other cares pressed him down, as well. You can see their shadows already gathered in his face, his body, in *Sunset Boulevard*. In Nancy Olson's eyes, her costar looked "frayed" on the screen and off. He had formed a friendship with the bottle. Liquor caressed all wounds, those inflicted by a shrewish wife and a harsh world.

The marriage of Bill Holden and Brenda Marshall (a.k.a. Ardis Holden) lasted from 1941 to 1973. One wonders why. A vexed question indeed, considering that Hollywood was the easiest place in the world to get a divorce. Perhaps Holden's predominant self-image—husband and father first, actor last—demanded a bourgeois life uncluttered by failed marriages. If publicists hadn't thought up "Wholesome Olson" for another star of *Sunset Boulevard*, they might have dubbed the male lead "Wholesome Holden."

For many years Bill and Ardis lived in Toluca Lake, a San Fernando

Valley suburb distant in all respects from Hollywood and Beverly Hills. To outward appearances, the couple and their three children could have passed for neighbors of Ward and June Cleaver. Holden's biographer, Bob Thomas, describes the years after *Sunset Boulevard* as a time when writers for national magazines stressed Holden's qualities "as a sound, normal, public-spirited citizen who was active not only in industry and city affairs but attended PTA meetings at his children's schools, as well. Holden himself contributed to this impression in interviews."

Two of the Holdens' closest friends were fellow actors Ronald Reagan and Nancy Davis. Bill and Ardis encouraged the romance of this pair by inviting them to dinner almost every weekend. When finally the alliance was ready to be joined, "Ardis made all the arrangements. The wedding was to be held March 4, 1952, at the Little Brown Church in the Valley, a tiny nondenominational church on Coldwater Canyon Boulevard. Ardis would be matron of honor, Bill best man. No one else was invited."

The bride—not exactly blushing, from what we hear—no doubt possessed something old, something new, and all that. So did Ardis, at least something old: the same old malice toward her husband. Furious at Bill for some minor infraction, she refused to speak to him. She flounced to the other side of the church, determined not to sit beside him in the pew.

Once united in holy matrimony, the Reagans celebrated at the Holdens' home in Toluca Lake, where Ardis had arranged a wedding cake, a photographer, and a reception for a few friends. Everyone felt happy, everyone smiled, even Ardis, who smiled at all but Bill.

At the time of *Sunset Boulevard*, Holden already had begun drinking heavily. For the next three decades, often deluded and half-destroyed by alcohol, he lived through a zigzag of binges and hospitalizations. Even so, in a heroic effort to keep working he made more than forty pictures between 1950 and his death thirty-one years later.

Holden found no peace from suffering. Because he was a star, every insecurity, every torment, was there in close-up. He had many friends, yet no one was allowed near enough to help.

According to David Seltzer, a screenwriter and director who worked with Holden in Kenya, "He complained about being recognized. When he was asked for his autograph he would say afterward, 'Why can't these goddamn people leave me alone?' But if he wasn't recognized, he'd put a monkey on his head until people gathered around."

Though he and Gloria Swanson seldom met after working together, a bond of affection remained between them. Once in the 1970s she was in Palm Springs and dropped by Holden's house. He was away, but his housekeeper showed her around. When Holden returned, he found this message taped to the toilet seat in his bathroom: "Dear Joe, I'm leaving this note where I know you'll find it. Where is Max? Where is DeMille? Where is Hedda? Where has everybody gone? Love, Norma Desmond."

Swanson, in her autobiography, wrote that Holden "was brilliant in our picture, and I adored him." Like many others, she must have been very sad when he died in 1981. She saved his obituary from the *New York Times*.

Holden said in an interview in 1971 that his favorite role was Joe Gillis in *Sunset Boulevard*. Most moviegoers would agree, though he gave fine performances in many other films: *Stalag 17, Picnic, The Bridge on the River Kwai, The Wild Bunch, Network*. Speaking to another interviewer in 1978, he put forth a very bad idea for a *Sunset Boulevard* sequel: "Norma Desmond has been sentenced to life for the murder of Joe Gillis and she is now eligible for parole. She gets out of Folsom Prison in California, rehabilitated in society again. That would have to be Hollywood. Now to me that is fascinating. And certainly Gloria can do it at her age. Now her problems of adjustment to a normal life. It is, what, twenty-eight years later? Of course she would still be seeking a career. Isn't that a great idea? And an opportunity to examine Hollywood today as against the time when she was a star in the twenties. I heartily endorse that idea."

Holden should have known better. That scenario sounds like a speech on prison reform by his buddy Ronald Reagan.

Holden, like Norma Desmond, had "moments of melancholy." Too many to count. But he also had moments of brilliant comedy. Onscreen, they were too few. I've always thought that in the right roles he could have been as droll as Cary Grant, or perhaps warm-and-cool funny at the same time like Paul Newman. In the hands of a brilliant director, Holden might have revealed the same glimmers of repressed madness that make Bill Murray a great comedian.

Holden's best comic role was on TV, in 1955. If you poll *I Love Lucy* fanatics on the funniest episodes, you'll almost always hear "Lucy at the Brown Derby with William Holden." (Officially titled "L.A. at Last.") Lunching with Fred and Ethel, Lucy spots Holden. She stares relentlessly at him until he stares back. And stares and stares. Lucy is so flustered that she loses control of a plate of spaghetti, which Ethel helpfully snips with a pair of scissors she just happens to have in her purse.

Later that day, Ricky surprises Lucy by bringing Bill Holden to their hotel to meet her. Embarrassed by the lunch encounter, she disguises herself with eyeglasses and a false nose. When Holden lights her cigarette, the nose catches fire.

Holden's timing is brilliant. He evokes hilarity without doing very much at all; his face merely registers astonishment, dismay, total bewilderment, and resignation at Lucy's antics. Holden, a stud version of Jack Benny, builds a classic performance by underplaying. His face acts as Lucy's mirror. Reflected in that deadpan looking glass, she's even funnier—but she's no funnier than Holden. (Jack Benny apparently noticed Holden's resemblance to himself. He loved the episode. When he learned that none of his own writing team had seen it, he arranged a special showing for them.)

I'm convinced that this classic *I Love Lucy* moment—her false nose ablaze thanks to Bill Holden—is an allusion to the scene in *Sunset Boulevard* where Holden waves a cigarette lighter in front of Nancy Olson's face to examine her nose job. Camera angles are similar, and so is Holden's facial expression.

If we start rounding up suspects, I'd finger Desilu cameraman Karl Freund as the comic culprit. As a director of phototography, first in Germany and later in Hollywood, he's in the same league as *Sunset Boulevard*'s John F. Seitz. In fact, Freund was one of the greats. Among his credits are Murnau's *The Last Laugh* (1924), Lang's *Metropolis* (1927), Tod Browning's *Dracula* (1931), and Cukor's *Camille* (1937).

One thing only in this Lucy episode isn't funny: the way Bill Holden seems to have aged ten years between 1950 and 1955.

It's hard to think of a movie with more right-wingers in it than *Sunset Boulevard*. Holden was one, though moderate compared to the rest: Hedda Hopper, Jack Webb, DeMille. Charles Brackett, producer and cowriter, leaned to the right, the opposite direction from Billy Wilder and Nancy Olson. (Swanson had capricious ideas in politics; she's best described as a pick-and-choose liberal.)

In 1956 Holden and a political bedfellow, Hedda Hopper, clashed because she considered him soft on communism. When Columbia announced that he would appear in *The Bridge on the River Kwai*, Hedda phoned him in a lather.

"You're not really going to make that picture for Sam Spiegel, are you, Bill?" she demanded.

"Hell, yes!" Holden answered. "It's one of the best scripts I've ever read."

"Yes, and you know who wrote it."

"Sure. Carl Foreman."

"A damned Red."

"I don't know anything about his politics. All I know is he has written a crackling good script."

"Bill, you can't do it! We can't let those Commies get their feet back in the industry now. And you, especially. You're one of the pillars of the community. You're respected as a solid, straight-thinking American. I'm telling you, Bill, you can't do that picture."

Holden exploded. "Goddammit, Hedda, since when are you or anybody else telling me what I can or cannot do? I've seen what you vigilantes have done to Larry Parks and a lot of other people. Well, don't start meddling in my life, because I won't stand for it." He slammed down the phone.

The outburst resulted in a permanent estrangement between Holden and Hedda Hopper. In the end, Columbia had second thoughts about Foreman. The *Kwai* script, on which Calder Willingham, Michael Wilson, and Pierre Boulle also worked, was credited only to Boulle.

Holden's salary for *The Bridge on the River Kwai*—$300,000 plus ten percent of the profits—made him the highest-paid film star in the world at that time.

About the same time as the Holden–Hopper quarrel, Wally Westmore, head of Paramount's makeup department, wrote an article for the *Saturday Evening Post* titled "I Make Up Hollywood." Here's what he said about Holden: "No actor now working in Hollywood has a harder or more athletic body than Bill Holden. If you saw him without his shirt in *Picnic*, you know what I mean.

"But Bill has human limitations, and when he's exhausted from making too many pictures in a row, the makeup artist who works on him must do a little highlighting under his eyes. Bill's tiredness shows there more than any place else. I don't say that he actually has circles under his eyes when he's bushed—let's just say his skin gets dark there. . . . Bill also needs a little makeup on his chin because his beard is so heavy that he must cover his five o'clock shadow."

Bob Thomas's *Golden Boy: The Untold Story of William Holden* opens with a scene that evokes *Sunset Boulevard*: "Monday morning, November 16, 1981. Police cars raced along Ocean Boulevard in Santa Monica, sirens shrilling, and converged on the Shoreham Tower, a thirteen-story apartment building overlooking the Pacific. An hour later, the news was released: William Holden, the movie star, had been found dead in his apartment."

But this time there was no voice-over. Instead, the Los Angeles County coroner theorized that Holden "had slipped on a throw rug, hit his head on the sharp corner of the bedside table, and fallen on the bed. . . . When the body was discovered, four or five days later, the television set in the bedroom was on, a movie script nearby." The coroner concluded that "the telephone had not been picked up." Bill Holden was too drunk to call for help.

The previous Saturday, November 14, Billy and Audrey Wilder had planned to visit Holden at his home in Palm Springs. They had already packed. Wilder wanted to get away, not only to visit Holden but also to take a break from *Buddy, Buddy*, the last film he would direct.

When Billy phoned Holden's home to confirm that they were on the way, the housekeeper told him Holden wasn't there. Nobody knew his whereabouts. Billy and Audrey unpacked and spent the weekend at home.

Two days later, when he learned of the death of his old friend, Wilder sounded like a character in one of his own *films noirs:* "To be killed by a bottle of vodka and a night table—what a lousy fadeout for a great guy."

Many years later, Billy Wilder spoke tenderly: "My love will always be with Mr. Holden."

Even the fickle heart of Hollywood is still with Mr. Holden. In 1999, the American Film Institute named him as one of the fifty stars who qualify as legends of American movies. The same year, film critic David Denby, writing in the *New Yorker*, summed up the appeal of Holden (and also of other male stars such as James Cagney and Spencer Tracy): "To become a movie star, an actor needs a certain density, a stubborn, immovable mass of being that an audience can rely on."

In Holden's case there's much more than density. Observe him in *Sunset Boulevard* and you see intense vulnerability. It's not on his sleeve, like James Dean's, nor does his emotional anguish burn through, like Brando's. But the pain, and his stoic repression of it, never depart. We can say of Joe Gillis, and perhaps of Bill Holden, that only at the end, when the body is empty of life, does the face uncrease. No longer frayed, the features have been washed and smoothed and laid out, as though for pleasant dreams.

chapter 19

Popcorn in Beverly Hills with Nancy

$\mathcal{I}$ visited Nancy Olson at her home on Alpine Drive in Beverly Hills on April 30, 1999. By happy coincidence, the date was a fiftieth anniversary of sorts, for *Sunset Boulevard* was filmed from mid-April to mid-June of 1949. Not even Olson, however, with her deep-focus memory, could pinpoint exactly what had happened on that midcentury April 30.

A movie star doesn't answer the door herself when you go to visit. A maid greeted me and led me to an understated sitting room whose sofa, armchairs, tables, paintings, and objects didn't proclaim themselves. I hadn't walked into *Architectural Digest*, I felt, but rather into a home. A few minutes later Nancy made an entrance, as actresses always do.

She strode briskly through the door as though onto the set of her own television show. I imagine that show as *Leave It to Nancy*, with Nancy playing a very youthful Golden Girls actress, her husband making the occasional droll appearance (as her real husband did that day), and their son, who's an independent filmmaker, popping up now and then with a one-liner such as "My mother's a narcissist, you know," as Nancy's real-life son did that afternoon.

In the virtual sitcom running through my head, there's a peculiar neighbor up the hill. Or maybe she's a tenant in some outlying room at Nancy's place. Either way, she's a weird old glamour puss who used to be big in silent pictures, and though she never appears full-face we hear a lot about her antics. In every episode the camera catches Mona Almond, let's call her, in long shot. Once she was dragging something heavy across the lawn toward the pool. Another time she swooped down Nancy's staircase, flinging and flailing bejeweled arms while she mouthed soundless words, then traipsed out the door to vanish in the leafy haze of Alpine Drive.

Every show needs a symbol, and this one isn't hard to figure out. She's the neurosis in the attic, the symbolic old age of starlets who never reached stardom—and of great stars who collapsed into black holes. She's the potential future that awaited Nancy Olson, a California sunbeam trapped in a Gothic nightmare, if Olson had veered off the Yellow Brick Road and onto Sunset Boulevard.

"I knew I couldn't handle Hollywood," Nancy says. "I survived it because I was so naive, and because I left town." And then she laughs. "I'm now too old to play Norma Desmond." (The extraordinary thing, from my point of view, is that Nancy looks too *young*. She has stumbled on the secret of the Gabors.)

Perhaps the most important thing to note about Nancy Olson (or Nancy Livingston, as she calls herself, using her married name) is that she inhabits Los Angeles but not Hollywood. By that I mean she never bought into the myths of Filmland, Tinseltown, the studios . . . or *Sunset Boulevard*. To the extent that Los Angeles is a "normal" city, Nancy Olson Livingston leads the regular life she might in Chicago, Atlanta, or Seattle.

She's a pianist, she and her husband often attend concerts and plays, and she's better known around Los Angeles as Nancy Livingston, board member of Gordon Davidson's Center Theatre Group and of the California Institute of the Arts, than as Nancy Olson, film actress.

When we met, Nancy was a couple of months shy of her seventy-second birthday. Her unlined face hasn't been drained of character, as sometimes happens to actresses of a certain age, and her petite, svelte figure implies lots of fresh vegetables and hold the red meat. (I forgot to ask whether Gloria Swanson gave her diet tips.) To my eyes Nancy Olson is more attractive now than at twenty-one, when she played Betty Schaeffer. She's lost that dollop of baby fat, and life has guided her—gently, I'd say—far beyond "Wholesome Olson" and an ingenue youth.

Show business always does a number. After long years in it you're either jaded—if you've retained some measure of success—or bitter if you haven't. In rare cases, when the ego finds offstage or offcamera nourishment from life, and when there's plenty of non-box-office money, one retires from show business as from industry or nursing. It's a slow glide back down, with no bumps. Deanna Durbin comes to mind, reportedly happy for the past half century and living in wealthy retirement in France. Dina Merrill is another. Extremely rich, she is now, as always, an attractive socialite for whom Hollywood seemed an avocation, like orchid growing or scrimshaw.

And yet the word "retire" doesn't quite fit the usual retreat from show business. Except for Garbo, one steps back while remaining available. Although Nancy Olson's last significant film role was in *Making Love* (1982), she often appears in TV documentaries about Billy Wilder, William Holden, or Paramount. She speaks at tributes and talks to interviewers about costars from the past. Curiously, no one seems to have queried her before in depth about filming *Sunset Boulevard*.

Now that age and infirmity prevent Billy Wilder's attending most functions, Olson, the only surviving cast member apart from bit players, has become ex officio spokesperson, the authority on matters pertaining to *Sunset Boulevard*.

The day after I met her, she made an appearance at the Alex Theatre in Glendale, a restored movie palace from the twenties. On May 1, 1999, an audience of fourteen hundred filled every seat in the house to watch a new print of *Sunset Boulevard*. At a wine and cheese reception in the theatre lobby before the screening, Jane Withers rushed over (as though making a guest appearance on *Leave It to Nancy*) and exchanged air kisses with Olson and two or three others. Once the theatre had filled up, L.A. TV and radio personality Tom Hatten, the emcee, interviewed Olson onstage. Then the curtain rose, a hush fell over the house, and the ominous *Sunset Boulevard* music accelerated every pulse.

In a phone conversation several days later, Olson told me she hadn't seen the picture on a big screen for about twenty years. "I hadn't planned to stay that night," she said. "But I started watching, and I became fascinated by the audience response. So I stayed until the end. What surprised me was the laughter, and in all the right places." She had remembered a darker *Sunset Boulevard* but realized that evening, perhaps for the first time, that it's full of laughs, and each one intended.

The day I called on her at home, we talked at length about filming *Sunset Boulevard*. Much of what she told me appears earlier in this book. But I wanted to know everything, including the filler. For example, "Did you and Gloria Swanson actually talk on the phone during that scene near the end when she tips you off that Joe Gillis is her gigolo?"

"Yes," Olson said. "And earlier, when I phoned Norma's house asking for Joe, I talked with Erich von Stroheim in real time." Asked about working with Swanson, Olson describes her famous costar as "extremely cordial. Gracious, excited about the film, and determined to make it wonderful."

All of Olson's comments indicate harmonious filmmaking by an ensemble of pros. There were no star turns, no demands, no tantrums. All of this helps explain how Wilder and his cast were able to work with an unfinished script under conditions that might have led to chaos.

Specifically, most scenes in the film involve two or three actors, viz. Swanson, Holden, Stroheim, each one razor sharp, disciplined, and experienced. Another important point is this: all in the cast so closely resembled the characters they played that they could bring off their performances almost by instinct, without really knowing where the script was headed. Seen from this angle, Norma Desmond is the darker side of Swanson; Stroheim had sunk from greatness to menial servant roles; Holden had already begun to unravel. And Nancy Olson was indeed an ingenue.

"I'm going to get a Diet Coke," Olson announces. "Would you like one?"

This breaks the intensity of our interview. We lighten up. "This might interest you," Nancy says. "The cameraman and Billy would go into a little huddle, they would discuss where they wanted the camera, how they wanted the angle, where they wanted the over-the-shoulder shot. They put me in profile a lot. One day the cameraman told me, 'The camera likes you in profile.'"

I had arrived at Nancy Olson's under the impression that she was a widow. Although I had read about her two marriages, none of my research came from recently published sources, so that when a friend in Los Angeles told me he thought her husband was deceased, I accepted the information. I knew that the name of her second husband was Alan Livingston.

At a certain point in our conversation a door to the sitting room slowly opened. The door paused, then opened a little more. I glanced up but saw no one. Then Nancy exclaimed, "The ghost of Alan Livingston!" And a man well on in years entered the room.

For an instant I spun offbalance. Fortunately, I had the aplomb not to blurt something gauche. (After all, I'm only a guest on *Leave It to Nancy*.)

Alan Livingston joined us. He sat down beside me on the sofa and promptly dozed. Nancy and I went on talking. When she noticed the nap in progress, she called from her armchair in an Ethel Mertz voice: "Alan, are we *boring* you? Go and sleep somewhere else."

"I've heard this story before," he drawled.

It's obvious they're crazy about one another. That's why they're so good at this Ma and Pa Kettle in Beverly Hills routine. She told me more about how she survived studio-era Hollywood.

I realized that on one level working in the movies granted me privileged access to the world. I would know people I never would have met had I married a doctor or lawyer and stayed in Milwaukee. I had entree to a world of artists. That's the positive side.

But I understood, also, what went with it: a distortion of my life, my relationships, of my own family. I would be tainted by the system that created me as a movie star. Those who wanted to use me for their own purposes would exploit me.

You see, I was never an artist, I was never a great actress. I was good at it, I had a flair. I was smart, for me it looked like a great adventure. I believe I would have been better off as a writer. Or a pianist. I'm very musical. That's much harder, though. Much harder. Acting is easy because it feeds the ego like forbidden fruit.

As though we're nearing a commercial break, the star of our show announces, "Who wants popcorn? I'm going to make a big bowl." She leaves the room to her husband, who's managed to keep napping during our solemn colloquy.

It takes only one cue—"I'd like to hear about your career, also"—to jolt Alan Livingston from understudy to star performer. He springs alive, full of pep and ten years younger.

"I came to Los Angeles in 1946 and took a job at Capitol Records," he said. There he created a character called Bozo the Clown. "I designed an album where Bozo talked to the animals," Livingston explained. "Bozo on the record said, 'Every time I blow my whistle you turn the page.' It was a smash hit and sold over a million copies, which was unheard of in children's records." In 1955 he moved from Capitol to NBC, where, as vice president, he produced the hit Western *Bonanza.*

Nancy's back. "I made popcorn. Would you like some?"

We don't hear her. We're on the Sinatra years, for Livingston has back-tracked to the early fifties, before he left Capitol for NBC. "Frank was broke, in debt. Ava Gardner had left him, so emotionally he was a mess. The president of the William Morris Agency called to ask if I would consider signing Sinatra. He went on to record 'Young at Heart,' which was a hit." Later, Alan Livingston released the bulk of the Sinatra library on Capitol LPs.

One day in 1964 Livingston got a phone call. His secretary announced that a man named Brian Epstein was on the line from London. He told Livingston he represented a singing group called the Beatles. Epstein said, "Will you listen to some of their records?"

"We decided on one," Livingston said, "and I brought it home to Nancy, who is musical."

He played it for her.

Livingston: "I think these boys will change the whole record business."

Nancy: (imitates her 1964 incredulity) "'I Want to Hold Your Hand'? Are you kidding me?"

Livingston: "And the rest is history. Biggest thing Capitol ever had."

Long before the Beatles, however, Nancy Olson's years were filled with music.

In the fall of 1949 Alan Jay Lerner happened to be in Hollywood to write the story and screenplay for *An American in Paris*. One day he picked up the *Los Angeles Times* and read an item in Hedda Hopper's column: "Everybody's talking about the new girl at Paramount. She's from Wisconsin, her father's a doctor, and she's quite a . . ." Hedda ran a picture of the new girl in town.

Nancy Olson married Alan Jay Lerner on March 10, 1950—five months before *Sunset Boulevard* was released. He said later that he finished the script of *An American in Paris* the night before their wedding. "I sat down at eight that evening and wrote sixty pages. Somehow I ended it and I never changed anything."

Neither her Academy Award nomination as Best Supporting Actress nor her loss to elderly Josephine Hull impressed Nancy unduly. That's because in the early fifties she came close to personifying every romantic song in the repertoire, by Lerner or anyone else. Love, youth, happiness, moon-June-spoon, and making whoopee. Two daughters, Liza in 1951 and Jennifer in 1953, made Nancy the ideal fifties woman. She had curtailed her career even before she really had it to be wife to one of the most successful men in America, and mother to his children.

The couple lived in New York, where Nancy often appeared on television. She commuted to Hollywood for the occasional film assignment.

From the start, Nancy fell in step with Lerner and his musical friends. "We used to go to Ira Gershwin's every Saturday night," she recalls. "There was Oscar Levant playing the piano, with Judy Garland beside him, singing. Ira would make up lyrics about everybody in the room. For instance—" and Olson sings one of those impromptu Gershwin tunes: "Could you coo, could you care/For little Nancy in that chair . . ."

The roster of others in attendance at those soirees sounds like a Tin Pan Alley roll call: Arthur Schwartz and Howard Dietz, Burton Lane, Harold Arlen. Olson says, "They sang their old songs and their new ones. And Vincente Minnelli would sit quietly somewhere while Judy was singing, and their enchanting little girl, Liza, would play under the piano. Sometimes Oscar would play this"—and Olson sings another Gershwin song, this time a few bars from "Liza," beginning "Liza, Liza, skies of gray." (That's how Nancy's daughter got her name.) Olson's singing voice is very pleasant, her phrasing sophisticated. You can tell she learned from the best people in the world. (When I phone later with follow-up questions I pretend I don't recall the lyric just so she'll sing it for me.)

While married to Lerner, Nancy Olson watched the birth and development of *My Fair Lady*. Lerner, the lyricist and book writer, and his collaborator, Frederick Loewe, wrote much of the show in a studio near the Lerners' country home in Rockland County, New York. Late one night during a snow storm Nancy Olson woke up to find Lerner and Loewe, in mufflers and boots, standing at the foot of her bed, clamoring, "Nancy, wake up. You've got to come over and listen to this! Please!"

So at 3:00 A.M. she trudged through a blizzard to hear their new number. "They started to read the dialogue for me and explain the scene," Olson remembers. "Eliza Doolittle's accent is hopeless, Henry Higgins and Colonel Pickering are exhausted, they've given up, when all of a sudden she says, quietly, 'The rain in Spain falls mainly on the plain.' Perfectly.

"Okay, all of a sudden Fritz [Loewe] races to the piano and starts to play. And they start the song: 'The Rain in Spain.' Alan picks up a pillow. He says, 'This is Eliza, Nancy.' And he waltzes the pillow around the room. They end it with Fritz jumping up from the piano, grabbing Alan's hand, and they collapse on the sofa. They were beside themselves with excitement.

"I said, 'You've got one terrible problem.' They screamed, 'OH NO, WHAT DO YOU MEAN, NANCY, THIS IS BRILLIANT.' I said, 'You've got a terrible problem. You're going to stop the show dead in its tracks. The first time the audience hears this, they'll go beserk. The actors won't be able to continue.'

"And of course the first night in New Haven, that song stopped the show. People yelled, stomped their feet, they loved it so much the show couldn't go on. Rex [Harrison] panicked. He whispered to Julie [Andrews], 'What are we going to do?' She said, 'Get up and take a bow.' From then on, of course, 'The Rain in Spain' always stopped the show."

Alan Jay Lerner, in his 1978 book *The Street Where I Live*, tells a different version of how this show-stopper came to be. "Walking to the office from auditions one day, we began to discuss how to end the sequence of Eliza's lessons. I said to Fritz, 'Why don't we just do a number in which all that she had done wrong she now does correctly?' Fritz nodded approvingly. 'Like what?' he asked.

"'Well,' I replied, 'her main difficulty is with the letter *A* so why don't we call it "The Rain in Spain?"' Fritz thought for a moment and said, 'Good. I'll write a tango.'

"We went up to the office. He sat down at the piano and somehow, from somewhere, he played the main theme of 'The Rain in Spain.' I took out a pad and pencil and wrote the next two lines. He set them immediately. Then the next two. Then the conclusion. I do not believe the entire effort took more than ten minutes."

Normally one would trust a songwriter's memory more than his wife's. But Lerner, after ditching Nancy Olson, expunged references to her from his life and writings. Less than an ex-wife, she became a non-person in Lernerland. By 1978, when he set down his memoirs, Lerner had been married eight times, like Bluebeard. Olson, wife number three, gets scarcely a word in the book.

The real reason I find his account unconvincing, however, is because it's prosaic. No matter whose memory works better, "The Rain in Spain" deserves to have been written in the middle of a blizzard, with composers jumping to the piano and waltzing pillows around the room while begging approval from a sleepy actress. The song is too witty and wonderful to have been born in an office, like ad copy. That show-stopper needs a story behind it that stops the show. But Lerner's only retards it.

———————

In February 1955 Nancy appeared in a live television production of *The Women*. Two cast members from George Cukor's 1939 film also appeared in this version: Paulette Goddard, this time as Sylvia (played by Rosalind Russell in the movie) and Mary Boland, recreating the Countess. Shelley Winters played Crystal. Mary Astor, Cathleen Nesbitt, Ruth Hussey, and Pat Carroll costarred, with Valerie Bettis as Miriam, Paulette Goddard's role in the film.

Olson told me a story about *The Women* that I've revisited again and again, like a box of chocolates. My question was, "Did the TV production have as much wit and bite as the movie?" The memory, not my question, startled her.

"Shelley Winters and Paulette Goddard got into a fist fight and hair pulling," she said. "It frightened me so much. I've never witnessed anything like it."

"Do you mean as part of the show?"

"No! During rehearsal. Oh! It was unbelievable. Two women leaping, trying to scratch each other's eyes out."

"What was the cat fight about?"

"I don't remember. Something stupid. But I was horrified. I just couldn't believe it."

"Did they duplicate the fight oncamera?"

"It's a blur. At that point my marriage was already in a lot of trouble, and I had two little girls."

Olson, to judge by the look of stupefaction that crossed her face, still sees that fight in jungle red. The only reason I cross-examined her, that day and later, is that the story duplicates the famous bitch fight in the movie. Could life so sublimely imitate a script? If so, the imitation erred in one detail. In the play and the film, the brawlers are Miriam and Sylvia, not Sylvia and Crystal.

The reason I wondered whether Nancy's recall might have veered is because Shelley Winters and Paulette Goddard worked together again, apparently without a snarl, in the Italian film *Gli Indifferenti* (1964). Here's Winters on Goddard in her second memoir, *Shelley II*: "I think my scenes with Paulette Goddard were very funny. I had worked with her in *The Women*. . . . She was indeed fun to work with in this [later] film, rather zany, and she would tell me long, rambling stories about how stingy Charlie Chaplin was."

It's possible, of course, that nine years after their knock-down-drag-out, the two high-octane ladies decided to air-kiss and make up.

Later in 1955, when Lerner and Loewe were in the middle of *My Fair Lady* and Mr. and Mrs. Lerner had moved into Manhattan for the production, one song remained for the show. Lerner called his wife from the office and asked her to come over. He was stuck.

"It was about four o'clock in the afternoon," Nancy recalls. "Alan said, 'I have the hardest thing to do. I don't want to tamper with Shaw's play so I can't have Higgins just express that he's in love with Eliza. On the other hand, I can't let the audience feel that he's not smitten, or that he isn't truly in love with her. So I have to write a love song.'"

"I said, 'Well, Alan, I don't know how you'll solve it but would you like a cup of tea?' So I went to the kitchen and organized the tea tray. As I came down the little narrow stairs in his studio-office, he looked up at me and said, 'You know, Nancy, you really are a very pretty girl.' I said, 'Thanks a lot' and I set the tea tray down. He said, 'I wake up with you every morning, I'm with you all day, I go to bed with you at night—I forget that I've just become accustomed to you. Can you believe it? I've become accustomed to your face.'"

Boing! Boing!

"And he raced over to the desk, grabbed his paper and pencil and wrote down, 'I've . . . grown . . . accustomed . . . to . . . her . . . face.'"

My Fair Lady opened in New York at the Mark Hellinger Theatre on March 15, 1956, and ran for 2,717 performances. The published score bears this dedication: "For Nancy, With Love."

But Alan Jay Lerner didn't stay accustomed to her face. One afternoon he came home and "just like that, no warning or anything," he asked Nancy for a divorce. In Paris, where *Gigi* (scored by Lerner and Loewe) was being filmed, he had met Micheline Muselli Pozzo di Borgo. He brought her home with him.

Devastated, Nancy Olson phoned her mother in Los Angeles and said, "I'm in serious trouble, but I'd like to be alone for twenty-four hours. Then, please come and see me." Twenty-four tear-drenched hours later, her mother found her in a state of semishock.

Naive girls from the heartland usually keep their wits about them, even when they're no longer girls, and even in Hollywood and New York. Nancy Olson picked herself up, brushed herself off, got a divorce settlement reported at the time as three million dollars, and sailed for Europe with her two young daughters.

She resumed her screen career: *Pollyanna* (1960), *The Absent Minded Professor* (1961), *Son of Flubber* (1963). In 1962 she married Alan Livingston, and their son, Christopher, was born in 1964.

Life has been good to Nancy Olson, and she knows it. The things she told me about her life with Alan Jay Lerner had the ring of an old silver chime that summons mellow, vanished days. She recalled the high-toned life of Broadway hits and country houses, of melodies composed and plays in rehearsal, of being seen around New York in all the smart cafes. But, like anyone who has been betrayed, she carries antibodies formed by anguish. In all such cases, a trace of hurt will always brush the lips just when it's least expected, often in a litany of well-being.

"My big regret," she said, not bitterly but with an emotion echoing nostalgia, "is that I married Alan Lerner, who tried to extinguish the spirit of that girl I was."

"Hi, beautiful," Nancy's son greets her when he makes his entrance.

She giggles, then croons, "Oh, thank you."

She tells Christopher, "I had just said that you never saw *Sunset Boulevard* until you went to college."

He confesses that's not quite the case. Referring to his half sister, Jennifer Lerner, he says, "Jenny showed it to me once when I was probably eight or nine. I kept saying, 'Where's Mom? Where's Mom?' I didn't recognize you."

Nancy, to Christopher: "I didn't know that. But when you saw it in college, you said I reminded you of Granny."

Christopher Livingston is an independent filmmaker. When our conversation took place, his film *Hit and Runway* had just won an award for best screenplay at the L.A. Film Festival. His next project, he told me, had the working title *Alpine Drive*. I was all ears for his synopsis: "It's about a young man directing a star, who's his mother. I think the movie will open with the mother floating in the pool, facedown. The opening line would be, 'I'd like you to meet my mother.'"

Nancy chimed in as though auditioning: "The body is floating, you see, so it looks dead. But—" And she clued me in, but I promised not to reveal a word of it.

Christopher added, "Just as *Sunset Boulevard* took a silent star and brought her to a movie set with sound equipment, we're going to take a Golden Age star and bring her on in the present day."

Alan Livingston has joined us again. Another bowl of popcorn has appeared, along with Diet Cokes.

This leads back to Nancy's escape from Hollywood's depredations. "In my family we were all very close, very straight with each other," she said. "Then suddenly, after I got a contract at Paramount, my brother, my father, my mother—they assigned me to a special category. Part reverence, part resentment. Their attitude went something like this: You have so much; you are being given so much; you are so singled out."

I asked whether that led to actual conflict with members of her family.

She paused for a long moment. "Yes. In particular with my mother. That relationship was difficult anyway. My mother treated me as if I were her younger sister, and as though I must share everything with her."

For a little while we trod the Oprah path of movie star daughters and the mothers who siblingize them. At the end of what must have been a difficult reminiscence, Nancy Olson made a deft turn out of the spotlight. Befitting a mother who's not at all in competition, she focused on her son.

"One night Chris called me from Connecticut College and said, 'Mom, a group of us from the dorm are going to the Classic Film Society. They're showing *Sunset Boulevard*. I'll call you later and let you know how they like it.'

"When he called later he said, 'Mom! You know what I thought when I was watching that? You look so much like Grandmother,' meaning my mother. He told me he understood his grandmother much better. Because when she looked up on that screen, she saw herself."

Christopher spoke. "That must have been hard for her, to look up at her daughter on the big screen and think, That should have been me."

Nancy's fillip brings us to an upbeat ending. "At the end of the phone conversation Chris said, 'Some of the guys in the dorm would like a picture.' I said, 'Christopher! Of your old mother?' And he said, 'Oh, not a picture of you now, a picture of you then.'"

She shrugged. "You see how it gets?"

The camera pulls back from *Leave It to Nancy.* "How did I come off?" laughs Nancy.

Suddenly I realize—all these hours, with Nancy starring, and not once did she demand a close-up.

chapter 20

"Buttons and Bows"

S heldrake, the Paramount producer who has just turned down Joe Gillis's pitch of his latest story idea: "Of course, we're always looking for a Betty Hutton. Do you see it as a Betty Hutton?"

Gillis doesn't, of course. And another script for Betty Hutton would have been superfluous; she was all over the place at Paramount. She even had a past and future connection with *Sunset Boulevard* other than a throw-away line in the script.

In *The Stork Club* (1945) she belted out "A Square in a Social Circle," composed by Jay Livingston and Ray Evans. Hutton was the first major star to sing one of their songs in a picture. She was by no means the last, for this composing team wrote some of the most famous songs to come out of Hollywood, including "Que Será, Será," "Buttons and Bows," and "Mona Lisa."

They're also the men at the piano in Jack Webb's crowded apartment on New Year's Eve, when Joe Gillis makes a failed attempt to escape from Norma's claws. And Jay Livingston is Alan Livingston's older brother. (Alan Livingston, coincidentally, was once married to Betty Hutton.)

In a sense, Jay Livingston and Ray Evans have maintained for more than sixty years what Billy Wilder and Charles Brackett claimed for a decade: the happiest marriage in Hollywood. Surely theirs is one of the longest collaborations, and one of the most successful, in show business.

Although the men say that away from work they're not best friends, they've spent their lives as close as twins.

Livingston was born on February 4, 1915, near Pittsburgh, Evans on March 28 of the same year in upstate New York. They met in Philadelphia at the University of Pennsylvania in 1933. Later, in New York and then in Los Angeles, they roomed together. In 1947 these men whose first names rhyme married women whose names also rhyme: Livingston married Lynne, Evans married Wynn. (Many years later Lynne died and Livingston remarried.) How can it be that they're not best friends? They believe that when a partnership works as well as theirs has, you shouldn't analyze it too much.

Success came in the midforties when Paramount hired them for the musical equivalent of odd jobs. They wrote special material for two-reel shorts, the kind of musical fillers that turn up on cable networks like AMC and Turner. (Livingston wrote the music, and both men wrote lyrics.)

Ray Evans explains that these shorts were often shown in theatres along with the main picture in lieu of a double feature. "The singers might be cabaret stars," he says, "or singers who weren't quite famous. We wrote whatever they needed. If it was a Latin number, we'd write a Latin song. Or a French song. Or a comedy song."

Betty Hutton's razzle-dazzle interpretation of "A Square in a Social Circle" put Livingston and Evans securely on the map at Paramount. What established them forever on the musical map, however, was another song they wrote for a picture—which wasn't used in the picture. Victor Young wrote the background score for Paramount's *To Each His Own*, starring Olivia de Havilland. He refused to write a title song, however, because, as Evans puts it, "he thought it was a dumb title. We were low men on the totem pole, so they came to us with the assignment. We wrote 'To Each His Own' and it became one of the biggest hits of the forties. According to the trade papers, for several weeks in 1947 five of the top ten best-selling records in the United States were different versions of that song."

Jay Livingston adds, "Few people realize that our song put the expression into the language. Since then, everybody says, 'Well, to each his own.'"

Their next song to enter the repertoire was "Golden Earrings," title song of the 1947 picture starring Marlene Dietrich and Ray Milland. "Buttons and Bows," sung by Bob Hope in *The Paleface* (1948), became a huge hit when recorded by Dinah Shore. Livingston and Evans won their first Oscar for it. (Oscar number two was for "Mona Lisa," from the film *Captain Carey, U.S.A.* (1950), and "Que Será, Será," sung by Doris Day in *The Man Who Knew Too Much* (1956), won them their third Academy Award.)

Livingston and Evans had been friends with Billy Wilder for several years before the spring of 1949 when he asked them to compose a number for *Sunset Bouelvard*. According to Jay Livingston, "Paramount was a friendly place, a democratic place, and everybody knew each other well there. We first met Billy in the commissary, where we all ate lunch. The writers' table was right near ours."

They Did Lunch

Pauline Kessinger, who ran the Paramount commissary for almost forty years, knew everyone at the studio. Interviewed in 1976, a few years after retirement, she recounted a culinary history of Paramount. "I went to work there as a waitress [circa 1928] just to see the stars," she said. In 1935 she was promoted to manager.

Like other studio commissaries, Paramount's had specialties on the menu named for various luminaries, i.e., turkey and eggs à la Crosby. Kessinger, who dreamed up many of these dishes, revealed a secret: "The only player that did *not* want his name on the menu was Bill Holden. He was a very unassuming person."

It was customary to throw a lavish party in the commissary at the end of an important picture. "On *Sunset Boulevard*," Kessinger remembered, "the whole dining room was converted into a beautiful nightclub with a dance floor. And we sprayed the place with perfume."

The writers' table, a more quotidian affair, might be said to have been sprayed with wit. Wilder and Brackett often lunched there, along with cronies. During the meal they played what they called "the Word Game." According to Kessinger, "Edith Head would often sit with them and she would nearly always beat them at their game."

Other specialty tables, according to Kessinger, included "a cameramen's table, Mr. DeMille's table, and a set dressers' table. At that time, until the last few years I was there, none of the big stars asked for reserved tables. They would just come in and take a table, catch as catch can."

Reading her reminiscences, it's easy to believe that "everybody liked to work at Paramount in the old days." She called it "a very friendly studio, and a very democratic studio." Her descriptions make the commissary sound like a perpetual movie set rather than a place people flocked to when they left work. "Oh, it was a glorious place! The dining room would be filled with people in full dress clothes. Men with white tie and tails, the women in evening gowns, others would be raggedy people, and miners," she said.

"It was a sea of tables. The reason they originally opened the commissary was to keep the personnel on the lot: stars, craftsmen, and everybody. Otherwise they would go off to different restaurants around Hollywood, the Brown Derby, the Montmartre. And the stars wouldn't come back to work. The studio didn't expect to make money on the commissary, and they never did.

"During the 1930s, we had eighty-two employees. And we had four cafes: a back lot cafe, a coffee shop, a private dining room, and the main dining room. And slowly, as the picture business went, you might say, on the rocks, they started closing the different departments. The back lot cafe went first, and when I left, in 1970, we only had the dining room and the private dining room open."

Ray Evans adds, "Billy wanted a song for the party scene in *Sunset Boulevard*. He told us to include as many inside references as possible. And he wanted us to perform it in the picture." The song they wrote was called "The Paramount-Don't-Want-Me Blues." It starts out, "I got those Paramount-don't-want-me/ Warner Brothers-only-taunt-me/ And-the-others-seem-to-flaunt-me blues," and matches *Sunset Boulevard* itself with references to the Hollywood establishment, including Selznick, Schary, Goldwyn, Zanuck, Metro, RKO, Hedda and Louella, and Schwab's.

Evans and Livingston, on a studio publicity junket to promote a Paramount picture with John Payne and Rhonda Fleming called *The Eagle and the Hawk*, had reached Texas when a telegram arrived from the studio. "We had to come back because they planned to shoot our scene in Billy's picture in a few days," says Evans.

"What do we do?" these polished songwriters who were amateurs before a movie camera asked Wilder. "Act like songwriters," Wilder told them, as though it's the most obvious thing in the world.

"We started the song," Evans recalls. "Billy said, 'Cut. Stop. You don't look like you're having fun.' Jay said, 'I'm not.' He's kind of withdrawn, not an exhibitionist like me. I was having a great time."

Wilder knew how to loosen them up. He herded several starlets and extras from the party scene over to the piano. "He put one girl in my lap," Evans says. "I was sitting there with her, two or three girls leaned over Jay, and several others sat on the upright piano and dangled their legs over the side. Of course we smiled, and Billy shot the scene."

They finished the song—neither man recalls whether they did it in one take—then Wilder said, "Just for protection and just for the fun of it, do some of 'Buttons and Bows.'" They did so, and Wilder filmed it.

Months later, at the disastrous preview in Evanston, Illinois, that almost sank *Sunset Boulevard*, the audience didn't get "The Paramount-Don't-Want-Me Blues." Wilder phoned from Chicago: "No one here ever heard of Schwab's Drug Store. Your song is out, it's *too* inside." The snippet of "Buttons and Bows" stayed in the picture. "So we're immortal because our names are in the credits," Evans laughs, "and we're seen as young men in 1950."

Songs by Livingston and Evans have sold roughly 300 million records and countless pages of sheet music. Besides the songs you might sing in the shower, there's the Christmas hit, "Silver Bells," from *The Lemon Drop Kid* (1951). By contrast, who wants to remember, but who can shake off, novelty songs done for *Aaron Slick from Punkin Crick* (1952): "Purt Nigh, but Not Plumb," "Chores," and "Saturday Night in Punkin Crick." Or Sophia Loren's goofy number from *Houseboat* (1958), "Bing! Bang! Bong!" Not to mention the va-va-va-voom "36-24-36" from *A Private's Affair* (1959).

Wilder called on the team again for his 1951 picture *The Big Carnival* (originally titled *Ace in the Hole*). He instructed them to write "the worst song you can, with bad rhymes and everything else bad." And they did. It's "We're Coming, Leo"—a promotional ditty to lure gawkers to the site where a man is trapped in a mine cave-in. (The picture flopped, perhaps because it told people too much about themselves.)

In 1959, Alan Livingston, as producer, hired his brother and Ray Evans to write the theme for *Bonanza*. Jay Livingston says they "knocked off 'Bonanza' in a few hours, and it has been very, very lucrative for us." They also wrote the theme song for *Mr. Ed*, with vocal by Jay Livingston. The show ran from 1961 to 1965.

Their real music, singable and sunny, drew Nancy Olson to their office at Paramount during intermissions from filming *Sunset Boulevard*. After she married Alan Livingston in 1962, he told her that his brother, Jay, used to tell him about "this girl from Wisconsin at the studio, and she doesn't seem like a movie actress. She's very attractive and very interesting. Alan said, 'Really? What's her name?' And that was the end of it, until about thirteen years later, when we were married."

chapter 21

Men in Uniform

*W*ith enormous and calculated irony, Billy Wilder cast Erich von Stroheim as a butler who once was Norma Desmond's director. In real life Stroheim, a supporting player grown old, had been a great director of silent films. He directed Gloria Swanson in the ill-fated *Queen Kelly*, still considered both a silent mastepiece and a notorious bomb.

Wilder's casting of Stroheim, like Stroheim's performance, exceeds most such brilliant decisions. That's because Stroheim as Max von Mayerling stands not only as a monument for those who know nothing of silent movies, but also because, for those acquainted with Hollywood's ancient history, this Babylonian monument (born in Vienna) comes with vast art history attached. Stroheim stands, but he also stands in: as *Sunset Boulevard*'s male Norma Desmond, he reflects himself and every other star/director who used to be big. Unlike Norma, who's still tops in her own eyes, Stroheim's sad face tells the whole truth. This genius, robbed of illusions, perceives how minuscule he's become.

In the Old World he was Erich Oswald Stroheim, son of a Jewish hatmaker who had emigrated from Prussian Silesia to the capital of the Hapsburg Empire. He debarked in the New World a self-anointed noble: Erich von Stroheim, soon a convert to Roman Catholicism.

Euro-American show business is full of such stock characters, bogus barons and countesses from Hoboken. But there's no Germanic equivalent of vaudeville, and so Stroheim's hefty myth assumed Wagnerian proportions. This notorious fabricator invented a distinguished military career for himself, implying brave deeds as an officer in the legions of Austria-Hungary. Later he postured as D. W. Griffith's assistant director on *Birth of a Nation*—a tale as unfactual as Tannhäuser or the "Sängerkrieg auf Wartburg."

Some charlatans drive you nuts, others make you want to spit, and a few gain absolution when greatness defeats deception. Who could begrudge Stroheim's hocus-pocus? By filming his own lies, he became a Founding Father of Hollywood. If anyone ever carves a gaudy Rushmore in Griffith Park, the noble heads enshrined will be D. W. Griffith, Stroheim, C. B. DeMille, and Charlie Chaplin.

Stroheim's beginning was inauspicious. In 1915 he appeared as an extra in a four-reeler, *Captain Macklin*, now lost. Soon he advanced to supporting roles and sometimes worked as assistant director on a picture. It's possible he served in some minor capacity on *Intolerance* in 1916, although the Stroheim expert Arthur Lennig states that he is not visible in existing prints. In 1919 he persuaded Carl Laemmle of Universal to let him direct *Blind Husbands*, the only one of Stroheim's pictures that escaped studio mutilation. Prior to release, Universal nevertheless dropped Stroheim's title, *The Pinnacle*, and added its own. Furious, the director said to Laemmle, and to the press, "It is my masterpiece and I will not let anyone spoil it." (Thirty years later, Norma Desmond defended her *Salome* script: "I will not have it butchered!")

Foolish Wives (1922) *was* butchered: from the original thirty-two reels to eighteen, then fourteen, then ten, finally seven. A 1972 restoration, by Arthur Lennig, came to eleven reels.

Merry-Go-Round (1923) was Stroheim's picture until Irving G. Thalberg, the new head of production at Universal, removed him because of budget overruns and general excess. Years later, Stroheim claimed a left-handed distinction: "I was the first director in the history of motion pictures to be taken off during the making of a film." The picture was completed by Rupert Julian.

If Stroheim is a Founding Father, then his Declaration of Independence is *Greed* (1924). In this case, alas, the Redcoats won. There was war in Hollywood. Stroheim fought against MGM, and prevailed not.

Only a madman would have filmed virtually every page, every subplot, every incident of the Frank Norris novel, *McTeague*. Stroheim was that madman. Originally forty-two reels, running time nine hours plus, the film was doomed. Stroheim cut it to twenty-four reels. When Louis B. Mayer and Thalberg (seemingly out to get Stroheim) finished whittling *Greed*, the release print ran about 135 minutes, or ten reels.

In 1999 film restorer Rick Schmidlin produced the closest possible approximation to Stroheim's greatest masterpiece. Using existing footage, the 330-page continuity script dated March 31, 1923, and some 600 stills from the Motion Picture Academy, Schmidlin and his editor, Glenn Morgan, added about two hours to this magnificent ruin. They even colorized certain scenes, as Stroheim intended, including the final one. Schmidlin's haunting guess at what might have been: "I don't think up until *Citizen Kane* there would have been a stronger film [than *Greed*]. I think cinema history would have been entirely different, and we might have had in this country a much more exciting cinema, a cinema that we lost."

At the end of *Greed*, Stroheim, like the vengeful Jehovah, punishes human folly with biblical finality. The judgment meted out surpasses any horrific irony in Poe, Hitchcock, Paul Bowles, or other masters of the dreadful. Stroheim's ending also transcends the novel's.

On the frying sands of Death Valley, two men, McTeague (played by Gibson Gowland) and Marcus (Jean Hersholt), lay claim to a wealth of gold. Water supply depleted, they vie for the gold they treasure over life itself. Marcus attempts to grab the loot. They struggle. McTeague shoots Marcus, killing him, but not before Marcus slips a pair of handcuffs on them both: a dead man and a man still alive, yoked by greed and both aflame in hell. *Greed* ends with the golden sun burning forever in the ghastly sky.

"The history of each Stroheim film is a nightmare," wrote Arthur Lenning in his biography of the prodigious, persecuted god. And yet Stroheim's vision underwent less mutilation in *The Merry Widow* (1925) than in any other film he made. Thalberg edited it, which displeased Stroheim, but at least he cut with scissors and not a chainsaw.

The story already verged on senility: A prince (John Gilbert) woos a rich American widow (Mae Murray). Under the wrinkles, however, *The Merry Widow* shimmers with the erotic play of *A Midsummer Night's Dream*. You can see how it influenced Billy Wilder, for it's full of unexpected directorial touches and sly gags, some of which manage to appear innocent and suggestive at the same time. The film is graceful, light on its feet. Every move by every actor seems choreographed. As always in Stroheim's films, the director's fetishes try to jump onscreen and displace studio-imposed morality. Wilder and many others may have learned a big lesson in subversive technique from this silent operetta. (Even mute it's more musical than Lubitsch's version of 1934, a fallen soufflé with Jeanette MacDonald and Maurice Chevalier.)

Stroheim's career is a museum of depressing exhibits. *The Wedding March* (1928), thirty-plus reels cut to twelve. *The Honeymoon*, also in 1928, was severely cut. And worse. Intended as a continuation of *The Wedding March*, it is, as Arthur Lennig points out, "a difficult film to assess for the simple reason that the sole remaining print was destroyed in 1957."

If you wish to see a silent picture about a convent girl in Europe who inherits a whorehouse in German East Africa, sails off to claim a legacy that includes an employee named Coughdrops ("A lady of the horizontal profession," per intertitle), is forced into marriage with a syphillitic old lecher by the bedside of her dying aunt while a leering priest reads wedding vows and last rites simultaneously—here's the picture to see: *Queen Kelly*, and that pious clip in *Sunset Boulevard* doesn't even hint at the demented arabesques of Stroheim's pen and camera.

At the outset, Stroheim conceived a story that he called *The Swamp*. The swamp is not a wet place in the jungle but rather the name of the brothel. Surely that suggests what was on his mind.

It told Gloria Swanson something quite different, however, for when Stroheim outlined the story for her and Joseph Kennedy—cautiously dubbing the Swamp "a dance hall"—Swanson felt relief that Patricia Kelly, the convent girl, was Irish Catholic and therefore likely to appeal to her married tycoon lover.

"The strange story reminded me of nothing I had ever heard before," Swanson said later. She had reservations, however, one being that she, approaching thirty, seemed "long in the tooth to play a convent girl." Stroheim probably guessed that Swanson's age scarcely mattered: she had always looked mature. More important, he knew that Swanson, unlike many actors in silent films, would underact. By so doing, she would not detract from *his* film, *his* direction, *his* obsessions. He was right. Not only did she not detract, she also gave one of the best performances of her career.

Kennedy seems to have ignored everything in Stroheim's synopsis save virtue, even though the outline included much to make a more conventional Bostonian blanch. For instance, the part about the prince's affair with the country's mad queen; the fire he sets in Kelly's convent so that he can kidnap her; the postkidnapping supper in his private apartment at the queen's palace; and the blacksnake whip the queen uses on Kelly when she discovers the—still intact?—virgin lass at a heavy-breathing moment with the prince.

The ability not to see certain things is a handy trait in political families. "I think that Mr. von Stroheim should begin at once," Kennedy announced before Gloria could voice her reservations about a picture whose "two major costumes are a novice's habit and a nightie."

Even using words such as "monumental" and "godlike," it's difficult to convey Stroheim's greatness. It's especially hard when you factor in the utter ridiculousness of some of his work. *Queen Kelly* is the best example of his gaga imagination. It's a magnificent hoot. Perhaps the best way to imply the measure of his genius is to contrast the ludicrous story and plot of *Queen Kelly* on the page with the corrupt grandeur of what Stroheim actually filmed. Indeed, so amazing is this mutilated masterpiece that the loss of big chunks doesn't really damage it. Imagine a couple of acts of *Macbeth* gone forever; we could still marvel at what remains.

Stroheim possessed the most lurid imagination in silent Hollywood.

Not many moviemakers have topped him to this day. If Dickens had filmed his most septic visions, they might have resembled a picture by Erich von Stroheim. To cite one example: Jan, the lecher who claims Kelly as his bride, hobbles to the whorehouse on crutches. By casting Nosferatu lookalike Tully Marshall in the part, Stroheim got not only a grotesque performance, but a visual allegory of disease. When Jan dies of overarousal just as Kelly becomes his bride, he staggers like a double-jointed skeleton, gnarling his limbs in the air in a repellent exterminated cockroach dance of death.

At this point filming ended. Here is Swanson's account of the calamity. "Mr. Von Stroheim began instructing Mr. Marshall . . . how to dribble tobacco juice onto my hand while he was putting on the wedding ring. It was early morning, I had just eaten breadfast, and my stomach turned. I became nauseated and furious at the same time. 'Excuse me,' I said to Erich von Stroheim, and turned and walked off the set." Swanson phoned Joe Kennedy in the East. She never returned to the set, and when Kennedy arrived in Hollywood he fired Stroheim.

An ending was eventually cobbled together from footage previously shot: Kelly, her virtue saved and her dying aunt now dead, becomes the new madam. Before she can ply her trade, however, the mad queen is assassinated back in Europe and the prince marries Swanson on the day of his coronation, making her Queen Kelly. For Stroheim, happy families are all alike.

Long before this convenient ending, however, on the night the prince kidnaps Kelly from her convent and the queen catches them one step from flagrante delicto, we have witnessed a whipping scene unequalled in any of the pseudo-daring movies made about de Sade.

The harpy queen, aging but strong-armed, thrashes her straying lover. Then she turns on Kelly. The whipping starts in the prince's boudoir. Blows and lashes rain on Swanson outside the bedroom and onto the landing, down the marble stairs, out the palace door, and into the night. The length of the sequence, and the brutality, recall the murder of

Nancy in *Oliver Twist*. Whatever S&M fantasy Stroheim started out with, it's hard to think of him getting off, for this sequence is as unerotic as the beating of Lillian Gish in *Broken Blossoms*.

Queen Kelly's overdose of fetishes, morbidity, and "immorality" might easily have ended up like the silly excesses in a Ken Russell movie. Instead it haunts any true cinephile who sees it, for it's a silent opera (including outlandish plot) and a fragment of grandiose architecture. It's also a weird ballet which, in some way I can't quite explain, seems to prefigure the final shot in Bergman's *The Seventh Seal*, when Death leads a line of mortals dancing toward eternity.

It was said for years in Hollywood that those who saw Stroheim's original nine-hour *Greed* never stopped talking about it. *Queen Kelly*, also, must have impressed the few who saw it. The very few, for it was never released in the United States, and abroad it attracted only connoisseurs. (Among them Billy Wilder in Berlin, who reviewed it in 1929 for the literary journal *Der Querschnitt*.) Had Stroheim not been fired, the picture left unfinished, and if it had not dealt a horrid blow to Swanson's career, it might be discussed in the same breath as, say, *Way Down East* or even *Citizen Kane*. But he was fired, his directing career finished. Swanson didn't regain her professional balance until 1950, and the only principal left undamaged personally and professionally was Joe Kennedy.

No director ever had better reason to pay homage to an earlier film than Billy Wilder, for here, in *Queen Kelly*, was the fabled collaboration of two main stars, Swanson and Stroheim. We're surely meant to make the parallel inference that the unnamed silent picture on Norma Desmond's home screen is her collaboration with Max von Mayerling. That isn't said, however, because at the point in the film when Norma shows *Queen Kelly* to Joe Gillis, it hasn't been revealed that Max was once her director.

Why, though, did Wilder choose this comparatively ordinary clip from *Queen Kelly*? According to one source, the suggestion came from Stroheim, no doubt with Swanson's assent. Wilder might have used to greater advantage some footage of the convent girls out walking when the prince rides by on horseback. Swanson's close-ups in that sequence reveal more of her young beauty and nuanced acting than the passive bits used in *Sunset Bouelvard*.

In Wilder's clip, Swanson's right profile is prominent—not her best angle because her nose sticks up. Left profile works better. Better still, for Swanson, is full face, which flatters her offbeat beauty.

It's unclear exactly what footage Wilder, Stroheim, and Swanson had to pick from in 1949. Existing prints of *Queen Kelly* may well have been in shambles. Not until 1985 was the film restored, with certain footage added, some deleted, and passages bridged by production stills.

In the clip used in *Sunset Boulevard*, we see only one intertitle: "Cast out this wicked dream which has seized my heart." (The context is Kelly praying for deliverance from lust after meeting the prince.) Then Swanson lights the candle. Only a few of these shots are used in the restored version of *Queen Kelly*.

In the restoration, however, the entire sequence plays brilliantly. Swanson, alone, kneels in front of a statue of the Virgin and Child. The sequence includes numerous shots from different angles, including Swanson photographed behind the dripping candles. The angle shifts, candles drip, then she lights a fresh candle and adds it to others already burning and dripping. This sequence has three intertitles: (1) "Holy Mother—Forgive me—"; (2) "Please make my wish come true—to see the Prince again!"; (3) "Please!"

The clip Wilder might have preferred, had there been no censor, was the startling sequence where, during the prince's ride-by, Swanson's panties fall to the ground. The prince laughs. Embarrassed but defiant, she tosses them at the mocking prince . . . who pockets them, then takes the garment out and kisses it as though it were made of flesh. (When Stroheim proposed a similar incident for Max in *Sunset Boulevard*—washing Norma's underwear—Wilder nixed it.)

Stroheim's work appealed more directly to fellow moviemakers than to the public, and Wilder belonged to the partisans. "I've always been his great admirer," Wilder said. They first met in the Arizona desert in 1942 when Wilder directed *Five Graves to Cairo* and Stroheim played Nazi Field Marshal Erwin Rommel. Their famous meeting has the legendary aroma of Stanley's jungle encounter with Livingstone.

Wilder perceived the delicacy of the situation: he, young and on his way up, must direct the fifty-seven-year-old eminence who had no hope of comeback or return. "I rushed over to him," Wilder recalled, "and told him how moved I was, an insignificant director, to be working with the great Stroheim. Trying to say the right thing, I said this: 'You know, Herr Stroheim, why they won't let you direct pictures anymore? It's because you've always been ten years ahead of your time.' He looked at me and said, 'Twenty.' "

Wilder's assessment of Stroheim belongs on a monument: "He possessed grandeur. Even his mistakes were grandiose, and when he succeeded he had real class."

Wilder, of course, didn't fall for Stroheim's jiggery-pokery. Being Viennese, and Jewish, Wilder spotted the real story like Brooklyn spotting Queens: "His accent was working class."

By the time of *Sunset Boulevard*, Wilder had risen high in Hollywood while Stroheim remained low. Paramount summoned Stroheim from France, where he had settled with his companion, Denise Vernac, in a house at Maurepas, about forty minutes by train from Paris. Anita Loos, an old friend from silent Hollywood, used to visit "Von," as she fondly called him, every year during her trip to France. She described the house where Stroheim spent his final years: "The interior was always dimly lighted and it had an atmosphere of such heavy-footed *Gemütlichkeit* that one felt it belonged in the Black Forest of Germany. The dun-colored, pock-marked plaster walls were hung with sabers and guns arranged in patterns, together with some German officers' tunics, and over the huge fireplace of the living room was a collection of enormous beer steins."

Stroheim, like Gloria Swanson, poked relentlessly at the Brackett and Wilder script, attempting to inject his personality into it and also to redeem what he called "that goddamned butler role." He resisted the idea that his life and career might even obliquely have suggested the story of this artist turned lackey.

Although Brackett and Wilder were thoroughbreds who sought no barking tips from Stroheim, they seem nevertheless to have followed as many of his suggestions as they rejected. A soupçon of this generosity might have sprung from pity, though it's probable they recognized the artistic value of the Master's collaboration. In every instance *Sunset Boulevard* is richer for the Stroheim touches.

Arthur Lennig, an authority on Stroheim's life and career, has catalogued these touches in his biography, *Stroheim*. I have incorporated some of them in the following paragraphs.

Lennig suggests several reasons why Stroheim felt compelled to ennoble the role of Max. For one thing, the part was neither heroic nor grand. "This was no Rauffenstein or Rommel [Stroheim's memorable roles in Renoir's *La Grande Illusion* and Wilder's *Five Graves to Cairo*, respectively] but a has-been, a man no longer important, someone similar enough to himself to be unsettling to Stroheim's ego. Furthermore, he was afraid— and correctly so—that this was the way he would be remembered." Another writer has stated the outcome of Stroheim's premonition: "Today he is remembered, if at all, as Norma Desmond's butler. This is like remembering Orson Welles for his television commercials."

DeMille, though indirectly, might account for Stroheim's additional motivation to revise Max. Lennig speculates that "to be back in Hollywood was bad enough, but to play a servant to a woman he had once directed and to accompany her onto the Paramount lot where she visited the still active C. B. DeMille must have been galling. Here was a lesser talent still making films, still a success, still a foremost director, and here was Stroheim playing a butler."

On the set of *Sunset Boulevard*, according to Swanson, Stroheim "kept adding things and suggesting things and asking if scenes might not be reshot—very much in his grand old manner of perfectionism regardless of schedule or cost." A possible Stroheim embellishment, which cost nothing, helped characterize Max, and also aggrandized Norma, is Max's servile use of the third person when speaking to her: "Madame is wanted on the telephone"; "Madame will pardon me. The shadow over the left eye is not quite balanced." (Only once does he call her by name, at the end when he's "directing" her for the newsreel cameras: "Are you ready, Norma?")

Like so much in *Sunset Boulevard*, this trope has its roots in Hollywood

soil. In the twenties, when Swanson and Joe Kennedy approached Stroheim about creating a vehicle for her, he deferred to Paramount's reigning
goddess, addressing her obsequiously as "Madame la Marquise" (which
she still was). The queenly part of Swanson lapped it up; another—the
democratic, Midwestern side—surely winced.

Stroheim, like a bird constructing a nest, built Max with twigs from
his old films. When Gillis reads Norma's script, Max moves a lamp
closer, "a solicitous gesture that Stroheim had used twenty years earlier in
Three Faces East," in which he played a major role. In the same sequence,
"Max wheels in a cart containing champagne and caviar, pure Stro-
heimian fare."

Several references in the script to December and to the Christmas season may have been plucked from an incident in Stroheim's past. Lennig
explains that after his arrival in the United States in November 1909,
Stroheim found a job gift wrapping holiday packages. On Christmas Eve
the job ended, and the penniless immigrant spent his first hungry
Christmas in America "alone, far from his family and his homeland."
Lennig pinpoints that bleak day as the reservoir from which Stroheim
drew, in his films and scripts, a long dynasty of dreadful events, all of
them occurring near December 25. A few examples cited by Lennig: "In
Greed, Trina is murdered on Christmas Eve (it occurred a few days later in
the book), in *The Merry Widow*, the heroine (in the script) spends the holidays with her semicomatose husband." In *Walking Down Broadway*, a character standing under a sign wishing "Peace on Earth, Good Will to
Men" is told she is fired. Was there no joy in Stroheim's world? If he had
written *A Christmas Carol*, Tiny Tim would have died, Scrooge's heart
would have hardened, and God would have cursed them every one.

December doom in *Sunset Boulevard* is comparatively benign. Gillis's
birthday is December 21. When the roof leaks over the garage, it is during "the last week of December." Surely the darkest December night in
this film is the final one: Norma's suicide attempt takes place on New
Year's Eve, the same night she sinks her inextricable talons into Joe's flesh.

The maimed and crippled turn up often in Stroheim pictures, but
Wilder balked when Stroheim wanted to give Max a limp. In the script,

Max is described as "semiparalyzed. The left side of his mouth is pulled down, and he leans on a rubber-ferruled stick." Apparently, though, Wilder had second thoughts either on the set or in the editing room.

"Such a limp you've never seen," Wilder exclaimed years later. "The first step would carry me off the platform where we were shooting." An echo of Stroheim's suggestion remains, however. When Max leaves Gillis in the bedroom over the garage, Gillis says in voice-over: "I pegged him as slightly cuckoo, too. A stroke maybe."

Wilder also forbade cigarettes to Max, since butlers may not smoke. But Stroheim did wear his trademark white gloves, even when playing the organ.

I pause here to pick a bone with Arthur Lennig, albeit a wee bone no bigger than a toothpick. Referring to Stroheim's beloved geranium motif (often present in pictures he directed and sometimes in those he appeared in), Lennig finds one such reference in *Sunset Boulevard*, viz. the New Year's Eve party at Artie Green's apartment. When Gillis enters, Artie announces him to the other guests: "Fans, you all know Joe Gillis, the well-known screenwriter, geranium smuggler, and Black Dahlia suspect."

What Artie actually says is, ". . . uranium smuggler." Earlier versions of the scripted scene use "opium smuggler," a word sure to rile the drug-free Production Code censors. Otherwise, Lennig's arguments in favor of Stroheim's influence resound with probability. It's possible, of course, that Wilder and Brackett recalled many of them from Stroheim pictures they admired, and included them as tributes.

Lennig doesn't make this connection, but I suspect that the monkey funeral in *Sunset Boulevard* (with Max and Norma, in long shot, forming the abbreviated cortege) is an oblique nod to *Greed*. There, McTeague and Trina get married as a funeral procession passes in the street. We see the mourners first in long shot through the second-story window, then in medium shot from street level. Wilder, despite his reputation, shows more restraint than Stroheim. In the funeral scene in *Greed*, a small, one-legged boy follows the coffin, italicizing the ironic juxtaposition of wedding and funeral. The heartbreak is almost unbearable: we realize that the child is following a dead parent.

The Black Dahlia

Artie Green's allusion to the Black Dahlia puzzled no one at the time of *Sunset Boulevard*. Throughout the country, and especially in Los Angeles, the name evoked the same shiver of recognition as Nicole Brown Simpson's almost half a century later.

On January 15, 1947, the body of twenty-two-year-old Beth Short was discovered in a vacant lot at 3925 Norton Avenue in L.A. The woman's corpse had been severed at the waist. One half lay on the sidewalk, the other in weeds. The head was battered; the body had been slashed all over and burned with cigarettes. The murderer was never found.

The "Black Dahlia" nickname came from the woman's luxuriant black hair. For several years she had been a drifter and a "Victory girl"—a World War II euphemism for a prostitute specializing in servicemen. She was also said to be popular in certain Hollywood lesbian circles. Like Joe Gillis, Beth Short lived for a time in the Alto Nido apartments.

The Black Dahlia is rumored to have been secretly buried in Mountain View Cemetery in Oakland, a site designed by Frederick Law Olmstead. Others who rest there are novelist Frank Norris (*McTeague*), San Simeon architect Julia Morgan, and members of San Francisco's family of chocolatiers, the Ghiradellis.

The Black Dahlia story is covered in nauseating detail in Kenneth Anger's *Hollywood Babylon II*, with illustrations to match the prose. John Austin's pulp primer *Hollywood's Unsolved Mysteries*, published in 1970 by Ace, tells the story better and with a modicum of restraint. A recent book, *The Cases That Haunt Us* by John Douglas and Mark Olshaker, also takes up the case.

Not every Stroheim anecdote depresses. While filming *Sunset Boulevard* he played a comic turn—though out of camera range, and Stroheim himself was not amused. In the scene where Max drives Norma and Joe to Paramount, all went smoothly except for the chauffeur. Stroheim had never learned to drive a car. "And so," said Billy Wilder, "we had to pull him through, we had to put a chain on something and pull him." Even with the chauffeur chauffeured, a mishap took place. He crashed into the Paramount gate. Swanson recalled that this episode humiliated him. She said that every take exhausted him, even though the Isotta-Fraschini was towed by another vehicle.

In earlier years Stroheim's chauffeur was Valerie, his third wife. In a letter sent to him in France the year after *Sunset Boulevard*, she brought up her unpaid labors in an attempt to grab additional support money. "Of course, I did not receive a salary for my services from the studios or from you, nor did I receive a chauffeur's fee for driving you to and from the studio as far back as 1918—nor did I receive a stenographer's salary for taking dictation."

Sunset Boulevard was Stroheim's last American film. For his performance, he received an Oscar nomination as Best Supporting Actor. He lost.

But then he always lost in Hollywood. Maybe Stroheim took the place too seriously. Reportedly insulted that he wasn't nominated as Best Actor, he threatened to sue Paramount for daring to enter him in the lesser category. Stroheim the Great was without honor in his adopted country, but elsewhere he towered like a cinematic Alp. Retrospectives of his work took place in London in 1954 and in Brussels in 1955. On his deathbed, in 1957, he was visited at his home in Maurepas by an official delegation of the French government and awarded the medal of the Légion d'Honneur.

Even in death, however, Stroheim looked back at Hollywood. And why not? The town had long ago turned him to a block of salt. A friend reported that, even through pain and paralysis and the fog of heavy sedation, Stroheim muttered these words: "This isn't the worst. The worst is that they stole twenty-five years of my life."

The Man You Love to Hate

Hollywood press agentry dreamed up this nickname for Stroheim, and it stuck. It wasn't farfetched at the outset of his career, for he played so many cruel Huns during and just after World War I that audiences booed him almost as energetically as they booed Hitler in newsreels a few years later.

Stroheim gave his most damning performance in *The Heart of Humanity* (1919). In a town invaded by the enemy, Stroheim, as a German lieutenant, picks up a wailing baby and throws it out the window. In an interview in 1943, he recalled the notorious scene. It was all genuine, he said: the baby and the toss. An assistant director stood on a mattress out of camera range to catch the terrified infant. "I felt badly about that," Stroheim admitted. "That child screamed madly after the fourth take and went into hysterics on the sight of my gray uniform. I was the villain in the picture, but the real villain was the mother who would let her child suffer like that."

At least one famous colleague, however, didn't love to hate Stroheim. When he appeared with Garbo in *As You Desire Me* (1932), he reportedly caused numerous delays because he couldn't remember his lines. Hedda Hopper, who played Garbo's sister in the film, said that "Garbo never complained and, on the occasions when Stroheim was ill, she herself would claim an indisposition, thus covering for him. On the last day of the picture, he surprised everybody by serving vintage champagne. It may have been his way of apologizing to the star, who never showed a bit of annoyance at the many hours' delay his actions had caused her."

The unanswered question of this ancedote is: Who cast Hedda as Garbo's sister? They didn't look alike, they didn't sound alike. Perhaps someone noticed a resemblance because both women were tall and gangly, even horsey. (Garbo almost neighs in *Susan Lenox, Her Fall and Rise.*)

Though Hedda's face looked anything but Garboesque, she was considered a pretty woman circa 1908 when, as a vivacious teenager, she gallivanted about New York. Charles Brackett claimed that in his youth Hedda had "the most beautiful legs in the New York theatre."

Unlike Garbo, Hedda hadn't a shy bone in her busy body. Some years after *As You Desire Me*, and after Garbo's retirement, Hedda spotted her dining at Chasen's. Rumors forever circulated that Garbo might return to pictures. Hedda charged over to her table and asked if she intended to do so. "Do you really think the people want me?" she asked. "I don't think," replied Hedda. "I know. Because your fans have never stopped writing to ask when you're going to return."

If some of these lines sound vaguely familiar, they are. Hedda recounted this story in her book *From Under My Hat*, published in 1952 when *Sunset Boulevard* was still fresh in her memory. Her prose had undergone temporary improvement from exposure to the script.

Though he worked in the undersize medium of television, Jack Webb obsessed as much as Erich von Stroheim over details. In *Dragnet*, the noirish series that made him famous, Webb—producer, director, star—insisted on realism down to the smallest prop. On Stage 11 at the Walt Disney Studios in Burbank, where the show was filmed, Webb reconstructed the lower floor of the Los Angeles Police Department. The set was an exact replica: room for room, filing cabinet for filing cabinet, even locks on the doors.

According to a reporter who visited that set in 1954, "The phones have the same extension numbers as the LAPD. The calendars are alike. He wanted to reproduce the old-fashioned knobs on the doors. But the firm manufacturing them had gone out of business twenty years ago. So he had a plaster cast made of each knob at police headquarters and duplicated it down to the last screw."

Webb's reason for perfectionism matched Stroheim's. An audience watching *Dragnet* on the home screen of course couldn't see the telephone numbers, and those forty million viewers would neither know nor care about doorknobs at the LAPD. But actors knew. Webb believed actors gave more honest and more convincing performances in authentic settings.

Jack Webb, of course, had the advantage of controlling all aspects of his show. And unlike Stroheim, whose pictures stretched for months, years, in production and ended up with Tolstoyan running times, Webb had to package every episode in a neat thirty-minute format, minus a few commercial minutes. (Stroheim, notoriously, would stop production until precisely the right button was found for an army officer's jacket, or to replace an incorrect doily on a table in a dark corner of a room where the camera would never travel. His actors *absolutely had to* wear the exact historical undergarments, meticulously sewn, embroidered, and pressed.)

Webb (1920–82) grew up in Los Angeles in desperate poverty. As a child he suffered so severely from asthma that his mother or his grandmother often had to carry him up the stairs to their third-story flat.

Shy and withdrawn, the boy found substitues for childhood. He read pulpy police stories. He rummaged in garbage cans for such flotsam as a red pennant with the words "Souvenir of Lake Tahoe," or Chianti bottles in straw holders. At the time, such finds were not objets trouvés but trash. His mother tolerated his collection, however, because it seemed the sole pleasure in her son's constricted life.

A broken-down, alcoholic neighbor in the apartment house once had been a horn player. Adolescent Jack Webb learned about jazz from him. Eventually, when he had money, Webb assembled an extensive collection of jazz recordings. And in 1955 he directed and starred in a jazz movie, *Pete Kelly's Blues.* Others in the offbeat cast: Peggy Lee, Andy Devine, Jayne Mansfield, Lee Marvin, and Ella Fitzgerald.

The teenage Jack Webb also took up drawing, and worked in the realistic style of Norman Rockwell. Graduating from high school, he was offered two college scholarships to study art. The scholarships were not full, however, and so he had to turn them down and go to work. Webb's health improved, he joined the Army Air Corps, and three and a half years later, in San Francisco, he started his show business career as a radio announcer. In 1945 he married bourbon-throated singer Julie London. Their marriage lasted until 1953, despite Webb's physical abuse. Afterward, he married twice more.

B-movie queen Mamie Van Doren (*Forbidden, Untamed Youth*) said in a recent interview that Webb once drugged her wine and "the next thing I knew, I was naked, lying spread-eagled on a four-poster bed, my arms and legs tied to each bedpost. As the fog in my brain lifted, I looked up and saw Sgt. Joe Friday having sex with me with a wild look in his eyes." The incident was not turned into a *Dragnet* episode.

Webb's first film was *He Walked by Night*, in 1948, followed by *The Men* (1950) and *Sunset Boulevard.*

Billy Wilder must have had a reason for casting Webb as Artie Green, the flighty assistant director who's like a pushy comedian panhandling for laughs. Wilder's reason, however, remains occult. Surely Nancy Olson speaks for all when she snarls, in the scene at Schwab's, "Oh Artie, shut up!"

If you look ahead from *Sunset Boulevard* to Wilder's career from the mid-1950s onward, you'll see many variations on Artie Green. Jack Webb started the trend, Tom Ewell in *The Seven Year Itch* (1955) advanced it, and Jack Lemmon, in *Some Like It Hot* (1959) and *The Apartment* (1960), perfected the type, playing nervous, prissy, hyper, insecure characters who won't buzz off. The list grows from an occasional bug to a swarm: Horst Buchholz in *One, Two, Three* (1961), Ray Walston in *Kiss Me, Stupid* (1964), Lureen Tuttle in *The Fortune Cookie* (1966), Gianfranco Barra in *Avanti!* (1972), and Lemmon again and again and again.

Attack of the Fifty-Foot Starlet

No list of Billy Wilder's annoying minor characters is complete without Yvette Vickers. At Artie Green's New Year's Eve party in *Sunset Boulevard*, she's one of the blondes giggling wildly into the phone. When she's finally off she announces to Holden, "You can have the phone now." That's her only line in her debut film.

Vickers's official year of birth is 1936, which means she would have been thirteen when she appeared in *Sunset Boulevard*. Even for Hollywood, where nymphets grow up fast, her development by 1950 seems advanced. Perhaps she was just precocious. She either knew the score, or if not, she gave the best performance in the picture.

Born Yvette Vedder, she was the daughter of Kansas City jazz saxophonist Chuck Vedder and Iola Vedder, a pianist. When jazz musicians like Harry James and Charlie Parker visited her parents, baby Yvette would stay up all night with the grown-ups, singing and dancing. At fifteen she did a TV commercial for White Rain shampoo, which became famous in its fashion. And very long-running. According to Vickers, the commercial must be still in use somewhere, since she continues to receive residual checks for it.

Until 1957 she was Yvette Vedder both personally and professionally (though unbilled in *Sunset Boulevard*). That year she changed her name to Vickers and was "introduced" in *Short Cut to Hell*, the only film James Cagney ever directed. (This Paramount picture was produced by A.C. Lyles, who turns up elsewhere in these pages.)

The year 1959 was her annus mirabilis. She appeared on Broadway in *The Gang's All Here*, with Melvyn Douglas, Arthur Hill, E.G. Marshall, and other male actors. She was the only female in the cast. "Al Hirsh", she said recently, put her in a drawing that adorned the cover of the *New Yorker*. Well, not quite. She meant Al Hirshfeld, who cartooned her and Douglas dancing on a tabletop. The caricature appeared in the *New York Times*. (And Kenneth Tynan, reviewing the play for the *New Yorker*, mentioned everyone in the cast *but* Yvette Vickers.) In July of that year she was *Playboy*'s centerfold (photographed by Russ Meyer), and while still riding high from her film of the previous year, *Attack of the 50-Foot Woman*, she made an equally stunning follow-up, *Attack of the Giant Leeches* (both for American International Pictures). Although Vickers was too young for the demanding role of the 50-Foot Woman, she did enjoy star billing in the latter film, which claims the hybrid distinction (in Leonard Maltin's *Movie and Video Guide*, at least) of belonging to both the white trash and monster genres.

Webb seems cast against type as chatty Artie Green in *Sunset Boulevard*. Everyone who has seen *Dragnet* imagines him self-possessed and stoic off-camera, like Sgt. Joe Friday. But that, apparently, was not the real Jack Webb. According to A. C. Lyles, "Jack had tremendous drive. He always had something going on. When he saw you, he'd talk, talk, talk. He was perfectly capable of calling you at midnight to say, 'Get right over here, I've got to see you! Listen to this idea.'"

A classic Type A personality, Webb seemed to keep a cigarette in one hand and a drink in the other, according to Lyles. Sometimes one cigarette seemed not enough. "Jack and I sometimes met for dinner at the old Cock and Bull, on Sunset," Lyles recalls. "He'd put two packs of cigarettes down on the table, one filtered and the other unfiltered. During the evening, he alternated."

Jack Webb's *Sunset Boulevard* contract stipulated that he start on May 10, 1949, at $600 a week with a one-week guarantee. A few weeks later, on June 3, the radio show *Dragnet*—created by Webb—went on the air for the first time. Webb, of course, played Joe Friday in that debut broadcast from NBC's Los Angeles Studio H. For the rest of his career, he was never far from *Dragnet*, not in reality and not in the popular imagination.

The show moved to television in January 1952 and ran though 1959. Then it resumed in 1967 and continued until 1970. A feature film, *Dragnet*, directed by Webb, came out in 1954. In a second film with that title, a spoof released in 1987, Dan Ackroyd played Sgt. Friday's nephew.

According to Max Allan Collins, writing in *The Big Book of Film Noir*, Webb's first movie, *He Walked by Night*, "not only set the tone for *Dragnet*, the term 'dragnet' can be heard in the film. Technical adviser was Los Angeles police sergeant Marty Wynn, with whom Webb struck up a friendship, and the actor—after Wynn chided him about Hollywood's phony version of cops and robbers—began doing research by riding around on calls in a police car with Wynn and his partner. From this, Webb picked up on the jargon of cops—'Go down to R&I [Records and Identification] and pull the suspect's package'—which became not only *Dragnet*'s trademark, but Webb's; even his non-*Dragnet* work always leans on inside jargon from some male-dominated profession."

Dragnet, like *Sunset Boulevard*, added several phrases to the American language, most famously "Just the facts, ma'am." Variations on such laconic shibboleths as "My name's Friday—I'm a cop" still pop up in the occasional commercial or in the speech of sixty-year-old adolescents. High school English teachers seem to have approved of Sgt. Friday's diction as well as his morals. A typical letter to Webb in the midfifties: "Our speech class wants you to know that you have been voted the personality with the most compelling voice on the air." Another facet of the show's legacy is the *Dragnet* theme. "Dum-de-dum-dum" is instantly recognizable, like the first four notes of Beethoven's Fifth, even to ears unacquainted with the source.

Less recognizable, however, though more toothsome to camp followers, are the "songs" on "You're My Girl," the album Jack Webb recorded in 1958. According to the liner notes, Webb "digs music deeply" but "cannot sing a lick." The obvious compromise: talk the songs.

I can't count this album among my blessings, but George Gimarc and Pat Reeder, in their dishy book *Hollywood Hi-Fi: Over 100 of the Most Outrageous Celebrity Recordings Ever*, describe Webb's voice as a "staccato monotone." They state convincingly that it's impossible to listen to these cuts as anything but imaginary *Dragnet* episodes set to music. For instance, the melancholy "Stranger in Town" from their perspective: "I was working the day watch out of Robbery. A call came in on a 211: Shoplifting. Merchant couldn't get a description. Said it was a stranger..." When they've had their fun, the catty authors pronounce "You're My Girl" "a dumb-de-dumb-dumb idea."

chapter 22

"We'll Make Another Picture, and Another Picture"

The English critic Kenneth Tynan wrote in his diary on October 19, 1975: "The most powerful influence on the arts in the West is—the cinema. Novels, plays, *and films* are filled with references to, quotations from, parodies of—old movies. They dominate the cultural subconscious because we absorb them in our formative years . . . and we see them again on TV when we grow up. . . . As the sheer number of films piles up, their influence will increase, until we have a civilization entirely molded by cinematic values and behavior patterns."

Some of the most influential sound movies are *Citizen Kane, 2001: A Space Odyssey, Nashville,* and *Blade Runner.* These influenced the structure of later films, and also the camera work, characterizations, even that elusive quality one might call the *attitude* of a movie. *Sunset Boulevard,* on the other hand, was not greatly influential in these respects. Instead, later films appropriated its grotesquerie, the situation of its plot, certain ones of its more memorable lines of dialogue, and most of all the persona of Norma Desmond.

Although highly polished and technically admirable, *Sunset Boulevard* is cinematically conservative. It lacks the pyrotechnics of many a lesser film—*Easy Rider,* for example—which quickly dated but nevertheless exerted lasting influence. Like several other character-driven pictures of Hollywood preeminence, *Sunset Boulevard* seems to possess some potent charm. Applied to filmmakers, that assertion explains why virtually every film made after 1950 that deals with Hollywood from any angle seems to have brushed against *Sunset Boulevard*. And why not? It's the grandest drama ever made about the place, at once the most preposterous and the most realistic.

To be sure, it's a film à clef with gossipy clues. But it's far more than that. If you watch it enough, you can find the entire history of motion pictures swarming below the surface of *Sunset Boulevard*, for encoded in it is the Hollywood cosmos from cinematic Big Bang—those first flickering images in the 1890s—to unmade films yet to come in the new millennium. It's an endless Borgesian reflection of itself.

One of the ironies of this supremely ironic movie is that *Sunset Boulevard*, from Norma Desmond's point of view if she could watch it, is one of those pictures that got "smaller" when the silent image was sacrificed to "words, words, more words." From every other point of view, *Sunset Boulevard* was "big" when it came out in 1950 and, in the half century since, has surged and redoubled, so that today it's on everybody's list of the greatest films of the studio era. (It's number twelve on the AFI's rather slaphappy list of the 100 Greatest.)

Since Norma Desmond is, among many other things, a Bette Davis role, how appropriate that the first movie to bow before the altar of *Sunset Boulevard* was *The Star*, released in 1952 and starring Bette herself. This milestone in the cinema of excess not only kowtows to its superior ancestor, it grovels and drools.

Bette seems to have aged ten years in the two years since *All About Eve*. As Margaret Elliott, she is, like Norma Desmond, a bundle of raw nerves. Margaret is also a has-been, and every bit as neurotic as Norma. Although she's no pistol-packing mama, you just know she would shoot anyone who stood between her and a comeback. (She's been away only three years, Norma more than twenty.) Margaret Elliott is a star in extremis. Unlike Norma, she's broke. She's also locked out of her apartment, her possessions have been sold at auction, and hangers-on cling like dead lice.

There's a great deal of yelling, slapping, smoking, and running about, even for a Bette Davis picture. It copies the car-chase scene from *Sunset*

Boulevard—cops are after Bette for drunk driving; maudlin masochism could also be one of the charges. They throw her in the slammer, and when her young daughter, played by Natalie Wood, gets wind of it, Mom tells her it's all a publicity stunt.

This picture is so much in thrall to its worthier predecessor that Bette and her agent go traipsing to her former studio to see J. M., the executive who can put her in a comeback role. Like Swanson, she has to take a screen test. She loses the part she wants—the eighteen-year-old—and agrees to play the older sister, who is "fortyish." Poor Margaret Elliott—she loses even that, probably because she plays it like *Cabin in the Cotton*.

This terrible picture, a paragon of mean-spirited hilarity, is really lower than it sounds. That's because it's a merciless humiliation of Bette Davis and other actresses of her vintage in fifties Hollywood. If, as some have claimed, Bette thought of Joan Crawford when she played the role, she should have realized that Joan would have brought more heart to it than she did—ersatz, but heart all the same. ("Bless you," Bette says several times, using a famous Crawford shibboleth.)

A few Desmondesque lines from *The Star*: Bette to her agent, "Don't touch me with your ten percent hands!" "One good picture is all I need." "You see, the public remembers." "If you're a star, you don't stop being a star."

This picture, so shameless in its theft, even trots out a DeMille surrogate named R. J. When Bette encounters him at a party, he reminisces long-windedly, "And when the Red Sea parted . . ."

Stuart Heisler directed *The Star*. He was the most egregious of Wilder's pasticheurs, at least until Robert Aldrich and *What Ever Happened to Baby Jane?* came along.

Before that, however, Chaplin lifted a few ideas from *Sunset Boulevard*. He opened his mouth and out came words, words, more words. In *Limelight* (1952), Chaplin spoke. He had done so before, though for years he resisted talking pictures more aggressively than anyone else. Chaplin made silent films into the thirties, and even by the time of *Limelight*, a quarter century after talkies arrived, he and his pictures retained the look and rhythm of silents.

Here, and elsewhere in his later work, Chaplin's endless speechifying and sentimental platitudes breed nostalgia for the brief title cards in his silents. In *Limelight*, the formerly great comedian Calvero (Chaplin) attempts one tormented comeback after another in World War I London. He's not very funny, even by the standards of that era. When he finally triumphs (along with another old music hall star played by Buster Keaton), his routines are as corny and outmoded as those audiences had recently walked out on.

In dramatic terms Norma Desmond's "return" on the staircase plays more convincingly—though it's all in her head—than Calvero's. We believe she once had it. Calvero—he's *had* it. And poor Keaton. Here he's onscreen longer, but not as well used as he was by Wilder in those few seconds in *Sunset Boulevard*.

Apart from Holy Land camp, the reason to see the cockeyed 1953 parable *Salome* starring Rita Hayworth is that in a real sense Norma Desmond's script got filmed—at Columbia, not Paramount—three years after *Sunset Boulevard*. Rita plays Princess Salome, who, even for Rome, puts out too freely—the noble Romans expel her for "ill-repute" and send her packing back to Palestine. This Roman epic grafted onto Oriental romance turned out as ludicrously outrageous as anything from the feverish pen of Norma Desmond.

En route to stepdaddy Herod's wanton palace, spoiled brat with a heart of gold Salome and her escort of men on camels pass the River Jordan, where John and his fellow Baptists are singing the Judean equivalent of "Kumbaya" around a campfire. To curry favor with Eisenhower-era picturegoers, Hollywood revisionists departed from the Gospel account—and also Oscar Wilde's—by making Salome an early Christian convert. It's her wicked mother, Herodias, sternly played by Judith Anderson, who demands the head of John the Baptist.

Salome, reformed and unaware of the high stakes, dances before lubricious Herod (Charles Laughton) like a fleshy combo of Little Egypt and Ricky Martin. As the last veil is flung off—or the last veil but one, since Hayworth remains chastely wrapped—the head of the holy man is toted in on a tray, like some monstrous antipasto.

This Salome, unlike Norma's, does not kiss "the cold, dead lips." Instead, she screams, denounces her harlot mother, and promptly elopes with righteous Roman Commander Claudius (Stewart Granger). On their honeymoon, the happy couple attend the Sermon on the Mount! (They must have loved it in Pomona.)

George Cukor's *A Star Is Born* (1954) pays graceful homage to *Sunset Boulevard*. Cukor and screenwriter Moss Hart seem to have dusted their picture with subliminal allusions to Brackett and Wilder's. Early on, someone mentions Sunset Boulevard, the street; someone else mentions "a little girl from Paramount." At Judy Garland's makeup test, she is scrutinized by cosmeticians, and the scene is shot like Norma Desmond's makeover. Garland's mouth, then one eye, are ruthlessly enlarged in a small round mirror set into a large rectangular mirror, recalling that startling pre-staircase close-up of Norma Desmond's epidermis.

Garland's Vicki Lester, a newcomer to the studio, stumbles into a photo shoot where a still photographer has rigged up artificial doves hanging from the ceiling. When she brushes into one of them, it suggests the Paramount microphone brushing the peacock feather in Norma's hat. In the studio head's screening room a projector blinds Garland the way that big overhead light on DeMille's set blinds Swanson in *Sunset Boulevard*. When Vicki Lester regales her husband, Norman Maine, with a parody of her film's production number, the sequence winks at Norma's Mack Sennett and Chaplin routines. Vicki and Norman screen a picture in their new home. We even catch a glimpse of Schwab's Drug Store as Vicki and the studio head drive down Sunset Boulevard to get her husband out of jail. Toward the end of the film James Mason, as Norman Maine, descends the staircase at the sanitarium like a grotesque imitation of Norma Desmond.

The theme of *A Star Is Born*, in every version, is: "I used to be big, and now she is." In the 1976 remake starring Barbra Streisand, that theme has swollen to the Ascent of Mount Ego. Apart from the story, this third iteration doesn't allude to the previous two. There was room for just one on Streisand Boulevard.

Rebel Without a Cause (1955) seems an unlikely source for *Sunset Boule-vardi*ana, but there's a verbal toast early on. "Life is crushing in on me,"

Natalie Wood tells James Dean as they walk to school. Dean's reply—
"Life can be beautiful"—was Holden's whimsical line to Nancy Olson at
the New Year's Eve party. Dean's line reading also copies Holden's.

Can Life Be Beautiful in Hollywood?

The line "Life can be beautiful" was a catch phrase all over
America in the forties and beyond. It's the exact title of a radio
soap opera that ran from 1938 to 1954. Each show began with
a hefty piece of philosophical profundity in the form of a
quote from Emerson, Ruskin, and other heavy hitters. Those
quotes ended with an added tout for the show, i.e., "When getting and spending happiness is your aim, life can be beautiful."

The Norma Desmond house also makes a surprise appearance in *Rebel
Without a Cause*. From the Griffith Observatory, there's a long shot of it far
away (in this instance, probably not the actual house, since the geography
would be too complicated, as well as the sight lines). Sal Mineo points
out the house to James Dean, telling him it's deserted.

Later Dean, Mineo, and Natalie Wood visit the empty mansion at
night. They find a ghostly ruin, with dangling window shutters and broken glass. (We can read this as a haunting allusion to Norma Desmond's
departure. Is she still incarcerated, we wonder, and where—jail? An asylum? Or did one of her suicide attempts succeed?)

The swimming pool is empty once more. It's photographed from
above, in a high angle shot that compounds the morbid desolation.
Dean, Wood, and Mineo cavort in it. By this point in the picture, however, teen anguish has become so viscous that it's a grim relief to specu-

late on Norma Desmond's fate. Will she ever return home? Where is Max? Does Norma grieve still for Gillis?

In *The Jeanne Eagels Story* (1957), Kim Novak, as Eagels, dupes an older actress named Elsie Desmond (played by Virginia Grey) in order to land a part in a play. The play, *Rain,* adapted from the Somerset Maugham story "Miss Thompson," made Jeanne Eagels famous (onscreen in this bio pic and also in reality). During a performance, Elsie Desmond waits in the wings to swoop on her usurper. Hissing venom, she decrees that the play will indeed bring Jeanne Eagels luck—"all of it bad." (In that scene Virginia Grey's face, like her character's name, alludes to the earlier Desmond.)

Traveling between *Sunset Boulevard* and *Mommie Dearest,* you'll pass a rest stop called *The Female Animal.* Pull in for a breath of stale air. But don't expect to leave feeling refreshed. The ads predict the climate of this low-budget 1958 melodrama starring Hedy Lamarr: "Once she was too hungry for love to be afraid. But now—it was too late!" Lamarr plays mother to Jane Powell; like Lana Turner and Sandra Dee in *Imitation of Life* the following year, both fall in love with the same man, in this case male animal George Nader.

Hedy pays the bills to keep movie extra and beach bum Nader happy. In the new clothes she buys him—and out of them—he keeps her very happy, though it takes a bit of doing for the stud to accept her sartorial presents.

NADER

What kind of a guy do you think I am, taking clothes from a woman?

LAMARR

An actor must make an impression. You can't get anywhere looking like a tramp.

NADER

If I took them, I'd *be* a tramp.

Like Holden, he keeps the fancy duds. To assure her gigolo's nightly comeback, aging beauty Lamarr puts herself through the equivalent of a Norma Desmond workout tape to maintain, or regain, an elusive menopausal youth.

Two other movies in 1958 waved to *Sunset Boulevard* from the Hollywood freeway. *The Goddess* stars Kim Stanley as a neurotic, Marilyn Monroe-type actress who lives in a house chock-full of framed photos of herself. At the end of *Suddenly, Last Summer*, Katharine Hepburn's final scene is a gauche mirror image of Swanson's. Hepburn's Violet Venable goes (more) insane while listening to Elizabeth Taylor spill the beans about Sebastian and what really happened to him "last summer." If Norma on the stairs turns into Salome, then Violet, ascending glassy-eyed in her private elevator car, evokes Jocasta.

If Wilder borrowed from Hitchcock the voyeuristic through-the-window shot into Gillis's apartment, Hitchcock perhaps glanced back at *Sunset Boulevard* when he made *Psycho* in 1960. The bedroom of Mrs. Bates, which Vera Miles examines just before the climax, is a middle-class Victorian version of Norma's high-toned baroque boudoir. By the fifties both styles had fallen out of favor because they were old, though the public, mad for newness, despised Victoriana most of all. The outmodedness, the antimodern grotesquerie of Norma's palazzo and of the Bates house, added an aura of depravity to both films. In *Psycho* and in *Sunset Boulevard*, the art directors encoded layers of sinister meanings into the respective houses and their contents.

Picture Norma Desmond in Rome and what have you got? *The Roman Spring of Mrs. Stone* (1961), from the novel by Tennessee Williams. José Quintero, the director, gets away with innuendos—in some cases, made graphic—that Billy Wilder wouldn't have dared a decade earlier. The carryings-on, the feast of gigolos, the lingering "depravity" of several millennia—this picture reads like a case history of forbidden desires.

Williams apparently finished the novel before he saw *Sunset Boulevard*. *The Roman Spring of Mrs. Stone*, written in 1949, was published in the summer of

1950. Williams did see *Sunset Boulevard*, however, at some point during 1950, later telling friends that he found it shattering and "wonderfully awful." A Williams acquaintance said that "Gloria Swanson was considered for *The Roman Spring of Mrs. Stone*, but it was thought that her brilliant success in *Sunset Boulevard* might raise unfair comparisons between the two films."

By the time *Roman Spring* was filmed, however, *Sunset Boulevard* had become a touchstone among filmmakers, especially gay ones, and a number of Wilder motifs leaked into Quintero's film. Declining actress Karen Stone (Vivien Leigh) takes her gigolo, Paolo (Warren Beatty), to a tailor to buy new clothes. They settle on "the finest cashmere"—not vicuna, but close enough. In a party scene, the pet monkey of a rich American woman rides the arm of her paid escort. Vivien Leigh sends Warren Beatty to buy cigarettes. Leigh, like Swanson, uses her hands to characterize the woman she's playing. Leigh clutches hers constantly—Beatty comments on them twice—in contrast to Swanson, who unfurls hers in melodramatic, stylized gestures.

Paolo shows home movies starring Mrs. Stone and himself. The star of these, however, is never Karen Stone but Paolo's butt, which upstages all else in the frame. When the romance begins to unravel, Paolo taunts Mrs. Stone: "How old are you, fifty?" (The same age as Norma Desmond.) Later, when she's alone, his words come back in voice-over echoes: "How old are you, fifty . . . fifty . . . fifty?"

Mrs. Stone even has her own Waxworks, though they're not called that. Bessie Love, once a silent star, plays Vivien Leigh's dresser. Ernest Thesiger (the mad scientist in *The Bride of Frankenstein*) appears as a wizened old man at a sour party at Mrs. Stone's. Lotte Lenya, in a much larger role, steals the show as the flesh broker who supplies gigolos to women and ladies of the evening to men. Lenya, as the Countessa Magda (born in Hungary), has an apartment even more elaborately too-much than Norma Desmond's house. And did screenwriter Gavin Lambert have the Gabors in mind for an in-joke when he had "Magda" talk about her young days in Budapest and how in the movie she "trapped" her first husband, a Turk, à la Zsa Zsa?

Billy Wilder's "tastelessness" is a will-o'-the-wisp accusation when you come to Robert Aldrich, whose directorial coat of arms should bear the device, "Any taste you make bad, I can make badder." His 1962 horror picture about family values, *What Ever Happened to Baby Jane?*, is one of the most sadomasochistic movies ever shown outside a grind house. (I confess that I watch it with as much demented pleasure as anyone.) It rips off *Sunset Boulevard* more than its other parent, *Psycho*, with Bette Davis playing the mutant Norma Desmond role. Ironically, Blanche—Joan Crawford—and not Baby Jane used to be big in movies, although it's Baby Jane who's planning the comeback.

Did Aldrich have a checklist to assure that he left out nothing from *Sunset Boulevard*? A few of his borrowings: bogus fan mail to Norma Desmond becomes real fan mail to Blanche, intercepted by Jane and dumped in the garbage. Each picture has its obsolete automobile—Norma's 1920s Isotta-Fraschini is about twenty years old at the time of *Sunset Boulevard*; an early-forties Lincoln in *Baby Jane*, which is set in 1962. Joan Crawford watches one of her old films on TV—proving, I suppose, that by 1962 pictures really had gotten small. Then cruel Bette stalks in and turns it off.

Here the equivalent of Norma Desmond's final scene on the stairs is Baby Jane waltzing down the beach at Malibu. Mistaking rubberneckers for fans, she performs a merry dance, overjoyed to be back in the limelight—the police limelight, as it turns out, just like Norma.

Geraldine Page, as faded star Alexandra del Lago, spends hours drunk in a hotel bed in *Sweet Bird of Youth* (1962). Her bedroom feels more claustrophobic than Norma Desmond's, one reason being that Page, despite much acclaim, is no Gloria Swanson. You don't buy the conceit that she was a movie queen. When a producer, in her comeback sequence, proclaims that "Alexandra del Lago is the sex symbol of America," it feels like a Carol Burnett skit. Page convinces as a symbol of the Actors Studio, but never of sex. Her Alexandra del Lago, nerves shot to hell, is the kind of neurotic actress less likely to evoke sympathy than fatigue.

In that same comeback sequence, a Stroheim figure—with monocle—lights Alexandra's cigarette as she descends the opulent staircase. But director Richard Brooks didn't pay close attention: the staircase upstages

Geraldine Page. When the comeback picture previews, the audience laughs at her close-up, and kids are overheard asking who she is and saying, "I thought she was dead."

Some lines from the script sound like reverberations in a *Sunset Boulevard* echo chamber. Geraldine Page: "There's a thing, God help us, called a close-up" and "There is no place to retire to when you retire from the movies." Paul Newman, her "employee" (i.e., gigolo), later demoted to chauffeur, tells Page, "I like you. You are a nice monster." Joe Gillis to Norma, in Wilder's version of this declaration: "You're the only person in this stinking town that has been good to me."

William Holden plays a screenwriter again in *Paris When It Sizzles* (1964)—this time successful and well-off, but as full of self-loathing as Gillis in *Sunset Boulevard*, and with plenty of booze to fuel self-contempt. Holden has come full circle: here he plays a lame, burned-out screenwriter version of Norma Desmond, with Audrey Hepburn functioning both as Joe Gillis and Betty Schaeffer. But the picture is far less imaginative or entertaining than those reversals imply. Its tiny allusions to *Sunset Boulevard* include Hepburn waving a pistol, though it's Tony Curtis who shoots Holden in the back. And in one scene Holden wears a white terry cloth bathrobe like the one Gillis wore in his seedy apartment at the Alto Nido.

In *Ship of Fools* (1965) Vivien Leigh, as lonely wandering widow Mary Treadwell, has a scene where, in drunken abhorrence, she regards her forty-six-year-old face in a mirror. She paints eyes and mouth in heavy clown-whore strips as a desperate remedy for the ravages of time. Plucked from *Sunset Boulevard* and strained through *Baby Jane*, the overripe scene was lifted not by the hand of an artist paying homage but snatched by the fingers of a vandal—in this case director Stanley Kramer.

In *Valley of the Dolls* (1966), every female character is trying desperately to avoid becoming Norma Desmond. That same year, a great silent star played a butler: Francis X. Bushman in *The Ghost in the Invisible Bikini*.

Robert Aldrich's disfigurement of fame, jolting in *What Ever Happened to Baby Jane?*, had become a rolling blackout by 1968, when he directed *The*

Legend of Lylah Clare. This one tries to be a cheap, dull, rip-off of *Sunset Boulevard,* but director and writers aren't up to such a feat.

The mansion where Hollywood director Peter Finch lives after the death of his lesbian discovery, Lylah Clare, resembles the Desmond house, and the movie-within-the-movie bears faint resemblance to *Queen Kelly.* Coral Browne, playing a vicious gossip columnist, asks Finch, "Aren't you borrowing a little heavily from *Sunset Boulevard?"* If only she were right. Everyone in it gives the worst performance of a career: Finch, Kim Novak, Valentina Cortese, Ernest Borgnine, Ellen Corby. One mildewed line sums it up: "I'll rummage through your soul like a pick-pocket through a stolen purse."

The seventies, a culturally unprepossessing decade, probably turned out no more bad movies than any other. And yet, a roundup of pictures that quoted *Sunset Boulevard* amounts to a dullish bouquet. Surely the funniest allusion came from the mouth of flaming Emory, in *The Boys in the Band* (1970): "I am not ready for my close-up, Mr. DeMille. Nor will I be for the next two weeks."

Heat (1972), produced by Andy Warhol and directed by Paul Morrissey, might be called a louche set of variations on a theme by Billy Wilder. It's an improvised, dead-pan, soft-core soap opera aimed at a twelve-year-old libido. Now it looks as passé as all else connected with the Warhol factory.

This title opens the picture: "In 1971 Another Film Studio, the Fox Lot on Sunset Boulevard, Was Torn Down." In the opening sequence Joe Dallesandro roams the bulldozed remains of 20th Century–Fox, an allusion to the famous 1960 photograph of Gloria Swanson in the ruins of the Roxy Theatre.

Vacuous, monotonal Dallessandro plays "Joe," as in "Gillis." Joe, a gigolo deadbeat, and blowsy Sylvia Miles (as forgotten actress Sally Todd), are both ex-TV stars. Miles's mansion has seen better days, though it vaguely resembles Norma's. "The days of your international stardom are over," says one of Sally Todd's four ex-husbands. She answers: "I need the money, Sidney. I'm strapped. I'm strapped in a white elephant with thirty-six rooms and a crazy daughter." Sidney: "And an eighteen-year-old Cadillac."

When Dallessandro walks out on star-yenta Miles, she goes to his fleabag motel, pulls a revolver, tries to shoot him but the gun is kaput. "Shit," she says and stomps away, ending this imitation of *Sunset* that might have killed Swanson ten years early had she deigned to see it.

Worse treats lay ahead in the Watergate era. The less said about *Mame* (1974) the better, but Edward Margulies and Stephen Rebello say this much in *Bad Movies We Love*: "*Sunset Boulevard* aficionados will quickly realize that this movie, rather than the *Salome* that Norma Desmond hoped would return her to glory, is the faded Hollywood star's vanity production nonpareil, and that Lucille Ball as Auntie Mame is a good deal scarier than Gloria Swanson as Desmond. The difference, of course, is that Swanson was *supposed* to be scary."

Before shooting *Eraserhead* in black and white in 1976, David Lynch screened *Sunset Boulevard* for his cast and crew. Asked why, he said, "*Sunset Boulevard* is in my top five movies, for sure. But there wasn't anything in particular about it that related to *Eraserhead*. It was just a black-and-white experience of a certain mood."

Paramount was always the most photogenic studio in Hollywood. It turns up in lots of movies, especially Paramount productions; usually the famous gate does an architectural star turn. *The Day of the Locust* (1975), however, like *Sunset Boulevard*, includes brief scenes shot elsewhere on the lot. So does *The Last Tycoon* (1976). Curiously, in the latter film the row of second-story offices where Nancy Olson and William Holden work on their script—the readers' department, in actuality and in *Sunset Boulevard*—has become the writers' department.

Among the many oddities credited to *Mommie Dearest* (1981) is the Dunaway–Swanson parallel. Faye Dunaway, like Swanson, will probably be best remembered for one picture. The ironic difference, of course, is *Sunset Boulevard*'s greatness versus the reeking camp of *Mommie Dearest*. In other words, Billy Wilder's artistry over Frank Perry's clueless direction.

This stock-car race of a movie shows paradoxical restraint in only one way: it barely swerves toward *Sunset Boulevard*, though you expect it to at every turn. That may be because Joan Crawford—in life and as portrayed by Dunaway—more than matches Norma Desmond. Hence, no borrowing needed. (Crawford, box office poison and kicked out of several studios, is still big at PepsiCo.) And maybe Frank Perry lacked what it takes even to copy Wilder.

If you think about *Sunset Boulevard* while watching *Mommie Dearest*, you deconstruct both Norma and Joan. Crawford's up at four in the morning so that her limo can pull through the MGM gate at five—none of that "I don't work before ten in the morning and never after four-thirty in the afternoon" Norma Desmond nonsense. The fanaticism of Dunaway/ Crawford lacks the angry nostalgia that drives Norma Desmond. Norma, fragile despite a waspish temper, might crumble any moment. Crawford was as delicate as a combat tank.

When Greg (Steve Forrest) walks out on Joan, it's the reverse of a Norma Desmond scene. No suicide attempt, no pistol; instead, Crawford uses scissors. With them, she castrates him right out of every photograph. Little Christina (Mara Hobel) observes to brother Christopher, "If she doesn't like you she can make you disappear." Which, in the most literal way, Norma does to Joe Gillis. Joan's appointment with L. B. Mayer, though harsh, amounts to the same as Norma's unannounced visit to DeMille: both women get the heave-ho, the Hollywood brush-off.

Other scenes in *Mommie Dearest* try to be *Sunset Boulevard* moments, but don't quite make it, perhaps because Crawford's beyond-the-grave possession of Dunaway brooks no competition. When Joan descends the staircase bearing Christina's uneaten rare steak, it's a muted, mad moment worthy of Norma. And when Joan greets her fans after winning the Oscar for *Mildred Pierce*, her big, masculine hands enact some strange Desmondesque drama of joyful desperation.

Those scenes of Joan signing photos seem conscious *Sunset Boulevard* quotes. And appropriately so; if you're making a movie about Hollywood, don't leave out fan mail and autographs. A history of movie stars could be written from the rear—that is, from "backstage," the privileged angle of those fans who kept the stars great, even after fame had lapsed and death had erased all but celluloid. The Norma Desmonds of Hollywood love signing photos and sending them out to adoring fans. Has-beens and starlets are especially generous. I know, because as a kid I targeted both groups. You should see the letters I got, along with luscious glossies covered with undying inscriptions of love and gratitude.

Gloria Swanson, like Joan Crawford, kept in touch with many fans over the years. She maintained files of addresses and preserved their letters, as she saved all else. Swanson was, of course, less obsessive than Crawford, who hired extra help and enlisted battalions of local fan volunteers to attend her far-flung admirers. Joan, beloved by those who never felt her wrath, looked upon answering fan mail as part of her discipline as an actress.

As a filmmaker, Rainer Werner Fassbinder was the child of Marx and Technicolor. I find most of his works unendurable, and yet *Veronika Voss* (1982) possesses a meagre charm, like a pretty weed on a desolate slag heap. This black-and-white Teutonic nosegay to the tragic dames of Hollywood might be called everybody's autobiography, with an oblique chapter on Norma Desmond.

Veronika is a spoiled, demanding forties movie star rumored to have been a protégée of Goebbels. Her story takes place in the midfifties, when her career is on the skids and she's addicted to morphine. So desperate for a comeback is she that she *begs* to play the mother role! The director of her comeback picture, *Blue Skies*, resembles Billy Wilder. But Veronika avoids the fate of Norma Desmond; at the end she offs herself with an overdose.

Trading Places (1983) includes two references to *Sunset Boulevard*, one literal—a clip from the film—and the other indirect: a sexual joke about a gorilla and a man, whom the gorilla mistakes for a woman. This sex joke also salutes another picture in the Wilder canon, the final scene in *Some Like It Hot.*

Had Gloria Swanson lived to see *The Cotton Club* (1984), I doubt that she would have been pleased. Set in the late 1920s, it has an appearance by "Gloria Swanson," played badly by Diane Venora, who seems unsure of who Swanson was.

You Can Take the Gay Train

George Chauncey, in his book *Gay New York*, writes about homosexual men who, with the increasing popularity of movies from around 1910 to the 1930s, borrowed the names of stars whose images struck sympathetic chords in gay culture. Theda Bara and Mae West were predictably in vogue, and "Gloria Swanson, an actress known for both her numerous marriages and her wardrobe, was perhaps the most popular of drag personas, and was taken as the *nom de drag* by the best-known African-American drag queen of the 1930s."

This man, né Winston, "was a female impersonator who had already won a clutch of prizes at Chicago's drag balls and had run his own club before moving to New York. He quickly found employment as hostess at a popular cellar club on West 134th Street. 'Here he reigned regally,' one gay Harlemite noted, 'so perfect a woman that frequently clients came and left never suspecting his true sex.' 'Gloria' sang bawdy parodies, danced a bit, and appeared in net and sequins, velvet-trimmed evening-gown skirts displaying with professional coyness a length of silk-clad limb."

Several movies released near the end of the twentieth century made intelligent and witty use of Swanson and of *Sunset Boulevard* as a thesaurus in which to find visual and verbal synonyms for their own topics. In *Soap Dish* (1991), Sally Field plays an aging soap opera star who's a bitch and not very smart. Her producer and various costars conspire to get her "killed" off the show. Field to her producer, Robert Downey Jr.: "I realize I'm not a young woman. However, could you *please* point out to our new costume designer that I don't feel quite right in a turban. What I feel like is Gloria fucking Swanson. What am I, seventy? Am I seventy? Why don't you just put me in a walker. Buy a goddamn walker and put me in it!"

Counting the *Sunset Boulevard* references in Robert Altman's *The Player* (1992) is like rolling pennies in paper tubes for the bank: at some point you must stop and leave the remainder uncounted. Coopting *Sunset Boulevard* to update Hollywood chicanery, Altman transforms Wilder's dark, gothic *Wuthering Heights* vision into a pastel, postmodern studioscape. Everything—thoughts, speech, deals, even murder—is an ironic quote, Hollywood mimicking itself. This is the Hollywood where pictures got small but high-concept movies, power lunches, and cosmetic surgery stay big forever.

The Player opens with writers pitching story ideas to studio execs, like Holden at Paramount. Griffin Mill (Tim Robbins), an executive stalked by a disgruntled writer, does the sensible thing and kills the writer—the wrong one. Unlike Norma Desmond, he gets away with murder.

One character mentions Wilder's *Witness for the Prosecution*, but an entire scene genuflects to *Sunset Boulevard*. In a screening room, watching rushes, a secretary addresses her boss (Tim Robbins).

SECRETARY

Griffin, a guy named Joe Gillis called and he said that he wants you to meet him at the St. James Club around ten o'clock on the patio. Know who this is?

GRIFFIN

Joe Gillis? Never heard of him.

SECRETARY

He said you'd know him.

GRIFFIN
(to others in the room)
Anyone know who Joe Gillis is?

STUDIO HEAD

He's the character William Holden plays in *Sunset Boulevard*. The writer who gets killed by the movie star.

FEMALE VOICE
Gloria Swanson. Fantastic movie.

GRIFFIN
(laughs)
That guy. Last week he said he was Charles Foster Kane, the week before that it was Rhett Butler.

Tim Burton didn't really need Norma Desmond fodder for *Ed Wood* (1994), since Wood himself provided sufficient loony subject matter. But Vampira (played by Lisa Marie) does owe her slithery hand gestures to Norma. So did the real Vampira in Ed Wood's *Plan 9 From Outer Space* (1959). It's not farfetched to say that Vampira herself owes her entire persona as much to Norma Desmond as to the vampire-movie genre.

Even when a film set in Hollywood works hard *not* to crib from *Sunset Boulevard*, as *Twilight* (1998) does, the allusions seep in. But since *Twilight* is nouveau noir, how could it not echo *Sunset*? Paul Newman plays Harry Ross, an ex-cop and private eye who now serves as handyman/houseboy for a Hollywood couple, played by Susan Sarandon and Gene Hackman. She's an ex-box office diva, he's a former action star. Like Norma Desmond, they retain their mansion and their millions.

And Newman lives over their garage. That's one of two direct quotes from *Sunset Boulevard*. The other is an empty swimming pool more forlorn than Norma's the night Joe Gillis spies rats skittering in it. But *Twilight* suffers from anemia; a Wilder transfusion would have helped.

Sonnenuntergang Boulevard

Several recent Germanic filmmakers plucked twigs from *Sunset Boulevard* to build their own rather odd cinematic nests. In 1980, Bastian Cleve made a feature film called *Exit Sunset Boulevard* starring longtime starlet Elke Sommer. This won't be on the shelf at your local Blockbuster, nor does the plot synopsis sound irresistably fetching: "A German citizen arrives in Hollywood to interview Elke Sommer. He tries unsuccessfully to pick up a black woman while rollerskating near the beach, then phones home from Death Valley to explain that he will not be returning to Germany. His surrealistic experiences collide with the gritty reality of life in Southern California."

Mit den Clowns kamen die Tränen (1990) might be translated as "Clowns Bring Tears." In three parts, with a total running time of 270 minutes, it stars Sunnyi Melles as Norma Desmond (apparently the only reference to *Sunset Boulevard*).

Sunset Boulevard (1991) an eight-minute documentary by Thomas Korschil of Austria, "is an attempt to simultaneously picture the two big contradictory American myths: the myth of individualism, and that of the melting pot. People alone in their cars remind us of similar boxlike containers such as houses, offices, factories, and coffins." Whatever.

Do these pretentious, angst-ridden plots sound like *Saturday Night Live*? Think what Mike Myers, as Dieter in "Sprokets," could do with any one of them. "Would you like to pet my monkey?" he might say. Or, more to the point, "Your cinema is morose but masturbatory."

In Alfonso Cuarón's *Great Expectations* (1998), Anne Bancroft plays Nora Dinsmore as a homage to Norma Desmond. The crest over her ruined villa in Florida, Paradiso Perduto, is ND—like the crest on Norma's Isotta-Fraschini.

Bancroft's Nora Dinsmore is also Miss Havisham by another name, just as Norma was Billy Wilder's Miss Havisham—Holden even refers to the grotesque Dickens character in voice-over. From the Dickens novel, through various earlier film versions, up to this latest *Great Expectations*, the durable role of Miss Havisham comes full circle from printed novel to cinema novel. If you doubt that movies have usurped literature, note that Anne Bancroft's Nora/Miss Havisham refers as much to Wilder as to Dickens. One reason, of course, being that many who have never read *Great Expectations* have seen *Sunset Boulevard.*

Desmond-like, retired director James Whale (Ian McKellen) in *Gods and Monsters* (1998) watches one of his old films, in this case *Bride of Frankenstein.* The clip we see him watching features a prominent portion of the Franz Waxman score. A double tribute: not only to Whale's work, but to *Sunset Boulevard,* since Waxman composed the scores for *Bride of Frankenstein* and for *Sunset Boulevard.*

Whale takes ironic delight in watching his old films, in contrast to Norma Desmond, whose rapture is literal, pure, and boundless. The one-sided homoerotic relationship between Whale and a young gardner (Brendan Fraser) ironically parallels that of Norma and Joe Gillis. Lynn Redgrave as Whale's crusty Central European servant serves as a comic version of Stroheim's Max.

Whale, dead in the swimming pool at the end, floats and bobs despite rigor mortis. Lynn Redgrave and Brendan Fraser, pulling him out of the pool, are photographed from the same angle as the cops fishing Holden out of Norma's pool. And Whale, like Holden in *Sunset Boulevard,* is photographed from underwater and also from above.

Christopher Bram, author of *Father of Frankenstein,* the novel on which *Gods and Monsters* is based, has pointed out that in his book Whale's body is at the bottom of the pool. He explains that a body must begin to decompose before it rises to the surface, and that takes time. Referring to the same unscientific phenomenon in *Sunset Boulevard,* Bram says, "It's biologically impossible, but it's such a great shot, who's going to criticize it?"

Glenn Close might be the Gloria Swanson of our day because of her deadpan imperiousness in so many roles. But it's her versatility—opera singer in *Meeting Venus,* manic killer in *Fatal Attraction,* vicious marquise in *Dangerous Liaisons,* first lady in *Mars Attacks!*—that crowns her as our Bette Davis. In *Cookie's Fortune* (1999) she plays Camille, a self-righteous, maniuplative small-town bitch in Holly Springs, Mississippi, where she's directing a play at the First Presbyterian Church. It's *Salome* by Oscar Wilde—revised and "improved" by Camille.

I read her role in *Cookie's Fortune* as a two-hour in-joke from in-jokester Robert Altman. Close played Norma Desmond in Andrew Lloyd Webber's *Sunset Boulevard* in Los Angeles and New York, and she's one of the few current film actors who can go over the top without really going over the top. Patchy Desmond fog moves in and out of Close's performance here, but she's too clever and too skilled to let it shroud her in.

Like Norma, Camille is a drama queen, whether directing this sanitized *Salome* or controlling everyone in Holly Springs. Her ego is Desmond-size, but she doesn't commit murder—she merely stages one, though in the end she's accused of the crime. Camille has no mad scene in the finale, or perhaps she does, though it's played under a blanket that she throws over her head. The implication is that she smothers herself.

When director Sam Mendes accepted his Oscar for *American Beauty* in March 2000, he thanked Billy Wilder in his speech, mentioning the comedy and drama in *The Apartment* as inspiration for his own work. But Mendes and his writer, Alan Ball, also borrowed a page from *Sunset Boulevard*. *American Beauty* opens with Kevin Spacey's voice-over narration informing us that he will be dead a year from now. That voice-over is fitting, since Spacey—in looks and as a solid actor—might be called the William Holden of current American movies.

chapter 23

Sunset Cul-de-sac

Sunset Boulevard was first shown on television in the early sixties. On the small screen, it looks reasonably good although, as always with "visual" movies, many details escape. In terms of temperamental compatibility, however, TV and *Sunset Boulevard* don't mix. The obvious reason: *Sunset Boulevard* is an epic, at least by implication—the epic story of movies, Hollywood, youth and age, treachery, and spoiled love. From Norma Desmond's point of view, carpetbaggers have marched through her glorious land of silent pictures and burned the plantations, leaving a ruinous swath of talk, talk, talk. In Desmondland, *yesterday* is another day.

The second reason why TV can't climb high enough to capture *Sunset Boulevard*, even in a small net of allusion or homage, is because those millions of couch potatoes out there in the family room won't grow up. They'll take Jimmy Stewart in *It's a Wonderful Life* and leave Norma Desmond to you and me.

Or, if they must welcome her into the home, let her come dressed as Carol Burnett. Serious TV shows have tried to channel Norma, usually with mawkish outcomes. Though Carol Burnett seldom got Norma right, certainly not the way she nailed so many Bette Davis and Joan Crawford heroines, and the way she created her own *Gone With the Wind* parallel universe, she did grasp the spirit of Norma Desmond. Burnett knew that only Gloria Swanson could ride the tempest of Norma, blow-ing tragic and comic in the same storm. Others must settle for caricature.

When I say that Burnett didn't get Norma right, I'm in disagreement with Gloria Swanson, who wrote in her autobiography: "I still collapse with laughter every time I see a rerun of her Norma Desmond takeoff." But then, I've been unable to track down Carol's first *Sunset Boulevard* parody, which ran in December 1971, with Steve Lawrence as Joe Gillis.

Swanson caught it, wrote Burnett a letter, and got an invitation to appear as guest star on *The Carol Burnett Show* in 1972. Swanson danced a tango with six Valentino chorus boys, sang a song, and performed a skit with Carol as a charwoman and Swanson as Chaplin.

As the seventies progressed, Burnett did Norma Desmond about six times. In one skit, Harvey Korman plays Max and Tim Conway an advertising man who wants Norma to do a TV commercial for bug spray. Now, if you're going to parody something, you must not entirely discard the original plot. Bug spray? The skit isn't funny, just depressingly silly as only lame TV can be. Bad writing, bad jokes, bad timing—how could they have missed the point so totally? (Several other Norma skits resemble that one.)

Not wanting to clobber Carol Burnett, I journeyed to the Museum of Television and Radio in New York in search of still another of her "Nora" Desmond turns, and indeed it has funny moments. Nora and Max, on a rare outing, enter a restaurant. Max rolls a red carpet for Nora, who pleads, "Don't let the autograph hounds hurt me." One spidery Carol Burnett hand, fingers twisted, makes an entrance on a doorjamb before the rest of her arrives. There are, of course, no autograph seekers to fend off.

Nora wears black and white furs, outrageous Pointer Sisters clothes and eyeglasses, and a black sequined turban. She has the clown eyes and runaway lips of Tammy Faye Baker. Harvey Korman as Max gets the best line: "Your performance as *The Sheep Girl of the Bronx* will live forever."

Sunset Boulevard on Radio: Words, Words, More Words, and No Pictures

On September 17, 1951, an announcer opened the evening's presentation of *The Lux Radio Theatre* with these credits: "Gloria Swanson as Norma Desmond, William Holden as Joe Gillis, and Nancy Gates as Betty Schaeffer, with John Wengraf as Max." Abridged to about forty-five minutes, this *Sunset Boulevard* retains the structure and a condensed version of the script. The first line is Holden's: "Twenty minutes ago, a murder was committed on Sunset Boulevard, at one of those great big mansions between Hollywood and the beach." From there to the end, this version resembles a *Sunset Boulevard* theme park where you whiz by on a monorail gawking at highlights, with no time to stop.

Many scenes and much dialogue have been sacrificed to the narration, which makes Holden the de facto star. He's on about seventy-five percent of the time, Swanson twenty-five. His voice compels on radio as it did in the picture, and Swanson, of course, is still Norma Desmond. The audience at this live broadcast laughed occasionally, especially at Holden's description of the studio's transformation of his script about Oakies in the Dust Bowl into a story set on a torpedo boat. There's an outburst of laughter when he says to Norma, referring to her *Salome* script, "They'll love it in Pomona."

When Norma goes to Paramount to see DeMille, Joe meets up with Betty, Max learns that the studio wants Norma's car for a Bing Crosby picture (audience laughter), then Norma returns from her supposed reunion with DeMille believing he can't wait to work with her again. DeMille's voice is omitted—the only time he, rather than someone in his movies, landed on the audio equivalent of the cutting room floor.

Years before Carol Burnett, however, and long before Wilder's *Sunset Boulevard* was televised, the networks produced their own versions of the film. The material would have seemed attractive because, throughout the fifties, genuine adult dramas were not the rarities they became with the advent of flaccid made-for-TV movies. These early television "plays," often live, sometimes bold, and not necessarily saddled with sunny denouements, were intended to lure traditional moviegoers away from the movies.

The first network *Sunset Boulevard* aired January 6, 1955 on NBC. A presentation of "Lux Video Theatre," it starred Miriam Hopkins as Norma and James Daly as Gillis. Two actors from the 1951 Lux Radio Theatre version played the same characters here: Nancy Gates as Betty Schaeffer and John Wengraf as Max. By then, Hopkins's film career having played out, she also echoed Norma Desmond in reality. Playing Norma on TV foreshadowed Miriam Hopkins's own sad finale. In 1969 she portrayed an aging movie star in an independent production called *The Comeback*. Her costars: Gale Sondergaard and Minta Durfee Arbuckle (sometime wife of Fatty). When Hopkins died in 1972, *The Comeback* hadn't been released. In 1976 someone reportedly dug it up and released it as *Hollywood Horror Home*.

Ratings for that first *Sunset Boulevard* must have pleased NBC, for on December 3, 1956 it showed another version, this one as a segment of *Robert Montgomery Presents*. Mary Astor starred as Norma Desmond, Darren McGavin as Gillis.

In her autobiography, *My Story*, Astor tells how she tried to repair her life after years of alcoholism, failed marriages, illness, and a suicide attempt: "I got a script of the old, wonderful movie that Gloria Swanson had made,

Sunset Boulevard. I took it to Father Ciklic [the priest who had been her therapist] and said, 'Would you mind reading this—tell me a little how this kind of person acts—why does she behave in such-and-such a manner?' He wrote a full diagnosis and analysis. I showed it to my director in New York, we worked and studied together, and when the show went on the air I was no longer a bundle of nerves waiting for it all to be over with."

It's curious that Mary Astor, of all people, would need third-party insight into Norma Desmond, for she herself had been through more than Norma. One would expect her to dig the character up by the roots the first time she read the script.

Round about that time, Sid Caeser on *Your Show of Shows* did a spoof called "Aggravated Boulevard." Predictably, he played an actor trying to make a comeback.

Rod Serling wrote the most serious, and in some ways the campiest, testimonial to the potency of *Sunset Boulevard*: an episode of *The Twilight Zone* called "The Sixteen-Millimeter Shrine," broadcast on October 23, 1959 on CBS, and starring Ida Lupino. In basso solemnity, Serling began the segment with this voice-over: "Barbara Jean Trenton, whose world is a projection room, whose dreams are made of celluloid. Barbara Jean Trenton, struck down by hit-and-run years and lying on the unhappy pavement trying desperately to get the license number of fleeting fame."

The story opens with Barbara Jean watching one of her pictures—a talkie, since she was a thirties star. The films she loves most from her vanished career are "A Farewell Without Tears" from 1933 and "A Night in Paris" the following year. Lupino obviously patterned her performance on Swanson's. Though less imperious, she uses similar sweeping gestures. She wallows in the same self-deceiving grandeur.

In place of Max, Barbara Jean employs a female butler, Sally. This story allows no younger man; it's all about Barbara Jean's self-love and self-deception, and being forever infatuated with her own screen images. When she watches those old romantic chestnuts on her home screen, flickering light caresses her adoring face as it does Norma's.

Barbara Jean's house and furnishings look only slightly less outmoded than Norma's. The art director, however, wasn't *Sunset Boulevard*'s Hans

Dreier but George W. Davis, who shared art direction credit with Lyle Wheeler for *All About Eve.*

Martin Balsam, as her agent, arranges an audition for Barbara Jean at "International." The part she's offered is that of a fortyish mother. She: "I don't play mothers. I never have and I won't start now."

The studio head blasts her: "All right, Miss—Miss Prima Donna, you I got news for. You may think you're still the number one lady on the top of the heap, but you got it wrong. You're just an aging broad with a scrapbook, and any part you get at this studio won't have to go through an agent. We can set it up with the Community Chest, because it'll be charity."

At the end, through desperate wishing, Barbara Jean takes up surreal residence on her home screen. Her butler and her agent discover her missing. Only her celluloid image remains. Up there on the screen she's giving a party for her old friends and costars. Barbara Jean retains her 1959 age, but her dead, retired, and forgotten friends are their younger selves, assembled for the party. She descends the stairs à la Norma to welcome them—their gaiety and happy laughter the only evidence that Barbara Jean Trenton has taken a one-way trip to the Twilight Zone.

Mitchell Leisen, Billy Wilder's colleague from the forties, directed. Franz Waxman composed and conducted the music, which echoes his *Bride of Frankenstein* score more than the one he wrote for *Sunset Boulevard.*

When Gloria Swanson appeared on *The Beverly Hillbillies* in the mid-sixties, TV audiences might have considered Granny Clampitt a typical Swanson fan: so out of date she thought Swanson's silent pictures, still on back home in the hills, were the latest thing Swanson had done. When gorgeous Gloria, age sixty-five or so, descends a carpeted staircase, you know what glamour means. Granny asks Swanson when she's going to make another movie like *Society Scandal* (1924).

The only *Sunset Boulevard* allusion in the episode is very submerged, probably unintentional: the Clampitts' ancient jalopy doubles as the hillbilly version of Norma Desmond's Isotta-Fraschini.

Eager to see more silent movies starring Swanson, the Clampitts finance a "comeback" picture for Gloria, *Passion's Plaything*, in which they costar. The premiere is held back in Bug Tussle, Tennessee. The silent footage, in black and white with Gloria as a vamp, shows off Swanson the comedienne as well as any real picture she ever made. Stump your friends with this trivia question: "Where did Gloria Swanson appear for the very last time in a silent picture?" The answer, of course, is, "On *The Beverly Hillbillies.*"

If someone at the trivia contest asks, "What actress made a second career playing Norma Desmond knockoffs?" answer, "Poor Ida Lupino." Poor Ida, indeed, for in 1977 she was eighteen years older than Barbara Jean Trenton on *The Twilight Zone*, and *Charlie's Angels* nabbed her to play Gloria Gibson in "I Will Be Remembered," a scrumptious piece of trash. This episode tries to ape *Sunset Boulevard* without coming close. Didn't anyone have a clue?

Years later, producer Barney Rosenzweig told Jack Condon and David Hofstede for their *Charlie's Angels Casebook*, published in 2000, "Ida could not remember two words in succession. This was beyond a memory problem. The editor and I struggled in the cutting toom to make that picture work. It was very, very sad."

Rosenzweig's old blame-the-victim trick may be true, but whatever Ida's difficulties the real problem was *Charlie's Angels*. The show opens with rain falling on a Motel 6 version of Desmondland. A flash of lightning reveals a hanged man dangling from a tree. This terrifies ex-star Gloria Gibson, who phones her old friend Charlie for help.

This segment is as cheesy as the dairy shelf at the A&P. It might be hilarious except that it's really no fun to see the wonderful Ida Lupino demeaned in what's probably the worst role of her career. No wonder she couldn't remember the lines: "My old studio is making an updated version of *The Heart of New York*. That was one of my most successful pictures. This time I'm up for the mother's role. It's much smaller, but I'll make something of it."

David Lynch packed *Twin Peaks* with movie references. Lynch himself plays Gordon Cole, an FBI inspector who wears a hearing aid that doesn't prevent his shouting when he talks. In *Sunset Boulevard*, it's Gordon Cole at Paramount who has phoned Norma's home repeatedly. Had she taken any one of his calls, she would have learned that the studio wanted her car for a comeback, not her. (A few years later, in *Mulholland Drive* [2001],

Lynch had the camera linger for a long moment on the street sign, SUNSET BLVD.)

A 1997 episode of *3rd Rock from the Sun*, the series about aliens posing as humans, has Sally Solomon (played by Kristen Johnston) becoming a minor celebrity who wears an outfit patterned after one of Norma Desmond's. Celebrity wanes, she wonders where her fans have gone, and Dick (John Lithgow) says to Harry (French Stewart), "She used to be big." To which Harry retorts, "She's still big. It's the planet that got small!" (The title of this episode seems destined for triple-X reuse: "Fifteen Minutes of Dick.")

Robert Townsend's 1999 movie on the Lifetime Channel, *Jackie's Back: Portrait of a Diva*, is a wild, camp-comedy great-granddaughter of *Sunset Boulevard*. A faux documentary, or, as it's called in the credits, a "mockumentary," it stars Jennifer Lewis as Jackie Washington, a Ross-like diva making a lowgrade comeback. It's full of guest stars—Whoopi Goldberg, Liza Minnelli, Isabel Sanford . . . and Diahann Carroll, who toured as Norma Desmond in Andrew Lloyd Webber's musical version of *Sunset Boulevard*.

Tim Curry is the ubiquitous "mockumentarian" who follows Jackie about while she readies herself for a trumpeted comeback. In her Missouri hometown, she declaims for the camera in desperate close-up: "I'm still big in Kinloch. Still huge in Kinloch." There's a flashback to 1972 in which Jackie is led off to jail for stabbing football player boyfriend Milkman ("He delivers") with an Afro pick. Townsend's wicked deconstruction of *Sunset Boulevard* shows more rollicking, loose-cannon wit than any other film that has cut a savory slice from the original.

chapter 24

Life Upon the Wicked Stage

"Take a good look—I'm not nearly so amusing as you're going to be when you imitate me." Norma Desmond might have said it, but she didn't. Rather, it's spoken by the headmistress of a London theatre school in Penelope Fitzgerald's novel, *At Freddie's*.

I thought about that Swanson line manqué when I saw *Miss Desmond Behind Bars* at the Court Theatre on La Cienega in Los Angeles in August 1999. This drag musical opens with Norma (Gregory Messer) at the start of her life sentence, which she must serve at the Hollywood Women's Correctional Institution. We learn that, during her trial, Miss Desmond thought she was playing yet another melodramatic part.

Enter Norma—to the strains of Strauss's "Salome." "This isn't Paramount!" she snarls, looking down her nose in regal drag-queen disdain. This play's theatre of the ridiculous shenanigans are a camp tribute to the Wilder film, and also a cross-eyed parody of the Lloyd Webber musical. In spirit, it dumps *The Women* onto *Women Behind Bars*, adds a dash of *Lakmé* and, as garnish, tosses in a soupçon of *The Snake Pit*. It's *The Green Mile* with hair pulling in place of miracles.

From prison, Norma writes letters to departed Joe Gillis. Maria, a fellow inmate patterned after Rita Moreno's Googie Gomez in *The Ritz*, becomes "Hogeye" to imperious Norma. As it turns out, Norma didn't really shoot Joe: the guilty party is Hedda Hopper—or so we're led to believe until the musical finale, the rousing "Front Page News." David

Bouzas, as the gossip columnist, belts out "I'm Hedda Hopper!" any number of times, each time evoking the same raucous reply from the chorus: "No one can stop her!"

But someone does—by yanking off Hedda's blonde wig. The culprit isn't Hedda Hopper at all but sinister bald-pate Max von Mayerling, who is hauled off to the pokey as Norma heads for her glorious *return* to pictures.

Long before this kind of giddy pageantry, the theatre had spotted Norma Desmond, though she made her grand recycled entrance there much later than in Hollywood films. The critic Ethan Mordden, in his book *Broadway Babies*, doesn't mention Norma, yet she haunts a certain paragraph like a poltergeist: "It's too bad nobody recorded [Carol] Channing's 1955 flop *The Vamp*, on silent Hollywood, for this was one of the great strange shows, every choice a wrong one. Steve Reeves, in a small part, thought the overture weak; everyone's a critic." The play's title suggests Theda Bara, but Channing as disphoniously named heroine Flora Weems might be expected to toss in a Desmond or two for the boys.

Although no one ever wrote *What Ever Happened to Norma Desmond?*, various theatrical personalities seem determined to answer defunct Joe Gillis's final question: "What would they do to Norma?"

In 1966, three years before Stonewall, the great Charles Ludlam, of the Ridiculous Theatrical Company in New York, wrote a camp theatre piece called *Big Hotel*. Among the characters are God, the devil, Lupe Velez, Mata Hari, Svengali, and Norma Desmond. This early work by Ludlam, which drew on dozens of movies, songs, comic books, television ads, and great works of literature for its material, merely suggests the lunatic brilliance to come in Ludlam's two decades before his death in 1987.

A theatre exercise more than a play, *Big Hotel* has a scene where Norma tries to cadge money from Lupe Velez: "Let's drop the shallow mask of pretense. I'm flat broke, I haven't got a dime. I haven't made a picture in years." These lines are a bit obvious, but later in the play it's equally obvious that Ludlam had mastered his technique of turning the divas of Hollywood, opera, fiction, the stage, and mythology into pop-up icons.

As portrayed by Ludlam, these ladies burst into flame as the tawdry parodies and wicked caricatures that fuel drag art.

By act three, Ludlam has invented a brand-new Norma Desmond, like a camp scientist producing a full-blooded Cleopatra from DNA scraped off a pyramid. *This* Norma, created in Ludlam's own image, reads a letter from DeMille: "Dear Norma, please come and see me Monday morning if you are free. I have something to discuss with you. It's about your car. It's the only one made that year whose chassis is still in such good condition. Yours truly, C. B."

In ecstasy, Norma looks up from the letter and breathes out her joy: "He's read my *Salome* script. He wants me for the part. I'm perfect for it . . . I will kiss thy mouth, O Jokanaan! I will kiss thy mouth! And remember, I never work before one o'clock and I'm driven to the studio in a chauffeured limousine."

Marc Huestis, a filmmaker and playwright in San Francisco, won't be upstaged by anyone when it comes to a Norma Desmond fixation. She turns up, in one guise or another, in these productions by his company, Outsider Enterprises: a 1977 short film, *Miracle on Sunset Boulevard*, in which a voluptuous madonna in flowing robes appears to Norma Desmond and presents her with a cherub. (If ever there lived an unfit adoptive mother, Norma must be she.); a 1984 underground soap opera called *Naked Brunch*, where a warbling drag queen named Miss X stops abruptly to wail, "I can't go on with the song. I'm too happy."; and a recent "Tribute to Billy Wilder" with chanteuse extraordinaire Connie Champagne singing "As If We Never Said Good-bye" from the Lloyd Webber musical.

Huestis's magnum opus of this sort, however, is *The Trial of Norma Desmond*. In this 1984 play, Norma stands before the bar of justice; Hedda Hopper hires Philip Marlowe to investigate; Norma shares jail space with Barbara Graham from *I Want to Live*; Baby Jane Hudson testifies against Norma, her next-door neighbor; Philip Marlowe discovers Betty Schaeffer drunk in some dive à la Susan Alexander in *Citizen Kane*; Betty agrees to tell what happened and is rushed to the courtroom just as the jury is filing out; she swears that Norma's gun fired blanks and that a jealous Max really killed Joe Gillis; pandemonium in the court, Norma goes free, walks out on the arm of Cecil B. DeMille as they make plans to film *Salome*. (And the trial publicity has made the world eager for Norma's comeback.)

The inimitable Charles Pierce, who imitated the great icons beloved by gay men, was also reluctant to let Norma go. In a show called *The Return of Norma Desmond*, he portrayed her as an elegant, imperious jailbird speaking lines like these: "My prison sunsuit was designed by Edith Head, my ball and chain by Cartier, and my prison cell lined in black tile. Valentino came in and we tangoed for days."

Why the recurring rescue fantasy vis-à-vis Norma Desmond? No one seems willing to leave her to the inevitable consequence of her ending. Maybe the myth of Norma parallels that of Marilyn Monroe. In both cases, whatever the lady's culpability, the real villain is Hollywood.

The myth of Joan Crawford, by contrast, casts Hollywood as a shrinking violet wilted by Dragon Joan. But not in *Christmas with the Crawfords*, a campy musical parody by Wayne Buidens and Mark Sargent that has been a holiday favorite in San Francisco for years. In this, Joan gets to bless them every one. She, naturally, seeks to bolster her fading image with a Christmas Eve broadcast from her home on Bristol Avenue. Every drag icon in movie history drops by en route to Gary Cooper's bash next door, including Bette (in Baby Jane getup, of course), Mae, Carmen, Judy . . . and Gloria, who serenades Joan, Christina, and Christopher with "O Little Town of Hollywood," "God Rest Ye Silent Movie Stars (The Talkies Did You In)," and "Glooooo-ria" minus the "in excelsis Deo."

The first thing to know about Lypsinka is that she, too, is a silent star. A *New York Times* reviewer described her as a "mute stage persona" who moves her mouth "to artfully arranged recordings of songs and movie dialogue," but the word "mute" diminishes her extravagance. Surely Lypsinka, like Norma Desmond, can say anything she wants with her eyes. Or her hands, which the same reviewer called "graceful, cheerful hands" that sometimes "take on lives of their own, becoming angular and weaponlike."

Lypsinka was neither silent nor mute when I phoned her recently. I wanted to know about Abnorma Desmond. How did Lypsinka run across her?

"I wrote an article for *Interview*," said Lypsinka. "I was trying to figure out how to get an interview with Jacqueline Susann. So Lypsinka visits a medium to call up the ghost. . . . Hold on a minute, let me read it to you." And she did.

"So one dark and sultry summer night, in suffocating humidity, myself and my companions, the renowned folk choreographer Illness DeMag and the reformed murderess and health food guru Abnorma Desmond, slip inconspicuously into a Manhattan taxi cab. We pull up in front of the macrobiotic restaurant the Sybil of Cumae, for it is here above the eatery on the second floor that Abnorma has located the most divine medium, Miss Eek, who will allow me to penetrate the veil of mystery and commune with the spirit of Jacqueline Susann. . . ."

Né John Epperson in Mississippi, Lypsinka fled to Denver at the age of twenty-one, where she first saw *Sunset Boulevard* at a midnight screening. Since then neither John Epperson nor Lypsinka can let go of Norma Desmond. John Epperson says, "The more I watch *Sunset Boulevard* the more I'm swept away. It seems deeper and richer every time. I think one reason gay men like that movie so much is because gay men are so narcissistic. And they identify with an aging broad."

Lypsinka uses several sound bytes from the picture in her act, but when she appeared in Paul Schrader's TV film *Witch Hunt* she had her say. On the set, though not in the film, speaking in her own voice and not lip-synched, she said: "All right, Mr. Schrader, I'm ready for my close-up."

Lypsinka leaves you laughing, onstage and off. "You know," she said at the end of our talk, "my little assistant wants to be a drag performer. I told him he *must* take the name Isotta-Fraschini."

Life Upon the Wicked Page

Since *Sunset Boulevard* has great literary merit in addition to cinematic and theatrical excellence, it grabs the notice of writers. One might expect frequent allusions to it in fiction and nonfiction, though this is not the case. Perhaps that's because the writing in *Sunset Boulevard* is so potent that it threatens to flood the prose of anyone other than Charles Brackett and Billy Wilder.

A few recent allusions: David Thomson, in his 1985 novel *Suspects*, imagines the life stories of dozens of characters from Hollywood movies, including three and a half from *Sunset Boulevard*: Norma Desmond, Joe Gillis, Max von Mayerling—and Julian Kay (the Richard Gere character in *American Gigolo*) who, we learn in astonishment, is the son of Norma and Joe.

Julian "was born in 1951, in an asylum hospital, taken with forceps from the small, irate body of his mother, Norma Desmond, the onetime movie actress." At the birth, Norma "had no anesthetics in labor, but screamed at the mysterious pain. Max petitioned the state of California to be appointed the boy's guardian. He was accepted."

Robin Lippincott, in a story called "If You're Going to San Francisco," included in his 1996 collection *The Real, True Angel*, describes a forty-year-old dancer: "Instead of looking elastic now, his face looked almost exaggerated, caricatured—like the campy face Gloria Swanson made as the aging silent-movie star in *Sunset Boulevard*."

In Andrew Holleran's story "Petunias," which appeared first in *Poz* magazine and then in his 1999 collection *In September, the Light Changes*, an older gay character says with disrelish of younger gay men, "But they don't have *faces.* . . . We had faces. These new guys don't."

Kenneth Anger's *Hollywood Babylon* books seem inspired by *Sunset Boulevard* in some ghastly way. To use Angeresque prose, they could have sprung from the loins of the monkey, who impregnated Norma Desmond to grotesque fecundity. Or is it that both *Babylon* books skitter through the Tinseltown sewers like graverobber rats?

Charles Brackett and Billy Wilder, "the happiest couple in Hollywood," completed the script only during the final days of shooting *Sunset Boulevard*. (Photofest)

Harry Gribbon, Gloria Swanson, and Bobby Vernon in the Keystone comedy *A Dash of Courage* (1915). (Photofest)

Above "I had an original story kicking around Paramount." (Photofest)

Left "There's nothing else—just us and the cameras and those wonderful people out there in the dark." (Photofest)

William Holden, Gloria Swanson, Nancy Olson, and Erich von Stroheim. *Sunset Boulevard* was the climax of four careers. (Author's Collection)

Cecil B. DeMille, Billy Wilder,
and Gloria Swanson filming on
Stage 18 at Paramount in 1949.
(Photofest)

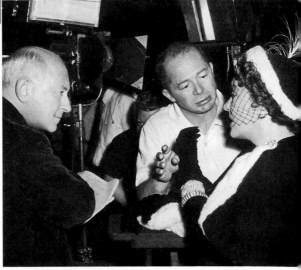

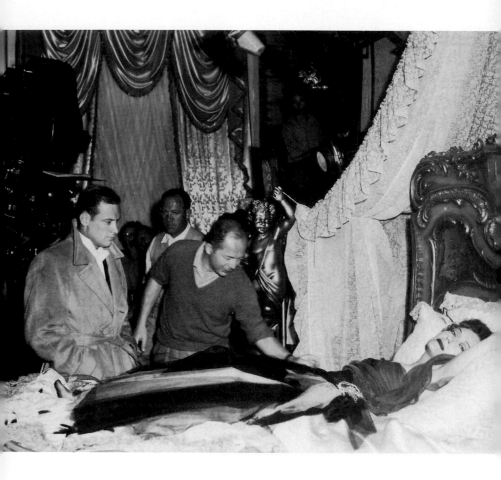

Holden, Wilder, and Swanson rehearsing the New Year's Eve sequence. (Photofest)

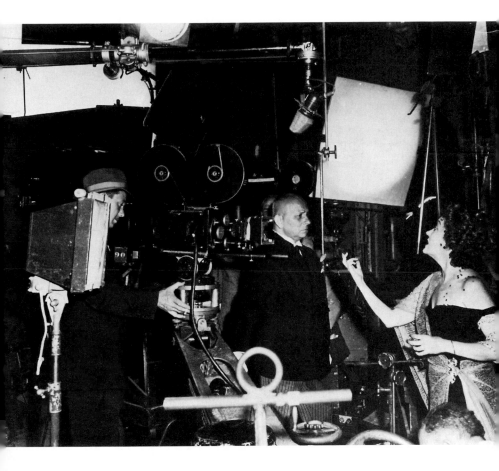

"The cameras have arrived." (Photofest)

The Waxworks and
friends: *(left to right)*
Buster Keaton, Anna
Q. Nilsson, Holden,
DeMille, Swanson,
and H. B. Warner.

"Harry Wilcoxon,
draw your sword and
raise that drape.
Samson's lying uncon-
scious over here."
Wilcoxon and
Swanson. (Photofest)

Chaplin fired Swanson in 1915 but she had the last laugh. (Photofest)

Mr. and Mrs. Holden—the unhappiest couple in Hollywood? (Photofest)

Jay Livingston, Ray Evans, Yvette Vickers, and a bevy of starlets. (Collection of Bob Grimes)

"Dear Joe, where is Max? Where is DeMille? Where is Hedda? Where has everybody gone? Love, Norma Desmond." (Photofest)

"I don't work before ten in the morning, and never after four-thirty in the afternoon." (Photofest)

Franz Waxman, composer. (Photofest)

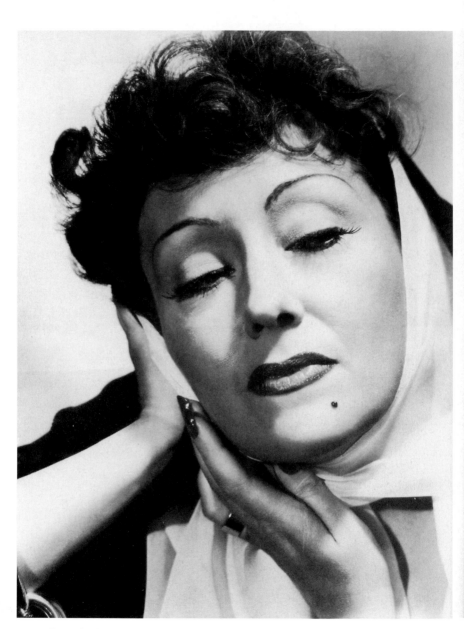

Will you look as exciting as Gloria Swanson when you're fifty? (Author's collection)

Erich von Stroheim: Who could really hate the Man You Love to Hate? (Photofest)

Judy Holliday, Jose Ferrer, and Swanson, Oscar night 1951. (Photofest)

Darren McGavin and Mary Astor in *Sunset Boulevard* on NBC Television in 1956.

The prison matron eyes Norma and Hedda in *Miss Desmond Behind Bars*. Los Angeles, 1999. (Ed Krieger)

Starring Norma Desmond…Glenn Close in Andrew Lloyd Webber's musical, *Sunset Boulevard*. (Craig Schwartz Photography)

chapter 25

Fifteen Minutes of Close-ups

R eady for Her Close-up"—*Newsweek* on Monica Lewinsky, March 15, 1999.

"Ready for my close-up, Mister"—package blurb for triple-X movie bluntly titled *White Trash Whore* (Vol. 10).

"Ready for Her Close-up"—*Time* on Laura Schlessinger at the debut of her short-lived TV show, September 18, 2000.

"America's teenagers are ready for their close-ups"—*The New Yorker* reporting on the Fox Network show, *American High*, August 21 & 28, 2000.

"Ready for His Close-up"—caption under photo of Russian president Vladimir Putin, *Newsweek*, September 18, 2000.

"We're Ready for Our Close-ups Now"—a January 16, 2000 *New York Times* article on Space Imaging, Inc., a pioneer company in the new field of close-up space photography.

"I'm ready for my close-up!"—an adult entertainment ad in the *Dallas Observer*, November 9–15, 2000 by "Mattress Actress—I'd love to be your leading lady!"

"The Antichrist is ready for his close-up"—lead of *GQ* article, "God's Moviemakers," March 2001.

"I'm ready for MY close-up"—bratty kid character Angelica, wearing feather boa and sunglasses, in TV ad for *The Rugrats Movie* in 1998.

"Are you ready for YOUR close-up?"—L.A. gay paper *Frontiers* in an

August 22, 1997 feature on gay porn director Mike Donner, reportedly "The Industry's Least Hated."

"The Republican gang that couldn't shoot straight on the economy is ready for its close-up"—Maureen Dowd, in the *New York Times*, reporting on "Bush 2" a few days before he was sort of elected president in November 2000.

"Ready for Their Close-ups"—an article on September 14, 2000 in the *Dallas Morning News* about finalists in "Model Search 2000." A color photo of the unprepossessing male and female aspirants suggests a better title: "Ready for Their Long Shots."

Edy, a gay character who has witnessed a murder in the February 20, 2000 episode of *The X-Files*, spots a camera crew following him, dashes off for a moment, returns in a new robe and turban to announce, "Ready for my close-up!"

"I'm (Not Quite) Ready for My Close-up"—Alistair McCartney, in the April 30, 1999 *Frontiers*, writing about "My Day as a Soft-Porn Centerfold."

"I'm ready for my close-up now"—teaser on page 1A of the *Dallas Morning News*, October 12, 2000. The actual article, in Section F, Personal Technology, is on "new lower-cost digital cameras."

"Ready for my out-of-court settlement now, Mr. DeMille"—Mark Steyn in his 1999 book, *Broadway Babies Say Goodnight: Musicals Then and Now*. He's referring not to Cecil B. but to Sir Andrew Lloyd Webber, who paid Patti LuPone a million dollars after he dumped her from his musical, *Sunset Boulevard*, and more than a million to Faye Dunaway after he dropped her from the show.

"I'm ready for my close-up"—Babs Bunny, a pink rabbit coed who favors Gloria Swanson/Norma Desmond outfits for schoolwear at Warner High, in Warner Bros. TV show *Tiny Toons*.

"Ready for my close-up now, Mr. DeMille"—the epitaph on an AIDS memorial quilt.

Richard Lederer, author of such books as *Anguished English* and *Practical Advice for the Grammatically Challenged*, was asked by a recent interviewer,

"What has popular culture done to the language?" He began his answer with a montage of movie quotes: "I'm going to make you an offer you can't refuse. . . . I have a feeling we're not in Kansas anymore. . . . Show me the money. . . . Hasta la vista, baby!" Lederer added that "people spend more time in front of a TV than they will ever spend in a college classroom."

The result of a lifetime of television watching and moviegoing—in lieu of reading books—is that Americans pepper their English with show business expressions. Once the language teemed with words and phrases from Shakespeare, the Bible, journalism, and politics. But since far more people have watched a single episode of *Seinfeld*, or the latest movie by Steven Spielberg, than ever have seen or read a play by Shakespeare, it's natural that "Yadda, yadda, yadda" and "E.T., phone home" should become catch phrases. Whether these will endure as long as certain lines from *Sunset Boulevard* and other Hollywood classics of the studio era is another matter.

In addition to "All right, Mr. DeMille, I'm ready for my close-up," Norma Desmond's immortal exit line, several other locutions from Brackett and Wilder's script have become naturalized citizens of the American language. An Associated Press dispatch titled "Academy Awards Going Back to Hollywood" opened like this: "The Oscars are making a Hollywood comeback—or is it a return?"

Michael Logan, writing about soap operas in *TV Guide*, gave a Bronx cheer to "The Worst of 2000." In the article he lamented a *Guiding Light* plot turn that was "pure hooey disguised as social commentary" in which Kim Zimmer "has become the Norma Desmond of daytime: She *is* big. It's her story lines that got small." In a January 2001 episode of *The Bette Midler Show*, Bette's manager, Oscar, misquoted Norma's line: "I am big, it's the *movies* [sic] that got small." In *The First Picture Show*, a stage musical about early Hollywood by Ain Gordon and David Gordon, a ninety-nine-year-old female silent-movie director, recalling her career before and after talkies, alludes obliquely to *Sunset Boulevard*: "The little studios where big things happened became big studios where little things happened." Tad Friend, reviewing William Goldman's memoir *Which Lie Did I Tell?* in the *New Yorker*, wrote that Goldman "is coasting, pretending to believe that he's still big and it's the pictures that got small." I confess that I, too, found this shorthand rhetorical device convenient. Assigned by *Publishers Weekly* in 1995 to interview a Japanese novelist whose novels and arrogance I disliked equally, I wrote that "Kenzaburo Oe believes he is big. It's literature that got small."

The subtlest exchange in *Sunset Boulevard*, and the briefest, takes place when Joe Gillis realizes that Betty Schaeffer has fallen in love with him. They're in the Paramount readers' department at night working on their script when she tells him she is no longer in love with her boyfriend, Artie Green.

GILLIS

What happened?

BETTY

You did.

I haven't heard it in other contexts, but Nancy Olson has. She says that sometimes, inquiring why a friend took a wrong turnoff or a colleague missed a cue, she'll ask "What happened?" and the smirking answer comes back, "You did."

Surely a smirk is inappropriate. This delicate exchange, shorter than a haiku, deserves esteem. And fame. After all, it sums up exactly what happens when love intervenes and detours two lives. Of all the tender utterances in Hollywood films, surely not one exceeds this perfectly balanced, highly compressed declaration. Its wisdom is classic, its passion romantic.

How long do ephemera last? There's a Goldwynism lurking somewhere in the answer, but I pose the question to emphasize that not all ephemera vanish overnight. For all I know, Toronto still has its own "Sunset Boulevard," the new name given in 1951 to Green Hills Road. This exotic Hollywood borrowing perhaps resulted from boosters spicing up their staid city. The presence of Gloria Swanson in town no doubt clinched the deal, and indeed someone took a picture of her on a ladder, still holding the hammer she had ostensibly used to nail the new sign onto a post. Lest municipal sovereignty be compromised, however, "immediately after changing the name, Miss Swanson planted a Canadian maple at the beginning of the street in memory of her visit to the city," stated a diplomatically-phrased press release.

In 1957 a French comic book version, *Boulevard du Crépuscule*, accomplished the feat of getting the story and its best lines into graphics, rather like an after-the-fact storyboard. Only the panels aren't drawings, they're actual stills from the film, greatly reduced. Holden's name, Swanson's, and Stroheim's are in lower case, preceding "Mise en scène de BILLY WILDER." Not surprising, since the French have always worshiped the auteur.

The first panel contains Holden's opening voice-over: "Voici le 'Sunset Boulevard,' le boulevard du crépuscule à Hollywood. Il est environ cinq heures du matin, et l'on voit accourir les agents de la police criminelle, au grand complet avec l'habituel cortège de journalistes. . . .'"

Famous translated lines explode from the page: "Je suis toujours UNE GRANDE ACTRICE. C'est le cinéma qui est devenu petit." On the cigarette case that Norma gives Gillis, "Mad About the Boy" turns into "Je suis folle de toi. Norma."

Norma Desmond's final speech loses no potency, even in comic book form. "Mais je vous promets de ne plus jamais vous quitter. Car, après *Salomé* nous ferons un autre film, et encore un autre. C'est que cela représente ma vie, et ce sera toujours de même. Il n'existe rien d'autre au monde à part nous, et les caméras. Et dans l'obscurité, le public qui admire en silence. Me voici, DeMille, je suis prête pour le 'premier plan.'" FIN.

It was bound to happen: a holiday card announcing "Christmas on SUNSET BOULEVARD," with a bewhiskered, Desmondesque Santa Claus descending the stairs, and a balloon caption that reads, "All right, Rudolph, I'm ready for my close-up." Another card, less seasonal, pictures a woman sitting before a mirror, holding an expressionistic Norma

Desmond mask over her face, with her reflection grinning back in a grimace, a huge Norma Desmond painting on a nearby wall, and Gloria Swanson photographs scattered across a table.

The comic strip *Heart of the City* recently showed a little girl sitting before a mirror, dressed in her mother's finery. Mom bursts in, shrieks, "My GOOD jewelry! My EXPENSIVE makeup! What have you got to SAY for yourself, young lady?" to which the child replies, "I'm ready for my close-up, Mr. DeMille."

These transmogrifications are not new. In the seventies, the *National Lampoon* ran a fake interview with Gloria Swanson that included (in her diatribe on health food) the coarse line, "We had feces then."

Close-up on "Sunsex Boulevard"

What's a good title for a gay porno flick about a middle-age muscle hunk named Norman Desmond who lives in a delapidated mansion attended by an S&M butler, and who takes in a young stud on the run from repo men? Why, *Sunsex Blvd.*, of course. Although sexual arousal and hilarity don't really mix, watch this and you may experience orgasmic laughter. For example: "There was a time in this business when all you needed was a big dick and tight ass. But that wasn't enough for them! No, they wanted stories and dialogue. Now it's talk, talk, talk when it should be cock, cock, cock."

Catalina Video, the Paramount of the male movie business, made this first *Sunsex Blvd.*, dazzling dialogue and all. Brad Austin, director of that 1993 release, shot all nonsexual scenes in black and white to evoke movies of the fifties. Sex scenes are in color.

The Catalina publicity department seems as energetic as Paramount's. A press release informs that "Zak Spears portrays former porn star Norman Desmond, and he does a hilarious job of emulating an aging prima donna. Muscular Brandon Wells is Joe, the writer Norman has called in to write the porn film that will mark Norman's cumback—er, return. Stunning Steve Maverick is captivating as Mr. DeVille, who likes to show his young actors exactly what it takes to be a star. Finally, we have Max Stone as Norman's loyal manservant Max, and with an impressive bald pate he looks quite like Max from the original movie—except perhaps for his tattoos."

Another *Sunsex Blvd.*, released by HIS Video, came out in 1994. In it, Steve Regis plays Dez Norman, a retiring porn star who decides that while the screen may have gotten smaller, he certainly hasn't. After all, as the promo advises, "He was a big star. In more ways than one."

In Catalina Video's 1999 sequel, *Return to Sunsex Blvd.*, Norman Desmond languishes in jail while Max, his assistant, takes care of Desmondland and its Desmondmen. The convoluted plot turns every way but loose and it hardly matters, for there are close-ups of all the things that make such movies big.

chapter 26

A Dethroned Queen

*B*ack in Chapter 17, Harold Prince telephoned Gloria Swanson after seeing her on the *The Steve Allen Show* in 1957. Something about Swanson, or her doomed musical *Boulevard!*, or Billy Wilder's *Sunset Boulevard*, kept revisiting Prince. Perhaps it was the potent combination of all three. At any rate, he couldn't shake the idea of Norma Desmond as the centerpiece of a big Broadway musical.

In 1961, *Variety* headlined, "Prince Gets B'way Musical Rights to *Sunset Blvd.*" The article led with, "Broadway producer Harold Prince plans a legit musical version of *Sunset Boulevard* starring Jeanette MacDonald in fall of 1962. Prince purchased legit rights from Paramount, which released film in 1950, with studio retaining a percentage of the show. Stephen Sondheim and Burt Shevelove are writing music and book, respectively."

In 1991, Harold Prince told MacDonald's biographer, Edward Baron Turk: "I had what I still think is a marvelous idea, and that was to star Jeanette MacDonald as Norma Desmond and Nelson Eddy as Max." Prince and his producing partner, Robert Griffith, visited MacDonald and her husband, Gene Raymond, in Bel-Air in December 1960. She mixed martinis for her guests, and eventually came around to asking Prince what he intended to call the musical version of *Sunset Boulevard*.

"*The Iron Butterfly*," Prince replied, using MacDonald's own sobriquet from earlier year.

The notion of Jeanette MacDonald as Norma Desmond seems outré until you peer past her screeching and find the comedienne. Carol Burnett could do Jeanette MacDonald, but Jeanette MacDonald might also have done Carol Burnett *doing* Jeanette MacDonald. When Swanson camps up Norma Desmond, it resembles a dance of death played for laughs. MacDonald, on stage as Norma, might have been mistaken for a very feminine drag queen, as in her 1936 pinnacle of cuckoo camp, *Rose-Marie*—which is screamingly funny, more so even than the *I Love Lucy* parody of it, with Ricky cajoling and Lucy squawking "By the Waters of Minnetonka" à la MacDonald and Eddy's "Indian Love Call."

When I asked Harold Prince about *Sunset Boulevard*, he reiterated what he had told MacDonald's biographer, adding that the star's ill health, and her death in 1965, probably helped to derail the project. He showed me a letter from MacDonald dated January 14, 1960, in which she wrote that Louella Parsons had announced the show "with a banner line" in her column, and that Hedda Hopper had phoned, miffed that she had been scooped. MacDonald ended, "I will be happy to hear how the first draft appeals to you—I'll keep my fingers crossed."

Nothing could derail Gloria Swanson, or so it seemed until fate finally had the last word. In the early sixties, however, several years after Paramount had flatly denied her entreaties for the rights to *Sunset Boulevard*, she still dreamed her impossible dream.

Swanson summoned Harold Prince and Robert Griffith, and they came. "I never go out to auditions," Prince said, "but because of her stature I made an exception."

Gloria had sublet her apartment on Fifth Avenue during an extended stay in California and although now back in New York, she had a suite at the Sulgrave Hotel on Park Avenue. On the big day, Dickson Hughes joined her and the producers in the hotel. He recalls "a brief social moment," at the end of which Swanson commanded, "Follow me into my boudoir."

There, in what Hughes describes as "her lavish star-type bedroom," was a rented spinet piano pushed into an alcove. Owing to the ungenerous amount of space, Hughes had to sit with his back to Swanson and her visitors while accompanying her and also performing the roles of Joe Gillis and Max.

Harold Prince recalls Swanson's presentation as "close to four hours." As though anticipating his remembered fatigue as he recounts the experience forty years later, she thoughtfully had him and Griffith stretch out on twin beds in the suite.

There was more to come. Some time after that, the dutiful producers trekked up Fifth Avenue to view, in considerable astonishment, a long roll of shelf paper on which Swanson had, in effect, storyboarded the musical. Prince said that Swanson "tossed" it at him. On the scroll were a breakdown of scenes with their respective sets; costume sketches; dialogue—a virtual frieze such as an ancient Egyptian star might have traced out on papyrus.

Show business, which can be strangely merciful, granted Swanson's wish in a very left-handed way. Although denied the musical of her desire, Harold Prince didn't forget. "Ten years later," he said, "*Follies* echoed *Sunset Boulevard,* and the famous *Follies* poster was directly inspired by the photograph of Gloria Swanson standing in the ruins of the Roxy Theatre."

I recently asked Stephen Sondheim about his own brief encounter with *Sunset Boulevard.* He was attracted to it, he said, because "it's a big romantic piece, and a friend of mine, Burt Shevelove, with whom I'd written *A Funny Thing Happened on the Way to the Forum,* and I, were looking for something to adapt. This movie is a favorite, and seemed like it would sing. So we started to work on it."

Shevelove wrote an opening scene that took place outside Norma Desmond's mansion, and Sondheim composed incidental music for it, which he describes as "some kind of mysterioso music that was to be the basis for singing."

Round about that time, Sondheim met Billy Wilder at a cocktail party. During their chat, Sondheim mentioned that he and Shevelove had embarked on a musical of *Sunset Boulevard.* Wilder said, "Oh, that's impossible."

Sondheim expected Wilder's next words to be, ". . . because you'll never get the rights from Paramount." A warning to be heeded, since word was out of Swanson's recent defeat and also because in the early sixties Stephen Sondheim, though a dazzling young newcomer, was not yet a Broadway titan.

But Wilder said this: "It can't be a musical. *Sunset Boulevard* has to be an opera because it's about a dethroned queen." Decades later Sondheim recalls how Wilder's words hit the mark: "The minute he said that it struck me as profoundly true. I realized that because *Sunset Boulevard* is so melodramatic and so over the top, it has to be done in the most melodramatic and over-the-top way available to the theatre: it must be an opera. But since I'm not interested in opera, I told Burt, 'Let's find something else.'"

Twenty years passed. In 1980, Angela Lansbury told a columnist for the *New York Post* that when she finished her tour in *Sweeney Todd* she would begin a "most exciting project," viz. a new musical version of *Sunset Boulevard*. Items about the show popped up in other columns for a year or so. Gloria Swanson, asked about this new candidate for "her" role, expressed doubt that the audience would accept Lansbury as Norma Desmond. "That's too soft a face," she said. Then she reconsidered. "Well, I don't know, maybe. . . . If I can do Charlie Chaplin, maybe she can do Norma Desmond."

The show died on the vine, and in January 1982 the *New York Daily News* advised: "Also scotch the story, once and for all, that the next Hal Prince–Stephen Sondheim musical will be *Sunset Boulevard* with Angela Lansbury in the Gloria Swanson role. That particular project was put to rest a good four months ago."

Sondheim's account: "A number of years later [i.e., after the early sixties explorations with Burt Shevelove], Hugh Wheeler, with whom I'd written a couple of shows, came to me and said he and Hal Prince had been talking and would really like to do *Sunset Boulevard* for Angela Lansbury. I told Hugh the story I've just outlined about why it shouldn't be done as a musical, it should be an opera, and Hugh asked if I would come and talk to Hal about it. Hal asked me the same thing and I told him the same story. He said, 'Well, then, let's do an opera.' I said, 'Hal, if there were any opera I'd want to do this would be it, but I don't want to do any opera.'"

In 1976, when Prince directed *Evita*, he and Andrew Lloyd Webber discussed a possible *Sunset Boulevard*. These forays, according to Lloyd Webber, "came to nothing."

During the 1980s Prince also talked about a *Sunset Boulevard* musical with Kander and Ebb. Other composers, meanwhile, were at work on the same material. In 1986 the *New York Times* reported that "Richard Barr and David Bixler, who will coproduce, now have a verbal go-ahead from Paramount Pictures and, if negotiations continue and things go without a hitch, the hope is that *Sunset Boulevard* will be on Broadway by next spring. According to Mr. Barr, the script and score are eighty-five percent completed, with Calvin Remsberg doing the book and lyrics, and Roger Ames the music. . . . The estimated budget for the show is $3.5 million."

Forty years after *Sunset Boulevard*, the film, *Sunset Boulevard* the musical had become a Broadway ghost. Many were haunted but none could touch it. On December 10, 1990, *Variety* carried this item: "A Musical Version of *Sunset Boulevard*? Andrew Lloyd Webber Is Ready, Mr. DeMille." The last sentence of the article stated that "the composer has reached an agreement with the studio for rights to the property, according to several sources close to the negotiations, and the deal was to be inked late last week."

Lloyd Webber had long since become the Cecil B. DeMille of musical theatre. Some would say the P. T. Barnum, as well. His blockbuster musicals, with their worldwide productions and marketing to equal a major studio release, already included *Joseph and the Amazing Technicolor Dreamcoat, Jesus Christ Superstar, Evita, Cats, Starlight Express,* and *The Phantom of the Opera.* He was big, and thirty million fans had *not* given him the brush. Sometimes it seemed, however, that every critic had.

Sunset Boulevard would surely intimidate a composer without the money, power, and box office magnetism of Lloyd Webber. If Puccini had lived long enough to write an opera about Hollywood, Wilder's picture might have appealed to him, since Norma Desmond resembles a

Lotusland Turandot. Or perhaps Gilbert and Sullivan, had they worked a hundred years later than they did, would have beaten Harold Prince to Jeanette MacDonald, the result being a burlesque of Hollywood with a tra-la-la finale sans pistol or dead gigolo. (I see Gene Kelly as her Joe Gillis and Groucho Marx as Max.) But *Sunset Boulevard* seems antithetical to the talents of traditional Broadway giants. It's difficult to imagine Cole Porter, Rogers and Hammerstein, or Jerome Kern finding the material anything but songless.

When Lloyd Webber began composing the score for his musical *Sunset Boulevard* in 1989, shortly after the London opening of *Aspects of Love*, he already had lived with the idea for two decades. "I first saw *Sunset Boulevard* at some time during the early 1970s," he said. "It made such an impression on me that it inspired a tune that I felt could be the title song. Unfortunately, I neither had the rights to the film, nor was I at that time likely to obtain them."

What on earth would Gloria Swanson have said had she been alive when Paramount granted Lloyd Webber an option on *Sunset Boulevard*? Struck by a thunderbolt, would she have taken cyanide or ordered champagne?

Between 1990, when Lloyd Webber and Paramount closed the deal, and 1992, when he was knighted by the Queen of England for his artistic endeavors, Sir Andrew Lloyd Webber composed the bulk of *Sunset Boulevard*, working closely with Don Black and Christopher Hampton who, collaboratively, wrote book and lyrics. The most important thing to state about the work of Black and Hampton is that they made the brilliant decision to retain the structure of the Wilder–Brackett–Marshman script, and much of the dialogue. More precisely, they created the illusion of retaining the film's dialogue while actually changing much of it, either to update the language or to meet the demands of music and the stage. This prestidigitation accounts for the magnificence of the libretto, which stands like a fraternal twin to the original script, although born forty years later.

To contrast *Sunset Boulevard* with other musicals based on famous films magnifies the rightness of Don Black and Christopher Hampton's choices. *All About Eve* turned into *Applause*; *Some Like It Hot* cross-dressed as *Sugar*; *The Wizard of Oz* changed shape and color to become *The Wiz*, and on and on. The point is, you'd never care to read one of these libretti, whereas *Sunset Boulevard*, the 1990s incarnation, could be staged as a non-singing play. Or, if all copies of Wilder's film vanished, the Black–Hampton version would reflect its greatness, like the Roman copy of some famous Greek statue.

In the early nineties, when media speculation climaxed on who would play Norma Desmond, it sometimes sounded like a latter-day search for Scarlett O'Hara. Certain names shone for their very unlikeliness: "Meryl Streep, Patti LuPone said to be neck and neck for Norma in the musical," panted *Variety* on October 12, 1992.

A year earlier a columnist for the *New York Daily News* had spread the most bizarre rumor of all: "Kathryn Grayson, the great MGM singing star of yesteryear, is said to be first in line for the Gloria Swanson role in *Sunset Boulevard*. . . . Sources say she's prepared to lose a lot of weight and get nipped and tucked by a plastic surgeon as soon as the offer is firm." Is it possible the Lloyd Webber team had Grayson in mind when they wrote "Eternal Youth Is Worth a Little Suffering"? That's the anthem sung by a phalanx of beauty experts who pound Norma into shape for her "return." As if in some mad infomercial, Norma's masseurs, beauticians, the whole team promise:

No more crow's-feet, no more flab
No more love handles to grab.

Lloyd Webber's magnitude having reached Wagnerian proportions, he set up his own Bayreuth, viz. a late-summer festival at Sydmonton, his four-thousand-acre estate straddling the borders of Hampshire and Berkshire in southern England. There, in 1992, within the walls of the ancient church situated on his land, the highlight of that year's three-day event was the first public performance of *Sunset Boulevard*. Although incomplete and lacking the fine-tuning required for such works, the show in effect fired a musical shot heard 'round the world. And the word "fired" soon claimed its full complement of meanings.

Patti LuPone, who sang the role of Norma Desmond, had perhaps already won the coveted part even before her plane touched down at Heathrow. If not, this dramatic audition splashed ice water on the ardent hearts of other contenders. For instance Meryl Streep, who sat in the audience that day and who was moved to tears by her rival's performance. Certain cynics in the cruel British press meowed that those tears, so Academy of Dramatic Arts, flowed not from a heart o'erturned but from Miss Streep's bleak awareness that the Norma Desmond jackpot had just been seized by the winning ticket.

LuPone had trumped La Streep once before, in 1979, when she snatched another role they both coveted: the lead in *Evita*. As Eva Perón, she opened the American run of the show in Los Angeles, then moved with it to New York a few months later. Rumors circulated in California that Harold Prince, the director, had his eye out for a replacement. This he denied, reassuring Patti LuPone publicly that he was not shopping for her replacement. She, however, made no secret of the damage done to her confidence by these wisps of noxious smoke, whether or not some underlying fire flamed up. Later she said, "I've never had doubts about my talents and how I affect an audience. I've been taught to have doubts by directors and producers and critics."

Whatever skirmishes LuPone and Lloyd Webber had during the *Evita* years, all was forgotten when she finally left the show in January 1981. She had won a Tony, she had lured publicity and crowds to the show, and she and Andrew Lloyd Webber parted friends. It was natural, therefore, that he should think of her a dozen years later when he cast *Sunset Boulevard*.

And so at Sydmonton on September 5, 1992, the lady went onstage as Patti LuPone. When she walked off, she was Sir Andrew's brand-new prima donna *assoluta*, anointed star of his nascent extravaganza. One writer summed up the great day: "When she sang the first solo, 'With One Look,' the acoustic effect in the tiny building was electrifying."

LuPone's voice might have electrified a few, but applause recorded on a videotape of the event sounds more like a subdued English response to candle power. This audience seems unsure how to react to these goings-on in faraway LaLa Land.

The event resembled a workshop version in Brooklyn of the latest spectacle from someone's brother-in-law or niece. LuPone, looking more like Anna Magnani than Gloria Swanson, performed, like others in the cast, without props or scenery. Costumes had a last-minute vagueness in period and fit. A tinny piano and small orchestra accompanied LuPone. That piano sounded like the one in Miss Kitty's saloon in *Gunsmoke*. The glorified audition seemed raw and undirected, more like a tired last performance than the first.

Nevertheless, eight months later, in May 1993, the cast of *Sunset Boulevard* assembled in London for the first time. A bird of ill omen, however, flapped its wings over New York even while Patti LuPone packed her bags. Just when the eyes of the theatre world should have focused on her, the announcement was made by the Really Useful Group, Lloyd Webber's production company, that Glenn Close would play Norma Desmond in Los Angeles when the show opened there later in the year.

In the code of theatre diplomacy, such announcements bear enormous import. And consequences. To newspaper readers they are little more than gossipy nuances, while those personally affected by them interpret these "coincidences" as full of significance. Each one is simultaneously pregnant with meaning, and inscrutable, like stylized gestures in Chinese opera as seen through occidental eyes.

As Patti LuPone's plane took off for London, trade papers and the dailies were full of Glenn Close. Suddenly the bride felt like a bridesmaid. Or a flower girl. As if to embellish an ill omen, it was announced that the American premiere of the show would not take place on Broadway but in Los Angeles. Lloyd Webber had taken the decision because, he said, *Sunset Boulevard* being a Hollywood story, his version of it should open near Hollywood. Also, critics and audiences there had flattered him in the past.

Patti LuPone wasn't thrilled. She said openly that she would have preferred the American premiere on Broadway: "I am, after all, a New Yorker." Broadway, she mused, might feel put down by a Los Angeles opening. Finally, however, she shrugged. "I'm too old for any bullshit and I don't want any," she stated with a soupçon of ill humor.

Even before these dour proceedings, LuPone had felt slighted by Barbra Streisand's recording of two songs from the show on her 1993 album, "Back to Broadway." The songs she recorded, "With One Look" and "As If We Never Said Good-bye," were indeed destined to become the show's most famous numbers. The Streisand preemption "apparently doesn't make Ms. LuPone too happy," the *New York Times* reported demurely on April 4, 1993, quoting two anonymous sources who had spoken with LuPone. Her agent, howevever, denied that his client cared at all. "That's absolutely not true," he said. "She's never mentioned it since I told her about Streisand doing it. Patti will be recording the original cast album very soon."

Touché.

"Hello, Norma, Well Hello Norma..."

In the booklet of her "Back to Broadway" compact disc, Streisand comments on "With One Look": "When I first heard this song, I was immediately taken with its strong melody. I couldn't wait to sing it—act it. The lyrics gave me the chance to play the character of Norma Desmond."

If rumors ever come true and a film is made of Andrew Lloyd Webber's *Sunset Boulevard*, Barbra Streisand might take a crack at it. Such casting is not unimaginable. She would overwhelm Norma Desmond with a screen ego bigger than Norma's own, pumping up the picture with her showy singer-actress starburst that includes a bag of old tricks: mugging, cute asides, upstaging of cast, scenery—and songs.

Those who relish the Streisand attack seem insatiable. Others, many of whom continue to admire her early work, find her interpretations in recent decades airless, predictable, and over-produced. Why must she dress up every song in lace pants, those loud Streisand frills and furbelows? For years it has seemed as if she's trying to coopt the composers she likes best.

Lloyd Webber's songs from *Sunset Boulevard*, tightly welded to the libretto, would seem to permit fewer histrionics than songs from his other shows. Even Streisand cannot invade them utterly, though she tries. Singing "As If We Never Said Goodbye," she chuckles twice; inappropriate grace notes. Of all the singers who have recorded songs from *Sunset Boulevard*, she conveys the least understanding of Norma Desmond, musically or dramatically. Her desire for "With One Look"—"I couldn't wait to sing it—act it" doesn't come true; she doesn't act it. Streisand's only vocal revelation is that Norma grew up in Brooklyn—which takes us back to Mae West. The classic Norma Desmond is invisible behind Streisand's bugle voice, with every crescendo a cue to blare "Reveille."

And that's where Streisand goes wrong. The subtext of *Sunset Boulevard*—even when Norma boasts that "with one look I can break your heart/ with one look I play every part"—is about endings, about sunset, not the dawn of a new day. If we hear a bugle, it should play "Taps."

And yet, suppose Streisand directed a film of Lloyd Webber's *Sunset Boulevard?* That would be an announcement to applaud. She's a gifted director who also understands the film-musical gestalt, no matter how she mistreats it on occasion. To watch a woman of Streisand's stature handle a character of Norma Desmond's pathos and vastness—it might resurrect the dead genre of Hollywood movie musicals.

Trevor Nunn, director of *Sunset Boulevard*, was a member of the Lloyd Webber stock company, having previously directed *Cats*, *Starlight Express*, and *Aspects of Love*. He also directed *Les Misérables*, the biggest non-Lloyd Webber musical in recent years.

At the time of *Sunset Boulevard*, Nunn had long been a towering figure in British theatre. In 1968, at the age of twenty-eight, he became artistic director of the Royal Shakespeare Company. His directing career also included operas at Glyndbourne (*Porgy and Bess, Peter Grimes*), numerous television productions, and three films. Nunn also wrote the words to one of Lloyd Webber's most famous songs, "Memory," from *Cats*.

John Napier, who designed the production, did too good a job: he has been critized ever since for stealing the show, dwarfing, with his powerful set, the successive divas who played Norma, of distracting and overwhelming the audience with decor. Did the set look like a giant red-and-gold jukebox, as one commentator claimed? Or did it resemble a 1920s movie palace more than the home of a movie goddess? Napier admitted that his inspiration came from those great dream emporia. Mark Steyn, in his book *Broadway Babies Say Goodnight: Musicals Then and Now*, argues that Norma Desmond "was a tiny stick figure lost in the scenery" of Napier's "huge stairway-to-paradise re-creation of her Hollywood mansion."

Surely, where Norma Desmond is concerned, more is more and too much is not enough. Perhaps the only problem with Napier's set was that it arrived eighty years too late, for it belonged in D. W. Griffith's *Intolerance* or some other screen-bursting panorama from the silent era. John Napier didn't taunt his critics by saying it, but he might have: "I am big, it's the theatre that got small."

Except for Andrew Lloyd Webber. Having settled on the Adelphi Theatre for *Sunset Boulevard*, he bought a half interest in the site and renovated the theatre to conform to his new work. Few plays have ever been so honored.

Previews were scheduled to begin on June 21, 1993, with opening night on June 29. Napier's grandiose set, however, had a mind of its own. Parts of the set were so intricate, so technologically sophisticated, that they began moving of their own accord. These ghostly, eccentric whims endangered actors and crew, and by the time they were normalized a postponement proved absolutely necessary. Previews began on June 28, and the show opened on July 12.

In the invited audience of celebrities: Billy and Audrey Wilder, Nancy Olson and her husband, Alan Livingston. When the show ended they, and all others in the audience, rose in a long ovation to Patti LuPone and her costar, Kevin Anderson.

An eyewitness gave this account of the first-night party at the Savoy, where a thousand guests celebrated in "four of the hotel's huge public rooms commandeered for the occasion." The menu included "Le Saumon Sunset, La Délice de Norma (breast of chicken on a bed of potato puree), and La Boîte de Chocolat Boulevard. Billy Wilder sat at the honored place at Andrew Lloyd Webber's table and expressed pleasure at the production. As each of the principals arrived they were cheered to their tables, Patti LuPone even jumping on hers to acknowledge the applause."

Diplomatically, Billy Wilder pronounced his benison on the production: "What they have done is so clever, when you make a film you choose what shot to have, long, medium, or close-up, you choose your lens, you have hundreds of ways to determine what the audience will see. On stage you cannot do that. Yet they have still managed to focus the attention where they wanted it to be focused. I wish I could do that."

Does Wilder sound disingenuous? His comments say the obvious and end with that frightfully mild, faint compliment about focusing attention where they wanted it to be focused. Certainly, the public Wilder did the gentlemanly thing: he toasted these theatre people with praise they wished to hear. But the real Wilder, speaking from the other side of his mouth, told a different tale. A person close to him got a typical earful later that night: "It's my movie in a permanent long shot."

Nancy Olson, speaking that evening, sounded like the Queen Mother: "Watching the show tonight was like seeing my young life again. I can't wait to get home to California to look at the film all over again. Working on it was extraordinary for a young actress in Hollywood." One could, of course, project any meaning at all onto those bland sentences. Imagine how the second one might come off if Nancy arched an eyebrow; cut her eyes or rolled them toward the ceiling.

Whatever her reservations about the production, however, Olson sent a bouquet to the show's Meredith Braun, who played the role Nancy created onscreen. Her note said, "From Betty Schaeffer to Betty Schaeffer."

Fast forward six years. I ask Nancy Olson Livingston about the *Sunset Boulevard* opening night in London. Her straightforward answer:

I must tell you something about Billy. As cuttingly witty as he can be, he is basically a very sensitive, polite man. He would never say anything to really embarrass Andrew or the production. He might make a few quips to his very close friends. The one about the permanent long shot is the strongest, you know, but we looked at each other after this opening night and were just kind of—we both obviously knew.

I'm sitting there and seeing the pitfalls very clearly and observing what happens and what doesn't work. The girl who played it in London, Patti LuPone, she's darling, she's a fabulous singer, but she is no more a famous beauty or a silent screen star than you are. Her voice, and the arias, and the songs she sang were wonderful, but you just simply did not believe her. You believe Glenn Close.

When the show opened in New York in 1994, Nancy told a reporter, "Glenn is obviously a more perfect casting. She is, after all, a movie star."

"But vocally?" asked the interviewer.

"Please," said Nancy Olson. "Let me be polite."

For more than a year, ever since England peeked at *Sunset Boulevard* during the 1992 Sydmonton festival, Fleet Street had chattered and gossiped about the show. At last, on opening night, the press confronted it face to face. The reviews were mixed, some praising this while others condemned that. Enthusiam and reservations balanced one another on the seesaw of critical opinion.

Frank Rich, at that time theatre critic for the *New York Times*, flew to London for the opening. He considered the "surprisingly dark, jazz-accented music" the "most interesting" he had encountered from Lloyd Webber. Rich found LuPone "miscast and unmoving as Norma Desmond."

The most fulsome praise came from the composer Malcolm Williamson, proud tenant of the title "Master of the Queen's Music." (Translated into American, the title means music director, rather like

Doc Severinson on *The Tonight Show Starring Johnny Carson.*) In 1992, Williamson had said, "Lloyd Webber's music is everywhere, but so is AIDS." Perhaps as antidote to his tasteless remark, he gushed over *Sunset Boulevard*: "It is technically marvelous. It also has spiritual and philosophical depth to it. This music is immortal. It must be taken every bit as seriously as the most significant developments in opera from *The Magic Flute* to Benjamin Britten."

A brief intermission for divas, emotional release, screaming, throwing things, and many tears.

Los Angeles: Glenn Close, nearing the end of her great success as Norma Desmond at the Shubert Theatre, looks forward to the time when she can rest after these months of eight grueling performances a week. At the end of her contract period, Faye Dunaway will replace her in Los Angeles. Patti LuPone will leave the show in London, come home to New York, and resume Norma Desmond on Broadway, no doubt to thunderous acclaim.

London: At the Adelphi Theatre on a night in mid-February 1994, Patti LuPone, in Norma Desmond costume and makeup, waits to go onstage. The phone rings in her dressing room. The call is from her agent in New York, who delivers such a devastating blow that LuPone's face twists into a strange witch doctor mask.

The voice from America reads a column by Liz Smith, breaking the news that Andrew Lloyd Webber has chosen Glenn Close over Patti LuPone for his Broadway Norma Desmond. Close's reviews in L.A. have been strong; she is perceived as performing better in the role; the show's investors are clamoring for her. Therefore, let the foul deed be done.

If one could travel back in time and enter the deepest heart of Patti LuPone, what message would one read? Did vengeance tempt her? *Come, thick night, and pall thee in the dunnest smoke of hell, that my keen knife see not the wound it makes, nor heaven peep through the blanket of the dark to cry, "Hold, hold!"*

She forbore to dagger the cad, though some would have spared him not. Rather, Patti LuPone wrecked her dressing room, she was a shrieking Fury in the hail of projectiles: lipstick rockets, wigstand bludgeons, perfume bombshells smashed on walls and mirrors. The *terribilità* of a fish-wife diva. As LuPone later said, "Things went flying into the street."

That night's performance closed, both literally and figuratively, on a funereal note: Joe Gillis dead in Norma's pool, and Patti LuPone profes-sionally disemboweled onstage. As the curtain fell, a shocked theatre world received the news of her humiliation.

Mortified, she missed three performances. Then she snapped her steel-trap nerves into position, stayed on to the end of her contract on March 12, and then went home.

Connecticut: Two years later, Patti LuPone swims in "the Andrew Lloyd Webber Memorial Pool," dug into the ground of her rural property. Sometimes, sunning in the sharp New England light, she toasts her benefactor, whose goneness from her life seems more permanent even than Joe's departure from Desmondland. "The best thing that could have happened was getting fired from that show," she tells a visitor. "I got all this money." More than a million, according to reliable sources.

But chlorine can't wash away pain and bitterness. LuPone's founda-tions were cracked from the magnitude of Lloyd Webber's deed, ungaugeable on the Richter scale of feelings. For a year she didn't work at all except in a concert version of *Pal Joey* in Manhattan. She saw herself as Lloyd Webber's scapegoat: "Because he didn't get good notices," she said, "he thought it was my fault."

Eventually she starred in her own show, *Patti LuPone on Broadway*. In it she sang "As If We Never Said Good-bye," and when she reached the line, "I've come home at last," she sang it like the terrible trumpet on Judgment Day. The audience sprang up in spontaneous ovation. Later LuPone replaced Zoe Caldwell in *Master Class*, playing another fishwife diva who believed herself persecuted and crucified by her employers: Maria Callas.

Gerald Alessandrini, creator of the parody show *Forbidden Broadway*, included the *Sunset Boulevard* hair pulling in the next update of his spoof. He said, "We decided that Andrew Lloyd Webber kept her in the show but made her play Max."

New York: On February 18, 1994, the *Times* ends a report on the

LuPone meltdown: "Ms. Close did not respond to an interview request, but Mr. Brown [a Lloyd Webber spokesman] said she was concerned that she not be seen as 'some kind of Eve Harrington,' referring to the coldly ambitious actress who is the title character in the film *All About Eve.*"

None dare call it voodoo. You can't help wondering, though, what Patti LuPone had in mind when she named her swimming pool for Sir Andrew. After all, Joe Gillis in the water is a potent image.

But *Sunset Boulevard,* though it ran for years, ultimately came to be labeled a "hit-flop." According to some estimates, it lost about twenty million dollars. Lloyd Webber's next show, *Whistle Down the Wind,* closed in Washington during pre-Broadway tryouts, and his production company, Really Useful, began downsizing, as though in the throes of a recession. He hasn't had a hit-hit since *The Phantom of the Opera.*

I wanted to know how *Sunset Boulevard* took shape onstage, and so I chose the Los Angeles production to reconstruct. This one seemed the right candidate for a basement-to-attic inspection because it was the "middle" production and therefore neither as complicated and problematic as London, nor as relatively crisis-free as New York. Los Angeles seemed auspicious also because the show's sunniest days—critically and meterologically—took place there. Many of those connected with *Sunset Boulevard* started out in L.A., and while most traveled with the show to New York, the ones I spoke with voiced more vibrant recollections of their initial California engagement with the musical. I attribute such afterglow to Hollywood, and the proximity of friendly ghosts.

I had the good fortune to encounter Sandra Allen and Colleen Dunn, members of the chorus who delineated the realities of an actual show in contrast to all those backstage screen musicals where conflict is formulaic and choreography conquers all. Even better, Colleen and Sandra told me what's what without destroying my illusions. Since theatre remains magical for them, they eroded none of my own stardust. I was allowed to retain my juvenile impression that choreography—along with composing, singing, acting, set building, stagecraft, and every other theatrical talent—rings down a happy final curtain.

"I had to audition four times for the show," said Sandra Allen, "as I'm sure everybody did. Johnson and Liss Casting in New York had seen me in other productions, so I guess they felt it was time for me to do an Andrew Lloyd Webber show. Also, ethnicity as well as talent might have counted—I'm half-Chinese, half-German-English." Sandra played a harem girl in the musicalized scene of DeMille's *Samson and Delilah*, so perhaps her Asian ancestry added a touch of old-Hollywood exoticism. Like all chorus members, she also doubled in various crowd scenes—in Norma's cosmetic makeover, for instance, where she played a beautician.

"This was my first Broadway show," she said. "There was maybe one other girl in the chorus who also had not done Broadway. We were the two youngest. I had just turned twenty-three. Everybody else had résumés out the wazoo."

Unlike the typecasting in old putting-on-a-show movies—a boy-next-door tap dancer with dimples, a saucy blonde, her roommate/sidekick who cracks jokes, a wolf, a doomed waif headed for heartbreak—these *Sunset Boulevard* singers and dancers came from unpredictable places. Sandra recalls "a couple of guys who had written scripts for TV shows, a piano player you wouldn't believe, and there were people of all ages. I remember one guy who was forty-nine or fifty, and looked about thirty-eight." One reason for such diversity was the requirement that chorus members portray a range of showbiz characters: agents, choreographers, managers, cosmeticians, and the like.

Auditions took place in a large hall at the Hollywood United Methodist Church. This venue—a gymlike building adjacent to the church sanctuary—is a frequent tryout and rehearsal site for Los Angeles musicals. Even Sandra, a relative newcomer, had already been there several times.

Here's how she auditioned for *Sunset Boulevard*: "You had to do a monologue, and mine was from *Fame*, about a girl who wants to get into the American Ballet Company but she's pregnant. For my up-tempo song I did 'Putting It Together' and for my ballad—it's been so long I can't remember. I want to say something from *Miss Saigon* or *Fame*. There was a dance call for everybody, then I did a separate dance for the harem girl role." Sandra was asked to repeat each one of these four times, except the monologue.

Colleen Dunn auditioned in New York in the fall of 1993. "They held auditions on both coasts," she explained, "because they wanted the crème de la crème." Recently cast in *Cats*, she had been performing for only a few weeks in that show. When she turned up at *Sunset Boulevard* auditions, a casting person said, "What are you doing here? We just put you in *Cats*." Colleen replied, "It's my job to show up, but if you don't want me here I'll leave." A bit of conferring, some whispers and nods: "No, wait a minute. Why don't you stay?"

She was called back once to meet Trevor Nunn, the director, and to sing and dance for Andrew Lloyd Webber. Colleen gave her notice to *Cats* and left the show after four weeks to go to Los Angeles. Like Sandra Allen, she played a harem girl, a beautician, and other supernumerary parts. Neither she nor Sandra had seen Billy Wilder's *Sunset Boulevard*. (They were like Glenn Close, who surprised me by saying: "I don't even know if I'd ever seen it all the way through before I played Norma Desmond.")

In Los Angeles, Colleen shared a furnished rental apartment for a month with another woman from the chorus. Then: "We drove around looking for places to stay, on top of rehearsals." Since rehearsals ran all day, from ten o'clock to six in the evening, Colleen's New York savvy with landlords and leases helped in finding new digs.

Trevor Nunn and David Caddick, the show's music director, had been at the auditions. Not until the first day of rehearsals, however, did Andrew Lloyd Webber show up. Rehearsals also took place at the Hollywood United Methodist Church. Now Glenn Close, who had been working separately, joined the rest of the cast.

"That first day was about meeting people," Sandra Allen said. "We also got a lot of background. Trevor Nunn talked about the original movie. He gave a plot synopsis, and he also told us personal facts about Gloria Swanson, and what happened in her life. On the first day we got the book."

In addition to the book—the libretto—they got their music and other materials, rather like the first day of school. "We all checked out who was there, who do I know, did any of my friends make it," said Sandra. On day one they also had a reading. "We sat in a circle and read the play," Colleen said. "The next few days, we played theatre games with each other. We improvised a party scene—Artie's party, obviously. We had to grade ourselves on our comfort levels, who was shy, who was confident. You know, introverts, extroverts. We also did a mirror game where we paired up and copied whatever the partner did. First one partner controlled the movement, then the other. After that, we broke into groups and did improvisations of being stranded on an island. Like *Survivor*. Who takes control? Who problem solves?"

Sandra recalled that, after a few days, "we started getting into our music. They split every day between music and choreography. For example, sometimes we'd do music in the morning, learn something new, then in the afternoon put it on its feet in the show."

Rehearsals started in September and continued for about two months. By the beginning of the second month *Sunset Boulevard* had assumed a coherent shape, so that an outsider who dropped in on rehearsals would have had some notion, although incomplete, of the way the show might unfold. Not until close to previews, however, did the cast begin full runs.

"At one point I considered quitting," Sandra confided. "The rehearsal process was very intense. The stakes were obviously high because of the money spent on the show and all the big names attached to it. Everybody felt on edge. Maybe part of that was because I was young and green."

Although confident of her abilities as singer, dancer, and actress, Sandra said, "I'm the first to admit that sometimes I'm a little slow. Dance is probably the area where it takes a second longer for me to catch on."

Once choreographer Bob Avian and his assistants had taught the dancers their steps, they polished every movement to assure that each dancer adhered to Avian's style. Sandra calls this process "cleaning the style."

One morning it was apparant to Sandra that an assistant to Avian "was having a bad day, for whatever reason." During a cleanup session of a routine with Sandra and two others, the entire cast observed the dancers as they worked on a particular movement. "It was a step," Sandra said, "a leg or something that I wasn't getting stylistically. I was in the spotlight. The assistant tried to explain to me, but I didn't understand exactly what she wanted. Now, this woman already has a reputation for not being terribly nice, and I'm a wreck. Everybody's watching and she's starting to raise her voice. The minute I said, 'Could we start from that—' she laid into me. 'No, we can't!!' she yelled. I burst out crying."

To the rescue came Bob Avian, or maybe it was Trevor Nunn. Sandra's tears fell so fast that in memory she couldn't sort it out properly. At any rate, one of the men suggested, "Let's take a break," and tears soon vanished. Legs did their stuff, and Sandra decided that her opponent "ended up looking like an asshole."

Generally, Glenn Close didn't rehearse with the chorus. Sandra Allen explained that "the chorus numbers revolved around her, so she was in only a couple of production numbers with us. We rehearsed with Glenn when we did specific scenes. A lot of those scenes involved us standing still while she went through her dialogue or her song."

"I remember the first time Glenn rehearsed with us," said Colleen Dunn. "We were doing the final scene. George Hearn [as Max] was directing her down the stairs; she thinks it's her comeback, her close-up. I was floored. I thought, My God, she's brilliant! And then later she turned in the same performance every night. She's amazing."

After two weeks of previews the show opened at the Shubert Theatre, on the Avenue of the Stars in Century City, on December 9, 1993. Brooke Young, Gloria Swanson's granddaughter, helped organize an opening-night benefit for Children's Hospital of Los Angeles. For her, the evening was not only extraordinary but extraordinarily busy.

She attended with her mother, Swanson's elder daughter, the late Gloria Daly. Also in the family party were Young's two brothers and her two children, who were in their late teens in 1993. (Swanson's other daughter, Michelle, who lives in France, was unable to attend.)

I asked Brooke Young about the emotions of the evening. She said, "I know my grandmother always wanted *Sunset Boulevard* to be a musical.

Then, to see someone else playing her role, it was like . . ." She gave a great sigh. "I think my grandmother would have been absolutely amazed and awed at the spectacle of it. I wanted her to be right there. But sitting next to my mother, and observing her awe of it, was also overwhelming."

I asked whether one felt the spirit of Gloria Swanson that evening, meaning that she must have been in everyone's mind.

"Yes," said Brooke, "I'm sure she was there in a certain way." Brooke herself had no time to ponder the matter that evening, however. She had promised Children's Hospital a full house and she filled it. She also hosted a preshow dinner, then a dessert intermission party, and in a sense stayed on duty for some two thousand guests throughout the long evening.

An off-key incident took place after the show. A member of the audience approached Gloria Daly and said, "Oh my God, did your mother really do that? Did she slash her wrists?" Years later, Brooke Young still sounds taken aback: "My mother tried to tell the woman that *Sunset Boulevard* is not the story of Gloria Swanson's life. I think that kind of reaction was hard on my mother."

A week later Brooke Young saw the show again, this time with Raymond Daum, her grandmother's friend. That's when they had time to visit Glenn Close backstage after the show. "She was charming," said Brooke. "She wrote on my program, 'I hope I did your grandmother proud.'"

The opening night party took place at Paramount. "It was lavish," said Colleen. "A great band, a million stars—and I can't remember a one of them! I think Billy Wilder came backstage after the show and said really complimentary things to the cast. But you know what I'll never forget? The red carpet at Paramount, and those huge studio arches."

Sandra said, "Opening night was great fun. The jitters had gone because the first night of previews had felt like opening night." Asked who came backstage, she recalled Barbra Streisand. "We wore these weird microphones," Sandra said, "that came up your back, through your hair, and rested on your forehead. Some people had microphones that came over the ear. Never on your body, because there you wouldn't get the best sound quality. So I remember Barbra Streisand asked, 'What are those funny little bumps on your forehead?' "

In the early hours of January 17, 1994, the Northridge earthquake hit the San Fernando Valley. Measuring 6.6 on the Richter scale, it killed sixty-one people and injured over 8,000. Damage in the Los Angeles metropolitan area was estimated at $13 to 20 billion. A natural disaster was the one phenomenon that could upstage Norma Desmond.

Every structure in town suddenly turned into a shaky question mark, and the Shubert was among the enigmas. The stage set—Norma's mansion, tons and tons of it—hovered above DeMille's movie set, Artie Green's apartment, Schwab's Drug Store. An elaborate system of hydraulics moved sets up and down and sideways. Always, however, that monumental palazzo dominated the proscenium, whether in view or not. Psychologically it loomed. Those in the show had spent many hours learning not to move an inch out of line lest they be crushed by Desmondland descending.

One performance was cancelled while engineers inspected the theatre. Finding neither cracks nor malfunctions, they green-lighted the next night's show.

As if to confirm our stereotypes, Sandra Allen's Angelino reaction to the earthquake is laid-back: "They said that house above us was more stable than if it were on the ground, but that didn't stop us looking. We got fifteen dollars per performance as hazard pay. But the show must go on."

And New Yorker Colleen Dunn:

Oh my God! It was horrifying! They brought in a therapist to talk to us because some of us were completely freaked out. I wanted to leave immediately for New York. That house, which flew above us, was suspended on seven bridge cables. We were so worried! It could kill you in an instant. They tried to reassure us that *one* cable could have held up the entire house, but—stress!

I was emotionally devastated. That therapist would ask, "How are you dealing with it? How's everything going?" A lot of us from New York stayed rattled. I was living between West Hollywood and Beverly Hills, and we'd go onto the roof and see fires and mud-slides. It was like the Apocalypse! I remember Glenn wanting to leave, too.

Following the quake, aftershocks continued for days. When these tremors happened during a performance, the show went on but the audience didn't.

"You'd hear them start to murmur," said Sandra, "then you'd look out there and an entire side of the theatre would empty out as they bolted for the exits. I thought it was funny; I almost cracked up on stage."

Colleen's nerves stayed raw. "They'd head for the doors and I'd start to think, Do I need to get out of here right now?"

A sign backstage, unrelated to the earthquake but strangely apropos, captured the macabre juxtaposition of Norma's delusions and the Los Angeles fault lines: "If the monkey hadn't died, the show would be over."

Colleen Dunn holds a unique and glamorous distinction. She was the first actress ever to play both Hedy Lamarr and Lana Turner in the same show. "I played Delilah," she said. "But since the harem scene was secondary to Norma coming back to Paramount to visit DeMille, they cut our *Samson and Delilah* down to an entrance, with DeMille directing us. That scene was all about Glenn as Norma Desmond.

"I started out as a harem girl at the beginning of the scene. Then I ran offstage, made a quick change into the Delilah costume, and reentered as Hedy Lamarr. I also played Lana Turner in the Schwab's Drug Store scene. And Lana Turner came backstage one night to tell me it's a myth about her being discovered in Schwab's. She wanted me to know that. Someone took a picture of us together. Even when you play a small role, you research your character, so meeting her was great. It's rare to meet the actual person you're portraying. Oh, by the way, at the New Year's party I played a Dorothy Lamour wannabe."

"What was Glenn Close like from backstage?" I asked Sandra Allen.

"She's sweet, funny, and very professional," Sandra answered. "She liked to have fun with all of us, but when it came to work, she worked harder than anyone. Glenn is down to earth. After I left the company I heard stories about other Norma Desmonds, her replacements, and everyone agreed that with them, the atmosphere didn't compare to when Glenn was starring."

After six months with the show in Los Angeles, Glenn Close was to leave. Faye Dunaway had been announced, with great fanfare, as her replacement.

While that fanfare still lights up the sky over Hollywood, and before fireworks change to gunfire, we'll attend the closing party given by Glenn Close at the house she had rented from Tracey Ullman.

"The entire cast attended," Sandra said.

Glenn hosted an afternoon barbeque. Now I have to tell you that a lot of cast members had children, and Glenn's daughter was about five at that time, and Glenn also had two dogs, cute and well-trained. She kept them with her all the time. So during the run various people brought their children backstage, and Glenn brought her daughter and her dogs. At one point somebody made a sign and hung it on the stage door: SUNSET BOULEVARD DAY CARE AND KENNEL.

Okay, so for the closing party Glenn ordered two big cakes. These she brought out after the barbeque lunch. The baker had written on one cake, *Thanks for a great run.* That one from Glenn. The other cake had, *Thank you for letting us have the run of the theatre* and it was from her dogs. These little paw prints ran all over the cake. They led around to the side, where the baker had decorated the cake with poop. Icing poop on top of the cake! As we're howling over this, Glenn scoops up a chocolate poop and eats it. That's her sense of humor.

The day I spoke with Glenn Close I found her shy at first, reserved, the sort of person who might enter a convivial room and hover for a time near the wall. Given the proper cues, however, that unobtrusive guest—a keen observer, a cautious yet eager participant in merriment—would warm like an open fire until, with artless resolve, she alternately blazed as raconteuse, great lady, and femme fatale, each flame locked within the grate of her self-control. I imagined a house party where Glenn Close entered as Emily Dickinson . . . and soon took over as Auntie Mame, serving outlandish cakes and dancing the Charleston.

Earlier, Close had told a reporter, "My main preparation for the role of Norma Desmond was to look at silent movies, because she was a great silent-movie star. I think the cliche about silent pictures is that everything was overdone, but I found, watching the silent Swanson and Garbo pictures, that they would stand up today as great performances."

I thought her approach smart and perceptive, so my first question was, "Which silent pictures did you watch?" She hesitated for a long moment, as she was to do after every Norma question. At first I thought something had distracted her. A dog? The doorbell?

Then I realized that traveling back to her Norma Desmond days required effort. A struggle, like hacking through an emotional forest to reach the forbidden tower she had escaped from. For Norma Desmond had captured Glenn Close, as she captured Gloria Swanson, Joe Gillis, and all who enter her charmed circumference.

"I watched *Sadie Thompson*," she said. Her tone struck me as flat, like a high school English teacher answering one more question after the two-thirty bell has rung. But then she switched from straight 2/4 rhythm to a catchy tempo. If it's possible to speak in a fox-trot, she did. "I actually . . . What I did . . . I watched . . . the old ones like Theda Bara. And I watched that incredible *Passion of Joan of Arc*. To get the gestures, and to see what that world was."

"What other things did you do besides watching silent pictures?"

Pause. "I took voice lessons," and she burst out giggling. I wondered why that struck her as hilarious.

"You were already a singer, weren't you?"

"Well," she said, "I was a singer . . . I never had been asked to sing the range . . . the kind of voice that Andrew Lloyd Webber writes for." Her tone toughened: "It's like getting ready for an Olympic event."

The time had come to chop the remaining forest and approach the demesne of Norma Desmond. I took a step: "How did you deal with the indelible performance of Gloria Swanson when your turn came to portray Norma?"

Her answer combined common sense and rhapsody: "Well, I looked at what was on the page." Suddenly she sounded deep in concentration, as if memorizing the part all over again. "I think Norma Desmond is one of the great roles ever created for a woman. Such a piece of writing, and a great role can stand many, many interpretations. So it wasn't about copying Gloria Swanson's performance. It was about trying to get into who I thought that character, Norma Desmond, was." (Some reviewers criticized Close because her Norma differed from Swanson's. "Glenn Close makes her sound nearer to age eighty than fifty," someone carped. "Less vulnerable than Swanson's spidery vamp," groused another.)

Glenn Close, across the moat, had reentered the Desmond fortress. I asked how she went about making Norma Desmond her own. At that point I didn't know how mutual the possession had been.

She paused as though getting ready to sing "The Star Spangled Banner," which she has done on occasion before a Mets game at Shea Stadium. "I wanted to watch a lot of silent pictures," she said, "to get in *my* mind the images that Norma had in *her* mind. I always felt that she was a character who, looking at herself in the mirror, saw someone different from what everyone else saw. For me, she became a heightened reality.

"Norma Desmond was considered a great actress, so I think she would move well. She had good posture and probably a certain kind of discipline, since she hadn't let herself go physically in all those years off the screen. I loved her very, very much."

"Why?" I asked, hesitant to intrude on those two Norma Desmonds: the imaginary one, and the real woman who embodied her.

Glenn Close spoke in a hush. "Because I think she is a noble spirit. She is deluded, yet her clinging to those delusions makes us respect her. And the fact that she has affected so many people, that she has been great. She was a great artist, and no one wants to see that art disappear."

A risky question remained. In typing my list I put it near the top.

But something warned me to postpone it. Near the end of our conversation I charged ahead: "Is it a role that haunts some actresses, who fear that they will turn into Norma Desmond as they reach fifty and beyond?"

Her bland answer surprised me. "Hollywood has changed," she said. "Image is still important, but surely people realize there's a person behind the image."

I didn't ask the shadow part of that question: "... the way presidents are dogged by JFK, wondering, Will I be shot?" In a sense, however, she read my mind and volunteered an oblique answer.

"Norma Desmond literally haunted me," she said. "When I left the show to spend more time with my daughter, who was then six and a half, I made a drastic change. One night the black limousine picked me up, I gave a performance, took my curtain call with an armful of roses. The next day I was making lunch for my little girl to take to school.

"At home, in my kitchen, being a mom, I swear I looked across the room and saw Norma Desmond sitting in a chair. She said—" and Close dropped into Norma Desmond's actressy lower register, with more than a touch of disdain: 'What am *I* doing here? Children? School? This is insane!'"

Glenn Close laughed. Did I imagine that she forced the laughter *not* to come out shrill? "That disturbed me. It was schizophrenic. I realized I had to go through a mourning period for her, because I loved that character so deeply. I didn't want to kill her off. She had to fade. Slowly fade away."

Then I asked a question that's impossible to answer, and yet I've often been asked it during my own involvement with *Sunset Boulevard*: "How might Norma Desmond have avoided becoming Norma Desmond?" I'm glad Glenn Close didn't say something obvious, such as, "She couldn't, that was her fate." Rather, she discussed Norma as a case history.

"Those around her propped up her dementia," Close said. "Max was a slave to the lie. I also think she was a true paranoid. Finally she passed the point of no return; reality would have proven too great a shock. No one ever said to Norma, 'Honey, the world is changing; let's do it this way.'"

And there's my answer to the earlier question also, the one about Norma Desmond haunting actresses over fifty. Her last sentence guarantees that no one ever need make the same plea to Glenn Close.

A large ad for *Sunset Boulevard* in the *Los Angeles Times* on May 29, 1994 announced: "Starring Glenn Close Now Through June 26. Starring Faye Dunaway Beginning July 5." At that point the only devastated diva was Patti LuPone, a Lloyd Webber survivor who had returned to New York from London two months earlier.

The Dunaway deal had been struck three weeks before that ad appeared. The *Los Angeles Times*, in an article titled "Faye Saves Her Voice for *Sunset*," reported that shortly after she was offered the role of Norma Desmond, but before she signed the contract, "her manager Bob Palmer talked to the Associated Press and Dunaway called *Variety* columnist Army Archerd." Nothing unusual about any of that, except that the boss apparently had told her to keep her mouth shut—and she didn't. The *Times* article explained that "Peter Brown, spokesman for producer-composer Andrew Lloyd Webber, expressed anger that the news had been released before contract negotiations were completed."

Lloyd Webber was cross. Otherwise his spokesman wouldn't have put so fine a point on his own angry reaction.

In an attempt at damage control, Dunaway issued a curious statement: "I love going back to the theatre, this time with music—a whole new dimension. But, while the details are being worked out, I want to stay as quiet as possible, stay in training and prepare for the work ahead. When I start talking I sometimes go to the point of exhaustion, and I mustn't do that."

Actresses often make self-serving statements, but hers is a rarity: a press release that's self-denigrating. Surely it didn't behoove her to dub herself a blabbermouth, which in so many words she did. What must Andrew Lloyd Webber have thought, far away in London but always tracking his farflung empire, when he read this humble confession from his new Norma Desmond? The Norma Desmond whose credo is, "Great stars have great pride."

Great composers have great pride, too. According to a piece in the London *Sunday Times* that appeared two days before the scheduled Dunaway takeover, "People who know him say he often speaks with the royal 'we.'" Elsewhere in the vicious profile, the paper's unsigned writer describes Lloyd Webber as sensitive, then instantly poisons the compliment: "For sensitive read paranoid, neurotic, takes umbrage, is a hyperperfectionist. Everything must be just so—just as he says so." Neither of our own polite cisatlantic *Times*—*New York* nor *Los Angeles*—would use such intemperate words, but London kept on stabbing. Other phrases in the piece called Lloyd Webber "curmudgeonly and mean," "arrogant," and quoted a theatrical colleague on the composer's "ferocious temper."

What might Faye Dunaway's sensitive employer have said, reading the faxes of Faye's premature disclosure and her subsequent retreat? One can only speculate whether Sir Andrew expressed his displeasure with "We are not amused," or "Kill the bitch."

Poor Faye. It's as though she worked so hard to distance herself from *Mommie Dearest*—omitting the picture from her professional bio, half pretending it never happened—that she changed from Joan Crawford's Doppelgänger into Loretta Young. Even so, her fans like to picture Faye Dunaway at one end of a corporate table, and Sir Andrew at the other. . . . She gives him a scrotum-shriveling look and then spits it out: "Don't fuck with me, Webber. This ain't my first time at the rodeo."

A few weeks later, she did more or less that.

Trouble was brewing almost from the day of her audition. All concerned seemed in agreement on two basic points: Faye Dunaway could act the role of Norma Desmond; she couldn't sing it.

But the inability to sing rarely keeps a name performer out of a musical, whether in Los Angeles, New York, London, or your local dinner theatre. Sometimes, though, an imperfect voice conveys the character perfectly, whereas a magnificent voice is all wrong. Carol Channing in *Hello Dolly* illustrates the first premise, Kiri Te Kanawa as Maria on a recording of *West Side Story* the second.

Faye Dunaway had sung onscreen only once, in the 1989 TV movie

Cold Sassy Tree, where she sat at a piano and sang ragtime. For whatever reason, though, Lloyd Webber chose her as the next Norma Desmond over an array of well-known actresses who either auditioned for him in Los Angeles or were rumored to be after the part: Cybill Shepherd, Diahann Carroll, Rita Moreno, Chita Rivera, Meryl Streep (again), Shirley MacLaine, Diana Ross, Raquel Welch, and Zsa Zsa Gabor.

Dunaway's voice being problematic, the obvious show business solution was: teach her to sing. Real singers, of course, spend years at it; how much vocal craft can anyone accrue in six weeks?

That's the question I asked Marge Rivingston, one of the vocal coaches who tutored Faye Dunaway during that high-strung, high-stakes interregnum in May and June of 1994. David Caddick, Lloyd Webber's music director, who knew Rivingston from a previous show, brought Dunaway to her with the question, "What can you do?"

Rivingston "listened to her trying to maneuver those songs" and replied, "I think we can do it because she has a lot of musical ability. But it's going to take a while." Rivingston asked for a minimum of two months. The Lloyd Webber company granted her three weeks.

Rivingston understood the reason for their short cuts. "Glenn Close was leaving. Her understudy, Karen Mason, is a fabulous singer but of course without the name value. They didn't want to put her on for three weeks between Glenn's departure and Faye's arrival."

Watching Dunaway in a couple of scenes from *Sunset Boulevard*, Rivingston thought, Oh my, this will be quite good if we can get the voice. Years earlier Rivingston had coached Linda Ronstadt on *The Pirates of Penzance*. Among her other students are Bette Midler, Meryl Streep, and Glenn Close.

I asked Marge Rivingston if it would be fair to assess Dunaway, when they started out, as an adequate singer and not much more. "Yes," she said. "She could definitely carry a tune, and she definitely had good pitch, all of that, but she didn't know how to put it together. She did not have the technique."

Marge Rivingston functions as the vocal equivalent of a script doctor; that is, she takes over a problem voice hoping to polish it to the point of utility, if not musical brilliance. She says, "I'm not trying to build a voice; I'm trying to make it work within the context of the material." To use an analogy from psychological counseling, Rivingston practices crisis intervention, not long-term therapy.

Seeking to discover why Glenn Close's singing convinced and Faye Dunaway's didn't, I asked Rivingston if Glenn's acting technique allowed her to create the illusion that she sang better than she actually did in reality.

"Absolutely!" she said. "I'd say that's the real truth of it. And I'm convinced Faye could have pulled it off the same way. She could have ended up singing the show in about two months."

But time ran out.

Faye's singing didn't please Lloyd Webber—or was it Trevor Nunn who shook his head each time she warbled? Both men claimed it was the other who wanted her in the first place. Each one accused the other of giving her the ax. Later, Andrew Lloyd Webber put it this way: "Faye was not ready. And to allow her to open in the role would be terribly damaging to her and to us." The real reason, however, was that tickets didn't sell as expected.

She wasn't exactly fired; she was made redundant. On Tuesday, June 21, Dunaway got word that the deal was off. Two days later Lloyd Webber announced that the Los Angeles production would close on June 26, the date of Glenn Close's last performance. He, along with most members of the cast, would soon depart for New York, where the next production was scheduled to open in November.

The decision to close the show was a brilliant stroke of low cunning. What better way to treat a surplus leading lady?

Three weeks earlier the *Los Angeles Times* had run a long, upbeat interview with Dunaway titled "Norma Dearest." Now the tune had changed. The latest headline: "Faye Dunaway Blasts 'Capricious' Lloyd Webber."

Calling the sudden shutdown "another capricious act by a capricious man," Dunaway stated at a news conference that Lloyd Webber "has been peripatetic throughout the entire process, changing his mind from day to day." Sounding exactly like the grand star she is—or like a scene from a grand old Hollywood movie—Dunaway addressed reporters: "Does he worry that his work is so fragile it might break apart if we moved the songs outside of a range that he feels comfortable with?" Then she gave a sensational Dunaway shrug. "I had more confidence in *Sunset Boulevard* than perhaps he." She made no secret of her intention to take legal action.

Imagine the climax of a contentious picture called *Norma Dearest*, in which Faye Dunaways plays herself. Picture her sitting there, prodigious, cool as an iceberg, while small, rumpled Lloyd Webber faces her from the opposite end of a corporate table. He clears his throat. Does he stammer? A powerful attorney takes over, offering to pay Miss Dunaway two weeks' salary—the amount required by Actors' Equity contracts when someone is dismissed during rehearsals. Two weeks' salary comes to about $50,000. That's when Faye Dunaway flares her nostils, neighs, and breathes fire to melt buttons on the roomful of Savile Row suits.

Such a face-off did not occur, of course; all was negotiated through agents and lawyers. Dunaway sued Lloyd Webber for a total of six million dollars: one million for breach of contract, five million on a variety of defamation and fraud charges, plus punitive damages. In a statement at the time of filing the lawsuit, Dunaway said, "I hope I am the last in a long line of artists who have come to this man's productions in good faith and have suffered great personal and professional injury at his hands."

In New York, Lloyd Webber spokesman Peter Brown again responded angrily: "It's a stickup, and we're not going to tolerate it." Lloyd Webber himself issued a statement in which he threatened to take "the severest action against her insulting, damaging, and defamatory remarks."

Legal and financial haggling stretched into the following year. On January 12, 1995, a joint press release announced that "a private settlement was reached today in the dispute between Faye Dunaway and Andrew Lloyd Webber.... The agreement stipulates that its terms will remain confidential."

Across a chasm of many thousands of miles, the two recent adversaries cooed a lovebird duet.

Lloyd Webber: "Faye Dunaway is an extraordinary talent. I hope our paths cross one day in happier circumstances where my regard for her abilities can be shown more fruitfully. I wish her every success in her future endeavors."

Faye Dunaway: "I accepted the role of Norma Desmond, in part, because of my admiration of Lloyd Webber's ability to put his finger on the pulse of the theatre-going public. He has created memorable musical theatre, and I have great respect for his achievements."

In her autobiography, *Looking for Gatsby*, Dunaway included the press release in its one-page entirety, adding a single sentence of her own: "The terms of this settlement prevent me from any further comment on this matter." Rumors put the payoff amount variously at one and a half million dollars, at one million, and "far, far less."

Marge Rivingston believes Faye Dunaway got "the sympathy vote," as well as a pile of money. "The public loves to side with someone who has been wronged," Rivingston said. "And Faye behaved like a lady through it all. That speaks very well of her."

After the final curtain on closing night at the Shubert, Glenn Close addressed the audience when ovations finally quietened. She referred cryptically to "the very dramatic developments of the past week," then brought virtually every member of the backstage team out onstage, mentioning them by name, from Trevor Nunn to carpenters and costumers. She thanked her "wonderful and incredibly talented" understudy Karen Mason, then handed her own large bouquet of flowers to Mason.

"We rehearsed a couple of weeks in New York before we put the show up," said Colleen Dunn. "A lot of it was teaching the new people what to do, and also refreshing our memories." Most of the Los Angeles cast moved east with the show. Judy Kuhn, who played Betty Schaeffer in L.A., was pregnant, so Alice Ripley took over the role on Broadway.

Sunset Boulevard opened November 17, 1994 at the Minskoff Theatre in New York. Reviewing the play for the *New York Times*, David Richards raved over Glenn Close: "When [the show] is good, it is outlandishly good. When it isn't, it is big. Both observations may be of secondary importance, however, since the musical allows Glenn Close to give one of those legendary performances people will be talking about years from now. As the film star Norma Desmond, a turbaned relic who considers herself the idol of millions, the actress takes breathtaking risks, venturing so far out on a limb at times that you fear it will snap. It doesn't."

Every spring, cast members of various shows perform in the revue *Broadway Cares-Equity Fights AIDS*. For the fund-raiser in April 1995, the *Sunset Boulevard* cast did a skit about auditioning for the role of Norma Desmond. Colleen Dunn directed a parade of famous stars who came onstage to grasp and claw for the part. Each "star" was played by a member of the cast. Sandra Allen, with her Asian features, played Connie Chung. Colleen said, "As the last one to audition, I came onstage as the Faye Dunaway of *Bonnie and Clyde*. I carried a machine gun and when I opened my mouth a donkey sound came out. Isn't that terrible?"

All the "stars" were rubbed out. After "Faye Dunaway" got hers, Glenn Close—the genuine article—made a grand entrance, proclaiming, "I'm the real Norma Desmond," followed by the real Whoopi Goldberg, who bumped *her* off.

In March, an exhausted Glenn Close took a two-week vacation from the show. Her understudy, Karen Mason, played Norma Desmond. According to *Variety* of April 13, 1995, "During that time the industry watched closely to see what impact the star's absence would have at the Minskoff box office." One reason for the scrutiny was that in the small, gossipy world of Broadway shows, everybody wants to know everybody else's business. Another, more pertinent reason in this case: Glenn Close would leave the show for good in July. The question on everyone's lips was, "How strong will the show be without her?"

Naturally, the closest scrutinizer of *Sunset Boulevard*'s box office during Glenn Close's absence was Lloyd Webber, in the person of his North American henchmen. Of these, Edgar Dobie occupied the top notch. And it was he who caused the scandal.

Dobie reported to *Variety* that the show sold $724,789 worth of tickets during the two weeks Close was on vacation, when in reality the show sold only $569,720 worth: a drop of $222,876 from Close's last week in the show. The implication being that Glenn Close was an expendable commodity and that an understudy without name recognition could as easily pack the house.

Too late for Sir Andrew to brush up his Shakespeare, though had he done so he might have recalled that "such an injury would vex a saint." And: "Though she be but little, she is fierce." Or his Congreve: "Hell hath no fury like a woman scorned."

Curtain up on Glenn Close—vexed, fierce, scorned—typing a letter. "I am furious and insulted," she wrote in the two-page, single-spaced missive, which she faxed to her boss and sometime friend.

> I don't think it's an exaggeration to say that my performance turned *Sunset Boulevard* around. I made it a hit. It has existed on my shoulders . . . and yet a representative of your company went out of their [sic] way and lied to try to make the public believe that my contribution to this show is nothing, that Karen's performance is equal to mine, and that my absence had absolutely no effect whatsoever on all the thousands of dollars that supposedly kept pouring into the box office. It sickens me to be treated with such disregard.
>
> If I could leave it in May, when my contract says I can, believe me, I would. At this point, what is making me stay is my sense of obligation to all the people who are holding tickets until July 2.

The dispute caused a feeding frenzy in the tabloids. For the *New York Times, Variety*, the news weeklies, and the entertainment press, the story became Broadwaygate. The feud was soon patched up, resulting in additional publicity. And of course the fisticuffs sold more tickets.

Lloyd Webber called Dobie's actions "idiotic," but did not accept his offer to resign. The Lloyd Webber machine blamed *Variety* for "sensationalizing" the incident, and took another trouncing from the paper. Glenn Close and Lloyd Webber issued a joint statement expressing dismay that "a very private communication between them found its way into public hands, especially since the matter has since been completely resolved."

A modification to their statement blamed the time difference for the fact that the spat wasn't quietly settled by telephone before the papers got it. The *New York Times* arched an eyebrow at this pretty nostrum: "London is only five hours ahead of New York, and Sir Andrew has certainly been known to call reporters unexpectedly from his home telephone."

The *Times* noted that "nearly every actress to touch the role of Norma Desmond . . . ends up in a public dispute with Sir Andrew," then quoted Broadway producer Arthur Cantor: "It can't hurt the show. The next thing is for Betty Buckley to get enraged at him." (Buckley was preparing to take over from Glenn Close in July.) A few days later, in a piece called "Faking It on Broadway" the *Times* poked more fun at Lloyd Webber: "The most powerful man on Broadway has some trouble keeping good help. It's easy to see why."

Not since Bette and Joan—or was it Margo and Eve?—had there been such a cat fight. Betty Buckley, as famous as she was going to be thanks to her role as Grizabella in *Cats*, told *New York Daily News* columnist Linda Stasi, "I play Norma *much younger* than Glenn." Stasi asked Buckley what she thought of Glenn's letter. "It's too bad people's mail goes public," she purred. "How *does* a thing like that happen?"

How indeed?

Theatre scuttlebutt claimed Glenn Close herself leaked the "private communication" to the press, though she sticks by her story: "I wrote a very angry letter that I stupidly faxed. I think it sat around the office, somebody found it, and that was it."

I refrained from prodding on this point for fear she might fax *me* a two-page letter, double-spaced.

But I did elicit the comment from her that "I just thought it was very bad producing. It wasn't only that one incident." Another irritant, according to Close, was "that they should blow up a review by somebody who came to see the show when I was out [and post it in the lobby]. I had an amazingly wonderful understudy, but what was written in that review kind of cast aspersions on me. I thought that was in incredibly bad taste, since I was getting out there eight times a week and making their money for them."

Another long pause, typical of Glenn Close. During these silences, she seems to be formatting her next paragraph. "I didn't mean to hurt anybody," she began. "I mean, it was stupid on my part. When you're angry you should sleep on it."

"But we don't, usually," I said.

She laughed. "Well, I've learned my lesson. I'll never do that again." And then the summing up. Close—nostalgic, generous, grand— sounded like a sane Norma Desmond who goes back to Paramount because they *really* want her and not her car.

"It was an amazing time for me," Glenn said. "One of the most grat- ifying things I've done in my career. We had an incredible company and we became a great extended family. I believe we gave the audience an emotional journey they'll never forget. I'm sad there was any controversy, because the show deserved only positive things. I consider myself a friend of Andrew and Madeleine's. [Madeleine Gurdon is Mrs. Lloyd Webber.]

"I learned how to sing in *Sunset Boulevard*. When we started rehearsals I was the weakest singer in the whole ensemble. For those high, belting notes, there were times I didn't know if I could do it when I went out onstage. I lept off the cliff every night until I mastered the music tech- nically. I did master it, but that probably wasn't until sometime in New York.

"We all had an amazing journey together, something that will last a lifetime."

chapter 27

If They Put All the Norma Desmonds on an Island, Which One Would Survive?

f there's a game called "Musical Normas," it's a roundelay played like this: Betty Buckley replaced Glenn Close on Broadway. Earlier, in London, she had followed Patti LuPone into the role of Norma Desmond. When Buckley left the show in New York, Elaine Paige took over. She, too, had sung Norma in London.

Eventually the game ended. *Sunset Boulevard* closed everywhere: in New York on March 22, 1997, in London a few weeks later, on April 5. It closed in Germany, in Canada, and on tour, even though Petula Clark seemed glued into the role of Norma, destined to play her on the road forever. (As I write this, a new tour is in progress in England starring Faith Brown—actress, comedienne, and impersonator best known for her rendition of Mrs. Thatcher.)

So many contenders, and the search goes on for the one who gave the great, the definitive performance. It's a question opera fanatics used to ask. They argued, yelled, debated, and fought over it: You're dirt if you think Tebaldi's a better Violetta/Mimì/Butterfly than Callas! Dame Joan? Gimme a break. Monserrat can sing it but she can't act.... Jessye has the most fabulous instrument.... You should have heard Zinka Milanov, now there was a great.... Bubbles... Leontyne... Schwartzkopf. Where are they now, the voices and the fans, the claques, the passion, the factions, the opinions, and the worship?

Divas are passé. Did you ever hear a screaming fight over Dawn

Upshaw or Eva Marton or Aprile Milo? Certainly these three, and their contemporaries, are divas in their fashion, enormously talented, but somehow they lack the enormity of offstage glamour. Kathleen Battle, either crazed or besotted by diva drive, sought to assume the persona of spitfire goddess—volcanic temperament, loud demands, queenly petti-ness. Ultimately, however, she proved that opera was still big; it's the sopranos that got small.

Or, more exactly, opera was big only in terms of the classic repertoire. Too often, the operas of present-day composers sound like grad school projects aimed at a doctoral committee. And no one leaves the commit-tee room humming the tunes.

Into the landscape of John Corigliano and David Del Tredici came *Sunset Boulevard*. It landed in an odd trough between operatic peaks and the heights of American musical theatre. In it, Lloyd Webber seems to have blended his many influences—opera, operetta, film scores, Broad-way tunes, church music, jazz, big band, pop, Latin rhythms, rock 'n' roll—into a postmodern idiom that quotes them all, sometimes deadpan and often ironically. More than anything else, however, *Sunset Boulevard* resembles an opera. *Resembles*, yes—or is it the first noir musical? Ironi-cally, critics eager to brand every new "serious" Broadway or West End show as opera squirmed when they finally got what they asked for.

Appropriately, echoes of the opera wars returned as soon as the show opened; for that we surely owe Sir Andrew a nod of thanks. Look at the list of incurable headliners who played Norma Desmond: Glenn Close, Patti LuPone, Diahann Carroll, Betty Buckley, Elaine Paige, Rita Moreno, Helen Schneider (who did the show in Germany), Petula Clark. Plus all those who have recorded songs from the show—Sarah Bright-man, Shirley Bassey, Streisand, and a dozen others. Someone should do a *Follies* revival with every one of them in the cast.

Having listened to many of these recordings, I offer not a discography but remarks on those I consider tops—and bottoms. I said earlier that the inability to sing rarely keeps a big star off the musical stage. For that reason, I rank the Norma Desmonds not for vocal purity but rather according to acting virtuosity, both spoken and sung.

Some singers who are technically perfect bore you because they can't, or don't bother to, convey emotion. They're like straight-A students who memorize the textbook but never express an original thought. I put Julie Andrews in that category, though her fans will howl in protest. Maureen McGovern is another one; and Kiri Te Kanawa. (Judy Garland is a great exception, a seamless blend of emotion and invisible technique.)

I prefer an imperfect voice, even a voice in trouble, that touches your heart or makes you laugh: Billie Holiday near the end, Callas and her famous wobble (which she labeled with the diva word "pulsation"), Ray Charles, Lotte Lenya, Mahalia Jackson, Mabel Mercer, Julie Wilson.

And Glenn Close. The reason I prefer her to the other CD Norma Desmonds is because she compensates for lack of musical thrust with acting thrust—octaves of dramatic range, shading, texture. Her singing voice, though small, and her speaking voice—theatrical and commanding—perfectly characterize Norma Desmond. Fearless, Close sends her voice flying on an operatic trapeze without a net. She makes it jump high and low on the Lloyd Webber trampoline, or twirl on his Pucciniesque jungle gym.

True, her upper register at times could double for Max's wheezing pipe organ, and true, her Norma Desmond sometimes sounds close to eighty. But what makes a grande dame grande? Not youth, not perfect bel canto. Better an out-of-shape pipe organ than a brand-new assembly-line spinet. Glenn Close told me she wasn't happy with the recording, which was made during the Los Angeles run. "I had two major break-throughs after it was done," she said. "I kept getting better and better."

Glenn Close's best song on the recording? I cast my vote for her first aria, "Surrender." It's a strangely haunting, nondenominational hymn. Norma, singing it over the corpse of her chimpanzee, moves the heart of any animal lover. Norma is also singing her own credo. Although it hasn't become a standard, "Surrender" may outlast the Streisand favorites, especially for use on memorial occasions. It's "You'll Never Walk Alone" for the New Age.

The imagery is of a World World I battlefield, stilled by death after the fever of fighting. "White flags fly tonight," poppies cover the hill, but Norma, unyielding, stays on in the fray; she and her pet will only meet again "when I surrender." (This threnody might have been more effective—and more accusatory of royal enemies—at Princess Diana's funeral than Elton John's retread of "Candle in the Wind.")

Patti LuPone has a strong voice, and she is famous for it. On her *Sunset Boulevard* recording she accomplishes the difficult feat of making the arias sound both operatic and Broadwayesque at the same time. But full-blooded singing is the alpha and omega of LuPone's performance. She doesn't *act* the songs; she only sings them. Her spoken line readings run the gamut from mechanical to lackluster, so you can't make the necessary emotional connection. LuPone takes control of Lloyd Webber's musical Norma, but she loses the Hollywood original. Hers is an Upper West Side Norma Desmond, a great teacher at Juilliard, say, but never a great lost star.

If only LuPone would cut loose and camp it up. She seems so inclined, but restrains herself. Or was it Trevor Nunn who threw up anti-camp barricades? Maybe the London production held her back. On CD it sounds unfinished and tentative. LuPone's Times Square belting sticks way out from the sedate production and unflamboyant costars. It's as if Sylvia Miles were cast as Desdemona in some demure, provincial theatre in Yorkshire.

Betty Buckley is an acquired taste that my own buds don't go for. Is she a reincarnation of Ethel Merman that backfired? As Norma Desmond, her strange diction recalls Tammy Grimes, but without Grimes's witchy-woman allure.

Buckley has a huge voice. Perhaps she'd be easier on the ears with a smaller one, since vocal size magnifies her unfortunate tremolo. When Buckley sings I can't help thinking of Dolly Parton, who apparently sent her own tremolo to obedience school. It behaves on a leash, while Buckley's knocks you over and paws your face.

To be sure, Buckley acts with her voice, but it's cheerleader theatrics. *Her* Norma Desmond has no grasp of silent pictures; more likely, she spent her youth on the midway barking, "Step right up!"

———

The award for best delivery of the line, "Shut up, I'm rich, not some platinum blonde bitch," goes to Diahann Carroll. It's from "The Lady's Paying." What she's paying for is Joe's new wardrobe. Carroll half speaks the first phrase, and sings the second one with an alley cat's hiss and the hauteur of a leopard. If I were casting à deux, I'd give four *Sunset Boulevard* performances a week to her, the other four to Glenn Close.

When Diahann Carroll played Norma Desmond in Canada in 1995, she was sixty. She had crow's-feet in her voice and a high-maintenance swagger in the role second only to Gloria Swanson's. Carroll also has Norma Desmond eyes—exotic, narrow, seductive, and dangerous. To borrow a phrase Pauline Kael used about another actress, Carroll is "a slinky, cat-eyed dame."

I've omitted the various Joe Gillises in Lloyd Webber's *Sunset Boulevard* because in a sense they're interchangeable. That's not to detract from them, only to say that the musical, unlike the Wilder film, hands everything to Norma Desmond. Holden was truly Swanson's costar. Musically and dramatically, the actors who played Gillis in the show—Kevin Anderson in London, Alan Campbell in Los Angeles and New York, Rex Smith in Canada—played juveniles. George Hearn as Max (L.A. and New York) is the memorable male in the show.

Which Norma Desmond really would survive an island ordeal? The first to go, aesthetically, is Petula Clark. Lawson Taitte, theatre critic of the *Dallas Morning News*, began his review of Clark's performance: "*Sunset Boulevard* is still big. It's the star who got small." I wish I didn't agree, but I do.

Clark, candid and witty and charming during our interview, has millions of fans all over the world, she's smart and down to earth—the kind of person you like spending time with. And so I'm writing "mea culpa" with one hand, and with the other pushing Petula into the water.

For several weeks in London in 1995, Clark filled in for Elaine Paige, who was on a break. When Trevor Nunn asked her to replace Paige the following year, she couldn't imagine a less likely choice than herself to play Norma Desmond.

"I asked Trevor what he thought I was able to bring to this role," Clark said. "He answered, 'Humor and vulnerability.'" Clark played the role for more than a year in London.

"No, I didn't see Patti LuPone in the show," she said. "I must have been out of the country when all that was going on. But mind you, I've heard her version of it. A long evening where we were supposed to be having dinner and she was—well, anyway."

"Go on," I prompted.

"You can get it from the horse's mouth," she demurred.

But I couldn't. Patti LuPone responded through her press agent, "I never want to talk about *Sunset Boulevard* again."

Petula Clark saw Glenn Close do the show in New York, and after that, Betty Buckley. What does Norma Desmond V say about Norma II and III? "With Betty it was softer, more ethereal," she said. Of Glenn Close, she stated frankly, "I was impressed by her performance, and by the production, but I didn't feel anything for her Norma Desmond. If she's just a monster and Joe is just a gigolo, what's the point?"

I said, "The song you sing over the dead monkey is a very poignant moment in the show. Are you an animal lover?"

"I am, actually," she answered. "Though I can't say I'm mad about that particular monkey." We both laughed. "I've never had a monkey of my own, not even on my back. My husband and I tend to be doggy people, and cats, too."

Clark made an interesting point about Norma Desmond that could apply to Joan Crawford and other female stars of the studio era, who seized the love of fans and wouldn't let go: "I think Norma's passion for her public is quite wonderful. She genuinely loves her people in the dark."

"You've probably never shot anyone onstage before," I said.

Petula Clark's answer might have come from the mouth of Dame Edna Everidge: "I haven't, no. It's rather good, night after night, to shoot a bastard."

I attended two performances of Clark's *Sunset Boulevard*, and this is what I noted at the time: "She seems determined to sabotage the character of

Norma Desmond by reducing her to rag-doll mawkishness. Her performance isn't camp, it's closer to sitcom predictability. Or worse: TV drama. Her line readings sound inspired by Ellen Corby in *The Waltons*."

Gloria Swanson—and Glenn Close—give Norma a tragic ridiculousness. They make you feel for the great, desperate woman crushed by that dark, demented ego. Clark, on the other hand, shrinks Norma with stock gimmicks: grumpy old-lady croaks, Margaret Hamilton cackles. Ultimately this Norma Desmond is a busybody from the reruns, scarcely more tragic than the Golden Girls.

Susan Shulman directed Petula Clark in the national tour. This one was, in a sense, national tour number two, since the New York production as directed by Trevor Nunn went on the road after closing on Broadway, made it to Chicago, then lumbered home because the thousands of pounds of scenery overwhelmed transport systems and theatres along the way. And astronomical costs gobbled profits.

When the Lloyd Webber machine called Susan Shulman about directing the *Sunset Boulevard* tour, she said, "Well, *wasn't* there a tour?" They catalogued the horrific problems.

Shulman responded, "If you're asking me to redirect the show on a smaller set, I'm not interested." No, no, what they wanted was a new show: "It has to be reconceived. It needs a new point of view."

Shulman, Petula Clark, Lewis Cleale as Joe Gillis, and everyone else started from scratch. The American tour would be as different from previous productions as silent film from talkies. Petula Clark said, "Susan told me to forget everything I did in London. She wanted a fresh start. That put me in the curious position of having to unlearn and learn at the same time."

What performer could survive such a wrenching turnaround? It might sound good, but the resulting show reveals a *Noises Off* schizo desperation. Psychologically, Norma Desmond is off (goofy, shticky) when she should be on (dark and tragic). Shulman turned a good deal of recitative from previous productions back into spoken dialogue, which helped neuter the show's operatic hormones.

I firmly believe Susan Shulman when she talks about *Sunset Boulevard*. Conversationally, her perceptions shine. For instance, her cogent grasp of

Lloyd Webber's musical intent: "The show is so cannily composed. It sounds like a period movie score, and the music that takes place inside the mansion differs greatly from the music outside the house, which sounds like fifties movie musicals."

And she told Lewis Cleale during rehearsals, "We know that Norma falls in love with Joe, but it's really important that Joe fall in love with Norma, even if it's for the briefest period of time." This is the one plot point where the musical improves the film.

After Norma's suicide attempt, Joe says (in dialogue virtually identical to the script), "I never meant to hurt you, Norma. You've been good to me. You're the only person in this stinking town that's ever been good to me." Norma responds: "Then why don't you just say thank you and go? Go, go! Go!" The libretto indicates that Joe goes to the stairs as if to leave, then returns to Norma. He sits near her on the sofa, leans forward, and kisses her. He says, from his heart at that instant, "Happy New Year."

And they kiss as William Holden and Gloria Swanson could not, because in Hollywood at that time gigolos did not fall in love with the boss, even for one evening. Only in Lloyd Webber's version do Joe and Norma exchange a real screen kiss—on the stage.

Susan Shulman faced a daunting task. Her physical production of *Sunset Boulevard* had to be svelte and nimble, and yet the story must retain all its emotional cream. Referring to the high-calorie *Sunset*s of London, Los Angeles, and New York, Shulman said, "People talked about the staircase. We were determined that in our production they would talk about relationships."

But remove Norma Desmond from the staircase, and what's left? You might as well stage a musical about Jill Clayburgh. Not that Shulman operated without the stairs, of course, although in her production it seemed less like a stairway to Paradise Lost than a way to walk to the second floor.

Shulman emphasized the comic elements of the story, at times minimizing the tragic. She even employed silent-movie slapstick as a way to set her production apart. Perhaps she was recalling Andrei Serban's legendary New York production of *The Cherry Orchard* in 1977, in which Irene Worth, as Madame Ranevskaya, and others in the cast played Chekhov as silent-screen farce, the way Chaplin or Keaton might have conceived it. There it worked. Ironically, it didn't work in *Sunset Boulevard*. That's because the show, like the film, eulogizes silent pictures. They're as dead as the pet monkey. Shulman's mistake was to raise that silent corpse, as it were, and make it a jerky, flickering presence on her stage.

And why on earth did Shulman and Clark decide that Norma Desmond's accent should be American? Petula Clark, born British, sounded more Chicago than Gloria Swanson ever wanted to. I asked Susan Shulman why, and she said, "Maybe Norma was a little girl from the Midwest. When she came to Hollywood they gave her speech and voice lessons so that she would sound as if she came from nowhere. She would have this flat, what I call Debbie Reynolds speech pattern."

But that's the crack in Shulman's *Sunset Boulevard* golden bowl. Norma Desmond *didn't* come from the Midwest; impossible. Such literal-mindedness must prove fatal.

Don't ask where Norma Desmond was born. The only answer available is this: She came from the country of movie stars, a city-state outside the geography of our understanding. And that's where she returned in the end.

chapter 28

Billy Wilder from Noir to Blackout

*W*hat diluted Billy Wilder? His 1940s pictures reveal a black-coffee director, strong and bitter and packing a jolt. Of these, *Sunset Boulevard* is the perfect cup.

His next picture, *The Big Carnival*, a.k.a. *Ace in the Hole* (1951), seems steeped in bile, but too much caffeine has been added in the form of Kirk Douglas, who gives his usual frothing, overwrought performance. Like Joe Gillis, he's a writer down on his luck—in this case, a newspaper reporter. Unlike Gillis, he's amoral and self-loathing to the core. And no one likes him, certainly not the audience. Covering the story of a man trapped in a cave, Douglas's character prolongs the victim's agony to boost his own media visibility and thus his career. Wilder once called *The Big Carnival* "the runt of my litter." Alas, he and his partners would birth many severely deformed progeny during the next thirty years.

The first draft of *The Big Carnival*'s script, by Wilder, Walter Newman, and Lesser Samuels, had a talking cadaver begin the picture in voice-over as his body was loaded into a railway baggage car: "Good-bye, Mr. Boot. So long, Herbie. Thanks for seeing me off. . . . When you write the obituary—lay it on the line! What I wanted and how bad I wanted it—put that in! What I did to get it—that goes in, too!"

Although this passage was later deleted, *The Big Carnival* remained too nerve-jangling for the American public. It flopped. Watching this savage satire a half century later, you realize that Wilder was trying valiantly to stand up on the artistic and critical Everest he had ascended the year before. But fierce winds howled, pushing him several degrees off the axis. Still Wilder, though wavering, held the peak.

Wilder and Brackett had split after *Sunset Boulevard*, never to reunite. And yet Brackett's absence from *The Big Carnival* resonates, as it would in many of Wilder's pictures until the end of his career. Motifs from their scripts recur in film after film, no matter who happens to be Wilder's collaborator. *The Big Carnival* opens with a coupé being towed; in it is Kirk Douglas. The car resembles Holden's in *Sunset Boulevard*. Douglas, aggressively Hedda Hopperish, phones in the lurid story of the cave-in to his editor: "Unless war's declared tonight, here's your front-page feature."

Even if Hedda's phone call in *Sunset Boulevard* was Wilder's exclusive idea, the way he uses it in the two pictures underlines the great guiding genius of Brackett on his volatile younger partner. Hateful as the real Hopper often was, as a character she's attractive, and her one brief scene in *Sunset Boulevard* reveals the dreadful power of Hollywood's gossip gorgons, Hedda and Louella.

As the years go by, the ghost of Charles Brackett's restraining hand seems to stretch toward Wilder, who never accepts the offer. And so Wilder's cynicism, bad taste, vulgarity—all those crass qualities he was accused of—take root and flourish. Brackett weeded the aesthetic garden daily, it appears, during their raucous and brilliant years at Paramount. Wilder's post-Brackett partners are less diligent. Tares spring up among the wheat.

In 1953, *Stalag 17*, an oddly misbegotten World War II comedy mixed with a concentration camp drama, was Wilder's offering. The two genres are oil and water, and Wilder's second film without the Brackett radar shows him veering further off-course. Wilder and Edwin Blum wrote the script, based on the play by Donald Bevan and Edmund Trzcinski. *Stalag 17* compares badly with *A Foreign Affair*, where the smart screenwriting decision was to set the picture in postwar Berlin. That way, Brackett and Wilder dealt with the Nazis after the fact by showing the corrupt legacy of fascism. Here, concentration camp brutality is jammed up against male bonding and barracks horseplay. (It seems odd, too, that Wilder, whose mother, stepfather, and grandmother died at Auschwitz, could set a film in a concentration camp and skip most of the horrors. American prisoners in this stalag are treated relatively well as long as they don't try to escape.)

As though nostalgic for *Sunset Boulevard*, Wilder cast William Holden as his star. He and the other camp inmates bet on the outcome of rat races—rats having appeared previously in both *The Lost Weekend* and *Sunset Boulevard*. Other faint *Sunset Boulevard* parallels: The only mail that prisoner Shapiro receives is from a finance company demanding payment for his Plymouth. A Christmas dance in *Stalag 17*, held under duress like Norma Desmond's New Year's Eve soirée, runs on the same false festivity. Since this is virtually a womanless film, Otto Preminger, as camp commandant Von Scherbach, assumes the role of diva. Berlin has put him out to pasture; by delivering a captured American saboteur he hopes to make a "comeback." In Preminger's last shot, his elongated face resembles Norma Desmond's, though his impenetrable look of cruelty and chilling composure lack her pathos.

Although *Sabrina* (1954) is widely considered charming, delightful, and fun, if you take a closer look you may find the plot laborious and the script pedestrian, with undertones of cruelty and misogyny. Audrey Hepburn's high-fashion effervescence distracts viewers from such weakness, however, and a handful of quirky Wilder touches add to the distraction. Here, as in *Sunset Boulevard*, Wilder employed former silent stars: Walter Hampden in a supporting role, Francis X. Bushman as Martha Hyer's father. Humphrey Bogart, as the scion of an immensely wealthy family, has a car phone, just like Norma Desmond. Hers rings only the chauffeur. This one, technologically advanced for 1954, lets Bogart phone Wall Street while motoring around Long Island.

You don't really think of *The Seven Year Itch* (1955) as a Wilder film. It belongs to Marilyn Monroe and her billowing white skirt. *The Spirit of St. Louis* (1957) is surely Wilder's most atypical picture. Perhaps for that reason, it's overlooked. Certainly it deserves attention for James Stewart's convincing portrayal of Charles Lindbergh, but even more for Wilder's ingenuity in capturing the exhilaration and the claustrophobia of that first transatlantic flight. Wilder cleverly turns the plane into Stewart's costar. A fly in the cockpit plays a supporting role.

In 1957 Billy Wilder teamed for the first time with I.A.L. Diamond for *Love in the Afternoon*, a Frenchified *Kaffee mit Schlag* of a movie. Unless you're a card-carrying member of the Gary Cooper, Audrey Hepburn, or Maurice Chevalier fan clubs, your most vivid memory of this one may well be "Fascination," a confectionery waltz played relentlessly. The unshakeable tune buzzes in your head for days, like a bumblebee in a jar.

Fascination, relentless and unshakeable, characterizes the professional marriage of Wilder and I.A.L. Diamond. With *Love in the Afternoon* as their engagement party, the happy pair stayed together until death (Diamond's) and retirement (Wilder's) did them part. From 1957 until Wilder's final picture in 1981, they wrote every film but one that Wilder directed.

That one was *Witness for the Prosecution* (1957), a one-picture stand Wilder had with Harry Kurnitz. This highly entertaining film, based on a play by Agatha Christie, proves what Wilder was still capable of, even without Brackett—provided he had good material, a solid cowriter, and inspired casting. Wilder believed that Charles Laughton had "the greatest range and power of any actor, man or woman," he had known. The rest of the cast—Marlene Dietrich, Tyrone Power, Elsa Lanchester, and the irrepressible character actors Norma Varden and Una O'Connor—make it one of Wilder's great treats. His cowriter, Harry Kurnitz, surely deserves a lot of credit for the picture's success. Kurnitz was an Anglophile, and also a mystery writer who published detective stories under the name Marco Page.

Looking back, one wishes Wilder had married that nice boy and settled down with him. Such a couple. Nu, the Wilder–Diamond troth was plighted, and so the wedding feast took place. But who's complaining? The marriage produced *Some Like It Hot* (1959).

If Billy Wilder had never made *Sunset Boulevard* or anything else, he'd be loved for *Some Like It Hot*. It violated so many taboos that it's still subversive.

In its famous ending Jack Lemmon as "Daphne" is headed to the altar with sugar daddy Joe E. Brown. Everyone knows the scene: Lemmon whips off his wig and says, "You don't understand, Osgood. *I'm a man.*" And the notorious answer is, "Well, nobody's perfect." (Who knew, in Eisenhower's twilight, that four decades later same-sex marriages would be a reality and also a Republican war cry?)

In 2000, *Some Like It Hot* placed number one in the American Film Institute's list of 100 best American movie comedies. Another drag picture, *Tootsie*, came in second. Both were selected by a panel of 1,800 actors, directors, studio executives, and critics polled by the AFI.

Wilder's résumé, during his first decade after Brackett, reads like a précis of every good Hollywood director's career: eight solid pictures in ten years, a couple not so good, several above average, and two first rate. And all eight films quite watchable, worth discussing, worth arguing and writing about.

In 1960, with *The Apartment*, the rift begins. From there to the end, you can start a riot by condemning—or defending—one of his films. As jury foreman, at least in this book, I take a hard line. For Billy Wilder's offenses I find him guilty—with recommendation of mercy. (I'm afraid the quality of mercy for his coconspirator, I.A.L. Diamond, is strained to breaking.)

The Apartment has legions of defenders, including those who picked the AFI's 100 funniest movies: it's number twenty on their list. The main reason I don't like it is hyper Jack Lemmon, whose tempo and twitches make me want to reach for a Valium. (I have similar adverse reactions to Betty Hutton, Robin Williams, Diane Keaton, and Jerry Lewis.)

To me, *The Apartment* is as dated and as threadbare as Camelot. I also find it jarring, for Wilder once again, as in *Stalag 17*, conflates incompatible elements—in this case, farce and ethics. It's a bit like casting solemn Gregory Peck in *The Bed Before Yesterday*.

Maybe the aesthetic dividing line in discussions of *The Apartment* is sexual orientation. Cameron Crowe, in his book *Conversations with Wilder*, dwells on this picture as though it were *Sunset Boulevard*. Perhaps for him, and for other heterosexuals who admire the film, Jack Lemmon equals the male Gloria Swanson. (Leonard Maltin's four-star assessment begins,

"Superb comedy-drama that manages to embrace both sentiment and cynicism.")

But what about heart? Having lost his own to I.A.L. Diamond, Billy Wilder had little left for the screen.

The next Wilder and Diamond picture, *One, Two, Three* (1961) is the smoking gun that proves Diamond did it. That is, ruined Wilder by downgrading his work to processed shtick. Today *One, Two, Three* is as dated as a rerun of *Pete and Gladys*. It was just as dated when it came out, at least according to Pauline Kael. Reviewing it in 1961, she wrote, "It was shot in Berlin and Munich, but the real location is the locker room where tired salesmen swap the latest variants of stale old jokes." A typical howler: The Russians reject a shipment of Swiss cheese because it's full of holes.

Beginning with *One, Two, Three*, Wilder films became increasingly, depressingly predictable. He and Diamond seem to have written the first thing that popped into their heads. (Good writers never do; sometimes they don't use even the tenth or twentieth thing that comes to mind.) For the next twenty years, they purveyed one-liners everyone had heard a hundred times. Eventually the mildew grew so thick that Neil Simon smelled like spring bouquets by comparison.

If you watch Wilder movies in chronological order, by the time you reach *Irma La Douce* (1963) you're numb from aesthetic novocaine. And, as in the dentist's chair and other unpleasant venues, you close your eyes and think about Desmond. If high schools put on plays about French hookers, *Irma La Douce* is the kind of low farce that might have the sophomore class in stitches.

Virtually everything Wilder did in the sixties could be lumped together under the title *Kiss Me, Stupid*, though he didn't actually make that one until 1964. It's an annoying mosquito of a movie, and yet Kim Novak's performance as a vulnerable, likeable whore in Climax, Nevada, wins your heart. She gives a Marilyn Monroe performance: wistful, intelligent, and used up by Hollywood. Doro Merande as Felicia Farr's old gripe of a mother is screamingly funny—for two minutes, then back to Dean Martin and Ray Walston at their unspeakable worst.

Actually, this picture deserves some kind of bad-movie cult status. Sufficiently bizarre to qualify, it's terrible with a few good scenes in it. And unforgettable. Every part of the picture wars with every other part, so that finally it's like a jigsaw puzzle with every piece in the wrong position.

In *The Fortune Cookie* (1966), Wilder paired Jack Lemmon and Walter Matthau—as lethal an odd-couple combination as Wilder and Diamond. And yet the picture isn't terrible, one reason being that Lemmon spends much of it confined to bed or a wheelchair. Restraint makes him bearable. Second, the writing depends more on plot than on cheap one-liners. And third, in some vague way it's a wan comic version of *Witness for the Prosecution*, though by no means as well written, well made, or entertaining. Perhaps I feel lenient toward *The Fortune Cookie* because of a clever *Sunset Boulevard* allusion. Lemmon says to a cameraman who is clandestinely filming him in his apartment for suspected insurance fraud: "Roll 'em, Max."

The Private Life of Sherlock Holmes (1970) has many good things in it. Wilder's cut lasted three hours and a half. The producer forced him to reduce it to the standard two-hour length, threatening not to release it otherwise. Until the picture is restored, it's unfair to evaluate it on a par with Wilder's other films.

The flaws in Wilder pictures of the sixties and seventies were never technical. He continued to use skilled cinematographers, editors, composers. The opening of *Avanti!* (1972) shows, however, the seemingly deliberate perversity of Wilder's directorial decisions. The picture opens with an establishing shot of Rome as Jack Lemmon's plane lands. That aerial shot makes Rome look gorgeous, but only for an instant. Then the plane's landing gear plops down into the frame like a giant bird in the act of elimination.

The same could be said of I.A.L. Diamond's approach to screenwriting: just when you want to bask in the artistry of Billy Wilder, Diamond plops into the picture as cowriter and stays right on until the crappy end. He has the sensibility of a headline writer for a supermarket tabloid, but without the gaga flair. If Wilder had written *Sunset Boulevard* with him, Norma Desmond would be no more sympathetic than Joan Crawford in *Queen Bee*. Asked to name the least attractive scene in any movie, I'd say Jack Lemmon's nude scene in *Avanti!* His rear end looks like a flayed carcass. Flayed, also, is poor Juliet Mills, who retains her dignity throughout—even playing Pamela Piggott, so named because she's fat.

———

Would anyone, even the most fundamentalist auteur critic, equate the twelve Wilder and Diamond pictures with the thirteen of Brackettand-wilder?

Apart from the inferiority of Wilder and Diamond—the gauche material, the facile dialogue that's often yelled by actors, the in-your-face crudeness parading as wit—many of their films rely on stereotypes. Those hoary old showbiz stereotypes that come in so handy for second-rate works by lazy writers. In *The Apartment* the stereotypes are Jewish: Dr. Dreyfuss, Mrs. Dreyfuss, Mrs. Lieberman. In *One, Two, Three* the Germans are loud-mouthed Krauts—and so are the Russians. The French in *Irma La Douce*, the Italians in *Avanti!*, the Greeks in *Fedora*—they're all generic "foreigners" as imagined by people who never turn off the TV. The Western small-town folk of *Kiss Me, Stupid* are citizens of Mayberry on Viagra.

None of this is shocking per se. It's just low-grade Hollywood product. You're speechless only when you recall Billy Wilder's former sensitivity, the nuances in his earlier characterizations, his humanity in evoking sympathy even for miserable offenders. In *Ninotchka*, Garbo as the head Russian is misguided but noble. Her Communist henchmen have their *Mittel Europa* charm, and the film pokes fun at all nationalities, not just "them."

The small-towners in *The Major and the Minor* (1942), Wilder's first American film as director, have more than one dimension. Lela Rogers—mother of Ginger, in the film and in real life—plays the role with warmth and feeling. She wasn't a professional actress, so one assumes Wilder shaped the winsome performance he wanted. *Five Graves to Cairo*, on one level a propaganda movie to boost the Allied war effort, stands apart from others in the genre because the Nazis—led by Erich von Stroheim as Field Marshall Rommel—are civilized, cultured human beings gone horribly astray. They're not a priori brutes.

Ray Milland in *The Lost Weekend* surely gives the definitive Hollywood performance of a hopeless alcoholic. We in the audience empathize with his human despair more than his pallid girlfriend Jane Wyman seems able to. We feel for him even when he double-crosses us. Marlene Dietrich in *A Foreign Affair* plays a cabaret singer with Nazi friends—some presumably convicted in Nuremberg, others still on the loose—but Wilder doesn't appoint the audience as her hanging judge.

Billy Wilder's bipolar partnership with Diamond seems to account for the curious character Luther "Boom Boom" Jackson in *The Fortune Cookie*. Jackson is the black football player who accidentally knocks Jack Lemmon down on the field, causing the injury that sets the plot in motion. Wilder's latest biographer, Ed Sikov, suggests that Wilder "either purposely created a cipher into whom audiences could pour their thoughts about black men, or else he simply couldn't deal with a magnetic black costar competing for attention with Lemmon and Matthau." Sikov concludes that "Wilder plays on contemporary racial issues without fully addressing any of them."

Although their paternalistic characterization of the black man would be offensive today, in 1966 it seemed mildly progressive. Hindsight is not only twenty-twenty; it's self-righteous and unfair. Even though Wilder seems uncomfortable with the African-American character, he avoids the typical white liberal condescension of sixties Hollywood.

When Wilder and Diamond wrote their adaptation of *The Front Page* (1974), the Hecht–MacArthur play had already been filmed twice: in 1931 with Adolphe Menjou, and in 1940 as *His Girl Friday*, with Cary Grant and Rosalind Russell. Surely the midseventies was rather late for still another version of this period piece. (Apparently not. In 1988 it reappeared as *Switching Channels*.)

Their *Front Page* is not a terrible picture; just tired, despite the frantic pace and newsroom shouting. It's here, however, that you'll find one of the few queer jokes in a Wilder picture. David Wayne plays a fussbudget priss named Bensinger. In case no one guesses his orientation, Jack Lemmon warns another reporter: "Never get caught in the can with Bensinger." It's an easy laugh—too easy for Wilder, in better days.

Maurice Zolotow, in his 1977 book *Billy Wilder in Hollywood*, asked Wilder about Mitchell Leisen, who directed three pictures that he and Brackett wrote. Wilder responded angrily: "Leisen was too goddamn fey. I don't knock fairies. Let him be a fairy. Leisen's problem was that he was a stupid fairy." Wilder's antipathy seems to have ignited only because Leisen favored fastidious set decoration over well-crafted scripts, not because he was gay.

A later statement Wilder made about homosexuals also suggests he loathed only "fairies" who were "stupid." While filming *Witness for the Prosecution*, Marlene Dietrich developed a crush on Tyrone Power. Years later Wilder said, "Everybody had a crush on Ty. Laughton had a crush on him. I did, too. As heterosexual as you might be, it was impossible to be impervious to that kind of charm." After the picture wrapped, Wilder, Laughton, and Power traveled around Europe together, no women allowed. As Sikov states in his Wilder biography, "The fact that a man was gay was certainly no reason for Billy not to enjoy his companionship."

"I wanted to stop the whole thing after we were shooting for a week or so, but I couldn't." Thus, Billy Wilder on *Fedora* (1978).

Wilder's penultimate film immediately earned the reputation of a *Sunset Boulevard* redux. Actually, it's more like *Dead Ringer* minus the galvanizing punch of Bette Davis. And very much minus Gloria Swanson, Norma Desmond, and Garbo, even though reviewers called Fedora "a reclusive, Garboesque actress."

William Holden, as director Barry Detweiler, travels to Greece in search of Fedora, the lost star he had an affair with in 1947 while working on her great MGM costume epic, *Leda and the Swan*. (The names L. B. Mayer might have called Billy Wilder at *this* premiere!)

They had faces *and* lily pads then—and Detweiler, an assistant director on *Leda*, performed the task of arranging the pads strategically during Fedora's nude bathing scene. This we see in flashback, but since affectless Marthe Keller plays Fedora-in-the-Tub, it's difficult to ascertain whether Leda's hot for the big bird or whether she's afterglowing from his shuddering loins.

Many years later Holden arrives at Fedora's musty Greek island villa. José Ferrer, the ex-star's live-in plastic surgeon, greets him with Max's words that fateful day at Desmondland: "Wipe your feet." So much for redux; from here on it's more like reflux. In this kind of rococo trash, Lana Turner should have played ripe old Fedora, for this picture belongs to the *Madame X* brand of screenwriting. (Hildegarde Knef chews scenery as the aged version of the greatest Leda of them all, wheelchair-bound because of a facelift run amok. Whereas Norma would have fired the butcher, Fedora generously retains him as a gatekeeper doc.)

What a great drag show this could be, with its preposterous plot twists, adulation of washed-up divas, and delectable camp lines: "I'll tell you what becomes a legend most," declaims Fedora in response to an inquiry from the Blackgama ad campaign. "Not to linger on beyond your time. Monroe and Harlow—they were the lucky ones."

Done deadpan, however, *Fedora* is film beige, coated with a sickly yellow finish.

Francis Veber, author of rancid scripts such as *Partners* and *Dinner for Shmucks*, is the I.A.L. Diamond of France. How depressingly right, then, that *Buddy Buddy* (1981), Billy Wilder's last film, was based on a play and story by Veber. A typical bad line: "Premature ejaculation means always having to say 'I'm sorry.'"

In a sense, every picture Wilder made during the last decades of his career turned into a sad mea culpa. Did Wilder know? Did he guess he was headed the wrong way? For after 1950, he traveled backward down *Sunset Boulevard*.

From 10086 Sunset, and the evocative shadows of Desmondland in high-toned Holmby Hills, Wilder should have headed west toward the Pacific. Charles Brackett knew the way. In that direction stretched Wilder's golden artistic ocean, with all Hollywood at his feet. Instead he reversed course.

Wilder took a wrong turn and headed east, back toward the flashy Sunset Strip and the fool's gold it represents. From there, he made a long, slow descent through the boulevard's seedy blocks of parking lots and graffiti-covered walls, pawn shops, and one-night cheap hotels. Billy Wilder's joy ride with I.A.L. Diamond was so exhilarating that he didn't see the jagged potholes. Ultimately, though, Sunset Boulevard petered out. Somewhere on the featureless fringes of downtown L.A., in the tangle of freeways and desert scrub, they reached the undistinguished end.

chapter 29

Lux Perpetua

In 1980, Gloria Swanson concluded her autobiography with these words: "Things are not clear yet, not by a long shot, but they are getting clearer . . ." She meant that the end of life, unlike the last chapter in her book, might melt shadows from her human riddle.

On March 20, 1983, exactly one week before her eighty-fourth birthday, Gloria Swanson entered New York Hospital after suffering a heart attack. She died there on April 4, and the following day her body was cremated at the Trinity Church crematorium in Manhattan. A private memorial service took place later.

On her hospital bed during the final two weeks of life she kept an E.T. doll that someone had given her. "You see," said her granddaughter, Brooke Young, "Grandma lived in the present. She was current and she had a keen mind. She didn't need to live in her past escapades."

In the last days, her persona least resembled that of another great silent-screen star. Indeed—what's the one item in the world that Norma Desmond would *not* have on her own hospital bed? An E.T. doll, certainly, nor anything else connected with the latest Hollywood picture. Poor Norma, in extremis, might command Max to bring her a very different sort of effigy: an N.D. doll from the past, dressed as Salome.

For more than thirty years, Gloria Swanson had tolerated an unwelcome visitor in her life, an alter ego she understood too well and who refused to leave when their mutual business had been transacted. But now, at last, Norma Desmond had departed.

Insofar as Norma Desmond possessed Gloria Swanson, she refused to give up her reluctant host without a fight. As though determined to prove that *she*, Norma Desmond, was in command, she engineered an affair more to her own liking than to Gloria Swanson's. Or so it seemed, though perhaps that encounter lay in Gloria's own horoscope all along.

I wish Billy Wilder and Charles Brackett could write the next few pages. If so, they would spare me a melancholy task, one I prefer to avoid. But in a sense they *did* write it. Their stars were Gloria Swanson and William Holden.

In the spring of 1978 a handsome man in his late youth phoned Gloria Swanson from California at the behest of Claire Trevor, the actress. Trevor was the wife of Milton Breen, director of *Three for Bedroom C*, the picture that Swanson made the year after *Sunset Boulevard*. Claire Trevor had told this man about Swanson the artist, who designed a postage stamp for the United Nations and who was also an amateur sculptor.

On the telephone the man suggested that, since Gloria took her work seriously, she should let art critics give it their appraisal. He mentioned the possibility of a one-woman show in London.

Arriving at Swanson's home on Fifth Avenue a few weeks later, the man said none of those Joe Gillis things like "You used to be big." There was no Max von Mayerling; the man of the house was William Dufty— or William the Sixth, as Swanson's daughters called their latest stepfather, for Madame had been married six times.

Philip Stanhope, Lord Chesterfield, wrote in the eighteenth century: "If you would particularly gain the affection and friendship of particular people, whether men or women, endeavour to find out their predominant excellency, if they have one, and their prevailing weakness, which everybody has; and do justice to the one and something more than justice to the other.... They are most and best flattered upon those points where they wish to excel and yet are doubtful whether they do or not."

To all the world, Gloria Swanson's predominant excellency was the art of being a movie star, and glamorous. Her prevailing weakness, if such she had, revealed itself in her sculpture. These pieces—representational, old-fashioned, pleasant but uninspired—pleased her, though she wondered if others would take equal pleasure in the viewing.

Her suave visitor set to work dispelling doubts. He told her he believed they could indeed mount a one-woman exhibition at a gallery in London.

Flushed with pleasure, she replied that she did not have enough pieces for a show. He encouraged her to accelerate her pace so that in six months she would have completed several additional sculptures.

In addition to his artistic entrepreneurship, Gloria Swanson's new friend billed himself as a writer and producer. He had worked on several scripts in Europe, he said. He had written a couple of TV shows. And a novel, under a pseudonym.

After the one-woman show she asked, "Where do I go from here? What next?"

He suggested that she write her memoirs. She considered it an extraordinary idea. Until now, she had been too interested by the present to revisit the past. But love opens new doors. Suddenly she was mad about the boy, who was forty years younger than she. William the Sixth, still Gloria's consort, was kept on, though under sufferance. Now old friends seemed dull in the gleam of this new male.

The memoirs, titled *Swanson on Swanson*, came out in 1980. For Gloria the fanfare and media buzz amounted to yet another comeback. By this time, however, the young man had become possessive, overly attentive, and apparently eager to isolate her from influences other than his own. Little is known about the man, though a view of him was captured by a reporter who came to Gloria's home to interview her about the book.

The reporter entered and the Swanson entourage dispersed. Among them were Raymond Daum, the archivist in charge of her papers and also her longtime friend, and the young man—Swanson's lover.

After two hours the lover stole back in. Gloria was still talking. She turned fondly toward her lover and said, "I was just telling him about—"

"Don't tire her," said the lover.

GLORIA: Don't tell her who? Me?

THE REPORTER: Don't tell her what?

GLORIA: The what?

THE LOVER: Don't *tire* you, Gloria.

GLORIA: Tire me? How many times have I told you *never* to use that word in connection with *me!*

THE LOVER: Darling . . .

GLORIA: Now wait a minute. Now just a second . . .

THE LOVER: I know, I know.

GLORIA: *I'm* not tired. Do you want me for some reason?

THE LOVER [to reporter]: Have you got what you want?

THE REPORTER: Not quite. I came with these questions.

THE LOVER [to Gloria]: What are the questions? Are they goodies?

GLORIA: Yes!

THE LOVER [to Gloria]: Call me if the questions are *impossible.*

GLORIA: He hasn't asked any impossible questions. And I'm *not* tired. Seven trillion cells in my body and each one knows what it's supposed to do.

This odd vignette, though oblique, conjures the sort of revelations captured by a hidden camera for an exposé.

———

A magazine editor in New York met Gloria and her lover at a party. According to the editor, the lover had "a Prince Mdivani look" and "came across as very cosmopolitan. He spoke in a British accent."

When the lover was traveling, he sent Gloria letters that fluttered her elderly heart. "Gloria darling," he wrote from a distant city, "I am flying in a rush to New York and cannot get a moment to say good-bye, but you know how much I love you and how grateful I am for all your kindness." A cable to her a few months before her death: "Be well. Be happy. We did it. Concorde confirmed for both of us to Paris September 24 for festival in Spain. Shall be returning Sunday night. A big hug."

They were seen around New York. Under the headline "Gloria Swanson Has Hubby #7 in Wings & He's Just Half Her Age," the *Post* reported: "He is confidently predicting to friends he will become Gloria's next husband." During the last week of Swanson's life the *Post* printed an erroneous report that she "was well enough to talk at length with her husband and business manager" from her hospital bed. Liz Smith in the *Daily News* corrected that item the following day: "That story gave the actress quite a laugh. She doesn't speak to the man any longer; furthermore, she has never been married to him and is still wed to husband number six, William Dufty."

Friends warned her that this man half her age could not be after anything other than material gain. She responded, "Don't do this to me! I can't hear talk like that."

Another source: "She kicked her husband, Bill Dufty, out of the house when the lover came along. The lover wanted her for his own. Exclusively." The source opined that he planned to market her.

Another friend of Gloria's said, "He involved her in projects that excited her. He told Gloria, 'You're going to do things,' and she said, 'Yes, I haven't quit.'"

Two young men from Greenwich Village approached Gloria about a cabaret act they wanted to produce, starring her. Enthusiastic, she jumped into preparations for the show. She took dance lessons and sang songs. She gaily laughed with the two young men, all of which reportedly made her paramour feel threatened. There was a break-up. Gloria phoned her old friend Raymond Daum. She wept as she said, "You warned me. All along I was a fool."

Years later Daum said, "I think that might have caused the heart attack."

The ex-lover came to the hospital room and Gloria's daughters refused to let him in. The man disappeared.

After a long and futile search for Gloria Swanson's last lover, I asked one of her daughters whether she knew his whereabouts. She said, "If you find him let us know. He raises his ugly head from time to time. I hope I never see him." I disagree. I would have loved to hear his side of the story to include here, along with his views on Gloria Swanson.

Raymond Daum, who witnessed the romance, said, "In the early days Gloria would say to me, 'Look at him—he's gorgeous!' When he walked out of the room she'd say, 'Look at that tush.' Then when he came back in Gloria would sit in his lap like a little girl. He'd call her darling. Oh yes, you couldn't fool Gloria about many things, but you can fool the heart."

The day after Gloria Swanson's death, newspapers in every country reported the story. Many of them quoted her immortal line: "All right, Mr. DeMille, I'm ready for my close-up."

Acknowledgments

Taking my initial steps on *Sunset Boulevard*, I scarely guessed the large number of travelers I would meet along the way. The kindness and generosity I encountered from every one of them made the two-year journey go by like a weekend.

My first stop was Nancy Olson Livingston's home in Beverly Hills, and she astonished me with her near-total recall of events so long past. Her husband, Alan Livingston, and their son, Christopher Livingston, added their good humor and their insights to hers.

She told Billy Wilder about my project. Although he was ill at the time, I later spoke with him by telephone. Reluctant to disturb him during recuperation, I said to his wife, Audrey Wilder, "I wonder if you might ask your husband about these aspects of *Sunset Boulevard.*" She answered, "Well, I'll let you ask him yourself. Hold on a minute." I heard her call out, "Billy!" A moment later he said, "Yes, sir?" Answers flew off his tongue as though he had been awaiting my call.

Nancy Olson also put me in touch with Jay Livingston and Ray Evans, the other surviving members of the cast, whose songwriting careers merit a tuneful, separate volume. I'm sad to report that Jay Livingston died as this book went to press.

Several persons involved in the various musical versions of *Sunset Boulevard* took time to speak with me at length. Without them I never would have gone backstage. Glenn Close, in my opinion the greatest living Norma Desmond, talked for forty-five minutes rather than the ten or fifteen I had agreed to with her publicist. To me, Glenn Close resembles a great star of the studio era because of her talent, virtuosity, and hard work. Part of her genius is transferring movie magic to the stage.

Petula Clark, Sandra Allen, Colleen Dunn, and Susan Shulman told me so many things of interest about the musical that I could have devoted several additional chapters to their stories. Three others—all surrounded by controvery during various productions of the stage show—declined to be interviewed: Faye Dunaway, Patti LuPone, and Andrew Lloyd Webber, although the latter answered questions through an assistant. Harold Prince and Stephen Sondheim recounted their own flirtations with *Sunset Boulevard.*

Gloria Swanson's daughters, Michelle Farmer-Amon and the late Gloria Daly, and her granddaughter, Brooke Young, extended every courtesy, as did her husband, William Dufty. Talking with them helped me to understand why Gloria Swanson had nothing in common with Norma Desmond—and everything.

Raymond Daum, Swanson's friend and archivist, spoke with me at length about many aspects of her life and career. So did Dickson Hughes, another key figure in the Swanson network. It's easy to understand why Gloria valued their friendship; so do I.

Cecilia Presley, Cecil B. DeMille's granddaughter; Richard DeMille, his son; and Ann del Valle, his secretary, supplied information not found in any biography. The same is true of James Larmore Jr., Charles Brackett's grandson; John Waxman, the son of Franz Waxman; and Michael Blake, the son of Larry Blake.

Other Hollywood children answered questions that might otherwise have gone begging: Joy Schary and Jill Robinson, the daughters of Dore Schary and Miriam Svet Schary, and Christopher Mankiewicz, the son of Joseph L. Mankiewicz.

Research took me to libraries and museums around the country. The staff of every one welcomed me and led me to material I hadn't dreamed of finding. The following persons also kept at it on my behalf long after I had left their institutions: Barbara Hall of the Margaret Herrick Library, Academy of Motion Picture Arts and Sciences; Steve Wilson, Pat Fox, and Carol A. Henderson at the Harry Ransom Humanities Research Center at the University of Texas, Austin; Ned Comstock of the Cinema-Television Library of the University of Southern California; B. Caroline Sisneros at the Louis B. Mayer Library of the American Film Institute, Los Angeles; Matthew Plumb of the Museum of Television and Radio in New York and Javier Barrios in Los Angeles; and all the librarians of the Dallas Public Library, my everyday source of film and theatre research.

At Paramount, the remarkable A. C. Lyles spent an afternoon answering questions. He has been at the studio since 1937, so my questions were numerous and wide ranging. I am grateful also to his assistant, Mary-Ann Dunlap, and to Larry Dukes of the studio's transportation department.

Almost every day I found a large envelope full of clippings, photographs, audio recordings, videotapes, and addresses of still more contacts in my mailbox. Most of these packages came from Ron Bowers and Vernon Jordan in New York, James Robert Parish and Steven Lieberman in Los Angeles, Bob Grimes in San Francisco, and Joann Kaplet Duff in Ohio. These friends spoiled me so thoroughly that if nothing arrived on a particular day I ran to the phone to inquire if the "clipping service" had shut down. Robert Sanchez in Dallas not only clipped and recorded, he read pages, offered gentle criticism, gleaned Hollywood gossip, and surfed the Net as if panhandling for gold.

In a separate category, equally valuable, are those friends who spent as many hours on the phone as telemarketers, only they weren't trying to sell me something—they were giving it away. I was the lucky beneficiary, for at every turn they encouraged, corrected, reshaped, and amplified both the style and content of this book. They are Leigh Rutledge, Evan Matthews, Glenn Russell, as well as several of those mentioned above.

Sometimes I joke that I'd like to write a book of acknowledgments minus any actual subject. When I do, I will specify all the ways the following friends and acquaintances have helped: Don Bachardy, Steven Baker, Kathy Bartels, Rudy Behlmer, Stacey Behlmer, Cary Birdwell, John Boab, Tim Boss, Carol Bruce, Warren Butler, Kim Campbell, Gary Carey, Randy Carter, Charles Champlin, Eric Comstock, John Conway, Sam Crothers, Bob Dallmeyer, James D'Arc, Jackie Davis, Ron Davis, the late Rick Dawn, Robert Eason, Brian Ellis, John (Lypsinka) Epperson, Roger Farabee, Esther Flores, Patty Fox, Laurie Franks, Hannah Frost, Laura Gottesman, Joe Guy, Tom Hatten, Harry Haun, Foster Hirsch, Joann Holt, Paulette Hopkins, Kelly Hoskins, Marc Huestis, Steven Hughes, John Inzerella, David Marshall James, Miles Kreuger, Steve Lambert,

Carlos Lamboy, Gaylen Larmore, Wayne Lawson, Arthur Lennig, Maggie Lewis, Peter Linden, Berri McBride, Adrienne McLean, George Marcelle, Arnold Margolin, Matthew Martin, Bill Mathers, Spencer Michlin, Roy Moseley, Catherine Olim, Phil Poulos, Shannon Raffetto, Peter Rawlings, Marty Richards, Philip Rinaldi, Marge Rivingston, Lester Roque, Elaine St. James, Beth Schacter, Gary Schwartz, Peter Sehnert, Tom Shell, Karl Silvera, Tom Stempel, John Tackaberry, Dan Talbot, Calvin Washington, Stan Wlasick, and Michael Zepeda. I also acknowledge those who spoke off the record.

My agent, Jim Donovan, and my editor, Elizabeth Beier, did everything right, as usual. Michael Connor at St. Martin's Press solved a hundred problems and kept me in a sunny mood all the while. Kevin Sweeney, production editor, kept the trains running on schedule. Alan Kaufman, of Frankfurt Garbus Klein and Selz, has the unusual knack of turning a legal vetting into an event to look forward to. Carly Somerstein did a top-notch copy edit of my manuscript.

And love to Wayne Irvin, who turned a new page.

During the thirty years I knew her, Pauline Kael remained a formidable presence in person and on the page. My last conversation with her, barely a week before she died, was about *Sunset Boulevard*. This made her death even more emotionally devastating. She was the most revolutionary film critic of the twentieth century, and probably the busiest. Yet she was always accessible to anyone who loved the movies.

A few years ago Billy Wilder said, "She never had a good word to say about my pictures. Maybe a little bit: *Sunset Boulevard*. But she was more often right than wrong. And she was always very positive about what she thought was bad. And she just said it."

Like many others, I feel her absence. This book is dedicated to her with love and gratitude.

Selected Bibliography

Several minor sources not listed below—books, newspaper and magazine articles, archival materials—are cited in the notes section.

Agee, James. *Agee on Film.* Vol. I. New York: Grosset and Dunlap, 1969.

Ames, Christopher. *Movies About the Movies.* Lexington: University Press of Kentucky, 1997.

Anger, Kenneth. *Hollywood Babylon II.* New York: Penguin, 1984.

Astor, Mary. *My Story: An Autobiography.* New York: Doubleday, 1959.

Banner, Lois W. *In Full Flower: Aging Women, Power, and Sexuality.* New York: Knopf, 1992.

Barsacq, Léon. *Caligari's Cabinet and Other Grand Illusions: A History of Film Design.* Boston: New York Graphic Society, 1976.

Basinger, Jeanine. *Silent Stars.* New York: Knopf, 1999.

Behlmer, Rudy, and Tony Thomas. *Hollywood's Hollywood: The Movies About the Movies.* Secaucus, NJ: Citadel, 1975.

Berg, A. Scott. *Goldwyn: A Biography.* New York: Knopf, 1989.

Blesh, Rudi. *Keaton.* New York: MacMillan, 1966.

Bosworth, Patricia. *Montgomery Clift: A Biography.* New York: Harcourt, Brace, Jovanovich, 1978.

Brackett, Charles. *American Colony.* New York: Horace Liveright, 1929.

———. *Entirely Surrounded.* New York: Knopf, 1934.

Brownlow, Kevin. *Hollywood: The Pioneers.* New York: Knopf, 1979.

———. *The Parade's Gone By.* Berkeley: University of California Press, 1968.

Burgess Wise, David, William Boddy, and Brian Laban. *The Automobile: The First Century.* New York: Greenwich House, 1983.

Burkhart, Jeff, and Bruce Stuart. *Hollywood's First Choices.* New York: Crown, 1994.

Carey, Gary. *Judy Holliday: An Intimate Life Story.* New York: Seaview Books, 1982.

Carr, Larry. *Four Fabulous Faces.* New York: Galahad, 1970.

Chauncey, George. *Gay New York: Gender, Urban Culture, and the Making of the Gay Male World, 1890–1940.* New York: Basic Books, 1994.

Chierichetti, David. *Hollywood Costume Design.* New York: Harmony Books, 1976.

Chiron, Michel. *David Lynch.* London: British Film Institute, 1995.

Christopher, Nicholas. *Somewhere in the Night: Film Noir and the American City.* New York: The Free Press, 1997.

Ciment, Michel. *Passeport pour Hollywood.* Paris: Editions du Seuil, 1987.

Citron, Stephen. *The Wordsmiths: Oscar Hammerstein 2nd and Alan Jay Lerner.* New York: Oxford University Press, 1995.

Clum, John M. *Something for the Boys: Musical Theater and Gay Culture.* New York: St. Martin's Press, 1999.

Cook, Pam. *The Cinema Book.* New York: Pantheon, 1985.

Corliss, Richard. *Talking Pictures: Screenwriters in the American Cinema.* New York: Penguin, 1974.

Craig, Warren. *The Great Songwriters of Hollywood.* San Diego: A. S. Barnes, 1980.

Crowe, Cameron. *Conversations with Wilder.* New York: Knopf, 1999.

Dick, Bernard F. *Billy Wilder.* Boston: Twayne, 1980.

Dunaway, Faye, and Betsy Sharkey. *Looking for Gatsby: My Life.* New York: Simon & Schuster, 1995.

Eames, John Douglas. *The Paramount Story.* New York: Crown, 1985.

Edwards, Anne. *The DeMilles: An American Family.* New York: Harry N. Abrams, 1988.

Eels, George. *Hedda and Louella.* New York, Putnam's, 1972.

Eisner, Lotte H. *The Haunted Screen: Expressionism in the German Cinema and the Influence of Max Reinhardt.* Berkeley: University of California Press, 1969.

Everson, William K. *American Silent Film.* New York: Oxford University Press, 1978.

Eyman, Scott. *Mary Pickford: Americas's Sweetheart.* New York: Donald I. Fine, 1990.

Finch, Christopher, and Linda Rosenkrantz. *Gone Hollywood.* New York: Doubleday, 1979.

Finler, Joel W. *Stroheim.* Berkeley: University of California Press, 1968.

Fox, Patty. *Star Style: Hollywood Legends as Fashion Icons.* Santa Monica, CA: Angel City Press, 1995.

French, Brandon. *On the Verge of Revolt: Women in American Films of the Fifties.* New York: Ungar, 1978.

Gänzl, Kurt. *The Musical: A Concise History.* Boston: Northeastern University Press, 1997.

Gardner, Gerald. *The Censorship Papers: Movie Censorship Letters from the Hays Office, 1934 to 1968.* New York: Dodd, Mead, 1987.

Gilbert, Julie. *Opposite Attraction: The Lives of Erich Maria Remarque and Paulette Goddard.* New York: Pantheon, 1995.

Gimarc, George, and Pat Reeder. *Hollywood Hi-Fi: Over 100 of the Most Outrageous Celebrity Recordings Ever.* New York: St. Martin's Press, 1996.

Golden, Eve. *Vamp: The Rise and Fall of Theda Bara.* Vestal, NY: Emprise Publishing, 1996.

Head, Edith, and Paddy Calistro. *Edith Head's Hollywood.* New York: Dutton, 1983.

Heilbut, Anthony. *Exiled in Paradise: German Refugee Artists and Intellectuals in America from the 1930s to the Present.* New York: Viking, 1983.

Heisner, Beverly. *Hollywood Art: Art Direction in the Days of the Great Studios.* Jefferson, NC: McFarland, 1990.

Higham, Charles. *Cecil B. DeMille.* New York: Scribner's, 1973.

Higham, Charles, and Joel Greenberg. *The Celluloid Muse: Hollywood Directors Speak.* Chicago: Henry Regnery, 1969.

Hirsch, Foster. *The Dark Side of the Screen: Film Noir.* San Diego: A. S. Barnes, 1981.

Holtzman, Will. *Judy Holliday.* New York: Putnam's, 1982.

Hopper, Hedda. *From Under My Hat.* Garden City, NY: Doubleday, 1952.

Hopper, Hedda, and James Brough. *The Truth and Nothing But.* Garden City, NY: Doubleday, 1963.

Isherwood, Christopher. *Diaries, Volume One: 1939–1960.* New York: HarperCollins, 1997.

Jablonski, Edward. *Alan Jay Lerner: A Biography.* New York: Holt, 1996.

Jolley, Willie. *A Setback Is a Setup for a Comeback.* New York: St. Martin's Press, 1999.

Jordan, Richard Tyler. *But Darling, I'm Your Auntie Mame! The Amazing History of the World's Favorite Madcap Aunt.* Santa Barbara, CA: Capra Press, 1998.

Kanin, Garson. *Hollywood.* New York: Viking, 1974.

Kaplan, E. Ann, ed. *Women in Film Noir.* London: British Film Institute, 1980.

Kline, Jim. *The Complete Films of Buster Keaton.* New York: Citadel, 1993.

Kobal, John. *People Will Talk.* New York: Knopf, 1985.

Koszarski, Richard. *Hollywood Directors, 1941–1976.* New York: Oxford University Press, 1977.

————. *The Man You Loved to Hate: Erich von Stroheim and Hollywood.* New York: Oxford University Press, 1983.

Lally, Kevin. *Wilder Times: The Life of Billy Wilder.* New York: Holt, 1996.

Larkin, Colin, ed. *The Encyclopedia of Popular Music.* 3rd ed. London: Muze U.K., Ltd., 1998.

LaVine, W. Robert. *In a Glamorous Fashion: The Fabulous Years of Hollywood Costume Design.* New York: Scribner's, 1980.

Lawson, Kristan, and Anneli Rufus. *California Babylon.* New York: St. Martin's Griffin, 2000.

Leider, Emily Wortis. *Becoming Mae West.* New York: Farrar, Straus and Giroux, 1997.

Lennig, Arthur. *Stroheim.* Lexington: University Press of Kentucky, 2000.

Lerner, Alan Jay. *The Street Where I Live.* New York: Norton, 1978.

Lloyd Webber, Andrew, Don Black, and Christopher Hampton. *Sunset Boulevard: Vocal Selections.* London: The Really Useful Group, Ltd., 1994.

Loos, Anita. *A Girl Like I.* New York: Viking, 1966.

————. *Kiss Hollywood Good-by.* New York: Viking, 1974.

Ludlam, Charles. *The Complete Plays of Charles Ludlam.* New York: Harper & Row, 1989.

McBride, Joseph, ed. *Filmmakers on Filmmaking.* Los Angeles: Tarcher, 1983.

McClelland, Doug. *The Unkindest Cuts: The Scissors and the Cinema.* Cranbury, NJ: A. S. Barnes, 1972.

Macdonald, Dwight. *On Movies.* New York: Da Capo, 1981.

Machlin, Milt. *Libby.* New York: Tower Publications, 1980.

Madsen, Axel. *Billy Wilder.* London: Secker and Warburg, 1968.

————. *The Sewing Circle: Hollywood's Greatest Secret—Female Stars Who Loved Other Women.* New York: Birch Lane, 1995.

Mann, Thomas. *Death in Venice,* trans. Joachim Neugroschel. New York: Viking Penguin, 1998.

Mann, William J. *Wisecracker: The Life and Times of William Haines, Hollywood's First Openly Gay Star.* New York: Viking, 1998.

Mast, Gerald. *A Short History of the Movies.* 4th ed. New York: MacMillan, 1986.

Meade, Marion. *Buster Keaton: Cut to the Chase.* New York: HarperCollins, 1995.

Morella, Joe, and Edward Z. Epstein. *Paulette: the Adventurous Life of Paulette Goddard.* New York: St. Martin's Press, 1985.

Negri, Pola. *Memoirs of a Star.* New York: Doubleday, 1970.

Paris, Barry. *Garbo: A Biography.* New York: Knopf, 1995.

Parish, James Robert. *The Paramount Pretties.* Secaucus, NJ: Castle Books, 1972.

Peary, Danny. *Alternate Oscars.* New York: Delta, 1993.

————. *Cult Movies.* New York: Delta, 1981.

Perry, George. *Sunset Boulevard: From Movie to Musical.* New York: Holt, 1993.

Poague, Leland. *The Hollywood Professionals.* Vol. 7. London: Tantivy Press, 1980.

Quirk, Lawrence J. *The Films of Gloria Swanson.* Secaucus, NJ: Citadel, 1984.

Rich, Frank. *Hot Seat: Theatre Criticism for the New York Times, 1980–1993*. New York: Random House, 1998.

Rodley, Chris, ed. *Lynch on Lynch*. London: Faber and Faber, 1997.

Roen, Paul. *High Camp*. Vol. I. San Francisco: Leyland Publications, 1994.

Rosen, Marjorie. *Popcorn Venus*. New York: Avon, 1973.

Rósza, Miklós. *Double Life*. New York: Wynwood Press, 1989.

St. James, Adela Rogers. *Some Are Born Great*. New York: Doubleday, 1974.

Schary, Dore. *Heyday: An Autobiography*. Boston: Little, Brown, 1979.

Schickel, Richard. *D. W. Griffith: An American Life*. New York: Simon & Schuster, 1984.

Seidman, Steve. *The Film Career of Billy Wilder*. Boston: G. K. Hall, 1977.

Server, Lee, Ed Gorman, and Martin H. Greenberg, eds. *The Big Book of Noir*. New York: Carroll and Graf, 1998.

Shipman, David. *The Great Movie Stars: The Golden Years*. Rev. ed. New York: Hill and Wang, 1979.

Sikov, Ed. *On Sunset Boulevard: The Life and Times of Billy Wilder*. New York: Hyperion, 1998.

Sinyard, Neil, and Adrian Turner. *Journey Down Sunset Boulevard: The Films of Billy Wilder*. Ryde, Isle of Wight: BCW Publishing, Ltd., 1979.

Spoto, Donald. *Camerado: Hollywood and the American Man*. New York: Plume, 1978.

Steen, Mike. *Hollywood Speaks: An Oral History*. New York: Putnam's, 1974.

Stempel, Tom. *Framework: A History of Screenwriting in the American Film*. New York: Continuum, 1988.

Stephens, Autumn. *Drama Queens: Wild Women of the Silver Screen*. Berkeley: Conari Press, 1998.

Steyn, Mark. *Broadway Babies Say Goodnight: Musicals Then and Now*. New York: Routledge, 1999.

Stoddard, Karen M. *Saints and Shrews: Women and Aging in American Popular Film*. Westport, CT: Greenwood Press, 1983.

Swanson, Gloria. *Swanson on Swanson*. New York: Random House, 1980.

Thomas, Bob. *Golden Boy: The Untold Story of William Holden*. New York: St. Martin's Press, 1983.

Thomas, Tony, ed. *Film Score: The View from the Podium*. London: Thomas Yoseloff, Ltd., 1979.

Thomson, David. *Suspects*. New York: Knopf, 1985.

Todd, Janet. *Women and Film*. New York: Holmes and Meier, 1988.

Turk, Edward Baron. *Hollywood Diva: A Biography of Jeanette MacDonald*. Berkeley: University of California Press, 1998.

Walker, Alexander. *Stardom*. New York: Stein and Day, 1970.

Whitfield, Eileen. *Pickford: The Woman Who Made Hollywood*. Lexington: University Press of Kentucky, 1997.

Wilder, Billy [Charles Brackett, and D. M. Marshman Jr.]. *Sunset Boulevard*, screenplay ed. Jeffrey Meyers. Berkeley: University of California Press, 1999.

Wilson, Earl. *Hot Times: True Tales of Hollywood and Broadway*. Chicago: Contemporary Books, 1984.

Winters, Shelly. *Shelly II*. New York: Simon & Schuster, 1989.

Zicree, Marc Scott. *The Twilight Zone Companion*. New York: Bantam, 1982.

Zimmer, Jill Schary. *With a Cast of Thousands*. New York: Stein and Day, 1963.

Zolotow, Maurice. *Billy Wilder in Hollywood*. New York: Putnam's, 1977.

Notes

A few secondary sources not found in the bibliography are included in these notes. Translations from French sources are mine unless otherwise noted. The designation "BW to RB" indicates Billy Wilder interviewed by Rudy Behlmer on November 8, 1976; a tape recording of that interview (the best ever done with Wilder, in my opinion) is now in the Margaret Herrick Library of the Academy of Motion Picture Arts and Sciences, Los Angeles. Similarly, "BW , AFI" plus date refers to two seminars held by Billy Wilder at the American Film Institute in Los Angeles. Transcripts are in the Louis B. Mayer Library of the AFI. "EH, AFI" refers to two Edith Head seminars at the AFI, with transcripts in the Mayer Library, as above.

The following abbreviations are used:

PERSONS
SA—Sandra Allen
RB—Rudy Behlmer
PC—Petula Clark
GC—Glenn Close
GD—Gloria Daly
RD—Raymond Daum
ADV—Ann del Valle
CD—Colleen Dunn
RE—Ray Evans
MFA—Michelle Farmer-Amon
PF—Patty Fox
DH—Dickson Hughes
MK—Miles Kreuger
JL—James Larmore Jr.
ML—Maggie Lewis
JL—Jay Livingston
ACL—A. C. Lyles

L—Lypsinka
CM—Christopher Mankiewicz
NO—Nancy Olson
CP—Cecilia Presley
HP—Harold Prince
MR—Marge Rivingston
JR—Jill Robinson
ESJ—Elaine St. James
SSh—Susan Shulman
KS—Karl Silvera
SSo—Stephen Sondheim
TS—Tom Stempel
JW—John Waxman
BW—Billy Wilder
BY—Brooke Young

INSTITUTIONS

AFI—American Film Institute, Los Angeles
AMPAS—Margaret Herrick Library, Academy of Motion Picture Arts and Sciences, Los Angeles
DPL—Dallas Public Library
SMU—DeGolyer Library, Southern Methodist University, Dallas
UTA—Harry Ransom Humanities Research Center, University of Texas at Austin

ENDNOTES

Voice-Over, 1948
pp. 1–2 D. W. Griffith, et al at Romanoff's: Berg, p. 447; Whitfield, p. 326.
pp. 2–3 Griffith's funeral: Schickel, p. 604. The phrase "brutal boulevard" is from Andrew Lloyd Webber's musical, *Sunset Boulevard*.

1. A La Recherche de Norma Desmond
pp. 4–5 sailed for the United States: Sikov, p. 98.
p. 5 "I came here because": Crowe, p. 19.
p. 5 "Billy and [his first wife]": Sikov, p. 114.
p. 5 "Wilder's marriage with Judith": Ibid., p. 116.
p. 5 the matchmaker in this case: Ibid., p. 115.
p. 6 "From now on you're a team.": *Life*, Dec. 11, 1944.
p. 7 "a new film about": Sikov, p. 281.
p. 7 Wilder told Garbo: Paris, p. 419.
p. 8 the time she and Garbo: *Vanity Fair*, April 2000.
p. 8 "The idea of Mae West": BW to RB.
p. 8 "She would certainly have wanted": ACL to SS.
p. 9 "a kind of Laurel and Hardy picture": Leider, p. 350.

p. 9 "We needed a passé star": BW to RB.
p. 9 "Mr. Brackett and I": BW to RB.
p. 9 "Pickford said she adored": Eyman, p. 282.
p. 10 "She would throw parties": Ibid., p. 247.

2. When Queens Collide

p. 11 the country next door: not a geographical error: Though Czechoslovakia later lay between Poland and Hungary, when these ladies were born Austria-Hungary bordered Poland, which existed technically only as a province of the Russian Empire.
p. 13 "every unkind thing": Negri, p. 210.
p. 13 "a herd of felines": Ibid., p. 213.
p. 13 "So far as the world knew": Swanson, p. 192.
p. 13 "Miss Negri is herself": Basinger, p. 244.
p. 14 "an Addams Family look": ML to SS.
p. 14 "sitting in an ornate chair": Basinger, p. 257.
p. 14 "Pola Negri later retired": Shipman, p. 421.

3. The Happiest Couple in Hollywood

pp. 15–16 "In the executive office": Behlmer and Thomas, p. 97.
p. 16 the young actress: Ibid., p. 118.
p. 17 "I loved *What Price Hollywood*": BW to RB.
p. 18 *A Foreign Affair* had wrapped: Sikov, p. 277.
p. 18 Brackett called it: Ibid., p. 267.
p. 19 "Hollywood's equivalent": *Life*, Dec. 11, 1944.
p. 19 "To them troop the most": Ibid.
p. 19 "Sunday lunch we went": Isherwood, pp. 494; 794; 880.
p. 19 "ladies and gentlemen sitting": Zolotow, pp. 99–100.
p. 19 Various government officials: *A Foreign Affair*, AFI Catalog, CD-Rom version.
p. 20 a string of bland substitutes: Ibid.
p. 20 The Department of Defense: Heilbut, p. 243.
p. 20 According to some sources: *A Foreign Affair*, AFI Catalog, CD-Rom version.
p. 21 "Whom God hath joined together.": *Life*, Dec. 11, 1944.
p. 22 "I remember Charlie": ACL to SS.
p. 22 "His only form of exercise": *Life*, Dec. 11, 1944.
p. 22 "Brackett conveys an impression": Ibid.
p. 22 "in everybody's office": ACL to SS.
pp. 22–23 "One of the best things": BW, AFI, Dec. 13, 1978.
p. 23 "a fountain of energy": Zolotow, p. 248.
p. 23 Wilder confessed: BW, AFI, Dec. 13, 1978.
p. 23 "At the end of the day": BW, AFI, Mar. 3, 1986.
p. 23 "they boast a kind of": *Life*, Dec. 11, 1944.
p. 23 $2,500 per week: Ibid.
p. 23 "Their office has": Ibid.
p. 23 "Work, talk, cards": Sikov, p. 216.

p. 23 "the volatile Wilder": Rózsa, p. 130.

p. 24 began "with talk": Screen Producers' Guild press release, AMPAS.

p. 24 "The only reliable peg": Ibid.

p. 24 "five years before": BW, AFI, Dec. 13, 1978.

p. 24 "a relationship between": *The New York Times*, 7-02-1950.

p. 25 According to Gloria Swanson: *Entertainment Today*, 10-10-75.

p. 25 Paramount interoffice memo: Paramount files, AMPAS.

p. 25 Paramount paid Marshman and Wilder: Sikov, p. 290.

p. 26 "He was bright": BW to RB.

p. 26 "What on earth": NO to SS.

p. 27 "Billy Wilder's Tips for Screenwriters": Crowe, p. 357.

p. 27 "For Limited Distribution": Paramount files, AMPAS.

p. 30 "It's a book about me": Paramount files, AMPAS.

p. 30 accompanying memo: Paramount files, AMPAS.

p. 31 "*Why* Frank Freeman": Crowe, p. 83.

p. 32 "It's possible he watched": NO to SS.

p. 32 "the original success kid": *Parade*, 7-01-62.

p. 33 "wanted a pool": BW to RB.

p. 33 "We had not written": BW to RB.

p. 33 Breen replied: MPAA file, AMPAS.

p. 34 Breen wrote worriedly: MPAA file, AMPAS.

p. 34 "There are times": McBride, p. 68.

4. Chaz

(Unless otherwise indicated, statements by James Larmore Jr. are to SS.)

p. 38 "He spoke excellent English": Wilder, *SB* script, p. ix.

p. 40 "In Billy's American films": Sikov, p. 79.

p. 40 Brackett, *American Colony*, pp. 9–11.

p. 42 "a friend of Scott Fitzgerald": Wilder, *SB* script, pp. xiv–xvii.

p. 42 "At the end of that novel": Wilder, *SB* script, pp. xiv–xv.

p. 42 "Narration or no": BW, AFI, Dec. 13, 1978.

p. 43 A character named Agnes: Brackett, *Entirely Surrounded*, p. 173.

p. 43 a son with homosexual tendencies: Ibid., p. 118.

p. 44 Brackett's letter to Swanson: UTA.

p. 45 "Billy smiled that sweet smile": Kanin, p. 178.

p. 45 "Billy got right into": Ibid.

p. 45 "like a box of matches": Sikov, p. 306.

p. 45 Louella Parsons reported: *Los Angeles Examiner*, 10-30-50.

p. 46 Billy Wilder called a press conference: Kanin, pp. 180–181.

5. Who Is Gloria Swanson?

p. 47 "I had just done a picture with Bill Holden": NO to SS.

p. 48 "I don't like it": Bosworth, pp. 174–175.

p. 48 "I don't think I could": Thomas, p. 59.

p. 48 "Bullshit!" Wilder yelled: Ibid.

p. 48 Later Wilder said: Higham and Greenberg, p. 249.

p. 48 liked young, pretty . . . men: Machlin, p. 12.

p. 49 "a dark purple menace": Bosworth p. 218.

p. 49 Montgomery Clift on a long leash: Bosworth, p. 227.

p. 49 decamped to New York: Swanson, p. 466.

p. 50 "I was hungry for knowledge": Kobal, p. 18.

p. 50 "surrounded herself": RD to SS.

p. 50 An unlikely guest: DH to SS.

p. 52 "That's awful": Swanson, p. 493.

p. 52 In her memoirs: Ibid., p. 494.

p. 52 "I've made two dozen pictures": Ibid.

p. 52 "no longer optimistic": Ibid.

p. 52 "The calls from Paramount continued.": Ibid.

p. 53 "I remembered Gloria": Crowe, p. 198.

p. 53 "Wilder saw Gloria": Zolotow, p. 57.

p. 53 "a dreadful Christmas": Swanson, p. 495.

p. 54 "on September third": *Saturday Evening Post*, 7-29-50.

p. 54 "Nobody else was considered": Ibid., p. 56.

p. 55 "her billing was the largest": Shipman, p. 525.

p. 56 "troops of policemen": Swanson, p. 8.

p. 57 "from floor to ceiling": *Saturday Evening Post*, 7-29-50.

pp. 57–58 "I went there for the first time": RD to SS.

p. 59 the family Bible: *Saturday Evening Post*, 7-29-50.

p. 60 "a tremendous sign": Ibid.

p. 61 "the brightest things": Swanson, p. 496.

p. 61 "We're working on it": Ibid., pp. 496–497.

p. 61 In it she spoke several lines: Crowe, p. 47.

p. 62 "another screen test": Swanson, pp. 497–498.

p. 63 "got credit for everything I did": KS to SS.

p. 64 "I rented a house": Swanson, p. 497.

p. 65 "Oh, when my mother": MFA to SS.

p. 65 "They didn't know": Kobal, p. 6.

p. 65 "Originally her role": MFA to SS.

p. 67 "Swanson sent him a telegram": CP to SS.

p. 67 pages dated April 26, 1949: Paramount files, AMPAS; a slightly different copy at DPL.

p. 68 "the purple prose": John Rosenfield in the *Dallas Morning News*, 9-08-50.

p. 69 "I have a vague memory": MFA to SS.

p. 69 "Gloria told me": RD to SS.

p. 70 "The script is there": BW, AFI, Dec. 13, 1978.

p. 70 "one of the best ideas": Ciment, p. 71.

p. 70 laundering Norma's underwear: BW to RB.

p. 70 "I remember you": UTA.

6. "The Cameras Have Arrived"

(Unless otherwise indicated, statements by Nancy Olson are to SS.)

p. 71 All contract and salary details from Paramount files, AMPAS.

p. 72 "He photographed like an actor": BW to RB.

p. 72 Holden said: Zolotow, p. 249.

p. 75 "didn't find joke very funny": Sikov, p. 297.

p. 76 "I never sat down": Crowe, p. 175.

p. 76 "He has such authority": Zolotow, p. 248; AFI program for Wilder tribute in 1986.

p. 76 "However despondent": Zolotow, p. 248.

pp. 77–78 Gerd Oswald oral history, SMU.

p. 78 "He never gave": AFI program for Wilder tribute in 1986.

p. 78 "He needed to know more": Swanson, p. 499.

p. 80 "Many people in Hollywood": Koszarski, *Hollywood Directors*, p. 272.

p. 80 "Veteran extras": *Saturday Evening Post*, 7-29-50.

p. 81 "When I walked on that film set": Kobal, p. 7.

7. The Bedroom of Norma Desmond

p. 83 Elaine St. James: ESJ to SS.

p. 84 the *Los Angeles Times* reported: 2-24-57; description of house, *Los Angeles Times*, 10-04-53.

pp. 84–85 John Meehan . . . said: *The Society of Motion Picture Art Directors Bulletin*, May/June 1951.

p. 85 "Baby, the shot I want": Ibid.

p. 86 the joke around Hollywood: *Hollywood Citizen-News*, 8-30-50.

p. 86 Lower-story interiors: Paramount files, AMPAS.

p. 87 "100 Swanson Photos": *Paramount News*, 1-02-50.

p. 87 Meryl Streep posed: *Vanity Fair*, April 1999.

p. 87 "My bedroom became": *Swann's Way*, p. 9 of Scott-Moncrief/Kilmartin trans.

p. 87 the address . . . didn't exist: *Los Angeles Times*, 12-26-93.

pp. 88–89 Schwab's Drug Store sidebar: Finch and Rosenkrantz, pp. 321–322.

p. 89 The parking lot we see: *Paramount News*, 12-19-49.

p. 89 Bullock's department store: BW letter to Richard Lamparski, 10-19-94 in file at AMPAS.

p. 90 *The New York Times* reported: 5-18-51.

p. 91 The picture was written: Victor S. Navasky, *Naming Names*, p. 328.

p. 93 "My mother adored Bill": Swanson to RD; reported by RD to SS.

p. 93 A legal document: UTA.

p. 93 telegram from Walter Futter: UTA.

p. 93 Scollard continued: UTA.

8. That's Why the Lady Has a Chimp

p. 96 small white coffin: Paramount files, AMPAS.

p. 96 asked Billy Wilder for guidance: Ciment, p. 72.

p. 97 "an affair with the monkey": Crowe, p. 303.

p. 97 "Somebody asked me recently": Ciment, p. 72.

p. 97 "Don't you understand?": Sikov, p. 489.

p. 98 Paramount . . . characterized: Everson, p. 315.

pp. 98–99 "I was never a bathing girl": Kobal, p. 10.

p. 99 "Chaplin's face": Mast, p. 93.

p. 99 "He picked me": Swanson, p. 42.

p. 99 Rehearsing a party scene: Ibid., p. 220.

p. 100 Next day, when she walked in: Ibid., p. 500.

p. 100 Chaplin apparently agreed: Kobal, p. 7.

9. "Ten Thousand Midnights Ago"

p. 101 "Louella and I": Hopper, *From Under My Hat*, p. 296.

p. 101–102 "I had in mind": BW to RB.

p. 102 Hedda told a slightly different version: Hopper, *The Whole Truth*, pp. 72–73.

p. 102 "I spent the day": unsourced clipping, AMPAS.

p. 102 exchange with Wilder: Ibid.

p. 102 "That bitch": DH to SS.

p. 103 "Skolsky not very good": BW to RB.

p. 103 "That was Grandfather": CP to SS.

p. 104 fond of DeMille: BW to RB.

p. 104 Originally the screenplay called: *Hollywood Citizen-News*, 6-10-49.

p. 104 When DeMille's scenes: Sikov, p. 296.

p. 104 *"The Greatest Show on Earth"*: Zolotow, pp. 235–236.

p. 106 Head didn't like: Head & Calisto, p. 81.

p. 106 "dirty bird feathers": Edwards, p. 196.

p. 106 he had angered Edith: Head & Calisto, p. 81.

p. 107 "He was a stickler": ACL to SS.

p. 107 Phil Koury, a reporter: *The New York Times*, 5-29-49.

p. 109 daily journey to studio: Edwards, pp. 197–200.

p. 109 "a minister from Omaha": ADV to SS.

p. 109 "It was wonderful": ACL to SS.

p. 110 H. B. Warner started out: Edwards, p. 103.

p. 110 "like old home week": Kline, p. 195.

p. 111 "When I was seven": *Dallas Times Herald*, 2-07-66.

p. 112 Keaton-Chaplin conversation: *The New York Times*, 10-06-96.

p. 112 "When I was a student in Vienna": Meade, p. 245.

p. 112 "unmatchable deadpan": Swanson, p. 500.

p. 113 "an absolute delight": Meade, p. 246.

p. 113 "the youngest flapper": Edwards, p. 93.

p. 114 "They said I'd never walk again: *Hollywood Studio Magazine*, n.d.

p. 114 "Anna Q. Nilsson is back": unsourced clipping, AMPAS.

p. 114 icy New York sidewalk: *Los Angeles Times*, 4-13-47.

p. 115 "we used to have such fun": *Hollywood Studio Magazine*, n.d.

p. 115 "Drop a cheery note": *The Hollywood Reporter*, 2-09-73.

p. 116 "Wilcoxon could do no wrong": Gerd Oswald oral history, SMU.

p. 116 "Anna looked splendid": Swanson, p. 500.

p. 116 "I saw you in *King of Kings*": TV8, 12-20-87.

pp. 116–117 "If I were ever": Ibid.

p. 117 "None of the stars": *Los Angeles Examiner*, 12-24-58.

p. 117 "One must be thankful": *Myra Breckinridge*, p. 37.

10. "All Right, Mr. DeMille, I'm Ready for My Close-up"

p. 119 "The forties were really Seitz's heyday": TS to SS.

p. 119 ". . . remember how foggy": Seitz to James Ursini, AFI oral history, Los Angeles.

p. 120 "hated to watch actors": BW to RB.

p. 120 "I never saw him do it": NO to SS.

p. 121 "That was true in another picture": BW to SS.

p. 121 "took some magnesium": Crowe, p. 55.

p. 121 "made some shreddings": Higham and Greenberg, p. 248.

p. 121 "strewn with years-deep dust": from Hardy's poem "Shut Out That Moon."

p. 121 "I doubt it": MFA to SS.

p. 122 "reports . . . out of Paramount": *The Hollywood Reporter*, 4-17-50.

p. 122 "It was mesmerizing": NO to SS.

p. 122 "clothes-and-jewel-bedrenched": Quirk, p. 118.

p. 122 "For the tango sequence": Swanson, p. 180.

p. 122 used a "dance dolly": *American Cinematographer*, Sept. 1950.

p. 123 "not the best dancer": Crowe, p. 29.

p. 123 "As inexperienced as I was": NO to SS.

p. 123 "spent the first day": unsourced Hopper column.

p. 124 "the staircase curved slightly": MFA to SS.

p. 124 "inside of the stairway": Swanson, p. 501.

p. 124 "I hated to have the picture end": Ibid.

p. 124 "At the end of the scene": MFA to SS.

pp. 124–125 "I had a party planned": Swanson, p. 501.

p. 125 "The focus gets thrown out": Crowe, p. 151.

11. Chiffon, Velvet, Chinchilla, Tulle, Brocade, Taffeta, Ermine, and Leopard-Printed Crêpe

p. 127 washing out Swanson's hosiery: Head & Calistro, p. 90.

p. 127 "I was apprehensive about working": Ibid., p. 90.

p. 127 "that she had requested me": Ibid.

p. 127 "he wanted Gloria to convey": Ibid., p. 88.

p. 127 Head translated Wilder's words: Ibid., p. 89.

pp. 127–128 "weren't exactly from the current era": Ibid.

p. 128 Patty Fox's views: PF to SS.

p. 128 "Because Norma Desmond": Head & Calistro, p. 89.

p. 129 "defined her wide waist": Ibid.

p. 129 Edith designed *with* Swanson: Ibid., p. 90.

p. 130 "Gloria showed me": Ibid., pp. 90–91.

p. 130 Head prepared and discarded sketches: LaVine, p. 116.

p. 130 "not one single white peacock feather": Ibid.

p. 130 "They also make the man": EH, AFI, 1972.

p. 132 "wanted me to be superplain": *Los Angeles Times*, 10-08-50.

pp. 132–133 "Our costuming in earlier days": EH, AFI, 1972.

p. 133 "I could take anybody in this room": EH, AFI, 1977.

p. 134 "the wife of Dore Schary": BW to SS.

p. 134 "Marlene Dietrich who gave": JR to SS.

12. If It's a Paramount Picture, It's the Best Show in Town

p. 137 "white-and-gold furniture": Leider, p. 279.

p. 137 "You'll notice the furniture": Ibid., p. 280.

p. 138 "It's appointments included": Ibid., p. 290.

p. 139 several art critics: Higham, p. 86.

p. 139 According to . . . Robert Clatworthy: Heisner, p. 168.

p. 139 "the art director is responsible": Heisner, p. 169.

p. 140 "sophisticated, polished": Ibid., p. 170.

p. 141 "You couldn't tell": ACL to SS.

p. 143 the ingenious composer: JW to SS.

p. 144 "French poetic realism": Christopher, p. 14.

p. 145 "the main theme": Thomas, *Film Score*, p. 57.

p. 145 "The final scene": BW to RB.

p. 145 "I had my favorite composers": Crowe, p. 214.

p. 146 "I worked with a very good cutter": BW to RB.

p. 146 taught Wilder how to preplan: Lally, p. 113.

p. 146 "always nearby to consult": Ibid., p. 114.

p. 146 "When I'm finished": Ibid.

p. 146 "I just shoot": Ibid.

p. 147 "a lanky, stoop-shouldered": Zolotow, p. 106.

p. 147 "didn't look very healthy": Sikov, p. 367.

13. Fiasco

p. 151 "When the morgue label was tied on": BW to RB.

p. 151 "Just enough to fire me": BW, AFI, Mar. 3, 1986.

p. 151 "a weird kind of framing sequence": Higham & Greenberg, p. 250.

p. 151 When Sherry Lansing: anonymous source to SS.

p. 151 "I don't know who": Crowe, p. 254.

p. 152 "Where they're not used to such things": Ibid.

p. 152 "Same goddamn reaction": Sikov, p. 301.

p. 152 "So we chopped it off": Higham & Greenberg, p. 250.

p. 152 Waxman made minor changes: JW to SS.

p. 152 "several sneak previews": UTA.

p. 153 "For many in the audience": Basinger, p. 234.

14. The Whole Audience Stood Up and Cheered

(Unless otherwise indicated, statements by Miles Kreuger are to SS.)

p. 158 signed himself T.M.P.: *The New York Times*, 8-11-50.

p. 158 Other New York reviewers: excerpts from *Paramount International News*, 8-11-50.

p. 158 *Variety* gave the picture a favorable review: *Variety*, 4-17-50.

p. 159 "will be studied years hence": *The Hollywood Reporter*, 4-17-50.

p. 159 reviewer Philip T. Hartung: *Commonweal*, 8-25-50.

p. 159 "morbid characterizations": *Christian Century*, 11-15-50.

p. 159 "Let no youngster ask": *Good Housekeeping*, July 1950.

p. 159 first critical discussion: Ames, p. 10.

p. 159 "the lost people": Agee, pp. 411–415.

p. 160 "were virtual premieres": *The Hollywood Reporter*, 8-03-50.

p. 161 "the first big screening in Hollywood": Swanson, p. 501.

p. 161 "morbidly restrained": Ibid.

p. 161 whole audience stood up: Ibid.

p. 161 "Gloria made a grand entrance": Head & Calistro, p. 91.

p. 161 "I could read in their eyes": Swanson, p. 501.

p. 161 Stanwyck . . . "had tears": Head & Calistro, p. 91.

p. 161 dropped theatrically to her knees: Swanson, p. 501.

p. 161 "there were so many people around": Head & Calistro, p. 91.

p. 161 "one of those ridiculous adulation things": Higham & Greenberg, p. 250.

p. 162 "Where's Mary?": Swanson, p. 502.

p. 162 Billy Haines quote: Mann, p. 328.

pp. 162–163 quotes from Joan Fontaine, et al: Paramount Press Book, AMPAS.

p. 163 "I thought Billy Wilder was a friend of mine": Paris, p. 431.

p. 163 Mae Murry quote: Kevin Brownlow in *Film*, (London), #41, n.d.

p. 163 Cher and Whoopi Goldberg quotes: AFI television special, 1999.

p. 164 he saw Louis B. Mayer: BW to RB.

p. 164 command performance, London: UTA.

p. 164 Paris opening of *Sunset: Paramount International News*, 4-28-51.

p. 165 the ersatz Cuban Swanson: Ibid.

p. 165 "sixth biggest-grossing picture": *Variety*, 9-27-50.

p. 166 "While *Sunset* is breaking records": *Variety*, 9-15-50.

p. 166 a thousand dollars a week: Sikov, p. 304.

p. 167 "Paramount and all other studios": Swanson, p. 502.

pp. 167–168 "Compartments glittered": Loos, *Kiss Hollywood Good-by*, p. 23.

p. 168 Swanson asked the studio: UTA.

pp. 168–169 radio script, handwritten cards, Swanson's letters to Paramount's sales force: UTA.

p. 172 gold key to publicity department: *Variety*, 8-21-50.

15. And the Winner Isn't Gloria Swanson

p. 175 in one scene of the play: Swanson, p. 505.

p. 176 "known in my bones": Ibid., pp. 265–266.

p. 177 sleeveless black dress: Ibid., p. 265.

p. 177 "media types": Ibid., p. 266.

p. 177 It was their first encounter: Ibid., p. 267.

p. 177 "George and I were": Ibid.

p. 177 "Celeste Holm moved": Ibid.

p. 177 "but they pestered me": Ibid.

p. 177 Wilder telegram: UTA.

p. 178 "Joe Ferrer couldn't possibly win": Swanson, pp. 267–268.

p. 178 "You're goddamned right": Ibid., p. 268.

p. 178 "Judy and I": Ibid.

p. 179 "I honestly didn't care": Ibid., p. 505.

p. 179 "Judy was overcome": Ibid., p. 269.

p. 180 "far less subtle": Ibid.

p. 180 "It slowly dawned on me": Ibid.

p. 180 "She was just about ten feet tall": Ibid., p. 270.

p. 181 "As the nominees were recited": Holtzman, pp. 148–149.

p. 181 "One of us": Kanin, p. 370.

p. 181 "creating the character": Ibid., p. 374.

p. 181 Swanson sweeping into La Zambra: Carey, pp. 117–118.

p. 182 "Ferrer and Swanson cooed": Ibid., p. 119.

p. 182 "Darling, why couldn't you": Wiley & Bona, *Inside Oscar*, p. 209.

p. 182 "the old warhorse": Osborne, *Academy Awards Illustrated*, p. 170.

p. 182 "No, not Gloria's personality": RD to SS.

p. 182 "her hands around Judy's neck": anonymous source to SS.

p. 182 Brackett's letter to Swanson: UTA.

p. 183 "On Oscar night in 1951": CM to SS.

p. 184 founding the Motion Picture Academy: Lillian Ross, *Picture*, pp. 162–163.

p. 184 at the party: Ibid., p. 163.

p. 185 She did lament to Brackett: Eels, p. 269.

p. 185 On arrival at the nightclub: Thomas, p. 65.

p. 186 "an icy woman": NO to SS.

p. 186 Paul and Ruth Clemens: Thomas, pp. 82–83.

p. 186 "Mrs. Holden, what's it like": Ibid., p. 64.

p. 187 "She was never properly acknowledged": RD to SS.

p. 187 exact wording on cigarette box: GD to SS.

p. 187 "*That* is my Oscar": RD to SS.

16. I've Got Nobody Floating in My Pool

p. 188 overseas awards: *Paramount International News*, 4-28-51.

p. 189 Miles Kreuger witnessed: MK to SS.

pp. 189–190 Bogdanovich analysis: UTA.

p. 194 Aschenbach "left the beach": Mann, *Death in Venice*, p. 321.

p. 194 "Like someone who cannot stop": Ibid., pp. 360–361.

p. 195 "pernicious image": Fischer, in Todd, pp. 103–104.

p. 196 "six years elapsed": Swanson, p. 519.

p. 197 Leisen wanted her to play: David Chierichetti, *Mitchell Leisen*, p. 272.

p. 197 "In order to spring back": Swanson, p. 270.

p. 197 "that corniest of theatrical cliches": Ibid.

p. 197 "More and more scripts arrived at my door": Ibid., p. 506.

p. 197 "I didn't want to spend": Ibid.

p. 199 "If you hear one intonation": Kobal, p. 7.

p. 199 "I've got nobody floating in my pool": Ibid., p. 4.

p. 200 "Gloria could play Norma Desmond": Ibid.

p. 200 "The ageless Gloria Swanson": Brownlow, p. 372.

pp. 200–201 Swanson visits Chaplin: Ibid., pp. 504–505.

17. *Boulevard!*

(Unless otherwise indicated, statements by Dickson Hughes are to SS.)

p. 202 "awful imitations": Swanson, p. 506.

p. 205 handwritten note to Zukor: Adolph Zukor collection, AMPAS.

p. 206 law firm of Gang, Kopp, and Tyre: UTA.

p. 207 Swanson wrote to Erich von Stroheim: UTA.

p. 210 "several top-flight producers": UTA.

p. 211 Swanson sent D. A. Doran a tape: UTA.

p. 214 "Since my return from Europe": UTA.

p. 214 Robert Fryer protests: UTA.

p. 215 February 12 telegram to Doran: UTA.

p. 215 Swanson's reply to Holman: UTA.

p. 216 Holman's reply: UTA.

18. "Funny How Gentle People Get with You Once You're Dead"

p. 225 "I'm a whore": Thomas, p. 228.

p. 226 "as a sound, normal, public-spirited citizen": Ibid., pp. 70–71.

p. 226 "Ardis made all the arrangements": Ibid., p. 70.

p. 227 "He complained about being recognized": Ibid., p. 171.

p. 227 Swanson's note to Holden: Ibid., p. 210.

p. 227 "was brilliant in our picture": Swanson, p. 267.

p. 227 Holden said in an interview in 1971: *Dallas Morning News*, 1-24-71.

p. 227 Speaking to another interviewer in 1978: *Dallas Times Herald*, 6-09-78.

p. 229 In 1956 Holden and a political bedfellow: Thomas, pp. 113–114.

p. 230 made him the highest-paid film star: Kevin Brownlow, *David Lean*, p. 366.

p. 230 Wally Westmore . . . wrote an article: *Saturday Evening Post*, 8-11-56.

p. 230 "Monday morning, November 16, 1981": Thomas, p. 1.

p. 230 "had slipped on a throw rug": Ibid., p. 7.

p. 231 "To be killed by a bottle of vodka": Sikov, pp. 567–568.

p. 231 "My love will always be": Crowe, p. 304.

p. 231 "To become a movie star": *The New Yorker*, 5-17-99.

19. Popcorn in Beverly Hills with Nancy

(Unless otherwise indicated, statements by Nancy Olson, Alan Livingston, and Christopher Livingston are to SS.)

p. 238 "I sat down at eight": Citron, p. 236.

p. 240 "Walking to the office": Lerner, p. 86.

p. 241 "I think my scenes with Paulette Goddard": Winters, p. 462.

p. 242 "no warning or anything": *Parade*, 7-01-62.

p. 243 "I'm in serious trouble": *Parade*, 7-01-62.

20. "Buttons and Bows"

(Unless otherwise indicated, statements by Jay Livingston and Ray Evans are to SS.)

p. 248–249 Pauline Kessinger oral history: SMU.

p. 251 "this girl from Wisconsin": NO to SS.

21. Men in Uniform

p. 253 "It is my masterpiece": Lennig, p. 104.

p. 253 "I was the first director": Ibid., p. 158.

p. 254 "The history of each Stroheim film": Ibid., p. 156.

p. 255 "a difficult film to assess": Ibid., p. 261.

p. 256 "The strange story": Swanson, p. 359.

p. 256 "long in the tooth": Ibid., p. 360.

p. 256 "Mr. von Stroheim should begin": Ibid.

p. 257 "began instructing Mr. Marshall": Ibid., p. 386.

p. 258 the suggestion came from Stroheim: Lennig, p. 446.

p. 259 "I've always been": Ciment, p. 71.

p. 260 "I rushed over to him": Ibid.

p. 260 "He possessed grandeur": Ibid.

p. 260 "His accent was working class": Ibid.

p. 260 "The interior was always dimly lighted": Loos, *A Girl Like I*, p. 127.

p. 260 "that goddamned butler role": Koszarski, *The Man You Loved to Hate*, p. 287.

p. 260 He resisted the idea: Ibid., p. 287.

p. 261 Lennig suggests several reasons: Lennig, p. 445.

p. 261 "Today he is remembered": Daniel M. Kimmel, the *Christian Science Monitor*, 5-31-84.

p. 261 "to be back in Hollywood": Lennig, p. 445.

p. 261 "kept adding things": Swanson, p. 499.

p. 262 "Madame la Marquise": Ibid., p. 358.

p. 262 "a solititous gesture": Lennig, p. 445.

p. 262 "alone, far from his family": Ibid., p. 17.

p. 262 "Trina is murdered": Ibid., p. 90.

p. 262 *Walking Down Broadway*: Ibid., p. 325.

p. 262 "the last week of December": Ibid., p. 446.

p. 263 "Such a limp": BW, AFI, Dec. 13, 1978.

p. 263 Wilder also forbade cigarettes: Lennig, p. 446.

p. 265 "We had to pull him through": Crowe, p. 304.

p. 265 every take exhausted him: Swanson, p. 500.

p. 265 "I did not receive a salary": Lennig, p. 338.

p. 265 "This isn't the worst": Lennig, p. 464.

p. 266 "That child screamed madly": Ibid., pp. 55–56.

p. 267 "the most beautiful legs": Eells, p. 62.

p. 267 "Do you really think": Hopper, *From Under My Hat*, p. 214.

p. 267 "The phones have the same extension numbers": Maurice Zolotow, *The American Weekly*, 9-19-54.

p. 269 Mamie Van Doren quote: *New York Post*, 1-05-01.

p. 271 "Jack had tremendous drive": ACL to SS.

p. 271 "Jack and I sometimes met for dinner": ACL to SS.

p. 271 Jack Webb's *SB* contract: Paramount Production files, AMPAS.

p. 272 "not only set the tone for *Dragnet*": Max Allen Collins in Server, et al, p. 363.

p. 272 a typical letter: *Radio-TV Mirror*, Dec. 1953.

pp. 272–273 "staccato monotone": Gimarc & Reeder, p. 87.

22. "We'll Make Another Picture, and Another Picture"

p. 274 Kenneth Tynan's entry diary: *The New Yorker*, 8-14-00.

p. 282 "wonderfully awful": Donald Spoto, *The Kindness of Strangers*, p. 231.

p. 282 "Gloria Swanson was considered for": photo caption in Richard Leavitt's *The World of Tennessee Williams*.

p. 286 "*Sunset Boulevard* aficionados": Edward Margulies and Stephen Rebello, *Bad Movies We Love*, p. 64.

p. 289 "Gloria Swanson, an actress known for": Chauncey, p. 51.

p. 289 Winston, "was a female impersonator": Ibid., p. 251.

p. 293 "It's biologically impossible": David Ehrenstein, *Open Secret*, p. 65.

23. Sunset Cul-de-sac

p. 296 "I still collapse with laughter": Swanson, p. 522.

p. 298 "I got a script": Astor, p. 322.

24. Life Upon the Wicked Stage

p. 304 "[Carol] Channing's 1955 flop": Ethan Mordden, *Broadway Babies*, p. 233.

p. 306 "mute stage persona": *The New York Times*, 9-16-00.

p. 306 "I wrote an article for *Interview*": L to SS.

p. 307 "So one dark and sultry summer night": *Interview*, Oct. 1997.

p. 307 "The more I watch *Sunset Boulevard*": L to SS.

p. 308 "was born in 1951": Thomson, p. 87.

p. 308 "had no anesthetics": Ibid., p. 70.

p. 308 "Instead of looking elastic": Robin Lippincott, *The Real, True Angel*, p. 81.

p. 308 "But they don't have faces": Andrew Holleran, *In September, the Light Changes*, p. 122.

25. Fifteen Minutes of Close-ups

p. 311 "pure hooey disguised as": *TV Guide*, 9-20-00.

pp. 311–312 "is coasting, pretending to believe": *The New Yorker*, 3-20-00.

p. 312 but Nancy Olson has: NO to SS.

26. A Dethroned Queen

(Unless otherwise indicated, all statements by Sandra Allen, Glenn Close, Colleen Dunn, Harold Prince, Marge Rivingston, Stephen Sondheim, and Brooke Young are to SS.)

p. 316 "producer Harold Prince": *Variety*, 9-19-61.

p. 316 Harold Prince to Edward Baron Turk: Turk, p. 318.

p. 319 "a most exciting project": *New York Post*, 12-09-80.

p. 319 "That's too soft a face": *Interview*, Feb. 1981.

p. 319 "Also scotch the story": *New York Daily News*, 1-04-82.

p. 320 "came to nothing": Perry, p. 8.

p. 320 "Richard Barr and David Bixler": *The New York Times*, 7-11-86.

p. 321 "I first saw *Sunset Boulevard*": Perry, p. 8.

p. 322 "Kathryn Grayson": *New York Daily News*, 10-13-91.

p. 323 "I've never had doubts": *The New York Times*, 7-13-96.

p. 323 One writer summed up: Perry, p. 89.

p. 325 "doesn't make Ms. LuPone too happy": *The New York Times*, 4-04-93.

p. 327 red-and-gold jukebox: Clum, p. 302.

p. 327 "was a tiny stick figure": Steyn, p. 274.

p. 328 An eyewitness gave this account: Perry, p. 106.

p. 328 "What they have done is": Ibid.

p. 328 "in a permanent long shot": NO to SS.

p. 328 "Watching the show tonight": Perry, p. 106.

p. 329 "I'm sitting there and seeing pitfalls": NO to SS.

p. 329 "Let me be polite": *New York Post*, 11-24-94.

p. 329 "dark, jazz-accented music": Rich, p. 934.

p. 330 "It is technically marvelous": Perry, p. 107.

p. 331 "Things went flying into the street": *The New York Times*, 6-30-96.

p. 331 "The best thing that could have": Ibid.

p. 331 "Because he didn't get good notices": Ibid.

p. 331 "We decided that": Ibid.

p. 341 "My main preparation for the role": *Los Angeles Times*, 12-05-93.

p. 344 Dunaway issued a curious statement: *Los Angeles Times*, 5-07-94.

p. 345 "People who know him": *London Sunday Times*, 7-03-94.

p. 345 Faye Dunaway had sung: *Los Angeles Times*, 5-07-94.

p. 346 well-known actresses who either auditioned: *Los Angeles Times*, 5-07-94 and 6-05-94.

p. 347 "Faye was not ready": *London Sunday Times*, 7-03-94.

p. 347 "Faye Dunaway Blasts 'Capricious' Lloyd Webber": *Los Angeles Times*, 6-25-94.

p. 347 "peripatetic throughout": Ibid.

p. 348 "I had more confidence": *Los Angeles Times*, 7-05-94.

p. 348 Dunaway sued Lloyd Webber: *Los Angeles Times*, 8-25-94.

p. 348 "It's a stickup": *The New York Times*, 8-25-94.

p. 348 "the severest action": *The New York Times*, 8-27-94.

pp. 348–349 Lloyd Webber on Dunaway: Dunaway, p. 387.

p. 349 Dunaway on Lloyd Webber: Ibid.

p. 349 "the very dramatic developments": *Los Angeles Times*, 6-28-94.

pp. 349–350 Reviewing the play: *The New York Times*, 11-18-94.

p. 350 "During that time": *Variety*, 4-03-94.

pp. 350–351 Dobie reported to *Variety: The New York Times*, 4-05-95.

p. 351 "I am furious and insulted": *Variety*, 4-10-95.

p. 351 "If I could leave it in May": *The New York Times*, 4-05-95.

p. 351 called Dobie's actions "idiotic": Ibid.

p. 352 "only five hours ahead of New York": Ibid.

p. 352 "It can't hurt the show": Ibid.

p. 352 "Faking It on Broadway": *The New York Times*, 4-09-95.

27. If They Put All the Norma Desmonds on an Island, Which One Would Survive?
(Unless otherwise indicated, all statements by Petula Clark and Susan Shulman are to SS.)
p. 356 She wasn't happy with the recording: GC to SS.

28. Billy Wilder from Noir to Blackout
p. 363 "the runt of my litter": Joseph McBride and Michael Wilmington, *Film Quarterly*, Summer 1970.

p. 363 "Good-bye, Mr. Boot": Sikov, p. 314.

p. 366 Wilder on Charles Laughton: Zolotow, p. 245.

p. 366 Kurnitz was an Anglophile: Sikov, p. 400.

pp. 367–368 "Superb comedy-drama": *Leonard Maltin's 2000 Movie and Video Guide*, p. 54.

p. 368 "shot in Berlin and Munich": Pauline Kael, *I Lost It at the Movies*, p. 150.

p. 371 "purposely created a cipher": Sikov, p. 504.

p. 371 "Leisen was too goddamn fey": Zolotow, p. 69.

p. 372 "The fact that a man was gay": Sikov, p. 405.

p. 372 "I wanted to stop": Crowe, p. 105.

29. Lux Perpetua
p. 374 "Grandma lived in the present": BY to SS.

p. 376 "Where do I go from here?": Swanson, p. 536.

p. 377 After two hours the lover stole back in: *Interview*, Feb. 1981.

p. 378 "a Prince Mdivani look": anonymous source to SS.

p. 378 he sent Gloria letters: UTA.

p. 378 "Hubby #7 in Wings": *New York Post*, 2-19-81.

p. 378 "was well enough to talk": *New York Post*, 3-27-83.

p. 378 Liz Smith . . . corrected: *New York Daily News*, 3-28-83.

p. 378 "Don't do this to me!": RD to SS.

p. 378 Another source: anonymous source to SS.

p. 378 Another friend of Gloria's: anonymous source to SS.

p. 379 I asked one of her daughters: MFA to SS.

p. 379 "In the early days": RD to SS.

Index